THE DANCE OF THE OPPOSITES

OTHER WORKS BY THE AUTHOR

'The Wind & the Mill'. Produced at West Wratting Mill in 1935 by the Festival Theatre Company. Cambridge. Directed by Joseph Macleod.

'He Was Like a Continent'. Produced at the Rooseveldt Theatre. New York in 1938. Directed by Nicholas Grey. Published by Adam Press in 1947 in London, with a Foreword by Dame Sybil Thorndike.

'The Brothers'. Produced & directed by Peter Zadek at the Watergate Theatre, London, in 1951.

'The Journey'. Produced at the Round House, London, in 1976. Directed by John Baliol.

'The Golden Thread'. First part of an autobiographical trilogy. Published by Skilton & Shaw in 1979.

'The Isle, the Sea & the Crown'. An epic drama. Published by Poets & Patrons Press in 1981.

'The Horses and the Charioteer'. The second part of an auto-biographical trilogy. Published by Charles Skilton in 1988 with Foreword by Lord Briggs of Lewes.

AN AUTOBIOGRAPHICAL TRILOGY

The author – Derbyshire 1981.

THE DANCE
OF
THE OPPOSITES

*A Biography of a World
in Crisis*

THE THIRD PART
OF AN AUTOBIOGRAPHICAL TRILOGY

Philippa Burrell

With an Introduction by
COLIN WILSON

CHARLES SKILTON LTD

Made
in Great Britain
and published by
CHARLES SKILTON LTD
Whittingehame House
Haddington,
Scotland

ISBN 0284 98836 7

Printed by
Hillman Printers (Frome) Ltd.
Frome, Somerset

INTRODUCTION
By COLIN WILSON

In January 1981, I received one morning a large blue-bound volume entitled *The Isle, the Sea and the Crown*. It was published by a press I had never heard of and, to my surprise, turned out to be a play about the abdication of King Edward VIII. I had never heard of its author, Philippa Burrell, but even the briefest dip into its pages revealed that she was a woman of remarkable literary talent. An allegorical prologue in which Britain emerges from the waves gave the impression that it was going to be a vast poetic drama in the manner of Thomas Hardy's *The Dynasts*, but an opening scene in front of Westminster Abbey on Coronation Day, 1911, soon made it clear that she was just as much at home in the style of Noël Coward's *Cavalcade*. I read on with admiration and a certain astonishment — the admiration for the humour and deftness of the characterisation, the astonishment for the foolhardiness of such an extraordinary literary undertaking. This 326-page play was positively Wagnerian in its dimensions; by comparison, Shaw's *Back to Methuselah* seemed unambitious. *Methuselah* had taken five evenings to perform; this, at a guess, would take about ten. So what had driven the author to write such a monster, with no obvious hope of performance, or even of reaching a wide audience? That was a baffling mystery — for it was fairly clear that, if she had chosen to write it as a straightforward political drama, and omitted the lengthy allegorical choruses, she would have stood an excellent chance of getting it accepted by a commercial management. What made it even odder was that the front of the book listed four other plays by Philippa Burrell that *had* achieved commercial productions, one of them in New York.

I wrote her a thank you note, congratulating her on a remarkable achievement, and received a warm reply in which she thanked me for my interest. But it contained no hint of what had led her to attempt anything so vast and impractical. I had to wait another eight years before my curiosity was to be satisfied.

In January 1989, I received another parcel from Philippa Burrell. This one contained the second volume of her autobiography, *The Horses and the Charioteer*, and a couple of photocopied chapters from its first volume, *The Golden Thread*. I began to read the photocopied pages, at first casually, then with increasing interest. She was describing how, in the mid-1920s, she and her mother were living in London, and her mother was painting a portrait of the wife of the Prime Minister, Mr Baldwin. One day, Baldwin's private secretary, Colonel Sir Ronald Waterhouse, and Mrs Baldwin's secretary, Miss Chard, came to call on Mrs Burrell to commission a portrait, and Miss Chard — a pretty and rather scatty woman in her thirties — took an instant liking to the pig-tailed Philippa, who was then seventeen. On subsequent visits she chatted with astonishing frankness about the goings-on at 10 Downing Street. And one day she took Philippa's breath away by asking her if she would like to become her assistant. The reason soon emerged when Philippa started the job. Miss Chard's real job was being Sir Ronald's mistress, and her skills as a secretary were minimal; soon, Philippa was Mrs Baldwin's *de facto* secretary. Philippa spent a two week holiday with Mrs Neville Chamberlain, whose husband was the Minister of Health, and it did not take Miss Chard long to sense that she had a rival rather than a partner. During the General Strike, Philippa — a secret socialist — was on the side of the strikers (as was the Prince of Wales), and Miss Chard became openly hostile. The break was precipitated by a Downing Street garden party which Philippa insisted on attending, much against Miss Chard's wishes, and after another violent row, Philippa resigned. . .

At this point, the photocopied section ran out. I wrote to ask Philippa Burrell if I could possibly read the whole book, and in the meantime, settled down to volume two. And here, on page 3, I discovered the central theme of the book. The year is 1932 and Philippa is twenty-four. As a result of reading a volume on the drama by Maurice Baring, she has decided that she will be a play-wright. But now, in the Canadian backwoods, she finds her original excitement evaporating. 'For no reason that I could see, the fire cooled and then went out; the fine creative power drained away, the ecstasy dissolved around me and I dropped from that bright mastering reality, deflated and half dead.'

This is the problem that baffles her and makes her miserable — the problem that had fascinated me from childhood: 'whither has gone the visionary gleam?', the problem that tormented the romantics of the 19th century. It had been the subject of my first book *The Outsider*. But in that book I had emphasised that this is not simply the problem of the artist and the poet. It happens to everyone. There are moments when life is self-evidently marvellous, and we feel that we would like to live forever; then we wake up the next day, and everything is back to normal; we are again trapped in the 'triviality of everydayness', and the infinite promise seems a delusion. Philippa goes on:

'As a child in California, I had had my first glimpse of reality and afterwards my high moods and my dull ones while I was searching for my task. Now that I had found it and seen reality again, I learnt how quickly it was lost, and that my task was going to lead me in and out of light and darkness, with more darkness to endure than light to breathe and leap in.'

This is quite clearly the central subject of the book, and I realised with excitement that she is a remarkable example of that relatively rare phenomenon, a genuine female 'Outsider'. When my book had appeared in 1956, I had received many letters from women asking me why I had not written about female Outsiders. I replied that I had not been able to find any important examples. I suppose I could have written about Emily Brontë or Marie Bashkirtseff or even Virginia Woolf; but I suspect they would have been diminished by comparison with Van Gogh and Nietzsche and Lawrence of Arabia. But if I had read Philippa Burrell in 1955 instead of 1989, I would certainly have included her — not because I think she is 'greater' than Emily Brontë or Virginia Woolf, but simply because her search for 'the golden thread' is so much the central theme of her life. In so many female Outsiders, unfulfilment is simply a matter of what Maslow called 'deficiency needs'; if Emily Brontë had found a real-life Heathcliff, she would have felt no need to write *Wuthering Heights*. Philippa Burrell's search for the 'golden thread' was like Novalis' search for 'the blue flower', a genuine craving for some form of fulfilment that *transcends* most of our everyday needs.

I was now eager to read the first volume, and when *The Golden Thread* arrived I settled down to it with enthusiasm. And in spite of the small size of the print, which made it rather a strain on the eyes, I found myself reading obsessively. The book is so good I was astonished that it is not better known. It opens with the positively Balzacian story of her grandmother, a brilliantly talented painter, who fell in love with a handsome and talented young artist named William Luker, and married him in spite of her father's frantic and agonised objections. At first all went well; his paintings of the Highlands were exactly the kind of thing the Victorians adored.

Then the fashions changed, and people ceased to buy his canvases; when he was finally rejected by the Royal Academy he was a broken man. But he placed all his hopes in his sons, believing passionately that the eldest was a genius; in fact, Willie was a second-rater, and the youngest was a sex maniac. (Even Willie tried to seduce his sister, Philippa's mother.) But, like her own mother, Philippa's mother, Louie, turned out to be a brilliant painter, and for a while it looked as if she was going to make up for the failure of the sons. But things soon turned sour; she married a handsome young adventurer who came from a wealthy family; and when he died Louie was left with the task of bringing up her remarkable daughter. In fact, Philippa inherited the 'dream of greatness'. 'I have dreamed their dream and believed in my own genius, as they did, and followed the same irregular road, climbing and falling and losing my way, losing my conscience, going without pity and doing the same mad, shabby things. And when I changed and gave the world away for the dream, I lived rootless and floating, more demented than they, anchored to nothing but the purpose and power in myself.

'Yes, I am one of them and, like the masters and monsters, all the ineffectual geniuses before me, I may fail in my turn. . .'

And this is what makes *The Golden Thread* such a totally absorbing work. In a garden in Los Angeles, when she was eight years old, she had her first 'visionary' experience. 'I was playing alone one day when everything around me suddenly vanished. I left my present self and leapt forward into the future where I could see myself raised up and looking down upon the world. And the figure that I saw was a military hero . . . riding a horse and leading a great column of men, while below in the vacant lots were my friends, grown no bigger, still grovelling in the dust playing the same childish games. . . I seemed to grow and grow in strength until I was filled with a marvellous power and I knew there was nothing that I could not do; that I could lift, I could lead, I could rescue the world.'

Understandably, this vision filled her with a sense of destiny, her own future greatness. But when Philippa and her mother returned to London during the first world war, life became hard and depressing. Philippa was sent to a school where her head-mistress developed a violent passion for her — she seems to have been an exceptionally pretty child — which was unrecognised as such by Philippa's mother; the lady was to pursue her insanely for many years. Then Louie was commissioned to paint a portrait of an industrial tycoon called Sir Vincent Caillard, and he also conceived a passion for the teenage Philippa. At first she was delighted, feeling that she had at last found a father figure — this is a thread that also runs through her life — but was soon disillusioned when he began luring her into empty rooms to give her passionate kisses, or persuading her to sit on his knee and trying to explore under her dress. She admits that although she jumped up, she did not slap his face and run away but endured all this because she felt she could not afford to alienate someone who might help her to get a start in life. It was soon after this that she met Miss Chard and accepted the job in Downing Street. . .

It would give me pleasure to continue to describe her life and quote from her remarkable book, but if I did so, this introduction would become absurdly long. I can only say that, by this time, I had become so absorbed in her life and experiences that reading her had become an addiction. She can be brutally frank about herself — about her desire to 'climb' in the world, about her 'acting and pretending' — and there are moments when she will remind some readers of Becky Sharpe. But the frankness is a part of her fascination, and makes her marvellously readable. In India she became engaged to a Gordon Highlander and lost her virginity. The trouble was that he bored her. She didn't like being 'owned and ordered', although she knew it would solve all her social problems. So she broke it off. She fell in love with a soldier-artist named John, and for a while they were deliriously happy; then his father ended the dream by threatening to disinherit him. Life seemed to be falling apart — and then, once again, she experienced the revelation that had come to her as a child in Los Angeles: the recognition of her failures and inadequacies, and the deeper sense of the reality of her true self. 'Gigantic, in a field of glory, I danced for the remainder of the night, and in the morning, someone else rose from the bed, someone newly-made and different.' And it was at this point that she discovered the book by Maurice Baring, and decided to become a playwright. Here ends the first volume of what is surely one of the finest autobiographies of the twentieth century.

In volume two, we learn of the success of her first play in New York (in 1938), and how she began to write her 'epic' about the sea and the abdication of Edward VIII — it was to take her sixteen years. When the war came she joined the ATS and fell in love with a major who was already married. But when the war ended, she returned to her 'epic', and the affair also came to an end. In 1950, she sent two of her plays to the actor-producer Gordon Craig, and then went to see him in Vence. Craig seemed to be exactly the kind of father-lover figure she had always been searching for, and the two embarked on a tempestuous affair, although he was 36 years her senior. But Craig himself was too mercurial — and too childish — for a permanent relationship. A few months later, she finally met the man she had spent her life looking for, the Indian statesman Sir C. P. Ramaswami Aiyar, whom she heard delivering a brilliant speech at the PEN Club Congress. Soon after this he invited her to tea, 'and I knew that, at last, I had found my father-teacher-lover'. He was almost thirty years her senior, but the relationship endured until his death fifteen years later. Finally, in 1954, she finished her 'epic'. Soon after this she had another strange experience. One day, while working, she had a vision of herself as a monstrous penis emitting seed. 'I could have been the bride and sustainer of men and mother of children if the opposite talent, equally sublime, had not been implanted in me at birth to turn me into a male begetter, a half-mad beater of thoughts into forms in a Promethean furnace.' The second volume ends with her description of reading most of the play aloud to an audience who crowded — uninvited — into the village hall, and who spent most of the night discussing it.

Inevitably, I began to read the third volume the moment the proof arrived. But since you are now holding it in your hands, I shall not even attempt to summarise it. I knew, of course, before I opened it that it was bound to be, in a sense, an anticlimax — after all, the only suitable climax would have been the triumphant stage production of the 'epic'. In fact, this failed to materialise, and the book itself was ignored. Yet if it *had* happened, it would have been the vulgar, obvious triumph. What actually happened was more tragic and more interesting. Her obsessive quest of 'the golden thread' continued, and took her again to India, then to communist China. Back in England, her involvement with an extraordinary guru ended in disillusionment, while her work on a play about 'spirit communication', based on someone else's book, ended in bitterness. Another play, *The Journey* — into which she poured all the money she could raise — was a failure in London. And the book ends on a note of self-questioning that has all her typically fierce and brutal honesty. It sounds almost as if she is subscribing to Yeats' comment that life is a long preparation for something that never happens. And I can understand why, to an eighty-year-old playwright whose work still remains unknown, this should appear to be so. But I can also see what she fails to understand: that in capturing her extraordinary life in such detail on paper, she has left behind a monument to herself that can bear comparison with

xii

Jean Jacques Rousseau. What happens to her plays is unimportant; they are a mere part of her. This autobiography, if not the whole, is something very close to it, and it is her justification. She has, after all, succeeded in leaving the most important part of herself behind.

AUTHOR'S FORENOTE

I was English — but I am no more.
I answer now to every name
And belong to every neighbourhood and clan.

The Earth has many images and offices
And chambers: a school or place of learning;
A garden of achievement and utmost joy;
A court and place of trial and punishment;
A place of exile and the ground of sorrow;
The Cathar's hell; the Hindu's great Illusion;
A place provided, in the Beginning,
For Creation and the state of Being.

I know them all — and know that I AM.
And clinging to a senseless faith,
Help build the road to a new and finer age.

CONTENTS

PART I

xvi

ILLUSTRATION PLATES

THE DANCE OF THE OPPOSITES

PART I

1

I WAS SURPRISED that the 'I' that was my body did not die — that only the 'I' that had lived in that work for so long, died when it was done.

I had had so many spiritual deaths and rebirths, turning-points, stops and stages on the journey followed by new intensified travel, but this time I was sure that the crisis would be final. When only the artist died to be reborn, I lived as actively as ever, working on the house and for the Peace Movement, and it was two years before I was ready to return to India — this time as a Seeker.

In March 1955, another great peace demonstration took place and my mother was keen to see it. She was eighty-two now but very vigorous and I did not try to dissuade her and I told her where to stand and watch.

I went to my assembly point and the march was uneventful until we reached St Martin's Lane where the mounted police were waiting. And all at once there was pandemonium. No distinction could be made between the marchers and the bystanders and those who backed into doorways were trapped and half crushed. The police reared their horses as they drove them into us and we ducked and scattered and ran down the side streets. But every time they cleared the street and then moved off to break up another section, we returned and reformed and marched again until eventually we reached Trafalgar Square. There, the police left us and from the plinth of Nelson's Column the leaders of the Movement delivered their passionate speeches and the huge gathering responded.

When I arrived home I listened, astonished, to my mother's story. She had not stood passively watching when the marchers appeared but had joined them and, evading the trouble when it came, had marched into Trafalgar Square at the head of the column.

The next day, there were protests in the press against the action of the police. Their very brutality now showed how important,

1

how much of a threat to the system, the Peace Movement had become.

From Banaras on March 28th, Sir C. P. commented:

"I read with intense fascination & also with pained surprise your account of the peace demonstration . . . I thought such things were outmoded & obsolete in England which, in my opinion, is the most balanced country in the world & which still retains a keen sense of proportion & humour . . . The World Peace Movement is gaining strength & the sheer folly of alternative (atomic) methods is beginning to be realised. Bravo! and all power to your elbow!
. . .'

The majority of the AWPA committee had boycotted the demonstration as being Communist inspired, just as they had refused to adhere to the Vienna Declaration, and had ignored my report on the Odense Conference and, thoroughly exasperated now, I tried again to shake up this precious group of self-isolating writers. At meetings, in letters and even in long telephone talks, I challenged their political timidity.

In a letter to the secretary, dated April 19th, I wrote:

"When I signed the Appeal four years ago I belonged to no church or political party and I believed that AWPA would provide the broad, enlightened substitute that I needed. It appeared to me as a spontaneous, novel and revolutionary movement of great significance in which I could at last express my views and feelings and through which I could go into action. Had I forseen that it would do no more than engage in various non-controversial, respectable and long-term activities (useful as these are) I should certainly not have been so excited.

"I now realise that even if the other 800 signatories had signed as I did — desiring and expecting action — the original Appeal was far too vague and the membership far too broad for it ever to have been possible for the handful on the E.C. to have plunged the whole movement into action every time a crisis flared up. To have done so, AWPA would have to have been organized like a political party or Trade Union with a mandate on every issue obtained from Conference each year.

"But having admitted this, I am still not capitulating altogether to Mrs Mitchison and abandoning my quest for action . . . some way must be found, I am sure, for AWPA writers to move forward as artists *and* citizens — undivided . . . And I think that finding this way forward should be the main purpose of the forthcoming conference.'

I made two suggestions. Education was one of them.

"After a long historical period of relative security and no radical change, many writers need to be awakened in their ivory towers, aroused to the realities of their situation and reminded of their power and of the role they should be playing. Apart from actual politics, the basic distaste for action inherent in many writers (for reasons good and bad) should be studied. To educate is to lead . . . Not only the extension of the bulletin but regular meetings should be initiated when discussions, readings, lectures etc would be carefully planned.'

And direct consultation.

"Could some simple referendum system not be devised by which all the signatories could express their views in a crisis, thus enabling the executive to act with strength when the voice of each progressive group becomes so vital to the outcome. . .'

I had suggested that AWPA should appeal to other liberal bodies for their support in the fight over visas. One of these was the National Council for Civil Liberties which Mrs Mitchison immediately condemned as Communist and, because no one knew much about the organization, the 'smear' went unrefuted, I felt that it was unwarranted and up to me to put it right. And I continued my letter:

"I have now ascertained that the NCCL is an all-party organization with countless Labour peers, M.P's, churchmen, etc, among its members and a Liberal general secretary. It initiates campaigns of all kinds, irrespective of party, and is in an expanding state with a growing reputation for most excellent work. It has already done a great deal more about visas than AWPA and we stand to benefit considerably by consulting them . . . I enclose their 1953 report and would draw attention to Sections V and VI on Freedom of Expression and Freedom of Travel. This report alone is sufficient to refute such a 'smear' . . ." And I ended:

"In case I don't see you before the conference I think I'd better say now that I don't think there is really much point in my being re-elected to the committee. I always feel like a fish out of water and so I play no part and do no good and it just becomes a waste of time and energy. I'd like to transfer to the new Meetings cttee if it is ever set up. If not, well, I'll keep in touch with you all and criticise noisily from the outside! . . ."

I was fed up with writers. Ostracised by the PEN Club and at loggerheads with most of the AWPA committee members, my real allegiance now was to the British Peace Committee where I found positive people (albeit Communists!) and made new friends.

I could not attend the next meeting and the secretary wrote:

"I brought your letter up at the meeting and the general feeling was in favour of having, not a series of discussion meetings, but a series of informal gatherings with a special guest who might be invited to speak if the occasion seemed ripe. We thought the first Thursday in each month would be suitable and we propose asking Cecil Day Lewis as the guest of honour. Wine and light refreshment would be provided and a charge of 5/- made. What do you think? The feeling was that it would be more workable than organised discussions and its results probably just as valuable. But it's up to you to say how you feel about it.

"About political action . . . it is fairly certain that all signatories wouldn't think alike in a crisis. I suppose we could over-ride the minority; but any action would send me, personally, out of AWPA, so it's not a course I could recommend. I don't think we can ever be a politically effective body; I think we have a quite different job to do.

"We had another talk about the NCCL and it was generally agreed that it was unlikely to be much help in arguing our visa cases . . . I've never known Naomi smear anything. If she says it's Communist, it probably is, in spite of its annual report.

"I feel this is probably not a very good reply to a long and thoughtful letter — but do think over the monthly meeting idea. If we could have your house, it would be fine."

On May 1st (1955) I replied:

"Your letter made me feel rather hopeless and helpless as I always do at Cttee meetings. However, I'll answer two points briefly.

"I am dead against plutocratic exclusive 5/- meetings. We'd never get people dropping in regularly at that price. It should be 6d and a cup of tea. An occasional expensive snob-type gathering — yes — but not every month . . . The doctrine of the 'infallibility of Naomi' I find not only rather ridiculous but dangerous and offensive. . ."

On the 3rd he wrote again:

"I didn't mean to depress you . . . You quite misunderstand me about Naomi. There is no 'doctrine of infallibility'. She is as likely to be wrong as any of us; but I know her well enough to be sure that she wouldn't be malicious."

To which I replied on the 5th:

"I could not possibly misunderstand your words, 'If she says it's Communist, it probably is' . . . If that isn't 'infallibility doctrine' then I don't know what is . . . And you are repeating or echoing the smear because you do not bother to disprove it for yourself or even consider any other opinion or testimony . . . I never said she was malicious. She just sees Communists everywhere. . .

In that letter you say . . . 'we have a quite different job to do'. I would like to know what it is, why you joined AWPA, what course you had in view and whether you think AWPA is carrying it out? These are the sort of questions that should be debated at one of the meetings. We might get to understand each other and so work together better."

I pursued the correspondence with another committee member.

"Your caution and Naomi's doubts and questionings and hesitations exasperate but do not surprise me. I understand her unwillingness to be committed but, perhaps because I am temperamentally different, cannot sympathise . . . At every vital historical moment I think that even the writer must ultimately be committed, for he is not a detached philosopher although he is philosophical, nor is he a cold analysing intellectual, although intellectuality is one of his components: he is, before all, an artist who *feels* more strongly than anyone else the dramatic pressures of his time and so is able to interpret them with power and importance.

"When she says that 'we writers should stick to our writing' (for peace & all that) I don't really know what she means. Without committment how can we write at all? If she means that we should turn our talents to mere political writing then I would say that this is the worst mistake of all that a writer can make — far better to fling ourselves into political action than our talents into the swirling gutters.

"As for AWPA, I think that the organization of the writers of a country on the basis of an Appeal is the first step and if their purpose can be achieved by such a joint statement plus some practical measures for the reform of literature, so much the better. But if it can't and the world moves rapidly on from one crisis to another, then the organization must move too or remain at the starting point, its influence decreasing the longer it lags behind. But from statement to action is a hard jump, I well realise, which not all will be willing to attempt and if the jump becomes still harder, few will follow to the end . . . Should the writers of our time be forced to jump only to scramble back in a fury to their original positions? Should they be challenged, a flinty stone lobbed into the sweet sun-scented places where they lie so that they spring away like grasshoppers, in all directions? Or should, and could, they be persuaded and led. . .? I don't know.

"The combining of all the peace groups for joint action on

important issues is a logical development and the first of these jumps. That is why I am anxious that our position be reconsidered as soon as possible that we may keep our place in the forefront. "

And so it went on.

I heard from Helena Maxfield. She was still at Keele where she found that learning in England was pursued only for learning's sake and for the honours which were the evidence of academic achievement, without any concern for its usefulness in actual living. It was not just the utilitarianism of America that she found wanting but the spirituality of India. What she called "this dead weight of English culture" she saw reflected everywhere; in resistance to economic change and to change in traditional attitudes and she felt that she was living in a country of "doomed dinosaurs". The vitality of the world, she thought had shifted from Europe to Asia and Africa.

She was still without a passport, unable to make plans, her money going and fearful that when she returned to the U.S. she would not be allowed to leave again. The American Council for Civil Liberties had stopped helping her and she disclosed a desperate idea and asked for my advice.

To force the State Department to renew her passport, reveal its reasons for withholding one and clear the calumnies against her, she planned to adopt the Gandhian technique of fasting and satyagraha.

Her long and tortuous paragraphs cut and condensed, she wrote:

"Would Home Office protect my right to public protest against U.S. Gov? Would the police protect me against violence instigated by my Gov, to get me out of the news as a dangerous element? I would be pitting myself against cruel & powerful forces, determined to maintain the U.S. 'Way of Life'.

"Were I in the U.S. . . . any publicity might well be suppressed. But in England, if I could obtain it & endure it with dignity & the newspapers took up my cause, the U.S. papers could hardly ignore it. And if the Indian papers picked it up they would be tickled to see my Gov harried by a U.S. citizen applying Gandhian techniques. A wonderful furore could build up. . .

"But unless I succeeded there would be no point in sticking my neck out, being branded a Communist & ruining all my chances of ever living peacefully in the U.S. again. But if I succeeded, I would halt the trend towards arbitrary Gov & the infringement of civil liberties & give courage to other Americans in my position. . . "

Her underlying fears and revelations followed.

"My Gov would not hesitate to haul out gossip & accuse me of all sorts of things & so drag red herrings across the real issue. Could a passport be withheld on grounds of pseudo-immoral conduct? One man can rightly claim I was his lover . . . but half a dozen others, out of malice, could allege I had seduced them. There are people in India who hated me & want to make trouble . . . I will not sign my name & you may tear this letter up. . ."

I loved heroic acts but all this self-dramatising alarmed me. I asked an influential friend to investigate her case and find out what the "real issue" was, and for several months I heard no more.

While all this was going on, my mother had been suffering from persistent diahorrea, apparently incurable, and as her wonderful vitality ebbed I was sure that she was going to die.

She had been examined in several hospitals but when she was finally seen by a specialist in the Middlesex Hospital in Acton, "who did unmentionable things to me", she came away feeling better and soon afterwards she returned to spend a fortnight being observed. She went alone and wrote the same day.

"It is hideous all round that part and the straggling hospital covers no end of ground. But the atmosphere inside is so nice & so human. One does not feel one of a 1000 at the mercy of callous awful doctors — like Grays Inn Road.

"It would have been crazy for you to come with me — just a long boring bus ride . . . I am now settled in — on a very comfortable bed — dozens of pillows & back rack — most luxurious . . . How foolish I was to come in my best clothes but I thought my other skirt was too ragged even for a hospital! Anyway my new things & best hat are all safe in my locker . . . I feel this is just a week of lazing in bed & being waited on . . . Do promise not to visit me. It will only bring my complaint on again. We always think that if anyone is in hospital they must be visited — with an expensive bunch of flowers. So keep away. . ."

The next day.

"This is really a beautifully run hospital — spotlessly clean — the ward with sun on three sides — a wide open window — my head is practically *out* of it. Freedom. I roamed all over the place after breakfast & sat on a bridge — got the milkman to move a seat for me & I was flooded with sun & lovely morning Acton air.

"The patients look a miserable lot, poor things — really ill — some would be better with a little pill to help them to 'pass on'. Mostly elderly. Comparing Grandma (pink & white & wholesome looking) gasping for breath & fighting thro exhaustion — always plucky. These old things wallowing in their miseries. One next to me her face lined by years of self pity. Nevertheless, some still have a spark of sex appeal left! My vis-a-vis — stone deaf, spoon fed, utterly helpless, has her wisps of white hair tied with little pink bows behind each ear. Another fat lump. a few beds off, also bedridden, straight greasy brown mane has it tied on top with 2 magenta lovers knots. I feel quite out of it in this beauty parlour. Their doctors must be more susceptible than mine. All that I am sure would be lost on him so I don't regret not having brought my pearls . . . During the night I was waked by weird snorts & snarls. I might have been in a jungle — sick humans reverting to animals in old age — but I slept again & waked in the morning refreshed. . . ."

She had no respectable dressing gown and I could not buy her one — only a Shetland shawl so that she could at least sit up in bed comfortably. And a book. She wrote the next day:

"I loved your visit yesterday but I hope you will never do it again & anyway, I can't be here very long. The funny thing is I have to take medicine to bring on my complaint. I am dosed at every meal . . . and I feel stronger in consequence . . . I simply adore my lovely shawl & I could not put down *Holy Deadlock*. I've finished it . . . I am perfectly well, waited on hand & foot with two doctors & a specialist ready to cure my trouble which has cured itself! . . . The young woman next to me has looked so ill all day & now she is being wheeled away. She gave me a vase of daffodils that her Jew boy had brought her. . . ."

When I went again it was to bring her home and the mysterious complaint only occasionally returned.

I went regularly to the Theatre Royal in Stratford East. Joan Littlewood had no use for my plays (they were not social realism) but I admired her and the company. She was still trying to give high drama to the people and still the people did not want it. The actors played to empty houses and were so poor that they could barely eat and could not pay for lodgings and were camping illegally in the theatre, not daring to keep on any lights after the doors closed and in constant fear of being discovered.

In May of that year (1955), Joan obtained the money to take the company with two plays, *As You Like It* and *Arden of Faversham*, to Paris for the International Theatre Festival. And I went with them.

On the 18th, on a picture postcard to my mother, I wrote:

"I always buy postcards of Notre Dame — I suppose I love it so. A long & riotous journey! the ship held up loading scenery — the Forest of Arden dangling from the derricks at Newhaven! to the consternation of unpoetical tourists! We all arrived dead tired but set off round the town . . . Such a lovely crowd they are but all half starving — I feel a vulgar plutocrat." With the money from my rents I gave them meals.

And 4 days later:

"They have made a great hit in Paris yet still they are penniless. Their story is fantastic. . ."

The foreign critics were enthusiastic and the London ones who had never troubled to go down to Stratford now filled their columns with long excited eulogies. Suddenly the company was famous. The British Embassy honoured them with a special reception from which several of the more uncompromising Party members stayed away, sorry to be missing the exquisite food and drink but pleased to be able to demonstrate their contempt for His Majesty's plenipotentiary and a fraudulent occasion.

When they returned to England the bourgeoisie flocked down to Stratford and the actors ate, threw away their rags, switched on the lights and slept in their own soft beds. But Joan Little-wood had failed. More than one brave missionary excursion was needed to convert the heathen, the disinherited, of London's East End.

A month later, at the invitation of the Committee for Cultural Relations with Foreign Countries and the League of Polish Women, I left for Poland in a delegation of twelve women drawn from different walks of life and professions and with different outlooks.

These package tours were a feature of the propaganda war as it was conducted then, and designed to counter the pictures of unmitigated misery and oppression in all the Iron Curtain countries, painted by the propagandists of the west.

They were very popular since they were free, with no strings attached and luxuriously arranged and so people were constantly setting out eastwards, "to see for themselves". It was worth the risk of being called a fellow-traveller, or worse, on return. They paid for these amazing holidays by just talking about all the good things that they saw and did. And for most of them this was easy. The not-so-good, which were never shown to them, had to be felt, guessed at and divined.

Everywhere, throughout the tour, we were greeted with flowers and embraces and given lavish hospitality and we came away with a picture of a warm and gifted people rising from their sufferings and re-building their ruined country with undiminished energy and courage and now wanting only to be left in peace.

I went on to Helsinki to attend the 1955 World Peace Congress

— on my own. This time, AWPA would not even send an observer.

On June 21st I wrote to my mother:

"I flew here with the Polish delegation protected and befriended to the last. Now I am sitting in the midst of hurdy gurdy noise & commotion greeting old friends from every quarter of the world. . ."

She wrote on the same day. The first of the snob gatherings had been held in our house.

"About fifty came. Mr StJ opened the door & collected the money. They made a 'small profit' but he said it was all very worthwhile — a great success. Cecil soon thawed & I am sure enjoyed himself — he was in the limelight all thro'. When he read — of course I could not hear a word (but I don't think I missed much) — his intonation was deadly monotonous. I watched the people & one & all looked politely bored. When *you* read one is alive. It is music — crashing *fortissimo* one moment & lovely emotional *piannissimo* the next. They want you to read at the next show . . . I made a point of talking to Cecil. When I told him where you had gone he was mildly interested & then, in the course of chatter, I said you had a book of his poems & that waked him a little. 'Oh which? May I see it?' So we wound our way through the fifty & he snatched it down, flicked over all the pages & put it under his arm — kept it the whole evening & then took it home. Mrs B wrote to him & yesterday he returned it, thanking me for my 'delightful hospitality!' . . ."

In Helsinki I was asked to broadcast my impressions of Poland. I had whirled all round the country with my group and seen the smiling, busy, glowing surface but at the end, when I spent several days alone in Warsaw, waiting to fly on, and I walked about and talked to people in the hotel — I saw and learnt much more. When submitting my impressions I tried to be objective — praise everything I could, yet speak the truth.

I spoke of Poland's tragic history and went on to say that revolutions are judged not only by their achievements, but by their methods, by the measure of their ruthlessness; that Poland was altering her whole way of life, grafting the new onto what is good of the old, with the minimum of oppression. But it was not the message that they wanted and it did not go out on the air to England.

After ten days of speeches, working commissions and entertainments, progressing upon an ever rising tide of fervour and flow of mutual love, the Congress came to a spectacular end. On July 1st I wrote:

"On the last day word went round that we were *all* invited to visit Russia before going home! (1800 of us!) And then, in a closing speech by a Chinese poet, we were *all* invited to China! I could stay away & wander the world as the guest of the new countries — paid for & feted indefinitely! What an extraordinary world this is! 400 of us are going to Leningrad & Moscow & then down to the Black Sea for a rest . . . But I shall not go on to China now — I am in the mood to come home, filled with new energy & zest for work. When I am ready I shall ask to go to China — & prepare the way, plan it carefully, take my own work, take English poetry, take something of myself & England with me — recite & lecture so that the traffic is not all one-way.

"I have found the world for which all my life I have been searching blindly. Instead of perpetually swimming *against* the current, alone — I am with it & surrounded by friends. Everything goes easily & everything comes to me. I want to travel the world without money. I can. 'Come, come to us, they say, & stay as long as you like'. They clamour for my work. Instead of being always on the outside, despised & neglected — unable to meet the people that I need to meet — I am accepted for myself without money or importance . . . This is the new sweet world springing up beside & within the old decayed & dying one — and I have found it & entered it & to it give myself & my work.

"Wonderful people I meet along the road. I don't have to be introduced nor step aside while the carriages pass by & through the dust from the wheels, catch the hard unfriendly faces. The people on my road walk confident & smiling & stop when I greet them & take my hand & talk to me — & I learn from them all the things I need to know & my life leaps — & the country is familiar for it was already inside me & I dance with understanding & dedicate myself anew. I am reborn.

"We leave for Leningrad tonight, travelling down the Karelian peninsular, away from the country of a 1000 lakes & light nights to the land of the Muscovites & red triumphant revolution.

"Poor little Susie — & poor *you* having to look after her for so long in London — let us all go down to Appledore & enjoy the salt seas of England & rest for a short while from the excitement of living."

The excitement of living. Another sighting of an ideal world and another rebirth. How lovely they were then and how pathetic they sound now; chasing all those appearances and changing as I ran, breathless and lyrical. But it was time that I stopped running and caught hold of something real.

The Peace train stopped, all through the night as well, at every town & village where people, mostly women, were waiting on the platforms or beside the track with flowers, food, gifts and embraces when we tumbled out.

To them, we were not just messengers of peace but gods with the power to impose it and their faith was pathetic — and distressing. They wanted tokens, something of us to keep and when I'd emptied my handbag I searched for things in my luggage. And when, each time, the whistle blew, they clung to us and kissed us as we climbed back into the train and when it moved, called out their hopes and wept and waved. The short journey took four days.

From Leningrad I went on to Moscow and then flew home and, at a joint meeting of the two organizations, Science for Peace and Teachers for Peace, gave a long account of the rise and development of the Peace Movement from the 1st World Congress in 1949 to the 4th at Helsinki — and into the great story I wove my own.

I described my arrival in Paris with 5000 others, all mad to get into the Salle Pleyel; the ticket sharing; the sharers vanishing; the storming of the doors; the chaos of the first days and my own good fortune in getting in and taking part in "a revolutionary gathering such as I had never before witnessed or imagined".

When I had traced the progress of the Congresses, these great meetings of the peoples of the world, from division and discord at the outset to love and convergence at Helsinki, I asked how such unity and agreement could be reached in Britain, how the distrust and divisions between the peace groups and between religious and political organizations were to be dissipated and healed. I pointed, finally, to the leads already given, to the statement of the scientists which had startled and brought hope to the world, only a few days before, and which was a direct outcome of Helsinki. And to Bertrand Russell's message to the Assembly. I concluded:

"After a long and ominous winter and a cold late spring the harvest is ripening and we must make ourselves ready to go out and reap."

The AWPA committee rejected my report on Helsinki and when, instead of resigning, I became the secretary (because no one else would take on the job) and I tried to turn those silly social gatherings into important meetings and No 10 Primrose Gardens into a centre of the progressive movement — I failed.

A different kind of demonstration now took place in London.

People came from all over the country to lobby their M.P.s and we stood outside the House of Commons in a queue, four abreast, which stretched as far as Lambeth Bridge. They would only let us in four or five at a time and we sang as we waited — until the mounted police appeared. Word came down the line that Churchill had ordered them out.

They rode into the queue, hitting and chasing people as they scattered, even beating up an M.P. who had come out to speak to his constituents. When the scrimmage ended there were bodies lying all over Palace Yard.

This time there was a storm of protest, the whole country was shocked and when we marched again the police marched with us. A year later, in 1956, I wound up the work of the committee and AWPA dissolved itself for, by then, a third world war, with atomic weapons, had been averted, peace was no longer a dirty word and even the cold war subsided for a while.

When it was resumed, the CND arose and the travellers, the delegates, the marchers all returned. Now, in the 1980s, we have a cold war even colder, a bomb even bigger, a fraternity of terrorists and a hundred little wars like running fires about the world. The same lovely people are in camps, still protesting — and in columns still marching.

2

I SENT A LONG account of my summer doings to Sir C.P. and, on August 31st, 1955, he replied from Banaras.

"What a stimulating letter. Your impressions of the Peace Conference & of Poland & Russia have aroused in me a desire to visit these resurgent lands. A desire quite independent of ideologies & political programmes. After all, what matters is the psychological renewal, the awakening of the soul of a people. . . "

And a month later:

"This morning I received a joint invitation from the Chinese & Indian governments to lead an Indian Universities delegation to China. . . And this evening your letter arrived wherein you suggest my visiting the 'Revolutionary countries' and especially China, 'the most stimulating of all'. 'Curioser & curioser' as Alice exclaimed in Wonderland. . . "

In November he sent long accounts of his five weeks tour. He had talked to Mao-Tse-Tung and Chou-en-Lai, to ministers and educationalists and been everywhere and seen everything.

"My conclusions may thus be summarised.

1) The attention paid to children's education, nurturing & 'learning through play' is widespread & most significant. 2) Spare time instruction to workers & peasants in schools & universities is wonderfully organized. 3) The pervasive discipline produced by a sense of crisis & ceaseless propaganda to be up & doing & on guard against 'US Imperialism & Chaing Kai Shek' is something to be seen to be believed. Crowds of half a million on the National Day, maintained periods of silence & order for hours on end . . . marched & cheered & sang in procession as one man with no jostling or pushing or impatience. This disciplined enthusiasm is specially noteworthy among students. . . Freedom as we understand it is simply not there & the uniqueness of human personality is not sought after. The 'liquidation' of opponents, 'counter revolutionaries' is not a figment of the imagination. . . They work to become a powerful nation able to stand up to the great powers. . .

And they are willing to pay the price. . . New China is an unforgettable phenomenon. . ."

With the help of an actor, I read excerpts from the epic to a number of people, including a barrister. It was well received, but I was told categorically that any publisher or management attempting to promote it would find himself in court at once. Although I had lifted and ennobled the still living and prominent characters in the drama, this verdict came as no surprise. But if the work had to wait indefinitely for a large public, there was nothing to stop me from reading it to small groups. And this I did.

Helena had had a busy and happy summer vacation attending courses on sociology and a fruit-picking camp, yet her long and frequent letters became more and more perplexing.

She had given up her idea of a fast having found "no support for it in any corner". When she was due to go on trial, the American Council for Civil Liberties took up her case again, but when the State Department dropped the case against her and offered her a new passport, she had refused it because "no apology for the infringement of her liberties and no admission of error and explanation" had been given her. Now she was at war with the Home Office. Her permit had expired — and would not be renewed. And it pleased her to find that "Eng Gov was no different from US Gov".

She had left Keele at the end of the academic year and gone to Dulwich Hospital to take up nursing training with the idea of going back to Asia as a social worker. After Christmas, advised by her solicitor, she left the hospital and asked the Home Office if she could remain until the summer to study chemistry which, if she had to leave, would be necessary for getting in to the University of Californis to study nursing in the Fall. In April, she wrote:

"H.O shocked me beyond telling by refusing this privilege. It seems inexcusable & flagrantly wrong . . . the Aliens Dept seems very angry. Why? What have I done? . . . and the bumbled efforts of fifteen M.Ps and not-so-clever attempts of the solicitor to get a sensible reason for expelling me have only produced the answer that the H.O. will not give one — only that it is *not* political. Exhausted & thoroughly disgusted with ENG GOV I have given up. . ."

On May 14th Sir C.P. wrote from Madras:

"Your letter portraying the currents & cross (very cross) currents within the PEN Club has shocked me. . . In the circumstances, I shall try hard to attend the Conference in July. . . Helena has, as you perhaps know, embraced the Catholic faith.

She is very restless & perturbed & I hope the Catholics will bring her some peace of mind. . . I have great respect for her integrity of soul . . . but she expects too much from people."

By this time, no less than twenty Members of Parliament had taken up her case, a deputation went to the Home Secretary and the press reported it in full. Maintaining that she had not only broken her contract but was also unsuited to nursing training, the Home Office now granted permission for her to remain, on condition that she return to an educational establishment. Then, feeling no gratitude and expressing none, towards all the "bumbling" people who had helped her, she threw away her victory and planned to leave. I didn't know if she was a victim of persecuting governments and "malicious" people — or just another sick, displaced person in a split society.

In June, Sir C.P. wrote to say that he had been elected a delegate and guest of honour from India to the PEN Congress. He was also one of the delegates to the British Commonwealth Universities Conference — and the dates clashed. Also, his fare was not being paid.

"I can manage to attend some sessions of both", he wrote, "but should I & need I? I am imposing upon you the ungrateful task of deciding for me. If I come I should like to meet Helena before she leaves. . ."

He came, whatever my advice was. He could never resist conferences. He met Helena (she was now working privately on chemistry), we talked about my forthcoming journey to India and I gave him a copy of the epic. And on July 23rd, before leaving for the airport, he wrote:

"I hope that your great play, so full of real poetry & yet compact of hard thinking & fervent desire to remould the world, may make the impression on the world that it richly deserves to make."

And two days later, from Bombay:

"Having cursorily read parts of your play, I definitely consider it an epically conceived & powerfully written drama of contemporary life & strivings with an immediate lesson for the world. May you be granted the opportunity to convey that lesson to the public of Europe & Asia!"

On the same day, I wrote about my journey — and he replied:

"Our letters crossed (telepathy?) . . . I look forward to greeting you in India. My grandaughter, Sakuntala, who is the Tourist Officer for the Government of India in Bombay, will receive you there & in Madras, I shall take hold of you & bundle you bodily to

Ooty for recuperation, discussion & the planning of your exciting itinerary. Your enthusiasm (intoxication you call it) is infectious ... The strike & the Suez Canal developments are epoch-making & the world watches half uneasily & half expectantly. . . ."

On August 10th he wrote from Ootacamund.

"I feel sure you will enjoy my art treasures & library. My main library is in Madras but my special favourites live with me here. Why should you marvel at *your* good fortune? It is *our* good fortune that, almost by chance, we were thrown together & able to reveal ourselves to each other during the Stratford-on-Avon visit. Our friendship & love have been deep & manysided. . . It is a thousand pities that Helena & you could not meet on a level of unreserved friendship. She has been living a hectic life of frustration & disappointment although her conversion to the Catholic faith seems to have given her some peace of mind & spiritual equilibrium. In truth, she needed (& still needs) comprehension & love & has had little of either. I wonder if she will be able, after her Indian & European experiences, to fit into the American set-up (of hysteria & dogmatism). . ."

The failure of "unreserved friendship" was on my side — my antipathy and intolerance. She left at the beginning of August, disenchanted with England and annoyed with Sir C.P. for disturbing her studies and, in her last letter, wrote:

"At sea — what a glorious privilege to have three weeks away from this so-called civilisation!... Terribly sorry not to see you... C.P. spoke truly when he said we terrified each other. On a deeper level I felt inevitably and irrevocably attached to one for whom I had discovered respect... U.S.A. frightens me so I refuse to think about it until I have to... Philippa, I do wish you well — it seems to me you deserve it. Affectionately, Helena Maxfield."

And so, Sir C.P's other woman, frightened and alone with nothing but her new faith, passed out of his life and out of mine.

On the 21st August (1956) he wrote again:

"The Suez controversy seems to be heading for a deadlock and the world is living in an atmosphere of ultimatum. The desire to clutch & retain power & at the same time to utter solemn appeals advocating peace & disarmament characterises both the opposing groups. Smaller nations follow this lead & words & assurances have lost their value. But out of all this confusion I am optimist enough to forsee *ultimately* the emergence of a chastened, a poorer but more balanced world . . . after a head-on crash, when the gospel of wealth will have to give place to the enthronement of simplicity or rather, of a sober idealism.

"I see your point about the consolations of Catholicism. Some see in their religion a challenge, others a tonic & some need feather beds & opiates. Each has to fashion his or her own hell or heaven!"

And the next day:

"Your brilliantly analytical postscript reached me today & some lines come to mind from your play, *He Was Like a Continent*. 'Poor Happiness, so much desired yet always in a crowd like this, pressed to the fringe & only talked of. Never once invited to the grand sophisticated parties of the great'. Helena Maxfield was symbolic, not of futility & despair, but of a constant & ill-fated attempt to square the circle. She craved the good things of the world yet worked to be out of the world. She loved champagne & yet spent months in Pondicherry & other asrams striving after short cuts to renunciation & communion with the Supreme. She expected the impossible from India (& from me) & failing to obtain it went to the other extreme of bitter disillusionment. Robert Bridges, in his *Testimony of Beauty*, says truly, 'Our stability is but balance & conduct lies in masterful administration of the unforseen'.

"You are among the fighters & crusaders & after many struggles are 'finding' yourself & 'administrating the unforseen'. I wish for 'more power to your elbow'. At the same time, may I ask you to remember in your quest for 'strength, courage & confidence' that we are living in a world compact of crises & confusions & welter of aims & ideals.

Judge mildly the tasked world; disincline
To brand it, for it bears a heavy pack.

"Yes. I agree that there are many things that need frank discussion & elucidation as between us . . . but I am confident that in the fundamentals of life & conduct we are consentaneous."

My answer and final word were in a scribbled note, written for myself — unsent.

". . . 'the glorious privilege of three weeks away from so-called civilisation'. How blind! What futile attempts & waste of living. I believe the circle can be squared. Will the Catholic Church wrench the forms apart & with its myths & doctrines of despair, finally negate the world for her while it denies man's passionate desire to leap & change it — here & now build the City of his Visions?

"The foundations have been laid, the scaffolding is rising, the cranes, the drills, the concrete mixers are at work; the bang of hammers & the ring of trowels; the shouts of the workmen; the lash of the overseer & disputes of the designers — can be heard. All the noise & confusion & danger which are frightening & from which she wants to run away. Do I brand — or am I branded?"

A month later I left for India to find out. If I could not square the circle either — if no one could — find out what else I had to do. And I was ready now to go on to China.

3

BEFORE I LEFT, I set my thoughts down on paper, perhaps to give some framework to my journey. And this was the beginning of my Asian notebooks.

When I finished the epic I felt utterly stale. I had written myself out of England — and Europe. Now, two years later, I still feel cramped, confined & suffocated by the spiritual & intellectual boundaries & the used-up mental atmosphere. Our ideas & ideals have grown dull or obscured or distorted. England has reached the end of her imperial period & Europe the end of her domination of the world & with these endings — all inspiration & spiritual advance. And so I go to new nations with cultures far older than our own but new because they are resurgent.

And if I go to obtain stimuli for myself, to live & feel so that I may work again, I also go as a citizen of Europe & the world to see & embrace the individual people who are awaking, willing & working the ground of the great global movements.

The integration of the world is the problem of our time; the uniting of races who, until now, have been separated & so have developed along widely different lines with the result that when the world suddenly contracts they meet & touch, not in friendship, but in repulsion; not advancing towards each other in wonder & delight but colliding — suspicious, envious & violent. They are not evil but ignorant (there is no original sin) and as Auden has written, "We must love each other or die". And love is the solution to the threat of the atomic bomb & the extinction of the human race. There is no other.

It is easy to love clean, nice people who are close to us & resemble us but hard to love dirty, dishonest, diseased & ugly people; cruel & tyrannical people whom we fear or, just stupid people whom we laugh at. We must learn to love them all & when we come to understand them — we shall. For humanity is one & when we despise, hate & laugh — we are despising, hating & laughing at ourselves.

When I was in India as a young girl I came to loathe Indians. I found them corrupt, unreliable, incompetent & cruel. But what

20

was I? Typical of the last generation of imperialists — arrogant, self-satisfied, deaf, dumb & blind. Ignorant & stupid. I go now to atone for my own sins and, in some measure, for those of my race — and to seek what I may find.

That is what I wrote, but in what I didn't write, because I couldn't, lay the more profound explanation. When I left India in 1932, after the experience which changed me and changed my life, I knew I would return. I began preparing then. And it took me twenty-four years to make myself ready; years of intense activity and wide reflective reading which conditioned me on the one hand and, on the other, led me through the grand avenue of my own culture until it brought me, excited but unsatisfied, to the edge of something else; round in a circle and to India again which now seemed eager to receive me back and give me what I sought.

I chose the old slow route because I loved the sea and believed I still loved boats, and because I wanted to invigorate myself before I had to face the rigours of the journey. Because it was the year of the Suez crisis when all British ships were being routed round the Cape, I chose the Polish ship, *Batory*, which I had sailed on before. Three days out at sea, on September 3rd, 1956, I wrote to my mother:

"It is ironical that British mail should be carried to India on Polish ships. All the P & O passengers who had to switch ships at the last moment, generals, colonels, planters, etc, are a reactionary lot & most indignant to find themselves on this reprehensible vessel!

"I couldn't be more comfortable. My cabin is so restful. I could write a book or two if my mental capacities were as good as my conditions . . . but within twenty-four hours I made up my mind that I don't like sea travel any more. It is archaic & stupid & utterly out of tune with the modern world & the modern mind. I am bored already & regretting it. . . I feel as if I've been away ages already. I have a dreamy, far-away exiled feeling as if I'd pulled up my roots again & gone off indefinitely — also a strange feeling of repetition — a return to my youth when we did this voyage so many times together — a nostalgic, sorrowful sensation. If I'd come by air I wouldn't have felt this. However, I must make effective use of this antique journey through time past. Why they make such a fuss about the Suez Canal, I can't think! The damn thing belongs to a past world. The real solution is to build passenger & cargo planes as fast as they can to hop the distance & the problem in a way commensurate with the twentieth century."

On October 5th I wrote again:

"We are approaching Port Said & go through the Canal at 11 o'clock tomorrow. I expect to go ashore for an hour or so before we set off. . . The voyage gets worse & worse . . . the peace & perfection of my lovely cabin were shattered & lost forever at Gibraltar. There, the Sindi traders swarmed on board & a woman with three children occupies a cabin close to mine. She never leaves it & her infernal children scream & shout from morning until night. I have appealed to her & complained to the purser but nothing affects her dumb, primitive, obstinate, anti-social behaviour. She belongs to another world . . . due to the crisis the ship is twice as full as usual, packed — & like a nursery. Hundreds of children running wild about the decks & lounges . . . & the Poles make no attempt to control them. . . My only consolation is that I have met several Indian professors who have invited me to visit them at their universities & read my work. . . One has told me to talk to Nehru who, they say, is very approachable. I had intended to get to him through C.P. Now I begin to think that I might read to him! Ideas pour through me & an exciting programme begins to form. But the hold-up on this ship maddens me. If I could rest & arrive fresh I wouldn't mind so much . . . but I shall reach Bombay exhausted. And so I fume & rage while everyone else seems to be enjoying every minute! However, I shall get through it, as always, & recover & forget & rush on.

"I enjoyed Gibraltar. I climbed the Rock & wandered through the alleys & went into the Cathedral & watched & discussed with a policeman the ever present & malign Levant cloud & thought of you & all your good & not so good far away experiences. . . I grow more & more debilitated & yet, in spite of everything, my mind soars, my imagination has been ignited again & this adventure & the work it will inspire lift me above my present irritations & I am in love once again with the struggle which is life. . ."

And on October 9th:

"The clenched fists of Egypt & the *Batory* got us through the sunken ships & abysmal politics & now we are out of the Red Sea. . . Although I spend half my time hunting for a quiet spot I am getting through the voyage studying the seething humanity around me & I have learnt a lot.

"When we came through the Canal I asked who the pilot was & the next thing was invited up to the bridge to meet him. The Captain gave up his chair to me but didn't look too pleased at the intrusion. I spent 1½ hours up there & he got so worked up & talked so hard that when the ships in front suddenly tied up — to let a

northbound convoy through — he nearly bumped into one of them! The passengers were all remarking afterwards on the extraordinary movements of the ship & concluded that one of the volunteer pilots, only half trained, must have been on board. In fact, he was an experienced Egyptian one — & I was on his side!
. . ."

At Bombay, the natives swarmed onto the ship, soliciting, and the passengers fought their way off it. On the quay below there was pandemonium. And later that day, October 16th, I wrote:

"I was very nervous about my arrival, not being sure if any of my friends would help me or whether, as always in the past, in both our lives, in all our adventures & struggles, I would be left entirely on my own & have to fight & pinch & scrape for what I wanted. But no! . . . I was met, not by Sir C.P.'s grandaughter, but by a relative of that fine old Parsee grandee in Harrogate — a Port doctor & commanding type who spotted me at once & dragged me through the raging crowds & queues to the VIP lounge & got me through the customs (which took 2½ hours!) & then out into her car. . ."

Sir C.P. had booked me a room at the Taj Mahal Hotel, the great international hostelry on the sea front beside the Gateway of India, the scene of all my comings and goings in the past. But as I drove towards it with the Port doctor, I grew nervous again for I knew I couldn't pay for it & almost wished that I was going to some backstreet lodging where I would feel safe.

At the reception desk two letters were handed to me and when the Port doctor left me with a friendly smile and invitations from the Bomanji family, I tore one of them open.

"You have timed your arrival well", Sir C.P. wrote from Ootacamund. "Just this morning our well-known poet-dramatist, Harindranath Chattopadyaya, called on me & told me that at the end of October, a World Theatre Conference will be held in Bombay. I spoke to him about you & read portions of your play to him. He was enthusiastic & promised to introduce you to the conference & to help you get your work known. This is a most providential contact. . . I have written to Sophia Wardhia of the Bombay PEN Club & arranged for you to read your work there. . . You need not be afraid of the expenses of a long sojourn in Bombay. The hotel bills will all be sent to me. . . I am sending you R500 now & more when your plans are decided. . ."

How could I have mistrusted him? And my letter continued:

"Really a wonderful reception . . . I *have* friends, *real* friends. I've never experienced anything like it before. . . I'm just sitting

back in my cool imperial room with private bath, marvelling &
giving thanks. . ."

And I loved her letter, the other one that was waiting for me,
ending with a little story about Susie, told in her inimitable way.

"Little Susie looked very reproachfully at me when I returned
from the boat train. Her face is so expressive — but I took her for a
walk at once. . . This morning in the butcher's shop, I was paying at
the desk for her meat when I remembered I had forgotten to ask
for some fat — the queue, by this time, longer than ever. I was
standing cursing & damning silently when, from under the counter
& the sawdust, out came Susie, 'thief' written all over her face,
slinking towards the door, a long trail of lovely suet in her mouth
which, as soon as she was out of sight round the corner, she laid on
the pavement & sat down beside it looking at me with a most
comic smirk on her face. . ."

While I waited for the conference, people called on me and
invited me to their beautiful homes on Malabar Hill and to their
marble mansions in the Parsee quarter, but before long the tone
of my letters changed.

". . . After the first reception & lots of promises, nothing more
happened & the people all seemed rather cranky & dull in one way
& another (especially the theosophists). They take a lot of understanding & I'm sure the climate has undermined their characters &
wills. Now, I am meeting new people who interest me more — but
I have to push my way a bit . . . C.P. too, has the failings of his race
— a tendency to make promises & not carry them out. . . But
I believe I *can* rely on him . . . the immemorial gap between
promise & performance. . ."

When I wrote about the Bombay people to him, he replied:

"I loved your letter (full of mixed fare & like all human
activities a blend of pleasant & unpleasant reactions). . . When you
reach Ooty, I shall insist that you spend all day at my house as I
have dozens of things & books & pictures to show you & talk about
including my own literary schemes. . . You should not be surprised
that nothing or very little 'happens'. India is too appreciative of
Eternity to worry much about Time & there is an age-old inertia
which has to be actively confronted & surmounted. Too much
delicacy is a handicap. What is the American saw about 'pull, push
& drive'. . ."

On October 27th I wrote again to my mother.

"The conference opens on Monday but people are already
arriving from all over the world — artists & scholars. It is exciting
although, so far, I sense nothing very original or new. I feel in

advance of everyone. This sounds arrogant & I deplore it because I
am always searching for keen lively, forward minds from which I
may learn. Of course, from India itself I am already learning. C.P's
mind is still the best that I have known. And he is wonderful. He
keeps writing to his friends here, making them call, entertain &
look after me. . ."

How unchanged I was. What did I expect? Revelation with
every encounter? Enlightenment in the first week?

And then my mother wrote again.

"Your arrival letter just come. It has put ten years onto my life.
I dreaded opening it, fearing that you had arrived exhausted & on
your own. . . If I'd been on that boat I would have moved heaven &
earth to get you a quiet cabin. . ."

Yes. I was meeting people and going to their homes and to
places of interest and talking and listening and, in between, as I
walked about I was seeing and feeling — from India I was
learning.

Nine years after Independence, Bombay looked unchanged.
The Gateway, (built for the arrival of King George V and Queen
Mary to attend the Durbar in 1911) the docks, the banks, the ware-
houses and refineries, the statues and street names and the Taj
Mahal Hotel made it seem as if the British were still there. It was
said that there were more British in India now than when they
were the rulers. Those buildings were not just a façade, crumbling
monuments, but the solid layer left by the last conquerors who
tried their best but could not move the massive load of suffering
which had always lain behind.

Whenever I stepped outside the Taj beggars sprang from
nowhere and with loathesome mutilations surrounded me, holding
out their skinny hands, rubbing their stomachs — and devouring
me. I kept my purse filled with coins — but never enough. I saw
that if I went on I would soon be one of them. And after them —
the dogs, starving and diseased. I kept my pockets filled with bread
— but never enough. When a soft-eyed creature followed me
about one day, I saw how cruel and stupid my compassion was.
And when a social worker took me round a shanty town where
animals lay dead and dying and people roamed in their rags until
they died too — I felt how hopeless it all was. It was a long time
before these sights became too many and too much and I grew hard
— as Indians all are. And I wrote in my notebook:

I see all this horror but because I am where I am — clean and well
fed . . . I am insulated like most travellers & remote from the acres

& acres & acres of misery & squalor. Not until I leave here & go down into the real life of India shall I truly feel what I am seeing & understand how they endure it & how I may endure it, too.

Then, still more remote — from across the world — another amusing little story came.

"This morning I was at the sink when I heard a scuffle & yelp of pain from Susie in the passage. Cat — thought I & crept along to see. Sure enough, the Black & White — the worst thief of all, sitting on the stairs. Quick! Quick! no time to think. I half filled your garden bucket & waited. Susie all bristles. I sensed rather than heard him stealthily coming. When he saw the blockade — Me, Susie & the bucket — a moments hesitation was his undoing. I aimed — *got him* — bang in the face! He dashed past, Susie shrieking after him, and whirled into my bedroom & out of the window! I, elated to think that I had aimed straight but poor little Susie — one heartrending howl of frustration, then yapping madly up & down the garden. He had nipped over the wall.

"I know that Bennett was waked several times one night by an irritating voice calling, 'Kitty Kitty Kitty' & Miss T banged her window up & down. . . I must tell them how I have soused Kitty Kitty. . ."

The conference opened and I did not write again until it was over. From Madras on November 11th.

"This last week has been hectic. Long sessions — drama, dance, ballet & film performances far into every night — talks with actors & producers & an excursion across the bay to the Ajanta & Ellora Caves, full of wonderful Hindu carvings. . .

"I flew here this morning. C.P.'s secretary met me at the airport & brought me to a beautiful hotel on the edge of the Indian Ocean, to a room booked for the day where I could bath & rest. Tonight he escorts me by train to Coimbatore where tomorrow C.P.'s car meets us & takes us up the mountain. Isn't C.P. wonderful! Such attention (except from you) I have never in my life received. To travel like this is not tiring & wearisome at all.

"I walked down to the edge of the tropical sea after tea. Very hot but I don't mind it — rich colours — palms — beauty — & now, as the sun goes down rapidly, the sound of crickets beneath my balcony. . ."

This lovely picture was only half what I saw. But I wrote to my mother about myself and of things that would please her and make her happy — not of the horrors of India. She had been there and seen them and I kept them for my notebook.

Those palms were growing in a cluster round a village and as I passed it, drinking in the colours and the beauty and loving every moment, I was suddenly brought to a stop when I found myself picking my way between lumps of human excrement. In this rural spot where simple holes could have been dug (the ancient system everywhere), animal habits persisted and the tapeworm infested the soil and passed into the children's feet and diseases blew about in the dust.

After a restful night in a luxurious, air-conditioned coupé, the car climbed out of the heat up the steep winding road to the beautiful undulating tops of the Nilgiri Hills — 8000 ft above sea level. When we reached Ootacamund, I was driven straight to a small stylish hotel owned and managed by an Englishwoman and full of permanent guests, British people who did not leave when Independence came. It might have been in Tunbridge Wells.

I was given a lovely chintzy room furnished with antiques. Only the bed, placed in the middle (as always in India) reminded me of where I was. I unpacked and bathed and changed and then the car came back and took me to my friend.

In front of "Delisle", his old and spacious wooden bungalow standing back from the road, he had built a stone annexe, connected by a passage, which looked like a small fortress — and was.

It consisted of four rooms. The heavy entrance door opened into a hall and a circular staircase, protected by steel bars, with a locked steel gate at the bottom. He slept in one of the upstair rooms and in the other, a stiff Victorian parlour, kept his library and treasures. Ivory and bronze carvings, gold ornaments and jewels, Mogul miniatures, Sanskrit treatises and English first-editions.

In a lawless country he had to protect them — and protect himself. There had been an attempt on his life when he was Dewan of Travancore. He was stabbed in the cheek and he still bore the scar. He was not a controversial figure now but a father of his country, yet it wasn't long before I learnt how unsafe life was — even mine.

He was now without a job. He had completed the reorganizing programme at Banaras — and left. He was a Madrassi and he didn't like the north and he didn't like the university, in spite of his long friendship (until she died) with Annie Besant, the founder. With 10,000 students it was turning out 'failed B.A's' (a quite valuable qualification in common use) and successful B.A's without jobs to go to — and there was much unrest. It was several years before he returned to the quieter and more scholarly atmosphere of Annamali.

I passed through the fortifications and into the treasure chamber where, standing in the middle of the crowded cabinets and shelves and tables, he received me warmly and proudly. I had expected to stay with him and to have to endure the ideosyncracies of his love making, but I was half a mile away at night and, to my surprise, reprieved by day. At last he was what I had always wanted him to be — a father teacher and nothing more. And I wrote to my mother:

"C.P. becomes more & more wonderful. He takes for granted that my whole winter's journey is *his* responsibility. Everywhere he will provide me with friends, places to stay and, on occasion, his secretary as escort. And the publication of the epic he also takes for granted, saying that he has power over all the publishers & it is only a matter of time. . . He is not only a powerful man in India but a marvellous amalgam of the cultures of east & west & a fascinating teacher as we walk & talk on this mountain top, every day.

"I am giving my first reading next Tuesday to a mixed audience of Indians & British. Ooty is full of reactionary British — relics of the nineteenth century. How it will go I don't know but I'm looking forward to it. . . For a few days, when the news of Hungary came, I ceased to be here. My whole mind was back in Europe & I was ready to fly to England to join the demonstrations & take my part in the struggle which seemed imminent. But as things have quietened down, I am once again abandoning myself to my great pilgrimage."

And she replied:

"He is a godsend in your life. Whatever is happening in the world outside — stay — don't leave him. He is old & you may not have him long. Stay — get published & known & then *write* for the world. With your talent, far better & more powerful than anything that you could *do*. . . What they are all fighting about seems like Bedlam to me. But I don't feel much sympathy for the Hungarians when I read Dr Edith Bone's account of her seven years in various prisons. They must be just as savage & brutal as the Russians. . . Yes. It is 'all too marvellous to be true'. Your future is coming — & soon. And I shall live in your reflected glory as was once prophesied. . ."

Her hopes rose again. She lived on hope. She had to for that was all I could ever give her.

Every morning I went to his house and we stayed there talking until lunchtime — a meal of curds and dhal, vegetables and fruits. Afterwards, the car took us to the starting place of one or other of his favourite walks and met us where it ended. And for ten days, as we tramped through woods and over bare green expanses, not unlike English heathland, often with a view of the plains below, he talked and recited. English and French poetry, whole books of the Indian epics which he first declaimed in Sanskrit and then translated. And from these to history, politics and people. His mind was overwhelming and when I wrote up my notes every night, how could I capture it on little scraps of paper? After a few days I didn't try. I began with these fragments.

1. Nehru is an Englishman. He loves English life & English people. He is also a Communist at heart. He is a split personality & so his foreign policy is split. He will not link India to either east or west. He leans towards Russia & China yet maintains his associations with the West. And so, neither east not west trust him. That is why I could not join his government.

2. America is pouring men & money into India for rapid industrialisation because she envisages India as a bulwark against China & these factories can be rapidly converted to munition manufacture.

3. India is attempting to restore the ancient village community — the Panchayat & collective ownership, labour, welfare etc — by persuasive methods & not by force as in the Communist countries. The results vary — some successes, some failures. Soft methods are always dubious & slow.

4. The Panchayat was self-governing. Only once or twice a year the tax collector came from the central government in Delhi. There was no bureaucracy over them. Their only obligation was to provide men for the troops stationed here & there. When Aurungzebe introduced twenty viceroys over the country, a bureaucracy sprang up & when the British turned them into ruling princes, the community was destroyed.

5. Communism will not come to India yet. The influence of the Hindu religion is still too strong. Reincarnation. The belief that present misery is punishment for misdoings in past lives, that the world is of no importance anyway & that only eternity has value. When all this weakens & the Indian masses *do* wake up — God help us. They will rise like the worst & most terrible of beasts.

6. India has never honoured wealth. The wealthy class (cf. the rich merchants of the Middle Ages & onwards in Europe) has never been looked up to.

7. India's wars (of which there have been many) have never been aggressive — for conquest or ideology — but personal & individual. Quarrels between brothers for their heritage or for a woman — conducted rather on the lines of the Age of Chivalry.

8. When Asoka conquered Orissa he was so remorseful that he erected a column condemning his own deed & all the loss of life & misery he had caused. The last words on the column state that in all wars it is the defeated who are the real conquerors.

9. Therefore, the twin ideas which dominate the rest of the world today — the pursuit of wealth & aggressive war — are both alien to India. She finds herself playing a major role in world politics while all the time she is out of tune & being tossed from side to side.

10. Before the British came the viceroys had absolute power — the power of life & death over their people & there was no justice. When the British introduced a legal code & set up courts & just trials, we said — 'these people are gods!' Is it a wonder that they ruled us by consent?

11. Ever since then, generation after generation of my family have been lawyers. Although my eldest son has now abandoned the law for politics, I am hoping that a grand-daughter will keep the long tradition unbroken.

And he loved reciting this little piece of comic verse.

> In my youth I followed the law
> And argued each case with my wife
> And the strength that it gave to my jaw
> Has served me the whole of my life.

It was when he gave me the text of a lecture which he had delivered, not long before, at the Indian Institute of Culture in Bangalore, that I finally stopped struggling to keep my own record. See appendix No. 1.

How much I had to learn and how much he taught me — my beloved guru. The cleverest man in India, Sir Edwin Montagu had called him. And when I looked back at Europe now, it seemed so immature and barbarous — for all its genius and achievements.

On the last night, bringing my visit to an exciting climax, I read excerpts from the epic in the old British club, now the cultural centre. Sir C.P. had already arranged for me to read in the university in Mysore and so this was not only a dress rehearsal but a test performance to see how an Indian audience would receive the work.

Two days later, I wrote to my mother from Mysore.

"The old clubroom was crowded. The local Maharajah & Maharani were there & the remnants of the British community. C.P. dressed up in his Indian clothes, turban etc & looked very fine. I dressed too. I read for 2 hours & they kept asking for more. C.P. was thrilled & said afterwards that he was proud of me. When I left the next morning he wept & I felt sad, too, for I am devoted to him. He has been so fine in every way — sensitive to my every wish & doing everything in his power to help me. And he *is* a power here. He is one of India's great men. But even *he* is a little vague & Indianish occasionally. . ."

Yes. He was vague and Indianish now. He showed me the bill for my month's stay at the Taj and although I could see that he didn't like it, he remarked with approval that I had not run up any extras. But when I left Ooty at 8 o'clock on the morning of November 14th, I went without money, his car did not take me down the mountain nor did his secretary escort me — all the things he had promised. I was taken to the bus, his secretary bought me a ticket, the driver lifted in my bags — and they left me.

Had he flung me into the maelstrom deliberately — for my own good, which would have been a typical European, morally motivated action or, while applauding my performance the night before and weeping when I left him an hour before (the first time that I had ever seen him show any emotion), had he slipped back over the frontier and resumed his Indian nature, expunged all practicalities and promises from his consciousness and let me go unaided but so sweetly, as in a dream or, could he love and simultaneously not care — and be so mean?

It was not that I minded. I wanted to plunge from the heights into the depths and I could do without the money. But if it was the old flaw in another context, the eternal gap between promise and performance, or something else — I needed to know and understand it.

The starting place was crowded with pushing shouting people. I fought my way to a seat and a fat woman rolled in beside me and spread over me and others, in front and behind, hung over me until I felt obliterated. When all the broken seats and the gangway were filled and overfilled and the struggles ended, the bus moved heavily away. I was the only white passenger.

I wrote in my notebook later:

> I came down the mountain in a bus, squashed by the people, choked by their strong smell & the dust & deafened by the noise they made. At every stop beggars — lepers, blind & mutilated creatures, pregnant women, children, even crawling babies pressed round & clambered in & stood over me in all their rags & dirt & diseases, blackmailing me, until I had emptied my purse.
>
> By midday we reached a large village at the bottom of the mountain & stopped for awhile & I got out and, followed by beggars, looked about for a lavatory of any sort. They are Tamil speaking people here & so my Hindustani (brushed up from the past) was useless. Only in English could I eventually make my need known.
>
> Although most of the people relieve themselves where they stand, I found a piece of canvas stretched round some posts, open on one side & full of uncleared filth & flies. I was at the bottom now — of the mountain & of Indian life — no longer clean, comfortable & well fed — fascinated & horrified & from that time on never free from the pain of seeking & knowing. But to understand one must feel & the more one can force oneself to feel & the further one dare sink — the better will one understand. . ."

The next day, I wrote to my mother from Dasa Prakash, Mysore, where Sir C.P. had booked me a room, telling me that the modern international hotel was full.

"After an eventful journey down the mountain, I arrived here at tea-time yesterday — a Hindu hotel — all noise & pandemonium — talking & shouting on the gallery outside my little bare cell half the night, all the dogs of the town barking & howling by way of background chorus & today, hundreds of people, one after the other, sidling in offering some alluring service — & crowds hanging about down below — holiness, cheating, scholarly learning, celebrating & incompetence all raging round me at once. . . I slept about three hours & this afternoon I am reading in the University! But I have given up worrying about what I feel like. Yesterday, after a cup of coffee with C.P. at 7 am, I fasted all day, not daring to drink or eat the fruit en route or take the highly spiced Hindu food on arrival. I subsist on tea & fruit (which I wash in permangate) but, as I say, I have given up worrying. I am *living*. That is the great thing. . ."

Mr Josyer, a Sanskrit scholar and author of many learned but obscure works of religion and philosophy had been instructed by

Sir C.P. to look after me and he called on me as soon as I arrived.

He was a solemn, detached, unapproachable old man who, like all fastidious Brahmins, would not shake hands for fear of physical and spiritual contamination and only waited on me out of veneration for Sir C.P.

In a letter to his "gracious master", he declined an invitation to Ooty saying that "somehow Milton's words, 'The mind is its own place And in itself can make A heaven of hell, a hell of heaven', have held me tied here", ending adoringly, "Travelling about, like Indragit, north, south, east and west one doesn't know from where the heavenly voice will next come — as he takes all in his giant strides."

He told me that the reading had been arranged for the next day, when he called for me in a taxi — a large battered but still dignified old car, with the hood removed, which must once have carried fine imperial people. We rode together in silence. But when, instead of leaving the city, we crawled into narrower and narrower and more and more crowded alleyways I grew concerned and asked him where we were going. He made no reply and the next moment we stopped before a tiny house and a horde of women and children rushed the car and, shouting and screaming, scrambled in. At least twenty — his extended family. They sat all over each other on the seats and on the floor — and all over me — and the children stood on the back seats and looked out backwards and hung out of the windows and looked out sideways. And I cringed in my corner.

"Are they all coming to my reading?" I shouted to Mr Josyer above the noise.

"They are coming for a ride." he replied calmly.

I should have been pleased to be able to give them all such pleasure, but I was nervous before my performance — and not amused.

Before the end of the long drive the ecstasy moderated a little and when we reached the University they all tumbled out and disappeared and I followed Mr Josyer into the main hall, where he left me. A few minutes later he returned to tell me that nothing was known of my reading and that I would have to wait in Mysore until a date for it was fixed. I spent the next few days walking about and writing in my notebook.

The Dasa Prakash Hindu Hotel stands in a large irregular compound surrounded by a high wall & entered through a gateway. An open space is in the middle & tall dark trees grow all round with a few small houses beneath them.

The hotel building is high & narrow, faced by tier upon tier of galleries with rows of little cell-like rooms leading off them — like a prison in construction.

My stark unpainted cell has a plank bed, a hard chair & a rough cupboard & behind, a typical Indian all-concrete bathroom — a hole in the floor, a tap & a bucket. Luxury all this.

The cells are all occupied, the guests & their servants coming & going noisily throughout the day & night & the compound below is perpetually full of pilgrims, musicians & wedding guests — noise, dust & commotion. A rich & wonderful scene by day and, lit by lanterns at night, a fabulous play on an immense stage with a dark mysterious backdrop.

Mysore is one of the old princely states & the city one of the most beautiful in the world — full of gorgeous palaces, lakes & hanging gardens but all round the Dasa Prakash is the teeming bazaar, so overwhelming that I cannot go & feast myself upon beauty. Instead, I roam the streets & alleys & try to lose myself, identify myself, with the poverty & suffering.

When I go out at night I see little lumps that look like sacks or bundles or even stones lying in the middle of the road or cast into corners, crevices, drains & ditches. And when I get near them I see that they are people — shrivelled up. And I do not know if they will be dead in the morning or, if they are dead already.

Sometimes, I see whole families creep into dark stinking places & covering themselves with dirty rags, sink into the dust — almost returned to dust themselves.

When I return to my cell each night, I lie on my plank bed & listen to the harsh shouts of the guests & their servants, the banging of doors, the chanting of the pilgrims in their saffron robes below & from all over the city, the barking & howling of the pariah dogs. A strange medieval world of heat & dust & noise, of crowded living, callousness, frustration, passivity, suffering & death.

I detest it but must stay as long as I can bear it; feel & experience as much of it as I am able.

And now, the gulf between the treasures of Delisle and the indigence of Mysore, between Sir C.P's beautiful philosophising and transcending of the world and the worms that crawled and died in the dust, angered me and I wrote him a protesting letter, asking why *he* wasn't doing something about it?

In the meantime, my reading was arranged and Mr Josyer called for me again. This time, we rode alone and in silence and, on arrival, I was taken straight into a vast hall where rows and rows of students, 1000 or more, the benches rising to the ceiling — sat waiting for me.

I climbed onto the platform and laid my script on the table. Behind me were open arches leading out into a cloister, with people tramping to and fro talking loudly. But I had to disregard this and begin, shout above it and reach those distant rows up in the gods.

I had not been going two minutes when some individuals rose and stumbled along the creaking boards. Then others. I shouted above the din behind and the din in front and tried to hold them, but soon there was only a descending mass before me until every bench had emptied. But still I did not stop and glancing up again, saw some isolated figures creep down and join the professors still sitting in the front row and, realising that the uproar behind me had abated, I now took heart and soared blithely into the fantastical world of my play. Afterwards, the noble few gathered close and hung garlands round my neck.

When I asked why they had walked out, they told me that the notices had got mixed up and that a science lecture had been expected in the big hall. I left Mysore the next day.

Situated on a plateau with a dry healthy climate, Bangalore was once a large and popular British station and, with its wide straight roads and public buildings, it still retained the style and much of the atmosphere of the Raj.

The Institute, founded and still run by the Theosophists, was now the most important cultural centre in south India and it was there, succeeding Sir C.P. himself, that his son, Sundaram, arranged for me to read, at the same time booking me a room in a modern hotel.

My reading glasses were stolen the day before and I was having to use a quickly made pair. But nothing else went wrong here. Printed invitations had been sent out and Sundaram and his wife gave a party beforehand, in their large, richly furnished bungalow.

The guests pressed round an enormous table covered with bowls and platters of the finest Indian food — loading their plates. I was set at a tiny table by myself and the rich and multifarious dishes were paraded up to me. I refused them all. I could not eat before performing. And they could not understand.

Not a seat was empty in the large hall and they were standing round the sides. I was introduced by an eloquent and dignified chairman and when I began, with eager faces before me, not a sound could be heard. Soon, the venerable old scholars in the front row began nodding and then participating — first muttering softly, then crying out at dramatic moments.

At first, I found this disconcerting but it was traditional and when I got used to it, I liked it. I loved it. And I loved them.

The next day, November 21st, 1956, I wrote to my mother.

"I leave for Delhi tonight. I have now given three readings in three different places in the space of one week! Each more successful than the last — a triumphal progress. . . This epic of England & the sea seems to appeal to everyone. . . Last night, before my reading, I was introduced to a woman who said, "Are you the P.B. who was at Graham Street?" She had been a teacher there when I arrived from America but had left soon afterwards. She said that she remembered my name at once & that my first essay began, 'England is a prison and this school is a prison within a prison'! What a remarkable memory. She is a funny old stick but said to be very clever. She has lived out here teaching English literature for the last thirty years. . ."

"C.P. had a bill for £60 for my month's stay at the Taj! As a result he let me go unfinanced saying only that as soon as I get short I must let him know. So, I'm having to be careful & stand on my own feet. Travelling & hotels are very expensive unless one lives in the bazaar — but I'm not worrying. . ."

But *she* worried and saved on herself and, after paying the mortgage and the household bills, sent me all the rents. And now, I received Sir C.P.'s answer to my accusing letter.

"I fully realise what you felt in the 'communal' & 'vociferous' atmosphere but in a way, it was right that you should have experienced that particular aspect of Indian life. It was equally incumbent on you to witness the destitution & dirt of the slums — as well as the inexpressibly marvellous patience & resignation of the persons concerned. When we meet I shall explain the genesis of this ghastly anomaly, the essentially unIndian & recently generated squalor & dirt & the heroic attempts being made to eradicate these evils. In Egypt or Mesopotamia or even Turkey you will see the same phenomena but without the underlying philosophy of life. Che sarà sarà."

"Joyser is a relic of the past & a survival from the Neolithic period, so to say. But he is a scholar & his letter about you is full of lively & surprised admiration. He was as proud of your being garlanded as if he had received that honour himself. . . You will meet many such contradictions which may be likened to a Rolls Royce & a bullock wagon. . ."

He was not concerned about the poverty and suffering but only

gratified to think how effective was the Karmic philosophy
maintaining it — as in archaic Christian theology the Good, seated
on the right hand of God, gloat to see the Wicked burning
everlastingly, below. But, in India today, these certitudes have
been shaken by the fear that the "patience and resignation" of the
sinners will run out and turn into revolt.

The poet, Mulk Raj Anand, had told me in Bombay about the
Asian Writers Conference — the writer's "Bandung" — which
was to take place in Delhi in December and it was to this that I
now travelled — and by train, to save money.

In the station at Madras, families were camping on the
platforms with their charpoys, cooking pots and bundles, waiting,
often days, for their train. When I reached my 2nd class compartment, reserved for women, I found my fellow passengers and two
dogs already established, their tin trunks and wooden crates
stacked between the bunks, to the roof. And at once I recognised
the Rolls Royce and the bullock wagon.

One of the women, an army officer's wife travelling to join her
husband, had lived in England. The other was attended by another
Mr Josyer (her father or her husband) and while the first moved
restlessly about talking all the time, she sat passive and silent in
her corner.

Indian trains have always been constructed without corridors or
footboards because of dacoits (train robbers) and the second Mr
Josyer, leaving his own compartment, kept reappearing at the
door with more and more comforts and provisions.

When we left, late on schedule, the passive girl bestirred herself
to make up a luxurious bed and the restless woman settled her dogs
and made up hers. I let down the upper bunk, a padded shelf, above
the girl, spread out my travelling rug and rolled up my coat for a
pillow. We went, by turns, to the wash place (even more dirty
than the compartment) and then settled down for the night.

As no food could be obtained on the trains, an ingenious system
had been devised by the British, long ago. Before starting, the first
meal was ordered and the order signalled through to the station
ahead and when the train reached it and stopped, smart
khidmatgars with loaded trays covered with clean white napkins
came racing out to meet it and before it went on the next meal was
commanded. After that, the bearers pulled out the tables in the
compartments, spread the linen cloths and laid the cutlery and
served the well-cooked dishes to their sahibs and the sahibs ate in
comfort and with undiminished dignity. It was a good system
while it lasted.

The girl had her own supplies but when the train stopped early the next morning, the woman and I waited for our breakfast (ordered the night before). When it did not come she made a fuss, excuses followed and then a makeshift meal was rushed out to us. We ordered the next one and the train went on. That was the beginning. The next shock was the lavatory. We found it blocked and broken.

A few hours later when we stopped again and no trays appeared, she called for the station master and angrily complained about the lack of service and the leaking lavatory.

A sweeper went in to clean up and then a man with a hammer. While he banged and crashed we walked along the platform buying food from the hawkers. I only dared buy fruit which I could wash in permanganate in my own little basin, bottled soda water and packets of biscuits. When the train moved, the man jumped out leaving the lavatory worse than before. When we stopped a third time and nothing came and another man entered with a hammer, the woman raged and the station master quailed before her. And still there was worse to come.

The dust was terrible, and now the water supply to the basin gave out. We could no longer wash, urine poured under the door and the stench seeped through it — and still the girl sat silent in her corner, eating her appetising food and, quite unconcerned, Mr Josyer came and went while the poor emancipated woman thrashed about in despair.

At the next stop we jumped out once again and to another station master I added my desperate voice to hers, but all we got was another sweeper, another man, another hammer and, before we left — a large bucket of water. She went in first to wash but, after a few minutes, burst through the door with a look of horror.

"It's a lavatory bucket! They've put the water into a lavatory bucket and I didn't realise it! And I've washed my face!"

After expressing my own horror and trying to reassure her, I surrendered to my Karmic fate and withdrew, silent, to my corner. But not for long.

"One must protest! Protest! And you must too. You must help me!" She cried out now. "This is not the New India!" At that moment the girl woke from her trance and, looking at me, shook her head imperceptibly — and spoke. One word, which only I could hear. "Stupid"! And for less occult reasons, I thought so too. But I had to support her and for the next two days, at every stop until we reached Delhi, we protested and protested and protested.

There, she fell exhausted into the arms of her husband, we said good-bye affectionately and I thought her troubles would be over for awhile but, that night, she telephoned me at my hotel to ask if one of her suitcases had got mixed up with mine. I think she knew it hadn't and just rang to talk and tell me that it must have been stolen when it stood beside her on the platform and, for one moment, she had looked away. Protest again? Who to? What was the use? Poor woman.

4

I SPENT TWO nights in a hotel that I knew, in Old Delhi, and then moved to New Delhi to stay with the writer, Balwant Gargi, whom I had also met in Bombay. On November 29th, 1956, I wrote to my mother:

"I am now leading a most wonderful & fantastic life. This little two roomed, flat-roofed house & courtyard with a high wall round it, is in the bazaar. People (always men) pour in & out all day & another writer has already arrived to stay & more are expected. It is an open house & numbers have no meaning.

"Every morning I work in the office of the Asian Writers Conference & every afternoon I have been listening to the discourses at the World Buddhist Conference. I have been blessed by the Dalai Llhama & today have heard the Dalai and Panchen Llhamas & Nehru wind up this amazing event. In between, I am rushed about to Embassy receptions, meetings, entertainments. . . I cannot sleep & am absolutely worn out but — I live!

"Sir C.P. is giving the Convocation Address & receiving an Honorary Degree at Banaras University next month & he has invited me to attend all the ceremonies with him — & read my play. It is all so exciting that I feel in a dream — in some fabulous Arabian Nights' Tale — or contemporary version. How long this amazing pilgrimage & adventure will go on, I don't know — for as long as I can keep it going, I suppose. At present I am just letting myself be carried along on the whirling wave."

Mulk Raj Anand was the inspirer and now the organizer of the conference and I was pleased when he asked me to help him. Dozens of volunteer writers like myself (but Indians & all men) came and sat about in the crowded rooms talking and then disappeared when they were needed. Mulk himself worked frantically everywhere — and nowhere. When you wanted him you could never find him and when you found him he was too distraught to stop and listen. And politics made things worse.

40

Already the conference was being torn in two by America and Russia.

My first job was to look up and send off invitations (which should have gone out months before) to all British writers. After that, quite senseless jobs were given me to carry through and sensible ones snatched away half done. And soon I was snatched away myself. An English presence Mulk told me apologetically, was offending some of the writers. But by that time I was glad to leave for I was achieving nothing and, I had gained all I needed of new experience. Later, I wrote in my notebook:

> The writers' conference was an example of the wholly intuitive method of doing things. No planning or organizing — a great idea & a wild, unthought out, desperate endeavour to achieve it, the idea almost wrecked before the start & carried through in such a capricious & haphazard way that essential objectives materialised on the spur of the moment — or by chance.

My mother was following the aftermath of the Suez affair. She wrote now:

"Eden has gone off to Jamaica. Didn't I say that his floppy fluttering useless hands, no-chin & his vanity showed what he was really like. 'I don't want to go but my doctor says I must', & goes to some luxurious place & lets all the damage he has done & the sorrow & misery he has caused take care of itself. . . This is what Susie looks like now — a ruffle round her neck & all down her back. Someone asked if I had shaved it like that. Someone else said she must be a pedigree for it to grow like that!! . . . Yesterday she stole a bar of the lodger's chocolate!"

I wrote to her at the same time.

"Gargi's hospitality has no limits but I've had more than enough. The tiny house is now crowded with guests, they roll out their beds everywhere & the noise & dust & smells of the bazaar flow over the wall & torment me. A Sikh M.P. has promised to arrange a room for me in a government guest-house but I wait & wait while he procrastinates. If he doesn't do something soon I

shall just have to move to a hotel & put up with the expense. There
is nothing in between the good hotel for the rich foreigner & the
squalor of the bazaar. . ."

I had to plead and nag, alternately, to make the young Sikh do
the easy thing. When, at last, he spoke the word I moved into
Constitution House and, on December 7th, wrote again.

"Built after Independence & reserved for M.P.'s & their guests
. . . rows of bungalow rooms — 200 of them . . . very cheap &
pretty rough but I am lucky to be here. . . The inhabitants alone are
worth coming for — amazing characters from all over India. . ."

And a few days later:

"I have settled down & am very comfortable in a rough dirty
ugly way . . . already falling down, these bungalows are symbolic
of the general cultural level. . . Bad food, bad service, dirty rooms,
dirty used linen — tepid water between 6 & 8 in the morning &
perhaps, for an hour at night — a charpoy for a bed, rough
furniture & no heating & everything broken & out of order. And
this for M.P.'s & their distinguished guests! I don't mind living
rough — I've done plenty of it at home, but I dislike dirt. I keep the
dirty sweepers out, hold on to the key & keep my room more or
less tidy & clean myself. And I am very happy here — it is quiet,
cheap, independent & interesting. . . I go here & there, meeting all
kinds of people & doing all sorts of things — Bohemian café life,
invitations to wealthy houses, chance meetings in the street — a
vivid, chaotic, unpredictable, friendly & amazing world. . . In
January, when the conference is over, it will be too cold to go to
China but I must prepare the way. . . Susie stole a bar of chocolate!
She has never done that before & she knows where I keep mine on
my table & sleeps all night in the room with it — but the lodger's
— that, of course, is another matter!"

The dining room in Constitution House was bare, stark and
enormous. One sat anywhere at the large, round, unscrubbed
tables, people talked from one table to another, instant friendships
sprang up, long confiding tales were told and invitations to come
to distant parts and stay indefinitely, were flung about. I soon felt
that I could wander forever, unroll my bed anywhere, live on
mangoes and bananas, some nuts and a little rice and drift through
life with these impulsive, natural people.

One of my dining room friends, a permanent resident, was a
young provincial journalist, named Gupta. Whenever we found
outselves together he talked. Indians love to talk. And, as with Sir
C.P., Nehru was in the forefront of his consciousness. I wrote in
my notes:

Nehru is both Indian *and* English. He cannot sever his links with Britain & the Commonwealth. His strength is as a foreign secretary — relations with the world. He is no organizer. He cannot build a mass movement as Gandhi did to implement the progressive ideas which he professes. He loves power & flattery & surrounds himself with scoundrels whom he believes are useful.

He represents a bourgeois revolution. His & Gandhi's promises of "land for the peasants & power to the workers when freedom comes" were betrayed. Ever since, he has been pushed by public opinion — by the very astute intelligentsia & middle class. He was to Gandhi what Vivekananda was to the saint, Ramakrishna.

All Indian M.P's will *talk* progressively but look deeper & you will find the talk meaningless. They do little work. It is a good, well-paid job with a free house & free travel. Two thirds of them are in it only for all that. When they asked for still further provision for their servants, travel allowances etc, Nehru replied, "In two years time, the institution of servants will not exist".

India has no individualist tradition like the West. The joint family systems & other Hindu customs have given no freedom to the individual. She is fundamentally sympathetic, therefore, to Communism. She is not a non-violent country — only non-violent & submissive by virtue of her situation.

India talks morality but does not practise it. Corruption, dishonesty & unreliability prevail everywhere. Indians are not open like Europeans & however much they may *appear* westernised — underneath, deep down, they are not.

Gandhi could have stopped the race riots in 1947. He should have called for volunteers to go with him & stop them. He did not move. Everyone said he would be killed. He was. He wanted to be & gave himself. The whole of India stopped breathing when they heard that he was dead. All waited to hear *who* had killed him. A Brahmin — & they breathed again.

Harindranath Chattopadhyaya, the poet & playwright, arrived from Bombay and we met again.

"You are seeing India in all her decadence", he said. "Go & look at her temples & ancient monuments & ruins for these are more alive than the living Indians. She stagnates, or moves too slowly, & movement & renewal can only come through pain & chaos — the *blood bath* must & will come one day. . . An 'outlook' on life really means an 'inlook'. This is the first & all-important thing."

And now, wherever I went I met these doleful talkers. Indifferent to the physical poverty around them, they loved to bare their souls and reveal the poverty of spirit around — and within them; each adding a dark brushstroke to the picture of India.

Two well-known Communists, P. K. Punoose and his wife, invited me to stay with them in Kerala. He was a member of the Union Parliament in Delhi and she was the Speaker in the Legislative Assembly in Trivandrum. When I talked to them on December 9th, Nehru was again the obsessional topic.

If Nehru dies — anything may happen. There is neither an individual nor a group trained & inspired to carry on. In a speech he said once, "I cannot sleep at night thinking of the great creative work we have to do — but it seems that only I am inspired by the thought of it. I inspire no one else." He inspired India during the liberation struggle — but not now. There is no inspiration & buoyancy anywhere. Even Congress members when talking privately express doubts about the great projects in hand & about the future generally. And the old fatalism rises up before them.

The Chinese, by contrast, are building a scientific socialism. They have a complete grasp of affairs & have inspired the whole country to follow & work for the future.

In the south, most Communists are still Hindus, attending the temples. They unite on specific economic issues only.

The New Delhi was built by Sir Edwin Lutyens. A viceregal (now presidential) palace, legislative and administrative buildings rise up in the centre with parade grounds, highways and bungalows for civil servants all round — the bazaar set down behind. And now, like a spiritual and physical contagion, poverty whirled through the imperial buildings and round Gargi's little house and the stalls where I bought my fruit, infecting everyone according to their Karma.

One day, followed by some whining lepers, I dropped a coin into the fingerless hands of a half blind woman sitting in a box on wheels, pushed by a child — already leprous, too. As I did so, the woman thrust her dreadful stump into my hand and leered at me with evil eyes and the touch was like a stab of black, confusing energy. I did not jerk away cruelly but I jerked away inside and went quickly back to my room and washed and washed — and washed.

There was a leper hospital outside the city but they would not go to it. They liked themselves and liked their lives — and condemned their children.

The British had compelled them to be treated. In Europe in the Middle Ages, they had to ring a bell but here, at this time, no attempt was made to enforce the law of isolation and deliverance.

After two months, I had become like a manic depressive. The moments when I glimpsed some light — high with excitation; in between, crawling over the surface of the planet in despair. And at 4 o'clock in the morning of December 10th, I wrote out a little of my pain and confusion.

Everything here is vague & dreamy — weaving & coiling unseen in the grass like a snake — no one really listens or really gives an answer — all seems indefinite & unfinished. I feel nowhere — suspended. There is no real warmth — no real contact & I do not trust. And yet, there is much friendliness & kindness — easy meetings & continuous talking about serious things — meetings tho' planned, appear fortuitous, talks which contain no passion or purpose & which reach no conclusion. Each individual seems absorbed in himself in a brooding, half sorrowful, half fatalistic & indifferent way. Self-absorbed yet self indifferent. And yet there *is* some trust — *some* motiveless trust, I think?

The crowds are colourful & lively yet cold & humourless. Life seems to exist in a different dimension from that to which I am accustomed. It is a nether world. A purgatorial world of shades & shadows.

I have not yet heard the sound of laughter; only the beggar's insistent mutter, the sad dirge of the street vendor, the wail of the temple singer and, after that — silence. Men's loud & ugly voices, the bird-like muted cries of playing children and, after that — silence; a high voice & then — silence; silence in & above the noise because all the sounds seem unconnected, unrelated, impersonal, without sympathy, uncoordinated — with silence over all as the result.

It is hard to find one's way, to enter into a world of everlasting pain. Do they like pain? If not, why has no effort ever been made to cure it? Pain is the clue — into the meaning of their pain I must search — for there seems little real desire to remove it — no real revolt against it. Am I just beginning to see & understand where I am?

And the next day.

One must walk with one's eyes on the ground or in the sky for if one meets another eye or rests upon some object, immediately one draws to oneself the devouring attentions of some creature — be it shop-keeper, tonga-wallah, servant, beggar, unemployed or half employed idler or other — begging, soliciting, offering & proffering. One is perpetually devoured. Hunger is everywhere — also greed.

Even the dogs are the same. Look at a dog — half starved, often diseased — it will meet your eye with a surprised, half hopeful expression, approach you slowly & suspiciously, wanting, wanting, wanting something from you — food, love — life! The only difference between the dogs & the people is that the dogs have finer faces — sad, intelligent, ungreedy eyes & one almost comes to believe in reincarnation.

I had to find the still centre where the opposites are reconciled. I had to feel the movement of the world and let myself flow with the rythym. I had to go on and find my own way.

And now, Rustogi appeared and his slithery, ungraspable character fascinated me. He was the chief correspondent of *The Times of India* and through the grass, like a snake, he pursued me. On December 12th I made notes of his first talk.

The British gave great & good things to India. Where would India have been without them & now that they have gone there is more corruption, more dishonesty, nepotism, poverty & squalor than before & everything is deteriorating. But it is better to be free with all these evils — than slaves. The three months that I spent in Europe — one of them in England were the happiest of my whole life. I like my job but I do not like my life in India. I have no friends. I cannot make friends either with women or men. I have no use for Indian women. It is impossible to talk to them naturally. They are timid & suspicious of one's motives. I do not like them. All Europeans are reliable — you can trust them. You can trust no one here. There are no outstanding women in India.

And the next day.

The Indian Communist Party is not a mass party. It is an élite & extremely difficult to get into. Members are admitted only after years of work & proof of devotion. They are well read, astute, extremely intelligent intellectuals. It works through peasant & worker groups which it trains & prepares.

At present it has no hope of coming to power — so long as Nehru is alive the Congress Party will reign supreme & since it has followed a pro-Communist foreign policy & a socialist policy at home, the Communists are relatively satisfied & quiet. It is when Nehru dies or gives up that all the present parties will disintegrate & the Communists may well come to power.

In the world struggle between Russia & America both are trying to fill the vacuum left by Britain in Asia & the Middle East. The Asian countries are weak & so in need of aid from these two powers for they cannot fill the vacuum themselves — & it must be filled. Russia has all the advantages — aid without strings at low interest rates & the moral advantage of a socialist ideology.

On December 14th I managed to have a meeting with Mulk Raj Anand when he talked about the difficulties he was having in organising the conference. He then went on:

Indian writers suffer from at least six complexes. Poverty. Insecurity. Frustration. Job seeking for security & position apart from writing. Importance without writing anything. And no understanding whatsoever of other peoples' attitudes & positions.

Their minds are tortuous, involved, sinuous & subtle. None are open & simple — like the Muhammadans. The Hindu mind is complex — abstract, hair-splitting & unrealistic.

In this conference, they are all manoeuvring for position, power & importance. All pulling apart — all self-seeking. And I spend hours & days lobbying various important people to make sure that the pullers & the quarrellers are kept in order & the conference does not break in pieces.

As well as this, there are the American agents. Indians in the pay of the U.S. & hoping for jobs, scholarships for their children, etc, are working to disrupt the conference — trying to bring in the Chiang-Kai-Shek Chinese instead of those from Peking.

The majority of Indians pay lip-service to Nehru's idealism, to Panchshila etc, but in reality are opposed to him & working for American domination — for the glitter of the 'Almighty Dollar'.

When I spoke about my visit to Sir C.P. and said how much I admired him, his expression changed and he burst out:

"Sir C.P. is a reactionary and he's very unpopular with many people. He broke away from Gandhi and joined the Viceroy's Council and, when Independence came, he tried to prevent the integration of Kerala into the Indian Union. And when he could have joined Nehru's government he refused because he wanted to see India aligned with the West."

"Surely", I said then, "the work of the constitutionalists was as important, in its way, as the Gandhian movement? And as Dewan of Travancore, he had created a modern state economically and socially in advance of the rest of India and it was natural that he did not want to see it absorbed and all the gains seep away into the whole?"

"They wouldn't have done — and they didn't", he replied hotly. "It was a betrayal of all that the liberation movement worked for."

"He would rather have seen India aligned with Russia, "I went on, defending my teacher with equal passion, "than remain unaligned and not trusted by either."

"When he went to Banaras he got the wrong side of everybody."

"The University was in a mess when he went there and he reorganized it and upset vested interests. They have invited him back to give the Convocation Address and to confer an honorary degree on him next week — and I'm going with him."

Into this steamy, factious, neurotic atmosphere, with dependable regularity, my mother's letters came like little winds of simple goodness, wisdom and humour. When sending me some new spectacles, she wrote:

"You have enough strain from lack of sleep & excitement — you must not strain your eyes with bad glasses, as well. Actors play only one part but you, when you read, play them all — a terrific strain. . . Eden returned from Jamaica last evening. I was hoping he would resign but no, he will 'resume his duties!' . . . It is too desolate & dusky to go to Primrose Hill now. I have a few streets where Susie gets a lot of amusement. She collects rubbish in one garden as we pass & buries it in the next! We went to Hampstead Heath the other day — ever so much more fun for her — but I lost her twice!! dashed away when I wasn't looking to the Rat quarter! I got her back quite easily but I dare not try again. Do you know — she reads your letters! When the post comes she always rushes to the door & then watches while I open the letters & when I open one of yours, plunges her nose inside & sniffs it keenly. Your scent must come right across the world! . . ."

Then Rustogi again.

I come from a poor family. I had to struggle for education in my village. I worked my way up, won a scholarship, etc., until at last, by luck, I got this job. Now, I am timid, I am a coward. I am afraid of what people will say about me. If I hear that I have been talked about by someone — I am dead for the whole day.

In India, to cheat, betray or steal are condoned. To steal 5000 rupees or a woman's ornaments & give them as a bribe to a government official is approved but to drink, to go about with girls or run away with one & marry her — those are crimes. Moral values are absolutely different here. In Germany I spent nine days — there I met a girl who wanted to marry me, was mad about me. I refused all her advances. I was so terrified that my improper behaviour — even the idea of marriage — would get to our ambassador & from him be reported to Nehru. I was so timid. Such a coward. All this about myself I would never tell to any Indian. I do it to a European because I know they will never betray a friend.

Under British rule many Indians were used, often given titles which raised & pleased them & cost the British nothing. They were employed by the police and, as informers, worked against the liberation movement, often giving false evidence causing thousands of people to be arrested & imprisoned. These same people, a whole class, are now in the Congress Party & in the pay of the Americans, obtaining scholarships & jobs & still gaining power. And they have penetrated close to Nehru. Important government documents are constantly disappearing. When he dies they will come to power & the Communists will come up to challenge them. But so long as he lives the uneasy balance will be kept because he has the support of the masses. They trust him. They know that he is incorruptible & will not sell the country.

During the riots & the exodus when thousands were murdered, raped & impoverished — three months after the Indian government took over, before the British had left & power was still not wholly in their hands — they cried out & cursed him & the new government. On one occasion, when it was announced that he would visit them, they dyed their garments black & made them into flags. They were so hostile & violent that three miles before he reached the place he was warned not to go any further. He was furious & went on & when he heard the shouting & could see the flags he stood up in an open jeep & drove straight through them. And they changed & cheered him. The masses will never desert him. He gave them independence & he is out to help them. He may make mistakes & not go fast enough but they will forgive him everything.

But what can one do with a country in which the people have such bad characters? No characters. How can one live in such a country? I am not a reformer. I am a timid, cowardly man, out only for myself — for my comforts & my pleasures. But I am unhappy here. Everywhere, in the towns, the cities & the villages people are dying from hunger. But what can one do with such a country? Many people wish that the British would come back — but dare not say so.

I cannot dominate anyone. The reporters under me — you — anyone. I allow people to do whatever they like with me, I am a weak & timid man. . .

I commented the next day, in my notebook:

He is not really timid. He tries to dominate me every time we meet, forcing food & drink upon me that I do not want; driving me out into the country against my will & with a lie; overstaying his time here & trying to make me drink again; using physical force to try to make me kiss him — & more. He is consumed by a primitive self love & lust for women & when he pleads, there is in his supplication a ruthless persistence. When he left me last night, I saw a dirty degraded beggar crawl in triumph from my door — albeit empty-handed.

If he finds Indian women timid it is because he treats them in a brutal way; if, in his work, he criticises both sides impartially, it is not policy but because he has no principles himself; when he says that his friendship & the help he gives me are given in gratitude for the kindness he received in Europe — he lies.

I found him interesting at first & I was sorry for him but now, I believe that he is what he says he is & what his face expresses — a hard, empty, self seeking man, incapable of loving & of any idealism — a fraud, saying what he does not mean & doing what he says he will not do.

Why have I suffered him so much & why shall I suffer him again when I know that he is trying to drag me down to his own degraded level. And why do I stay when they all hang on like leeches, sap, suck & destroy you? They seem weak but possess a subtle & destructive strength, the strength of the beggar, symbolic of them all. Giving nothing, only pretending, they take & take & take until they turn you into a whining, degraded beggar, too. But I must go on, get as near as I can without being destroyed — go on until I understand.

The same day, December 15th, I visited a hostel where Miss Dube and a group of girls all talked.

Indian men have one, & only one, idea about women. They have no feeling, consideration or respect for them & play fast & loose with them if they can. They try to dominate them & make them feel helpless & dependent. They *like* them to be stupid & easy. And most women are still subservient & cowed.

Most of the princes still have harems of as many as 100 wives. And rich men, too (Dalmia the great industrialist & Jain). They keep them shut up & the servants spy on them. They are often not even allowed to eat the food to which they are accustomed (Dalmia's young Bengali wife). If one of them should ever have the spirit to run away she would be pursued, brought back & persecuted for the rest of her life.

They are very much afraid of them escaping. It is said that Kapurthala's (aged 70 odd) young European wife committee suicide by jumping from the Kutab Minar. The truth is that she was thrown from it because she was known to be in love with an American & likely to escape.

And I added.

> These hostel girls have little chance of meeting men & when they
> do they are scared of them. But what can they do? How can they
> find husbands? The relationship between men & women of
> whatever caste is feudal, chaotic & horrible.

In 1951, a remarkable book was published in England, *The Autobiography of an Unknown Indian*, by Nirad C. Chaudhuri.

It is the story, personal and historical, of the struggle of a
civilisation with a hostile environment in which Britain became
involved, written with absolute honesty and fearlessness
regardless of the consequences; the work of a critical and
powerful intellect, completely detached from tradition in contrast
with Sir C.P. whose house and mind were still so filled with and
motivated by, ancient treasures.

He dedicates the book 'To the memory of the British Empire in
India which conferred subjecthood on us but witheld citizenship;
yet to which every one of us threw out the challenge — Civis
Britannicus Sum — because all that was good and living within us
was made, shaped and quickened by the same British rule." I
longed to meet him.

I soon learnt that he had not been invited to the conference and
every mention of his name, evoked fury. Mulk and all those round
him, regarded him as a traitor who should not be allowed to write.
When I also learnt that he lived in Delhi, I searched out his address,
wrote him a note and was invited to come and see him.

I made my way through the crooked lanes of the old city and
reached a house built close inside the wall. I climbed flight after
flight of rickety stairs to the top, walked along a parapet over the
roof of another house and arrived at his door. His wife opened it
and led me through several large, bare but pleasing rooms. When
we reached him he stopped working and greeted me and I sat down
and we talked at once. Later, his wife gave me an English
afternoon tea with delicious Indian sweetmeats. Afterwards, I
wrote:

> Even now I do not fully understand my own people. I am
> continually discovering new things about them. The Hindu mind
> is intuitive. He cannot intellectualise, rationalise, his beliefs &
> ideas. If he could, he would be understood by the West & so, I have
> really come to believe with Kipling, that 'east is east & west is west
> etc'. I passionately *dis*believed this until I went to Europe.

The 3 great historical movements which have forced their way into India & created 3 different types of civilisation — Aryan, Muslim & British (or European) — have all remained, in turn, essentially foreign. They have never fused with the natives as in all other great conquests & have ceased to be living forces as soon as they have been cut off from their base or the base has weakened. And no political order or culture has arisen in India unless a foreign power has come into possession of the country. Then, the struggle has not been, as is generally thought, between that power & the indigenous population, which has always been passive — but with the climate. The Indo-Gangetic plain is the vampire of geography, sucking all vitality out of its victims. Only the British avoided this fate by not settling, by constantly renewing their soldiers & administrators — & sending their children home.

The heat, the dust, the dirt & the crowds are atrocious for the sensitive individual & to endure them the majority become insensitive — dead & dull to everything & overcome by inertia. Before this happens the Indian is often bright, intelligent & receptive. Afterwards, he grows complacent, selfish & devoid of all ideas & idealism. And, too, after a certain age, so-called educated, westernised people often return to religion. Not to the first pure religion of the Aryans, to the great epics with their ethical inspiration, their concern with the eternal conflict between good & evil — nor to the spiritual teachings of the Vedas & Upanishads, but to the later forms with their accretions & impurities — to the worship of the lingam & the multitude of venal gods, to pujas & other ceremonies. . . And the diet, as well, is fatal to creative energy & conducive to emotional gluttony. . .

At this point, to help out my memory, I had recourse to his book and some passages I have set down in appendix No. 2. When he stopped talking I spoke about the conference. And he said:

I have not been invited. Indians live surrounded by myths & do not like the truth about themselves & so, they do not like me.

There is no freedom of expression. If you disagree with the policy of the ruling party you cannot get a book or an article published or broadcast — or attend their conferences. You are an outcast.

I left the roof-top dwelling the way I came and, after stopping for a moment to gaze over the ancient wall, descended into the lane and made my way to the buses which, always overloaded, plied between the old city and the new — the grand imperial city which the British built but never stayed to use. Each time a conqueror built another Delhi, the astrologers knew and the people knew — that he had built his downfall. And the prophecy was never wrong.

Chaudhuri had gathered all the puzzling and painful reactions of the last weeks into a unified experience which accorded with the long dark hopeless history of India — and I was more depressed than ever. Again I wondered why I had returned. To my notes on his talk I added some thoughts of my own:

> I have always believed that a nation's success is determined by the proportion of the intelligent people to the mass. Dr Radhakrishnan, the great philosopher, has written "A country's culture is carried forward by a small elite representing the soul of the people. When only the tip of the wick burns we say that the lamp is alight".
>
> This is an ugly, ungracious, cruel, uncomfortable country yet above the leaden mass of decadence, insensitivity & amorality, saints & sages dwell (albeit smeared a little with the general dirt). The tip of the wick has never been extinguished. No country in the world is composed of such unpromising proportions. Chaudhuri would say that the equation cannot last, that the mass will, in time, knock over the lamp. Perhaps that is going to happen everywhere?
>
> The tolerance that one hears about & seems to see everywhere is not what it seems. There is no feeling or consideration for anyone but as no one protests against anything — they call it tolerance. It is resignation, in fact.

However, a few days later, on December 19th, when I left for Banaras with Sir C.P, India changed — and so did my condition. I leapt out of the blackness, changing the location of my sickness and for 3 delighting days I danced in the sun. I described them to my mother.

Constitution House, December 22nd, 5 pm.

"I have just arrived back from Banaras & your letter of the 14th is here to greet me. These letters from you — from the only family & home & anchorage that I seem to have been able to secure for myself are so good — so sure, so firm, so strong arriving into the middle of this dazzling, dusty, shifting, unpredictable, sublime, degraded, painful, exciting, exotic & amazing land! At times I am drawn to it & at times I want to flee from it — but I must go on. I have still so much to learn — still to far to go."

"Leaving Delhi in the early morning . . . only 3 days ago (it seems like 3 months) we arrived to find a great concourse of people at the airport with garlands & flowers to greet him. And from that moment we never stopped. Each morning, starting at 7.45, we went from one ceremony to another with lunches, teas, dinners &

banquets in between. He made something like 10 speeches a day —
each one better than the last.

"The climax was reached with the Convocation Ceremony. He
received an Honarary doctorate & gave the Address & 3000 of the
11000 students received degrees. Thousands of people came from
the town, there were guards of honour etc, all held under acres &
acres of colourful shamianas. A wonderful event.

"Immediately afterwards a reception & immediately after that
— believe it or not — *my* reading to the literature students! C.P.
presided. The Vice Chancellor, professors etc. I read for 2 hours &
only stopped because we were rushed off to a banquet in the local
Maharajah's palace. I was besieged by the students, professors &
everyone — invited to return, presented with an inscribed tray,
embraced & received into the heart of the university. It was
wonderful — the warmth & enthusiasm. These small triumphs are
worth all the nervousness & pain which precede them. I am still
dazed & tired — but satisfied.

"Tomorrow, the Writers Conference will be opened by the
President, Dr Prasad, & C.P will be back in Delhi. I returned a day
ahead of him."

No writers came from Britain but because Monica Felton, the
well-known Communist, and I happened to be in India, we
became the two official observers, our meagre reputations as
writers ridiculously inflated. She, in the pocket of the Left was
politically sophisticated. I was just a naive, unattached adventurer.

I arrived at the Vigyan Bhawan, the new conference centre (the
whitewashing and furnishing alone costing 18 lakhs of rupees) and
sat down in the body of the hall. But at once I was hauled from my
seat and hustled up onto the platform where Monica, already
sitting in the back row, signalled to me with a baleful expression. I
had always avoided her, feared her, and now I found myself beside
her while we waited for the arrival of the President.

The opening time came and passed. Then, Mulk went to the
microphone and announced that due to sudden indisposition, Dr
Prasad would be unable to appear and he asked the delegates to
take the platform at once to deliver the messages from their
various countries. Then — he dashed up to me and dragged me
aside.

"Will you speak on behalf of Britain? Monica's politics are too
well known."

"But observers don't speak. And I haven't prepared anything."

"I know. I know. But we must have a speech from Britain and
there's only you to make it."

Only I! How could I fail them at this hour! I am not a quick thinker and I left the hall and went out onto a quiet terrace to collect my wits. When I returned I whispered my regrets to Monica, assuring her that *she*, with all her experience, should be doing this — not I. Her mouth smiled but her hooded eyes could have killed. A few moments later, the celebrated dramatist from Great Britain was called and I walked forward, in a daze, to address the writers of all Asia, a few Europeans and half the populace of Delhi!

I spoke on behalf of the many British writers who, I declared, were watching this conference with deepest interest, regretting that they could not be in Delhi to take part. I went on to assert that at this time of mounting crisis many of them felt that the politicians of the world had been too much and for too long in charge of human affairs and that it was time that writers made their voices heard and, rising above all barriers, distinctions and political passions, gave that lead to the world which it so sorely needed. I ended by congratulating the Indian writers for taking the initiative and convening this great conference which, for the first time, would project the views and feelings of writers whose first faith is in humanity and whose first allegiance is to the world.

I returned to my uncomfortable place beside my fellow observer believing that I had done my duty and could relax and watch the variegated march of speakers. But when the conference adjourned for lunch, Mulk came hurrying through the crowd.

"The conference *must* be recognised and officially opened even if it's a day late — tomorrow. I've just seen Prasad again but I can't make him come. And neither will Radhakrishnan. They're both terrified. The Americans are pulling them and trying to kill the conference before it even starts and unless someone important who will stand above the factions, appears — they will. Nehru would come but he won't be back from America until the end of the week. Sir C.P. could do it. D'you think he would? Or would he run away, too? Could you persuade him? Will you try?

And now the fate of the conference was in my hands.

I met him at the airport and drove with him to the house of his eldest son, an extreme pro-American member of parliament. I told him all that was going on and asked him to step into the breach. And he didn't hesitate. It was arranged that I would call for him in a taxi at 8 o'clock the next morning.

I reported my success to Mulk without being sure that it was as it seemed. Nothing was as it seemed. Had Sir C.P. promised, once again, something that he would not perform? Had he listened to

me and afterwards listened to his son? Everything around me
shook and no one could be trusted. When I called for him in the
morning I did not expect him to come.

The taxi drew up and I jumped out but before I reached the door
it opened and he marched solemnly before me to the car, looking
more than ever like the prosecuting counsel that he once was, on
his way to the High Court or, like the condemned on his way to the
gallows.

"My son did not want me to come" was all he said.

Mulk was there to meet him and the hall was full. He stepped
onto the platform, stood silent for a moment, a tiny powerful
figure — and then spoke. Spoke magnificently — and saved the
conference! Oh India! India the unpredictable!

He saved it from premature collapse but not from the battles of
its continuation. By the middle of the week the forces were so
polarized, the exchanges so bitter and the scene presented to the
world so ugly that, clutching in anguish at any straw, Mulk came
to me once more.

"It's being torn apart. We must have a cool impartial voice.
You're a Liberal. Will you speak tomorrow?

I sat up half the night putting my liberal thoughts together and
preparing to cry from the centre — unity, unity and again unity!

I was down to speak in the morning and the hall where the
working sessions were held, with the press but without the public,
was full when I went onto the platform. I had hardly spoken a
dozen words when the door flew open and Nehru walked rapidly
in and straight towards me and, as I melted away, took my place.
He had arrived back from America and come straight from the
airport to the Vigyan Bhawan.

He said a few words and then hurried away as quickly as he
came. His dramatic appearance, deus ex machina, lasted not more
than a quarter of an hour. But it was enough to notify the
Americans and the world that the conference had received the
solid stamp of his approval and enough to shock some sense into the
contenders, abate the violence and turn the tide. When the session
was resumed and I returned to the platform feeling dwindled and
deflated, a complete anti-climax, half the delegates had left.

I spoke to the conference theme, "A Crisis in Culture and the
Writer's role in it", and restricting my remarks to the English
scene, said that it might well be elaborated to read, "England is in
a permanent state of moral, cultural and political crisis and the
writer is not playing the influential role in it which we expect of
him — why not?" The full text I append (No. 3).

The next day, made bold by Nehru, Dr Radhakrishnan came out of hiding and addressed the conference and, on the last day, Dr Prasad gave a reception for the delegates in the presidential palace. Out of the chaos and alarms all came right in the end. I wrote in my notebook:

> The real theme of the conference was — the struggle for the soul of India going on between America & Russia. And the main idea which came miraculously out of it was — the transcendence of nationalism & the creation of a world society.

Long long ago, Sir Edwin Lutyens and my mother and I, stumbling over bricks and circling through unfinished rooms, could not find our way out of the Viceroys House that he was building. A few years later, when Lord and Lady Willingdon were the first tenants, I attended a reception in the great ballroom where we had wandered lost. Now, on the last day of the conference, I climbed the steps of the Rashtrapati Bhawan, passed between the liveried servants at the door, walked up the grand staircase and then into the ballroom again. And there I stood by myself, watching a vast company of ghosts reenact a scene from the imperial past upon a stage where nothing had changed; where only the dust of India and of the grave had settled on the furniture and darkened the faces of the actors.

As I watched, the guests formed themselves into two long lines as before and waited for the Viceroy to appear while an orchestra in the gallery played the waltzes of Strauss and Lehar.

Presently, the music stopped, the great doors opened and two trumpeters wearing the uniform of the Household Cavalry sounded a fanfare and a moment later, he entered and stood still while the national anthem was played. Then, in the same pale grey morning dress, with the same retinue of ADC's behind him, he walked slowly between the lines bowing from side to side and pausing occasionally to say a gracious word to someone whom he knew. At the end of it he stopped again and stood in all his dignity while important people were brought up to him to be honoured with a smile, his hand and a little conversation.

I had to shake myself and look again. They were not ghosts but the President of India with his court, his councillors and his Asian guests.

On December 31st 1956, I wrote to my mother:

"Your Xmas letter has just arrived & this is the first day that I've been able to pause for even 5 minutes. The 10 days of conference & other events have been fantastic. Morning, noon & night. . . . All the conflicts of the world focussed here — & pacifying universalism as well. I dragged C.P. along to try to balance the rocking ship at the beginning & the great sage, Rajagopalachari, addressed us, too. On the first day, at a few minutes notice, before the full congress & the public, I had to speak on behalf of Britain ! ! ! Imagine my panic ! . . . and speak again immediately after Nehru ! Imagine how difficult ! . . . at a party given by the Nepalese delegation in their shamiana, I read passages from my work. . . Yesterday, Mahindra Pratap, rushed me off to the country with Carlo Levi, the Italian novelist, & a Finnish poet to a zamindar's house. . . Tonight, Monica Felton and I are giving a New Year's Eve party here in my room. . ."

The dance was over! Beautiful selfless visions had been paired with passions that were mischievous and blind yet, out of the tangle, more good than bad had come. The foreign delegates returned to their countries, the natives settled back into their normal lives and I retreated to my room feeling that I had no place anywhere, or purpose; that my journey had been a terrible mistake, that I was finding nothing and the only lesson I was learning — was to hate India even more than I did before.

5

FOR SEVERAL days I walked about my grey unheeding room
wondering how to keep up the momentum that I had come to
loathe, how to make things happen that I did not want to happen
— in order to go on. For I had to go on. I was a typical European,
trained only to ride upon the surface — to be doing. And my
journey had not started.

I applied for a visa for China. I wrote to Nehru asking if I could
come and read my work to him and I hurried to the friends who
had helped, all unwittingly, to put me where I was. I went first to
Mulk and afterwards made notes.

The wretchedness of these top men. The President himself could
tell a lie & pretend that he had not been invited. I had to force my
way into him & confront him with the 5 letters I had sent him
inviting him to open the conference & then *make* him give the
reception — to put things right. And the Vice President,
Radhakrishnan, could be a coward & not come until he heard that
Nehru had. Only Nehru has courage & integrity.

It was the pro-Americans in key positions in all the ministries
who advised them both not to attend. Prasad's secretary is one of
them. And the embassies abroad were told to hold up visas for all
the people they did not want. Appealing to Nehru in Washington
was useless because of all the people in between, including his
sister, Mrs Pandit. American spies are everywhere.

One night, before the conference opened, I was warned that the
Ministry for Home Affairs intended to raid our office I got up at 3
am & went to a friend who knew the Minister (Pant). I dragged him
out of bed with a temperature of 104 & we drove to the Minister's
residence & persuaded him to call off the raid.

Radhakrishnan talks all that high-falutin 'non-attachment' stuff
but he is just as attached to all the vanities & pleasures of this life as
anyone. The Oxford dons got fed up with him & called him a
humbug. When his wife died, he admitted to me that when it comes
to oneself one *is* attached.

On January 3rd Sir C.P. wrote from Madras.

"A thousand thanks for your lovely letter which moved me deeply. . . . Well: the conference was rather formless & sprawling but, in the end, there was real enthusiasm for oneness of endeavour & the objectives underlying it and, after all, Carlyle was right when he praised those who had 'fire in their bellies' . . . I hope very much that you will be able to meet & talk to Nehru. He is a fascinating but (tho it seems queer to say so) a 'baffled' person but he has ideals & pursues them. The Madras University Centenary Celebrations take place at the end of the month when I am to receive another honorary degree (peanut gathering!). . . ."

Then Rustogi came again — and talked again.

The Times of India would have ignored the conference altogether. Until I met you we had not written a line. Then I ordered the reporters to cover it up but to pass over the conflicts.

There is no such thing as a contemporary Indian literature. Every little man who can read & write for the first time calls himself a writer. Their work is conventional, imitative, stereotyped, unoriginal & lacking in ideas — worthless.

Then, even more frankly than before, he poured out his journalistic secrets. The constant increase in the funds with which the Americans were buying people to work for them; the report to Nehru by the Intelligence Service that many of his ministers and other men in high positions were in their pay; the disappearance of top secret files from the Office of External Affairs; the sale of budget secrets and their duplicating and hawking on the streets at 5 rupees each; the swindling on a fantastic scale when the Vigyan Bhawan and the Asoka Hotel were built. My notebook continues:

Nehru is so out of touch that he does not know & will not believe that the country is riddled & rotten with corruption & nepotism which all began after Independence & is getting worse. He has the weakness of a dictator, liking & listening only to people who agree with him & overlooking competent people who sometimes don't.

He was betrayed to Abdullah of Kashmir by a woman who was in love with him & wanted to marry him & to whom he gave high posts & who is still in communication with Pakistan & considered by everyone — but still not by him — as a traitor.

In the U.N. they listen to him & take his advice & give way to him — & this he likes. He gave way to Gandhi & now he thinks that others should give way to him. But when he dies only technology & a veneer of western culture will be left with a deep, stagnant

reservoir of traditionalism beneath them which will only be swept
away when India is opened up in the world society of the future...

He went on and on and I filled pages of my notebook with the
unchanging story. At the same time I wrote to my mother:

"I went to the Chinese Embassy for my visa. They were very
friendly & said they were sure I would be very welcome in
China... I shall hear soon what they propose... C.P. is glad that I
am going. He says I ought to see the difference between their way
of changing their society, their revolution, & India's. He will give
me an introduction to the Vice Chancellor of Peking University &
suggest that I read to the students but he didn't help me to
approach Nehru. And so I went ahead myself & now I have
received a very friendly letter saying that as he is going away there
will be no time for a reading but he would like me to come & see
him at 6 pm next Friday... I shall need £100 for China. I have
enough until I go. I don't spend much. But when I return I shall
have to appeal to C.P. & I've warned him..."

And on January 11th, she replied.

"I will send £100 at once. Blew money! Don't go into cheap
quarters. We don't know China & Indian bazaars are horrifying as
I remember them. If you come home penniless it will not matter.
You can always sell this house... Sir Anthony Eden resigned at
last! I am glad Butler does not follow. He looks awful in the photographs. Most of them look brainless & barmy!... My pet butcher
is back — bursting with pleasure. We had such an amusing how-
de-do this morning. Susie will do well... Can Nehru write? does
he like music, is he an artist at all? Don't get lost in an opium
den..."

Then I went to see Nirad Chauduri again. We talked about the
conference and then about money. One of his sons was leaving
soon for England and we exchanged rupees for London pounds. I
wrote afterwards:

"The Indian writers who were invited are only important because
of the government & other jobs they hold. As writers they are
nothing. On the other hand, some good writers kept away because
they did not like the sound of it. Had I been invited I, too, would
not have gone.

The sudden stoppage of foreign currency without warning will
bring great hardship to Indians abroad & those about to travel & it
will open the way to new forms of bribery & corruption.

At present it takes at least a year to obtain all the permits needed
to send a student to a foreign university. Foreign degrees obtain

better jobs in India & so those unable intellectually to obtain them, try to block & delay the ones who can. One result of this is that large numbers of mediocre students are applying for British universities & the authorities are becoming very unwilling to receive them.

The withdrawal of British power is not leading Indians back to their own culture. The younger generation is becoming more & more divorced from the best Indian traditions & more & more a prey to the debased culture of the west — to films, drink, cheap magazines, comic strips etc. Young intellectuals no longer understand Sanskrit, nor do they read the Indian classics — even in English: standards decline & decline & the middle classes generally, read nothing — know nothing. This causes deep distress to western Indophils & Nehru is largely responsible. When he is gone, traditionalism with all its superstitions & ritual together with technology will become the over-riding pattern. What will happen to my sons trained in a rational humanistic way?

The Hindu's love of money is notorious. He loves & works for it for its own sake — not for the benefits it will bring him. A friend of mine works 6 days a week from 6am until 10pm money-getting & on Sundays from 6am until the evening when for 2 hours he comes to me for rest & relaxation. Some do not even take 2 hours off but on Sunday evenings will still be poring over their ledgers.

Although money is not honoured in the sacred teachings nevertheless, the secular Sanskrit literature of the most ancient times is *full* of the subject & its importance.

Indians in Delhi are the worst possible cadgers & they exploit Europeans. They write & ask to be put on the lists of Embassy 'invités' & if you ask an Indian to dinner once, he rings you up every week more or less asking to be invited again.

In the sphere of morals Hinduism has not progressed much beyond its primitive beginnings, has not been able to brush aside the doctrine that the universe is an illusion & that happiness lies in putting an end to the cycle of births & deaths. A doctrine . . . conferring no qualities & values upon reality. With such a philosophical background it is not surprising that the Hindu, ignoring distinctions & enveloped in mysticism, has been unable to develop a sense of moral responsibility & that he remains ethically immature. Even the popular gods are economic or utilitarian & demand nothing higher than commercial honesty.

The influence of Christian/European morality waned as English political power waned & now it has disappeared altogether & the Hindu has again become as dead to moral issues as he was before.

At this point I interposed a last anguished question.

"I came to India only yesterday and I can leave tomorrow — but you? How can you bear to stay? You don't surround yourself

with myths, you have kept your sensitivity, you don't anaesthetise
yourself with pujas — how can you live with so much truth, past
and present, and not give way to despair?" And he answered.

"My mood is not so dark as I have made it seem. As a student of
empires & civilisations in decline the time came when I decided to
explore what was going on all round me — & I did not like the
sights & sounds & smells. But soon I realised that I must experience
the decay that I was trying to understand & I became consumed by
a morbid curiosity to watch a sick & dying civilisation. But now my
curiosity has had its fill & conscious of the degradation & destruction round me I have at last gained an understanding of the history
of my country which I could not have obtained without personal
tribulation.

I have not needed to read books because I have lived & still live
this history in my own life & because of this, the achievements of
the ancient past & of the renascent period under the British have
become dearer to me & I can sympathise with the entire process. I
have only to look into myself to discover India, emancipate my
intellect and say: l'Inde-c'est moi."

I would never be able to say that — however long I stayed. It
was not morbid curiosity that kept me listening and looking — and
staying; unless to be fascinated and horrified by the spectacle of
unmitigated blackness, is morbid; nor was it academic interest —
for I was not a historian. Like Chaudhuri, I always need to
experience a place or a proceeding in order to understand it, but
for what purpose was I suffering, as he had, so much tribulation
here? I had to go on until I knew.

On January 10th Sir C.P. wrote again from Banaras.

"I was delighted to receive your letter & to see that you have
adopted the direct approach method with regard to Nehru . . . a
frontal attack & I feel sure that he will understand & appreciate
it... Your remarks about the peanuts 'exalted' me & made me
buoyant & happy. You are a wonderful friend & comrade."

"The departure of Eden from No 10 Downing Street is a
victory for the 'East' though I am sorry that England has suffered
what I consider to be 'excessive' humiliation. (After all, I am very
English.)

"If you land back from China 'penniless' I shall send you some
pence to Calcutta . . . to take you to Ooty to get the hug & kiss due
to a conquering heroine! . . . ''

The day came for my visit to Nehru and afterwards, on January
15th, I wrote to my mother:

"I have got my visa. They are ready to receive me, supply me with an interpreter & see that I meet all the people that I want & need to meet. I already know the Chinese writers who were at the conference. It will not be so cold in February. Quite moderate they say. . . My return visit to Banaras, on my way to Calcutta, is now settled. Dr Jha, the Vice Chancellor. writes, "It is heartening to learn that you will spend some time with us here. . . I have missed you ever since you left. . . "

"Last Friday, I spent 25 minutes with Nehru in his office in the Secretariat. He was *very* quiet & withdrawn & rather tired & dispirited, it seemed to me. He asked me all about my work & what I was doing & why I hadn't come to see him sooner & said rather sadly that there was no real theatre in India. Then a long silence fell — he looked down on the floor & I looked out of the window — I smiled to myself as we sat there but I was resolved not to burst out & break it! Eventually he spoke & in a rather disconnected & abstracted way, we continued. If I could have *read* to him I could have stirred him up & encouraged him — but just with idle words I felt unwilling to. We left the building together & he told me to let him know when I return from China & to propose a day for a reading. He went away the next morning. . . I'm sure I could have tied him down to a date then & there but there was that about him which made me diffident. Yes. He is a writer & is said to hate politics & to regard himself first & foremost as an artist. He has his weaknesses but he is a very great man. . . "

And she replied.

"You describe so simply & vividly your visit to Nehru. The long unbroken silence — two great people. Poor Nehru. His life must be a terrific strain for an artist. I'm sure your will is stronger than his & you'll get him if you have the opportunity. . . Little Susie is telling me so impatiently that it is time for our walk. . . I shall put a big map on the wall & stick little flags of your movements all over it & really feel that I am travelling with you."

I was 'great' now — great as Nehru and she, herself, so humble.

I met a lovely Muslim girl studying at the Jamia Millia Muslim University in New Delhi and listened to her story.

To do anything in India is impossible. People undertake things & then never do them — make excuses. To get things done you have to turn yourself into a raging bully, shouter & slave driver. They are astonished but they then do what you want. After my experience of organizing a concert, I shall never undertake anything again — never care if a thing is good or bad, a failure or success."

She took me to her home to show me what a joint family was like. The square flat-roofed, windowless house stood in a row of newly built middle class houses and consisted of 2 stories and many small dark rooms all turned inwards onto a courtyard, walling out the world like a little prison.

We went first to her modern student's room with a desk and shelves full of books, then up onto the roof from where we could look down on the teeming, noisy, primitive life below.

> There is no peace or privacy here as you can see. There is a clinging to & confining of, the individual. Everyone tolerates everything & in turn behaves intolerably to everyone. My father's refrain is, "Never mind". No one resists, protests, objects — they quarrel but make it up as if nothing has happened & then quarrel again. There is only the peace & harmony of non-resistance to all that is atrocious and frustrating.
>
> When I reported one of my professors for his lying, his incompetence & unreliability, the Vice Chancellor only said to me, "I have tolerated this man with all his faults for 30 years. Why should I notice them now, at your behest — you who have only been here 6 months?" But to save me from a nervous breakdown, he told me to deal direct with him in future, thus avoiding the man I so despised."

Another woman had protested.

I still went here and there like this, listening and looking but I stopped walking about my room wondering how to make things happen and I found, to my surprise, that when I sat completely passive, tuning in to the vibrations that now danced round me — things happened by themselves. I did not need to go forth and strive.

A sombre, ascetic character appeared one morning at my open door and walked in and sat down. His English was voluble but hard to understand while what he had to say differed sharply from the sophisticated conversations of my friends. He stayed with me all day and came back the next and said he would come back again but when I waited expectantly — he didn't. But someone else did. A venerable old Brahmin in a dhoti. And after him another and another. A quiet stream of mystic visitors regaled me day by day with primitive tales and Hydra-headed beliefs, always disappearing just when I wanted them to stay. They were Mr Josyers, atavistic spirits called up out of the dust to beckon me away.

And soon they did. I found I knew when they were coming and

waited for them to arrive and without any conscious thinking, knew things that I must do — and did them. My intellect retreated and my intuition so long repressed in my own rationalist society, rose to take command and as I flowed with my surroundings, a marvellous feeling of liberation spread through me. Was I wrong about myself? Was I, in truth, becoming an Indian?

When I heard about an old Muslim mystic from Gujarat who had lived in Gandhi's ashram and now belonged to the community of the Muslim teacher, Kuruktaler Saheb, an unknown person came at once and took me to her bungalow on the outskirts of New Delhi. Afterwards, I wrote down a little of what I saw and heard — and felt about her. I still retained my powers of critical observation and I was still a compulsive writer.

> Riohanna has a pied or mottled brown & white skin & a strong rough, squashed little face. She wore a dingy white wool kerchief round her head — voluminous skirts & a padded jacket and sat crosslegged on her bed (which she never leaves) with brown blankets pulled up round her waist — in an icy cold room. All the curtains drawn & light from one weak electric bulb. A bookcase was beside her bed filled chiefly with crime & detective paperback thrillers. She looked more like a Russian character than an Indian. And she talked for 2 hours without stopping; during the second hour, slowly eating her vegetarian lunch from a bed table on which she takes all her meals. Visitors were coming & going all the time & she embraced them all. Noise & distraction inside the room & out — unheeded by the mystic.
>
> A woman with strong, fixed views — although professing religious tolerance, very intolerant — dogmatic as she talked, admitting no argument. A preacher, widely read with many interesting opinions but all slightly outlandish, obscure — often not intellectually credible at all. An abstract, speculative, emotional & imaginative tinge to her talk. Good to witness & listen to once but too curious to return to. She does not attract me.

My notes ended there. Before I left, however, she plunged passionately into a new theme, an Islamic belief — Jesus in India.

During the unknown years of the manhood of Jesus, according to this legend, he had lived and studied in Kashmir under holy men who taught him the signs and sciences and mysteries which had been preserved there because Kashmir was not inundated by the Flood which had destroyed Atlantis. He had then returned to the Middle East and taught the ignorant masses of Israel and to impress and convert them had often used the powers which he had learnt, to perform what were called miracles.

When he was crucified he did not die on the Cross but was healed by the Essenes and returned to India where he lived with his masters and died a natural death and was buried, it was said, in Srinagar. His hermitage is even now a secret place of pilgrimage.

When she stopped she gave me a lengthy manuscript, exhorting me to disseminate the holy tale in England.

On January 15th, Sir C.P. wrote, assuming that she was a Hindu.

"Please write to me fully regarding your experience with the mystic. Sometimes these persons distract & tire one — oftener they bring mental repose. It all depends on mutual 'suitability' (being en rapport or not).

"I rejoice that my letters give you some peace of mind & comfort. My aim has been to help you maintain your equilibrium. You are so sensitive & highly strung that my best service is to give you a sense of relaxation & sometime, every day, I trust that you will follow my advice & empty your mind of all passing thoughts & concentrate on one idea or vision or image. This is an essential preliminary to all true Yoga . . . some lines of poetry or the mental image of someone, human or semi-divine whose aspect you can evoke whenever you feel like it. Apart from other results, this practise may lead to telepathic contact irrespective of space or time."

"I am not surprised at what you say regarding Nehru. He is mentally fagged out because too much is expected of him & he is on the borderline between normality & a megalomiac valley of shadows. Everyone feels this, even his cabinet colleagues. He is a dictator but does not know it & such men always suffer from mysterious complexes. But he is at bottom a fine & sincere person. Well — there it is & it takes all sorts to make a world! It is a consolation that we understand & 'intuit' each other."

Yes. We did 'intuit' each other and I believe now that it was his benign influence, exercised so much in meditation, which helped to bring about the change which lifted me out of the surrounding darkness and into the next circle of my journey.

All through the early difficult years in England when racial and other differences sometimes upset me, he was the father-teacher whom I loved and now, as I travelled through this Indian inferno, he was my guide — although I was still too immature to know it.

After rejecting one mystic, I now approached another.

Sri Ramakrishna, one of the religious geniuses constantly thrown up by India, lived all his life in the Temple of Dakshineswar on the banks of the Ganges above Calcutta where God is worshipped as the Mother of the Universe and, after studying and practising both Christianity and Islam, developed and taught the reformed Hinduism which his disciple, Vivekananda, carried to the whole of India and to the world.

After the death of the saint in 1886, the Ramakrishna Order was founded by his disciples and a Mission House where many cultural/religious activities took place, was now established on the outskirts of New Delhi. And one Sunday afternoon, I went to listen to a discourse on the Bhagavad Gita given by the head swami — Raganathananda.

In two large halls, connected by open arches, and spilling out into the cloister, 1000 people went regularly every week to hear him. In saffron robe he stepped briskly onto a small low platform and sat down cross legged on a mat and for an hour, without notes and without pause, expounded the Song Celestial.

The teaching and his spirituality and omniscience enthralled me and the following Sunday I went early to get a seat near him. Afterwards I talked to him and the next day went again to ask if one of his monks would give me daily teaching until I left. I felt foolish to be asking for a crash course in religion and I waited to be rebuked. But his expression was clear, uncritical and tolerant as he directed me to a swami living in the jungle not far from where we were.

"Can I go now? straight away?

"Of course. Follow the road outside the Mission until you come to a temple and then, half a mile beyond it, take the path on the right. Follow this until it forks. Take the left hand fork and go on until you see his hut. It will take you an hour.

It was raining. I put up my umbrella and set out.

I found my way along the jungle path and came out into a beautiful clearing where the hut stood and the ground sloped away into a dell. It was raining even harder now — crashing through the foliage and he could not have heard me when I walked up to the hut to read the half washed out words on a sodden scrap of paper pinned to the back wall — 'Open at 4 o'clock'.

It was 3.30. I walked on over the soft soundless earth towards a sheltering tree where I meant to wait but I had not gone more than a few steps when I heard the bolts being shot back and, turning, saw him standing at the door.

"Come in", he said. "I was expecting you. An hour ago I knew that you were coming."

The hut was about 6 ft square. I entered and sat down on a chair beside a small rough table and he returned to his charpoy and sat

cross legged on the blankets. I gave a needless explanation of why I
had come.

"Will you tell me about yourself?" he then asked and I
embarked upon a shortened version of my life story. After that, he
talked for 3 hours, expounding various aspects of the Hindu
scriptures.

"I cannot teach you Hatha Yoga here — the ground is too wet"
he said finally, "so I will come to you at 8 o'clock every morning."

And the next day Swami Vigyananda came, wearing a new pair
of white plimsolls purchased for the enterprise, looking rather
incongruous beneath his saffron robe — and for which he at once
asked me to pay. When that little matter was settled, he sat on my
bed and for an hour instructed me in the Yoga postures and then
for another hour, we meditated. After that, we left for Old Delhi,
travelling not in a crowded bus but by the higher class motor cycle
transport which he favoured.

There, we plunged into the crowds and wandered through the
intricate lanes and entering every temple that we came to, stood
before each piece of statuary while he explained its meaning and
place in the Hindu pantheon — and the essence of each Buddha
figure. We even went into the mosques. At midday we stopped
for a meal in a Hindu restaurant and afterwards, went on again.
Every day until I left, I served my novitiate in this peripatetic
school.

When he left me every day, at about 4 o'clock, I returned to my
room to write or sit receptive or wait for mysterious visitors or, I
went to meet my friends. But although my habits, my notes, and
my letters seemed unchanged, the subtle shift in the relative
positions of my intellect and intuition had altered my perceptions
and reactions and as I grew attuned to my surroundings a feeling
of unreality settled into me. I saw and heard just as acutely and
wrote just as logically but I did so as in a dream — and acted as
another person. And I liked this new tilted, other-side existence. I
felt lighter and more free.

I still recorded conversations and impressions but my writings
expanded and I filled pages and pages of my notebook with the
teachings I adored and which now possessed me.

"In Hinduism the aim of man is the discovery of the Universal Self.
In Buddhism the aim is the remaking of character. The first
declares that man is set free by knowledge & emphasises the End —
the Goal. The second emphasises the Way — the Path (Marga) —

to the Goal. It is *practical* for without a change of personality Man cannot attain to the knowledge with which to reach the Goal.

The Buddha's Nirvana is the same as the Hindu Moksa (release) which means the blowing out of all passions & reunion with the Supreme Spirit — with the Whole — when the chain of causation is broken forever & there is no rebirth. . .

Nirvana is not complete extinction — nothingness. The cravings & desires which sustain the fire of life are those of lust, hatred & bewilderment. It is these which are extinguished. . . Nirvana is a spiritual state attainable in this life & compatible with intellectual & social work.

The sense of selfhood is completely killed. "No one is better than I or equal to me or less than me. Even so", said the Buddha, "do men of the true stamp declare the wisdom they have attained. They tell what they have gained but do not speak of 'I'". . . A deeper different mode of life — not *being* in the ordinary sense but a reality in which thought has no idea, language no expression . . . where there is neither coming nor going, motion nor rest, death nor birth . . . and that is the end of sorrow.

He refused to define God — all Indian thought prefers silence. He set himself against all personal conceptions of God which tend to substitute faith for morals. Prayer becomes a selfish bargaining with God — earthly ambitions tend to influence the sense of Self. *But*, meditation is selfchange & reconditions the Soul.

He devoted his life to saving suffering humanity from sorrow thus confirming the great mystic tradition that true immortals occupy themselves with human affairs, even tho they possess divine souls. . .

Not either — or, but both. And a few days later.

I am being taught that the Goal is Eternity and the Way is Morality. Today, in human political affairs, the goal is unity — the integration into a world society of the disparate peoples suddenly raised up & brought together. How can this be achieved? At present, organization & coercion are the only energies being employed when the Way should be spiritual;. Only a synthesis of eastern & western religions will blow out the fires of lust, greed, aggression & fear & create the *Whole* man in whom the 2 hemispheres of the brain work in balance & being & doing are undivided & world society is lifted onto a higher level.

A few days later:

Love & Knowledge. Humanism & Eternity. Is western humanism the outcome of a belief in a personal God & crucified Christ? a god incarnate? a personal compassionate attachment to the Man of Sorrows? And did it lead to science & is it ending in the obscenities of technology?

At what point did the soma-drinkers, the god-intoxicated Aryans go too far, soar beyond morality, beyond good & evil, intellect & personality, deny & neglect the world & while sinking into the dust of the great Gangetic plain, create a society with too much religion, no humanism & rotten with corruption?

Too much religion is catastrophic, for both God & a redeemed Caesar must be served & only the God-filled & Love-filled together can bring unity & deliverance to the world.

And so I wrote and wrote.

Dr Abdul Aleem was a professor at the Muslim University in Aligarh and when we met now, he invited me to come and read my work to the students and when we talked, Nehru was once again the first topic. The interest in him was everywhere obsessional.

"If anything happens to Nehru now the reactionaries will seize power with American help.

Nehru considers himself a writer & thinker — not a politician. He hates politics & is incapable, therefore, of organizing & training a team of people first to carry out his soaring ideas & then to succeed him. He knows that the Congress Party is rotten — that Indian life is rotten but he cannot bear to step down into the heat & dust & root out the rot & put things in order. He is an idealist & talker — not a doer.

Now, since Independence & because of the rotteness, the best of the old fighters, all his friends, have deserted him & moved into the Socialist & Communist parties. He is, therefore, very lonely & his old friends should rally round him again. I am thinking of doing this myself.

The Congress Party never had a social policy & even the Gandhian policy of village industries was not carried out. The Indian people would accept regimentation, limitation of freedom — Communism — if they were given food, houses, sanitation — and energy & order".

Here, his friend, Roshan, joined in.

"Yes. The Americans are waiting & longing for Nehru's death. . . Indians all have such bad characters. What can be done while they prevail? They talk. Nehru talks — wonderful ideas, dreams — but no one *does* anything. We should rally round him & help him. He must be here, there, open everything, attend everything. He is our daddy & we are helpless without him.

And I commented:

> Aleem struck me as being an honest & intelligent man but complacent & without any dynamism & fire. Easy going & slack like everyone else.

I wrote to my mother:

"I leave for Aligarh on the 27th. Their Convocation Ceremony is on the 28th and the next evening I give a reading. On the 31st I go on to Banaras. I am looking forward to getting away from Delhi and from this amazing caravanserai although the 2 months here have been well spent."

"The exciting thing about this pilgrimage to India is that I feel once more young — because I am once again learning. Learning is the great adventure of life & I feel, truly, as if I am being reborn & beginning the adventure all over again — but with a difference. This time I have behind me the experience & confidence — the memory, that is, of previous changes.

"I believe Banaras is going to be the best of all my experiences here. The Vice Chancellor has already become a real friend — warm & responsive & to be able to spend quiet days with him & with the other professors discussing the whole gamut of human knowledge & human destiny is a prospect I look forward to with excitement.

"I am giving 3 readings on 3 successive evenings & some informal lectures to the post graduate & honours students. And the V.C. is going to take me round the ghats & alleys & into the magical mystical places of the old city. Even the local Maharajah, a great & much loved character, has written to me. I go to many sincere friends in one of the greatest & most significant religious, cultural & fantastic cities in the world. C.P. & my work have done this for me.

"I have booked an air passage for Hong Kong leaving Calcutta on February 17th but I am not satisfied yet as to what the Chinese are really going to do for me. I am still trying to settle my programme. Their promises are so vague. I could go on wandering about India indefinitely — as in a dream. . ."

And she replied:

"Your letters are always a thrill to me but this one is the most wonderful of all. You are in another world and in Banaras you will be in your own world at last. All your life you have been intensely lonely — always uncongenial surroundings & driven into yourself.

Perhaps it gave you more strength than even you were born with."

Then I met a variant, a rare strain of Indian — an optimist and positivist. Hans Raj Sharma was the leader of the Left wing in the Punjab Legislative Assembly.

In the Punjab, he began vigorously, all rajahs & land-lords have been removed from power in the Assembly — they are not trusted — & only 5 or 6% of capitalists are being left. And a ceiling is being put on landholding.

Throughout the Congress Party a silent purge is going on. Tickets are being witheld from all reactionaries. The character of Congress will be transformed after this election. The best Socialists & Communists will return & afterwards, the Administration will also be purged. Commissioners of known Socialist & Communist views & integrity will be placed everywhere to keep a check on government. All these measures will clean up the corruption, strengthen the Congress Party & accelerate progress.

The masses of the people are awake & enthusiastic about the changes & advances being made & Communist ideas come natural to them. They have never had individual freedom like western people. The joint family, poverty & autocratic & colonial forms of government have always suppressed them.

Material improvements are the reality. Collectivism will not scare them.

There is no 'after Nehru' problem. Young, good men are rising now & a strong collective leadership will be ready to succeed him.

There is still a great deal of superstition among the people. The core of our religions, the good & basic things have been overlayed by ritual & superstition. For them the real would be something new — they wouldn't recognise it.

The time for the opening of the Hirakud dam was settled after consultation with the astrologers. When Nehru arrived he brushed aside all the arrangements & opened it an hour earlier.

And I commented:

His religion — do nothing that hurts anybody else & then eat, drink & be happy.

I began recording little stories, sayings and impressions — sacred and secular. And Gupta, the journalist, had a fund of these. One day, in the dining room, he told me this tale of a village saint — a village near Madras. Tanks are artificial ponds contained by mud walls and depending on rainfall for replenishment. The people bathe in them, wash their clothes in them and drink the water.

When he was 12 years old he began praying every day, after his bath in the village tank. Before long, he rose still earlier — at 2 or 3 o'clock — and prayed until he went to work as a cook. His master then told him that he could come to work later & so need not get up so early. But he continued in his ways. When he was about 20 he took leave of his master & disappeared for 6 or 7 years.

Then he returned & lived without work or food, praying in the forest day & night. The villagers were suspicious & kept watch but when they saw rats & snakes pass over him without his knowing, they brought him food & his master built him a hut & they gathered outside it every evening. And soon they came from all the villages around until some 300 & 400 gathered every night for prayers & healing.

He performed miracles; restored the dead, appeared in two places at once & could travel long distances in a flash of time etc. He refused money, refused to have a temple built & continued like this for some 10 years. Then, he dug his own grave & one day went to it, lay down in it — and died.

Another of his little stories:

In Burma, the government appealed to all citizens to come forward & help build their country & the Home Minister addressed the beggars, in particular, exhorting them to work. As a result, a beggars conference was called & although it was not officially reported, it was understood that they expressed reluctance to abdicate their privileged way of life.

There was no way of getting to the Ramakrisha Mission except by car and one Sunday I took a taxi as usual and gave directions to the driver.

In the centre of the commercial part of New Delhi is Connaught Circus a one-way circle nearly half a mile in circumference with shops all round. When we came to where he should have turned, he drove on in spite of my protests and when we came round a second time, he drove past it again. When we reached the Mission I refused to pay more than the correct fare and he shouted and threatened me until two monks came out and drove him off. Afterwards I wrote:

When & where does morality stop? Can there be honesty where there is extreme poverty? Can one protest against violence in a situation of crisis & violence? How much must one condone? Indians tolerate dishonesty at every level. They fear & protest against *some* violence.

One cannot stand on principles when the conditions render them unreal. Do principles *ever* cease to be principles? The philosopher-poet-priest is the watchdog of morality. The situation may demand that he condone much but the moment will arrive when he must protest. That is the role of the writer.

How could I pit myself against that ragged, dirty ruffian who drove me twice round Connaught Circus? How much was dishonesty & how much just foolishness? Have I the right to make a poor & hungry man pay for the 50% element of stupidity? How could I judge & punish one of whom I know nothing? the reality of whose life seen from my position, I cannot understand?

One day, Mahindra Pratap & Carlo Levi took a taxi & the old Sikh driver drove them round & round & from end to end of Delhi, laughing ever more wildly the farther they went. And Mahindra laughed too, utterly tolerant — and kept the man on waiting when they finally arrived — but Carlo Levi paid. Would Mahindra & the old Sikh have laughed so much if they had had to pay? Were they both dishonest — or on the outside of honesty? I don't yet know the answer.

One of my neighbours, in Constitution House, was a distinguished judge who lived in a double flat with his family. When drama struck and the gossip reached me, I wrote it down.

The Judge's daughter. Of very good Bengali family, she ran away one day with a servant. Eventually, she was found by the police in a go-down somewhere and brought back. The judge denies what all the world knows, saying that his daughter was away working.

And:

The desperate young man, a minor civil servant & the only one working in his family of 10, had to support them all according to the unwritten law of the extended family.

And:

A Bengali proverb: Fortunate is the man who loses his wife but luckless is the man who loses his livestock.

I went to say good-bye to Nirad Chaudhuri and he talked more excitingly and generously than ever.

Before the coming of the British, he began, the Hindus had no recollection of their real past, nor any idea of the true character of their classical Sanskritic civilisation. The reconstruction of their ancient history by the European Orientalists exerted a powerful influence upon modern Indian nationalism which would not have developed as it did but for these researches.

It made them conscious of a heritage of their own with which they could confront not only the Muslims but the far more powerful & virile English. Psychologically, they jumped from being primitive people to civilised people, belonging to the same historical species as the Europeans. And during the 19th century, the culturual decline which had been proceeding steadily with every cycle, was arrested for awhile. At the same time, the political organization which became more perfect with every conquest, reached its highest point in Indian history, under British domination — although they never had time to complete their task.

This led him on to the history of Indian nationalism, to Gandhi and to his own passionate involvement.

When Gandhi first appeared on the scene, although he was eulogized by the press there were things about his character & ideas which I disliked & instinctively mistrusted. And when a nephew of mine who was at Tagore's famous school, Santanikitan, reported that a troop of half naked cranks, 'Gandhi & his gang', he called them, had descended on the school & persuaded Tagore to dismiss all the servants & set the boys to work in the kitchens & sculleries & would even have had them do the sweepers' work if Tagore had not felt that that was going too far, I was convinced that the man was a faddist & fanatic & out to attack social standards & civilisation.

But when, after the 1st World War, India's hopes of greater self government were dashed & disappointment & disillusionment swept the country, my doubts dissolved & I approved of Gandhi's plan to launch a campaign of passive resistance. But when I saw how this weapon immediately degenerated into mob violence & I saw orderly government coming to an end, I recognised the need for the suppression of anarchy. When, later, the Civil Disobedience movement arose, the repressive measures shocked me. In 1920, however, when Congress accepted non-co-operation, I became violently opposed until, in 1930, during the next Civil Disobedience movement, my mood changed again & I became a passionate supporter of Gandhi at the same time as all the old leaders had withdrawn from this new form of nationalism into silence & incomprehension. It was then that I realised that not until I set myself to make a historical study of Indian nationalism & to reach an understanding of the nature of Gandhism would I free myself from all these blind impulses. When I did this I was able to observe it with a dispassionate comprehension.

There have been 3 forms of nationalism & 3 periods. The first prevailed during the centuries of Muslim domination & was characterized by hatred alone.

According to the Muslim scholar, Alberuni, writing in the 9th century, the Hindus were haughty, foolishly vain, conceited & full of self-pity, believing themselves superior in every way. Their society was closed & exclusive & they had no compassion for each other & although they nursed a fanatical hatred for all foreigners they were ever ready to serve them & profit by them. They were impossible to make any connection with.

Alberuni's account of the Hindu's xenophobia & double faced hatred of their more civilised conquerors, shocked me, having been brought up on the myth of Hindu tolerance & catholicity.

In the 19th century the second form of nationalism simmered beneath contentment with English rule, dependence on it & praise of it until it crystallised in a movement led by a number of highly intelligent & idealistic men, based upon the new Hinduism which was itself based partly upon the Puritan Christianity of the west.

These men recognized that British rule was beneficial to India, that a broader & more generous conception of life had resulted from it, that the nations of the world had been linked by the genius of the English race & their maritime power & that Hindu spirituality should use all these roads to go out to conquer the world in its turn.

The true Aryan path was grounded on internal knowledge but without external knowledge it would die & as the English were masters of external knowledge, to join with them would help India with her external problems & the English with their internal ones. "So let us not fight them but make them kings to teach us", they said. But this rational & co-operative movement never attracted the masses.

Then came Gandhi & the third form of nationalism which completely overturned the last. Basing his movement on beggarly ascetism & Christian pacifism, he repudiated the new historical, political & religious consciousness & appealed to the intuitive, timeless & humble morality of the masses; to the common man who lives in the present, is governed by reflexes & is held in bondage to the past yet is incapable of learning its lessons. To these he gave what they could all accept — the lowest common denominator.

And the middle class which had never developed any political understanding, aptitude for representative government & capacity for working it, followed suit. "Let the dead bury their dead" they said & with no desire for political freedom were perfectly content with a one-party dictatorship.

Gandhi was the perfect representative of the masses, preaching the morality of the slave, of the early Christian (which attracted the West to him. Today, in Europe, in complete contrast to Greek morality, the servile elements, promised easy release from pain, are being given disproportionate power). Grafting Christian love onto this negative doctrine, rejecting reason, eliminating mind, he opened the way for the masses to reject not only western civilisation but ancient Indian civilisation as well & in the end he came to stand for nothing else but the atavistic horde.

When the masses took over his teaching — & he could do nothing to prevent it — & he realised that the one thing he cared for, his vision of truth & right, had been repudiated by his countrymen, he wished only for death & it came, swiftly & mercifully.

The assassin was not an individual fanatic, nor a member of a reactionary minority but the whole traditionalist society acting in unison as a murderous force against his principles & teaching & what triumphed was the primitive nationalism of the Hindus — the ghastly Indo-Gangetic plain & its degenerate inhabitants.

The Good that he was perished at the hands of the Evil he had helped to triumph.

I added:

The Good that he was triumphed because his opponent had a conscience; the Evil, because that opponent had lost the will to rule an empire.

This tragic story which I noted down as he told it and again reinforced by resorting to his book, contained and illuminated everything that I had seen and heard and felt in India — and myself become. All that was left for me to ask was — "Where are you in all this — now?" His answer and final message are in the last paragraphs of his book.

During the years of my education I was becoming a stranger to my environment . . . in the next 10 years I was oppressed by a feeling of antagonism to it, & in the last phase I became hostile to it. When I was young & immature, I was led by this maladjustment to strike a Byronic attitude. I thought I was born to be misunderstood & rebellious. I have been cured of this habit of posturing. Today I nurse no grievance because I have at last unravelled the genesis & growth of my maladjustment. The process was simply this: that while I was being carried alone by the momentum of our history, most of my countrymen were being dragged backwards by inertia. We had been travelling in opposite directions & are still doing so. I can now see both motions as from an independent point in space. I have found liberation from a nightmare.

Yet, this emancipation is not the whole story. I should be guilty of the blackest ingratitude to life if I were to say that on the eve of my exit from the universe as a conscient being I am only resigned to it.

For long years I thought that the best which that thinking reed, man, could do was to go on maintaining an unyielding defiance to the universe. I subscribed to a creed of intellectual Prometheanism. But in the last 5 or 6 years, through another miracle, I have been able to put an end to this duality & found peace in a new form of monism. I have come to see that I & the universe are inseparable, because I am a particle of it in every manifestation of my existence — intellectual, moral & spiritual, as well as physical. Thus on the one hand I have been disenthralled by knowledge. On the other I have believed in order to understand, & have been rewarded with joy. I have found that to sit by the rivers of Babylon is not necessarily to weep in Hebraic sorrow.

Today, borne on a great flood of faith, hope & joy in the midst of infinite degradation, I feel that I shall be content to be nothing for ever after death in the ecstasy of having lived & been alive for a moment. I have made the discovery that the last act is glorious however squalid the play may be in all the rest.

As I left, I saluted this great Indian; his flawless western mind, his integrity and his mastery of the English language who, through tribulation, had reached Nirvana without recourse to any of the trodden noble Paths or Brahminical incantations. He had a more critical spirit than Sir C.P. and was more of an Englishman — yet he was as much an Indian as the Mahatma. He was a man of east and west — the imperative synthesis.

As to his work, he said, "My views make some people angry and they brush them aside but the majority of my countryman can see nothing in them to object to or disagree with — and just ignore me." And he wrote, not of himself, "most great Indians have felt like strangers in their own land."

It is nationalism, traditionalism and some technology that Indians want today — not synthesis; nor do the western guru-chasers want it either.

Swami Vigyananda had promised to arrange for me to stay in the Rama Krishna Monastery when I reached Calcutta but he could never remember to write the necessary letter although I reminded him, delicately, every day. However, when he came to me for the last time, he told me that he had actually written it and also how much I owed him for his teaching. Not him, he assured me — but his Order. It was an outrageous sum. Mulk was indignant when I told him. And I wrote:

Conclusions about Swami Vigyananda.

He is chauvenistic, dogmatic, intolerant & half educated. He was never equal to a real argument & always became vague, inaccurate or opinionated, his statements constantly wrong & historically false. He believes that India is always right & every other country (except China) always wrong. He is vain, too, in a subtle way, very shrewd about money & careless about people, with no understanding. It was not the exorbitant amount that I resented so much as his crawling, gnawing, rat-like insistence.

Yet with all this, he has charm & sincerity & is tolerant of many things. His fervour for his Yoga & religious practises is great & he *has* understanding & knowledge of a wide & deep kind. He is interesting, often absorbing to talk to & at the same time irritating & unsatisfying.

Wise & ignorant, simple & shrewd — in short, an Indian holy man combining good & bad without concern for their incongruity, from whom I seem to have learnt nothing — and a lot.

So long as the teaching is carried on and given forth, what the vehicle is like does not matter, I was later taught. In the West, if the vehicle is faulty we do not trust the message.

January 26th was Republic Day. Starting early in the morning the great procession in which the armies, arts and industries of India were represented, moved slowly through New Delhi to the Maidan, the parade ground where, on a platform in front of the great public buildings, the President stood, taking the salute, with the rest of the nation's notabilities assembled round him.

I watched for hours from a humble position in the crowd while it straggled past, with many gaps in the continuum and long waits. Then, in the afternoon, I made my way to the Maidan which had now become a dusty, colourless and rather depressing fairground. Little stalls were dotted about selling food and offering pathetic entertainments, the largest of which was a travelling zoo. And to this I went.

A mangy, spiritless cheetah was chained on the top of a box at the entrance, to attract people in. And it did. Afterwards, in a rather stilted and unctuous letter to the 'Statesman' of Calcutta, I described the scene.

"Although a foreign visitor should refrain from publicly voicing his views about incidents which may occur in the course of his travels, I hope, sir, that you will be indulgent if I transgress this code of courtesy and draw your attention to something about which I cannot help but feel strongly.

"On Saturday afternoon, when the impressive and inspiring

Republic Day procession was over, I strolled about the Maidan and beside the green lawns enjoying the rich and variegated holiday spectacle until, near India Gate, a canvas enclosure attracted my attention. It was a travelling zoo for which the entrance charge was one anna.

"I entered and discovered inside a large number of wild animals confined in small boxes before which the crowd continually passed while, to give them their anna's worth of entertainment, several men and a boy constantly jabbed at them with sharply pointed sticks and iron rods to stir them into painful protest, evasive movement and, in the case of a tiger cringing at the back of its box — a forlorn growl. A few still displayed some spirit but most looked beaten, broken and wretched.

"I know that suffering is everywhere, that it is common to life and in itself begets cruelty and that this incident is only one of countless others which education and economic advance will eventually reduce. However, it was the sight of animals being tortured upon the very spot over which, a few hours earlier, India's proud legions had passed that provokes me now to break the silence incumbent upon me and protest — protest on behalf of these animals and in the light of the high moral and humane ideals which India professes and is striving everywhere to translate into practise."

I did not say what I had done; that I had walked round with the crowd until I could no longer bear the scene and, in a voluble mixture of English and Hindustani, had shouted at the men to stop torturing the animals and when they merely looked at me for a moment and then jabbed again, I had snatched one of their sticks and broken it. After that, shouting once more at them and at the crowd, I had turned and left — in despair. I doubt if my letter was ever printed and even if it had been — what good it would have done?

The next day I left for Aligarh with a letter from Sir C.P. in my pocket.

"Bravo! I wish you Bon Voyage & all manner of new exciting experiences in China. I am especially glad that, notwithstanding the 'Hardness' of the travel, you will be unfettered by embarrassing state-sponsorship or Communist hospitality. China is progressing rapidly towards industrialisation & agricultural development but is paying a heavy price in regimentation of the body & soul. The complete elimination of spiritual influences may have calamitous consequences in the long run. China has never been 'religious' in the Indian sense & never brooded on the

Infinities but along with her practical ethics she has had a highly sensitive artistic conscience & a feeling of oneness with Nature. Will she retain or lose these precious characteristics? You will judge for yourself... As you are not 'Imperialist' in outlook they will take to you kindly (of this I have no doubt). When you meet the Chancellor of Peking University please convey my greetings & best wishes. And write to me from Aligarh and Banaras... Au revoir then, & with all affection & kisses of peace & love."

But by this time I did not want to go to China. On the one hand, I had sunk deep into the ground of India and on the other, lay formless upon the waters of the intuitional life held up by the many arms of Nataraja. And I wrote in my notebook:

Man's goal is to live a life of divine activity after the attainment of liberation . . . which can be realised not only in Samadhi (trance) but also in a state of full waking consciousness."

As I became god-drunk and the swirling particles in the degraded soil relentlessly devoured me — I was happy.

6

BEFORE DESCRIBING my experiences in Aligarh I am setting down what I recorded afterwards, in Banaras.

With some fine exceptions among the staff & students, the general atmosphere is one of moral & intellectual laxity. Little serious work is done by the students & the professors do little or no research work. The students come only for prestige reasons & to obtain some sort of degree to enable them to get jobs. Even nepotism requires a degree of some kind. Holidays are incessant — every week there is some religious holiday & every excuse is used to get other days as well. Party-going among the staff is the thing.

The new Vice Chancellor, Zaidi, & his wife Begum Zaidi are both careerist types — ambitious & unscrupulous. He started as a school master, next was a colonel in the Rampur army, then Prime Minister of Rampur state, then he went into business & this year has been made Vice Chancellor.

It is known that, if nothing else, he is keen on building & even if he gets a rake-off of 50,000 rupees on building the new library it will be worth it, is the general feeling, for the job has been hanging fire for so long. Both he & his wife are energetic — and this is a high qualification.

The professors wage subtle & underhand war on each other, to prevent each other rising & all kow-tow to the V.C. & other V.I.P's in the hope of favours & privileges. At examination time it is accepted that the examiners must be bribed or otherwise played up to, if the student is to be passed. Whether good or bad, *both* have to ensure that they pass — the good more than the bad because the master will be jealous & afraid of him & more likely to fail him.

There is widespread grumbling & discontent but no one has the courage to speak up. With a few exceptions, all are weak & cowardly. There are a number of Communists among the staff & many more are sympathisers but they are not trusted — either in the university or generally.

The intellectual & spiritual orientation is obvious — the emphasis is on the Islamic tradition — on Persian & Arabic histories & cultures, although the Muslim religion itself is not, I should say,

83

very deeply felt. The ritual more than the spirit is preserved. The general outlook is that of progressive India although, I was told, the traditional ideas being revived in Pakistan, are to be found here.

Additional note — Audrey Ahmed.

There is no genuine non-violence in India. It is her policy only because it suits her & she has no other way. In the villages, life is anything but golden & philosophical & perfect — cruelty & violence are rife. It is the custom when anyone is arrested for the local police to beat him until he confesses. They beat the innocent & the guilty alike — often almost to death.

The so-called purging of the Congress Party won't amount to much. Nehru could be strong & ruthless & the people would be with him but he has no support immediately round him.

Democracy in India is all talk. In local government, in university life etc, an individual or a committee rules with out consulting anyone. Higher up, if anyone criticises Nehru, he has to go. India is struggling out of feudalism — that is what we see — & a corrupt & degenerate feudalism at that.

The V.C's first annual report — the wonderful progress made in all the departments was false — nothing but bluff. In the Muslim school in Aligarh there is stealing & cheating among the children & the headmistress just laughs — takes the view that the child who leaves things about to get stolen is a fool.

I have to watch, she said finally, while the examination papers are being duplicated or extra copies will be taken off & sold to the students.

I stayed with Dr Aleem and his English wife and met their friends and students and it was from their conversations that I compiled the above notes.

I attended the Convocation Ceremony and the next evening took my place in a hall with a lofty ceiling, lit by lamps, with the Vice Chancellor and his wife surrounded by professors and visiting luminaries on the right, a handful of male students on the left and before me, behind a purdah screen, an unknown number of women students. A marvellous curtain rise to a scene which ended as tragi-comically as it augured. I wrote the next day to Sir C.P. and, 'in the train on the way to Banaras' the next evening, to my mother.

"Your letter reached me in the University. Dr Aleem & his English wife are wonderful people. Most of the others I wasn't too keen on. The Muslim spirit so different from anything I've known anywhere else. . . My reading was atrociously organized — only about 50 people altogether. . . I was furious with the V.C's wife who fixed the day & time & knew that I would take 2 hours and then, after an hour, got up & after asking me to stay on 2 days longer to give them the rest of the performance, walked out with her husband to a dinner party & the professors & guests followed. I told them what I thought of them & there was chaos! Believing that the performance was over some of the students left too & there were stirrings behind the purdah screen. However, I sat down again & read on to the visible & invisible few who remained ... Leaving a blunt letter behind for the Begum I left according to my programme. But such experiences are valuable ... & my lovely hosts redeemed everybody else." (Most ignorant & ill-bred was her comment when she answered this.)

"18 hours trundling along in a slow train on a hard seat through the countryside is interesting & restful. I like being on the move again. . . As I have said before, one could wander on forever. . . I have been invited to come to Burma and, on my way home — to Persia! But just jogging about the world is not much good. One must stay in a place for it to be of any real value. . ."

I did not mention in the letter the extraordinary scene on the platform at Aligarh station the night I left — before the train came in, 2 hours late. All the middle class travellers carried guns and swords, with knives and pistols stuck into their belts and bandoliers hung round their necks. They looked like a citizen army or a guerilla force, and were frightening to behold.

In British times, when dacoits were known to be in the district, soldiers were put onto the trains. Now, the people had to defend themselves. But the train was not attacked and, on February 1st, I reached Banares, safely.

I had told them when I would arrive and I expected to be met and felt so happy to be back at last. But when I stood waiting, easily identified, the only white person in the crowd, doubt came into my mind and my happiness ebbed suddenly away.

Then, I saw an official looking person go up to an important looking person who had stepped out of the train when I did and was obviously bound for the university, and I was sure that he had come to meet us both. But when he greeted the important looking person and then, without so much as a glance in my direction, walked away with him, followed by a servant with the luggage, I was desperate. Not only hurt but bewildered and loathe to have to pay for a taxi.

I ran after them and asked the official looking person if there wasn't some mistake and the car was meant for me, as well? When he told me coldly that there was no mistake I had to sink my pride and beg him to take me. And we all rode uncomfortably together.

When we arrived, I asked to be taken to the Vice Chancellor's house and there a servant at once led me to the room where Dr Jha was sitting with some friends. After a momentary look of horror, he jumped up and seized my hand with joy and delight, introduced me to his friends, led me to a chair and ordered me some tea.

Of course he was expecting me, he said. He had been looking forward to my coming and that no one was at the station to meet me was due to some terrible mistake for which he would never be able to apologise enough.

The guest-house was next to his and after I had drunk my tea he led me through the gardens and as we walked I asked him about my readings and lectures. Mr Dar, the Registrar, would wait on me at once with my programme, he told me and, still glowing with warmth and pleasure, he then left me in the hands of the servants.

I was taken upstairs to a delightful suite of rooms and with my fears suppressed and excited by the thought of the traffic which would flow between the houses, the talks that I would have with this charming man, the walks and the trips into the city, I unpacked and settled down. And soon, Mr Dar arrived. He came to welcome me and to know if I was comfortable. My programme he would bring in the morning, he said, and leaving two letters, went away. I opened the one from Sir C.P. first.

"Your letter about Aligarh did not take me by surprise & if you had consulted me beforehand I would have tried to dissuade you from going there. It is the worst institution of its type in the East &, if possible, the students are even more casual & undisciplined than the professors (who are recruited on haphazard lines). The atmosphere is fanatically Islamic & medieval. I am glad, however, that you were favourably impressed by your hosts."

"The Madras University centenary was very well conducted & a number of foreign savants attended it. . . I prize this honour conferred by my Alma Mater because during the last 100 years only 30 such degrees have been awarded. (I am extremely conceited — am I not?). . . In China all letters are scrutinised. Therefore, write only formally. . ."

He knew that I was going to Aligarh but he did not tell me what an awful place it was and try to stop me and I realised, suddenly, that he, too, nursed the Hindu's ancient hatred for the Muslims. And his strictures were the more unreasonable since the indiscipline of the students was one of his reasons for leaving Banaras.

I then read my mother's.

"Annie Besant loved Banaras & called it her home. It must be a wonderful city — & now you are back there at last, among so many friends & interests. . . Fortunately it rained most of the time when Susie was at her height & it kept the dogs off the doorstep. Micky was the worst follower. I had to fight to keep them apart one morning. When at last I got Susie home I went to the library, Micky following *me* there — & *inside*! He kept leaping up & scratching my best coat with his sharp claws. I got fed up & picked up a book to bang him with! It missfired, hit a chair, whizzed across the room & fell at the feet of a horrified man! I could not help laughing. He *glared* at me — an uncontrolled brutal woman!! I settled to read & left him to pick it up! . . ."

How far away and blessed were her little stories.

I went out and wandered happily about and then returned to my lovely room, sat down — and waited. A meal was brought to me — well cooked and smartly served — the best that I had had for months. I ate, walked out again, returned and sat again — and wrote:

Here, at last, is what I have been looking for & waiting for — all concentrated & complete. The kindness, simplicity, naturalness, scholarship & spiritual awareness of India — the sweet, searching, pure spirit of India. Intellect, yes, immense intellect but combined with intuition & warmth.

The next morning, Mr Dar returned. My programme was being prepared now, he said, and would be ready by the afternoon. I expressed surprise that it had not been prepared before I came and reminded him that I was on my way to China and could only stay a week. He made excuses and hurried away. In the afternoon it was still not ready — and not the next day, or the next.

The huge campus was sometimes deserted and sometimes alive with moving figures whom I could watch but not arrest and talk to. Back in my room, I wrote letters, wrote in my notebook, read, meditated — and ate the meals served by my gaolers for although I was free to exercise, I felt like a prisoner in solitary confinement. When I called on Dr Jha I was told he was away.

Then, on the fourth day, I discovered another lonely prisoner in the guest-house — a Hungarian Orientalist and refugee (it was the year after the Hungarian revolution) — accomodated but ignored, like me.

He had been an officer in the first World War and then a university professor. Now, he was a cynical, embittered reactionary, ready to lecture but not make friends. India, the country of his exile which he hated, was one of his subjects and the other was Russia, which he hated even more.

> True Hinduism is no longer alive. What is living is superstition, ritual, rottenness & talk. The villages are permeated by this & educated Indians make no attempt to eradicate it, saying that all things suit all men according to their Karma.
>
> There are sadhus everywhere, 90% of them rascals. During a cholera epidemic one of them went about telling the people to pay *him* for protection. Then he went himself to be inoculated but was thrown out by the Hungarian doctor working in the villages. Barren women are still sent to the priest to obtain God's help in producing a child.
>
> Dams & industrial projects are not culture. Only when Indians restore their ancient culture & make it live again will they advance. But they look back, glorify the past & make no attempt to do this.

Then, about Russia,

> The Russians are a miserable people. They have no spirit & have made no attempt throughout their history to revolt... In war, they have to be driven, they fight in masses. They are warm, emotional but weak. They go to extremes — barbaric & stupid — play with children one moment & murder a man the next. Bolshevism has nothing to do with Socialism & there will be no peace until Russian Communism is destroyed. Thousands of people were deported from Hungary — just taken off the streets. Whole age-groups between 20 & 50 disappeared.

Then a comic but poignant little story.

> Mr Jones, once a tutor in a remote Indian state, still lives on there, year after year, seeing no one & with nothing to do. But in his room is a huge wardrobe full of the bricks & meccano sets of his former pupils & he passes his time building houses & palaces, railways & trains. When the Hungarian arrived there & was bored & lonely, the old man proposed a competition in building — & they both got down onto the floor.

And I understood why he was living on charity and suffering humiliation in this indifferent, unkind place. Out of my own neglect, loneliness and disappointment, I wrote:

> Where is India to be found? I am still searching. I think I have found it & then I lose it. I have lost it again. They say they want

what I can give them, promise marvellous things & then do nothing when I come — let me wait & wait upon their pleasure, kick my heels & waste my time. Now I hear that the V.C. wants to leave it for the students to *ask* for me! What does that mean? How can they? He heard me read. He invited me to come back & read again so why didn't he fix up my programme in good time & why doesn't he fix it now? My performances are not obligatory, plenty of people would come & they should be thankful for something new & entertaining & exciting in this deadly place. But if I left now in a huff — they would not care. . .

The V.C. wouldn't see me when I called again this morning at 9.30. I was told he was having lunch. Because he hasn't the guts to come himself, he has sent Dar again. The excuse now is that the V.C. has been away. I let fly at Dar.

Is the Vice Chancellor of the university of Banaras, the oldest & holiest city in the world, not one of Dr Radhakrishnan's elite? The 'tip of the wick' — upholding the ancient culture & representing the soul of the people? Is Nehru sincere when he says that he wants me to read to him when I return from China? or is he flabby inside like them all? Who can one trust? The kindness that one meets is only skin deep; ask anyone to help you & they slither away; they have to be coerced & the qualities displayed by those who have been to Europe are only a veneer; & as for the much vaunted Indian tolerance, there is so much of it that no one takes any line or stand on anything at all — let them all be as they are — even evil is preordained & nothing can be done about it. Real tolerance could save the world but this tolerance is just a cloak for weakness & a breeding ground for laziness & cruelty.

Mr Dar never returned. I wrote to Sir C.P. and the next day, set out on foot for the old city.

I followed a path until I reached an avenue of tall, shade-giving trees with little fields each side — not neat and hard like our mechanized farmlands but untidy and soft and beautiful. I passed a man on a bullock cart bumping slowly over the ruts and pot-holes but I saw no dwelling and when the trees ended and I continued along a track through a wide expanse of growing crops, I saw no one. A beautiful emptiness and purity informed the landscape and when eventually I reached the Ganges and, standing on the bank, looked down into the grey water and then across it to the fields beyond and then to where it turned and disappeared, a loveliness lay round me and something of that peace that passeth all understanding.

The water was low and the sandy bank sloped down to it. I walked along the edge, round several wide loops of the river, and then — and then — I saw it! Still far off, a tiny white excrescence.

Banaras the Holy! Banaras the Ancient! contemporary with Babylon and Nineveh, Thebes and Troy (now only archeological ruins) where the Buddha preached his first sermon and a multitude of gods still reign.

I walked quicker in my excitement, lost it round another bend, then saw it again in all its glory — the pointed carven roofs and domes and minarets, the palaces and houses rising finely cut and bonded, like a marvellous jewel.

Then, as I got nearer, I felt a change. I kept coming upon little mounds of excrement. I ignored them at first until they became more numerous and I had to pick my way between them. A quarter of a mile from the city the whole ground was thickly spread, even down to the water's edge — a sea of filth lapping round the houses. I waded through it and reached the first ghat and stood and gazed.

Stone steps, like wide staircases, led down into the water with buildings of all shapes and sizes perched along the top, some spilling over and here and there prised apart by narrow streets and alleys. One of these, a mere crack between high houses, was only 2 feet wide. And often the balconies on either side touched each other.

Further on, I could see little temples and burning ghats which seemed to hang half down the steps and little shrines, half submerged, and further on still, the palaces of the maharajahs and rich merchants rising high and straight out of the water. Boats and barges and rafts, moored by railings of stakes, clustered confusedly along the edge while thousands of pilgrims, priests and beggars crowded the steps; those in the water dipping their heads in it, immersing themselves totally or sitting in it and, praying, singing, shouting, gargling, drinking it — infused with mud and urine, corpses being washed in it before burning and the bodies of lepers floating past. Lepers are never burned but flung into the rivers everywhere.

It was said that the waters of the Ganges change, like life, from one moment to the next and are so holy that everything that enters them is mystically transformed and made pure.

I climbed to the top of the steps to avoid the throng and soon came upon a funeral pyre. The corpse lay upon a bed of logs which were well ignited and the mourners hovered round, some poking at the flames. Then, leaving the tumult of the waterfront, I walked on into the narrow streets even more intricate (like the Indian mind itself) than those of Old Delhi — the beggars even more various. Not just holy men, lepers half eaten away, the old, the dying and children — but dwarfs, monsters and grotesques proud

of their deformities, laughing at themselves and the people
gathered round them, laughing too. Laughing at the comedy of
Maya — the world that has no meaning and is nothing but illusion.

And fakirs with nails stuck through their arms and thorns stuck
in their bodies; a naked man with matted hair smeared with
excrement, another with coils of chain hanging round his neck,
ashes falling from his head and congealing on his face — and eyes
that leered and a smile that was obscene; a devotee who had been
travelling for months upon his stomach, lifting himself along by his
arms and hands, his goal now reached and bliss his reward; and
quietists who lined the streets siting in their own excrement or
lying in pools of urine while the notes of a flute rose above the
shouts of vendors, raucous chanting, clashing cymbals and temple
bells.

It was like a fairground in the underworld where unholy
mountebanks, misshapen and misguided, competed with each
other for titles presented by some fiend for feats of suffering,
perversion and uncleanness.

Although his father, the king, removed the beggars from his
sight, the Buddha saw them nonetheless and 2500 years ago, tried
to save men from the Wheel of Sorrow and from the cruelties of
Karma — and was rejected in his own land.

I continued, without a guide, until I came to a house out of
which came lamentations and the beat of drums. I stopped and
asked who lived in there and they told me — 'It is the House of
Widows'. These widows would have lain upon the pyres beside
their husbands if the British had not stopped the practise. Now,
driven from their homes and looked upon as dead, they lived
wretched lives, waiting for death in a less meritorious way.

I walked on until I met an ex-bank clerk from Calcutta who had
given up his job and left his family to cultivate his soul. He was a
forceful and distinguished looking man and for a long time, he
preached at me. Then, when I asked him more about himself, he
revealed his disappointment and resentment that his family would
not support him and he had to beg. And I wrote in my notes, 'the
same, frustrated, self-obsessed, devouring spirit that I find everywhere.'

I then reached a house where women students from the
university were living. A piece of paper pinned to the door gave
this information and I knocked. A girl opened it and led me to a
room on the first floor and asked me to wait there. After a long
time she returned and led me higher and asked me to wait again.
Both rooms were quite empty, the walls covered with short

lengths of patterned paper, patched together, each of a violent colour and design. The whole house had a flimsy papery feel.

At length, the girl returned once more and I was invited to ascend still higher where, finally, I met them all and was given a cup of tea in a room containing a sofa and a small table. They were refugees from Bengal and well-to-do, very friendly and very primitive. But we were not together long when a bell rang and they all rushed out through a door onto a platform suspended above a dark well in the centre of the house. Some monks had entered with their begging bowls and food was placed in a basket and let down to them by rope and pulley. They fed 7 or 8 Brahmins every day.

The Buddha did this; went from house to house with his begging bowl, accepting whatever was put into it until the day came when the offering was so rotten that it killed him.

Alms-giving has never been the child of Charity, in India. Giving brings merit to the giver and improves his future Karma, that is all. And suffering is so highly thought of that the sufferer is morally superior to everyone else. His misery is liberating him from his bad Karma, ensuring him a good life when he returns and conferring a favour upon those for whom he is kind enough to suffer and display his diseases and his degradation — providing an object for their alms.

Sir C.P. told me to observe the marvellous resignation of these people but often it is an expression of satisfaction, condescension and even a glint of diabolic pleasure that one sees in their eyes, springing from the certainty that they and the givers will one day change places.

The beggars of India are, in an insane way, happy in their suffering and to interfere with it, to effect any sort of fundamental amelioration would still, for many, be tantamount to an assault upon their souls. In Medieval Europe bettering the lot of the beggar did not extinguish his hope of heaven.

I walked on again, still without a guide, until I came to a large and ugly temple. (The most beautiful ones in Banaras were destroyed during the Muslim conquest 1000 years ago). Through the open doorway I heard, not chanting or cymbals — but angry shouting. I stopped and peered inside. Foreigners are not allowed into the temples but, growing more curious and perturbed, I crept a little way into the dark interior and from behind a pillar, peeped and listened. Then, over the streaming wet stones, I crept on again until I could see into the centre, into the holy of holies, where a huge stone lingam of Shiva, made visible in the gloom by a shaft of dim light, rose erect within the yoni of Parvarti, with oil and milk running over it. I believe it is women who perform these ministries and add perfume to the oblations.

A fat powerful priest stood towering over two skinny, cringing peasants, a man and woman. Their monetary offering was not enough to please the god and his faithful servant was trying to extort more by threats of present pain and future punishment — 'Indulgencies' terrifyingly bestowed. Then, as the man fumbled in his dhoti for another pice piece the priest looked round and spotted me and roared — and I fled before he reached me.

I went on and came next to the Temple of Kali — the goddess who, like Nature, devours all her children and is depicted in the sculptures as a fiend-like woman with blood dripping from her mouth and wearing a necklace of miniscule children strung together.

Until 50 years before, when the British stopped this practise, too, human sacrifices were carried out and, in secret, until much later. Now, goats were sacrificed and fed to beggars every day and although it was not the sacrificial hour, the beggars were already waiting in the courtyard where the altar on which the animals were slaughtered was covered with their blood and congealing on the dusty stones all round.

I stared and came quickly away and from there went to Sarnath to see the great stupa and the Bo tree grown from a twig of a twig of a twig of the tree in Bodhgaya under which the Buddha meditated.

It was late when I reached the place where some tongas waited. A tonga wallah ran up to me and I asked him how much he would charge to take me to the university and he named his price. But instantly, all the others followed undercutting him and each other, in a violent shouting match. Angrily, I waved them all away and climbed into his cart. He shouted at the pony and with a jerk, stung by the whip, it moved away and, from behind I watched the half starved animal take all the strain and pain. What use was my anger? And what escape was there from pain?

In my room that night, I wrote:

Religion gone mad. A favourite saying is — 'Man proposes but God disposes. I must try my best, of course, but only God can decide if I shall succeed or not'. And this is repeated in a doleful, hopeless tone of voice, making success out of the question from the start.

Are poverty, hunger, disease & degradation the work of God? or the work of Man? They should turn the proverb back to front &

say, 'What God proposes Man disposes' & clean up & change the
whole horrible creation that is Indian society.

When I recounted my day's experience to the Hungarian, he
replied with another long lecture.

Indian thought at its highest is the greatest in the world. It soars
above the world, beyond ethics, morality & common actions *but* as
practised by the masses it has become unlivable. The timeless
cosmos translated into action becomes dreamy & indifferent &
leads to callousness & inertia; the tolerance of the high altitudes
becomes tolerance of ugliness, obscenity, cruelty & evil. The
enlightened are said to be above morals — they can do no wrong &,
this leads the way for everyone to consider themselves above
morals; they live their culture but in a debased way. Energies
directed only to religion make for conservatism & stagnation.

He expanded this all too familiar theme and then added:

Judging from the stories of the Mahabharata etc they must have
been the same then — a minority living on a tremendously high
level — the rest very low. The practical religions of the West lack
philosophy & all intellectual content but they make for common
sense living — for good living on a mundane level.

And later, I wrote:

When I entered the Holy City, I should have had a guide to lead me
to the quiet Upper Room above the unholy tumult where a man-
woman with a beautiful face sits on a white sheet, in the lotus
posture, looking with open eyes upon Infinity as he-she rests in the
Knowledge of the Ultimate, beyond good & evil, pain & rebirth;
one of the elite upholding the ancient Hindu culture and
embodying the soul of the people — the tip of the wick, hidden but
still alight.

The next day, by express delivery, there came a letter from Sir
C.P.
"I read your letter with great mental discomfort but not much
surprise. Not only in India but in university meetings & PEN
Conferences in Europe & USA people look to personalities rather
than causes. Scott, in his Rob Roy, speaks of a Highlander who
made his way through a crowd acting on the principle, 'whenever
you see a head, hit it'. That is evidently your disappointing

experience. You have begun to hit Dar's head & I hope something will come out of the impact.

"My very dear Philippa, do please give up taking people for granted, expecting too much. Most people are self-centred & indifferent to all things beyond their small horizons. The exceptions are the salt of the earth & they reconcile you to the world at large.

"It is true, as you say, that the Aligarh lot are not really Islamic fanatics but they have not shed the Islamic intolerance which Muhammed discouraged but his successors in the Caliphate fostered. . ."

He was annoyed — and touchy. He did not mind, when I hit a Muslim (the Begum) on the head in Aligarh, 'that lot', but when I did the same to a Hindu in Banaras, he did.

He was right about the West where people are individuals & 'looked to', but wrong about India where there are so few and Indians, generally, are *not* 'looked to', not held responsible and he was telling me that I was wrong to do this, to expect anything from 'most' people and wrong not to be more tolerant of their nothingness and of the gaps between promise and performance. He, too, was condoning amorality. I had always taken people for more than they were.

There is, surely, a contradiction in this moral morass? If causes, not people, are responsible and people regard themselves as being helpless or beyond good and evil, then how can there be bad Karma? But Indians believe passionately in Karma, the spiritual law of Cause and Effect and the inexorability of its working; that suffering is Effect, the price of past sin and cannot and should not be avoided. Yet if people are not 'looked to' and their sins are tolerated why should the same sins be punished by the law in a future life? Sin without morality? Popular Hinduism seems to have tied itself in knots.

It was true that I went about 'hitting people on the head'. But I am a born protester and even when I became dreamy and indifferent myself, in the air of India, I went on protesting.

In England, when I climbed more eagerly than ever, I protested even more. And when I dropped, rather than dreamed, out of the community I still witnessed to the reality of the created world — to its truth, its beauty and its goodness. Back in the community now, I am still witnessing and protesting.

I wrote in my notebook:

I am travelling through Hell where all values are turned upside down and behaviour is insane; where evil is tolerated, suffering is enjoyed, defecation is beautiful; where this world is illusion and life is somewhere else & a cloud of false spirituality rises off the plain, envelopes everything & hides the sun.

I am lost in the darkness, my guide has left me & I cannot find my way.

.   .   .   .   .

'Something *did* come' from hitting Dar on the head! Suddenly I was told that the readings had been arranged and the next evening I walked over to the hall. About 6 people sat waiting. When no one else came, I read as if the hall was full. I would have read to *one* person having the desire and courage to turn up.

The next evening, Prem Lata Sharma, of the Women's College, came up to me afterwards. She was indignant for the notices had not been put up until that morning and no one knew that I had been in the university for over a week. She invited me to the Music School the next day and I spent several hours with an old blind tabla player.

Sitting on the floor together, he explained and demonstrated the complicated rythyms of the drum. It was a lovely lesson and at the end he asked to hear my work and I read some choral passages from the epic. When I stopped, he looked at me with his blind eyes and held out his arms, "I never knew", he said, "that English was such a beautiful language."

I wrote to my mother from Calcutta.

"Whatever one expects to happen in India — *doesn't*; & what one *doesn't* expect — *does*. Banaras was disappointing & maddening in some respects & then consoling & compensating in others. I learnt more from what did *not* happen than from what *did*. . . The readings were badly arranged & badly publicised. . . On the first night hardly anyone came. After that, I had from 60 to 100 (mostly professors) . . . & I had them literally spell-bound. The whole front row of professors got up one by one on the last night & made speeches — which were quite overwhelming — tho' one must never believe quite all that Indians say. . ."

Dr Jha was the first of the eulogists and afterwards he invited me to walk with him the next morning before breakfast. For an hour, then, before the sun grew hot, we strolled about the campus and he talked about himself, his hopes and fears and difficulties — and marital problems. He was so affectionate and so charming —

and so sorry for himself — such an unpredictable, unaccountable child.

I spent the afternoon with Prem and while we talked she prepared the most delicious food for my journey. And I left for Calcutta that night. A few weeks later she wrote to Sir C.P. and, very nobly, he showed me the letter when I reached him in Ooty.

Revered Sir,
   Kindly permit me to address a few lines about Miss Philippa Burrell.
   Miss Burrell came here in the beginning of February and none of us knew anything about her arrival until more than a week later. . . I had the good fortune of coming in close personal contact with her in the last days of her stay. . . She was very anxious to meet Pandit Omkarnthji but by the time that we knew that she was here he had left for Madras. He highly appreciated her reading in December. . . When he returned he was deeply pained to learn that her programme could not attract large audiences this time, for lack of due publicity. He is keen to arrange a programme for her in our college and hopes she will return and waits anxiously for news of her. . . It will be very kind if you will give me information about her. . ."

She had protested. Another woman. It is the women of both east and west who are going to change the world.

. . . . .

It was not dacoits on this journey but bridges that the travellers feared. Another bridge had collapsed, the third in a year, and a whole train had plunged into a ravine. They were not being inspected and maintained and before setting out, people consulted the astrologers even more anxiously than usual.

There were no compartments reserved for women and I climbed into an empty one, locked the door, turned out the lights and pulled down the blinds. In the middle of the night when we stopped at the first large station, the doorhandle rattled. I peeped out and when the man began to hammer and shout, I still did not open it.

He went away and I thought that I had won but a few minutes later the station master arrived, a crowd gathered and the shouting and hammering were redoubled. When, overcome by superior power, I opened the door, the surprise at seeing that it was a white woman defending a compartment and holding up the train, stilled the anger outside as the man climbed in with all his bundles.

He did not look like a robber or a rapist but I trusted no one and stayed awake for the rest of the night watching him. But when dawn came and I pulled up the blinds, we were soon sitting on the same bench and he was telling me about his life.

When we arrived in Calcutta I boarded a crowded bus which wound through the northern slums of the city and then out into the suburbs, stopping at length before the gates of Belur Math, the Ramakrishna Monastery.

The swami in Delhi had never written and the monks were not expecting me but they received me kindly and one of them escorted me through a door in the wall and "down a beautiful perfumed winding lane", as I wrote to my mother, to the guest-house.

I was given a stark clean room, containing a plank bed covered with a piece of cotton and surmounted by a mosquito net, a chair and a small rough-hewn table. I was the only guest and servants were summoned to look after me and bring me my meals. I unpacked my simple needs and then returned through the wall to find the monks with whom, for the next five days, I was to dwell.

I wrote to my mother:

"The whole scene is very beautiful. The monastery is surrounded by a high wall & the temple is in the centre, close to the river, with wide steps leading down to the water's edge. Ancient, grimy old boats, looking half like gondolas & half like triremes, ply for customers up & down the sacred river & across to the other shore. Great banyan trees grow almost out of the water & the boatmen huddle under them before their fires at night.

"One lives in the past everywhere in India, moving in & out of every historical age & adjusting oneself quickly is really most difficult & exhausting. One could go on & on. I have got to the point where I should settle down & *live* in Asia for several years — or come home. I've been meeting so many people & seeing & hearing & taking in so much; been hit on the head or pierced by so many shocks & sharp experiences; been lifted up & flung down incessantly; been so moved, so stimulated, so horrified, irritated & disgusted alternately, that I'm quite worn out — dreaming of reaching home again changed & enriched & reinvigorated — dreaming of rest — and then of new work.

"Of course, I could stand still somewhere here & rest — but there'd be no point to that. I still have more to do, more conclusions to strive for & I'd better keep going until I've achieved my immediate goal. After that, staying at home or returning here, I shall take up the quest where I left it off — in quite other ways & by other means. . ."

Every morning I went into Calcutta and returning in the afternoon, spent some time with the crowds in the temple until the monks were free and I could walk up and down with them beneath the trees.

Several of them had lived and studied in England and at first were pleased to hear about London and to recount some of their own experiences but when these preliminaries were over, they preached. I knew by this time that Indians do not discuss. I asked my questions — and joyfully listened. At 7 o'clock the gates were closed and I withdrew to the world outside the wall. And I wrote in my notebook:

> I walk up & down with the monks beside the Ganges with harsh chanting voices & an orchestra of drums & vinas coming from the temple — the mosquitos buzzing.
>
> This evening an old monk unlocked the door & came out to call on me & we sat on the veranda outside my room while he talked, gazing across the vast grey waters to the Dakshineshwar Temple, both of us almost invisible inside a cloud of mosquitos — he quite unconcerned, barely conscious of them.
>
> When I am alone & locked out, I watch the ferry arrive — a grimy gondola — & see the ferryman push it up with a pole onto the mud & the passengers step out up to their knees & wade through it to dry land. Why don't they build a small jetty? I watch the boat repairers in their encampment under the banyan trees & listen to their wild music which goes on all night — bells & drums & singing.
>
> Mosquitos, mud, dust, poverty, dirt & depression — a purgatorial scene. And when darkness comes I roam round the unlit deserted lanes, meet & talk to a neurotic Bengali boy & absorb into myself the dark, hopeless, haunting, ominous night — the silence punctuated constantly, as everywhere, by the screams of kicked & stoned dogs.

Sir C.P. had given me an introduction to some wealthy friends of his — and I called on them. And wrote:

> The poverty, misery, hunger & disease are worse here than anywhere else — aggravated by the refugees from East Bengal. People lie about the streets starving & listless. There are camps & help is given but the problem is too great for the government.
>
> Today, I had lunch at the club with Mrs Sekhar & other wives of eminent Calcutta men, all in gorgeous saris, all dabbling in social

work. The newspapers complain that no selfless people come forward. The atmosphere is enervating, slack & demoralised.

I have been to the great Temple of Kali where, as in Banaras, animals are sacrificed & 400 beggars are fed daily. Beggars were everywhere amid the squalor & degradation. I walked into a dusty, dried-up garden where, in the middle, stood the Tree of the Barren Women before which they come to pray for a child while staying in the Temple with the priest. The Tree was dead but loathesome looking objects were stuck like leaves onto its dessicated branches — the gifts, together with money, brought by the supplicants or by successful devotees returning to give thanks.

I have visited the home of some prostitutes and, in the street, met an elegant Edwardian Anglo-Indian, a sad nostalgic old man left stranded by the departure of the British.

Another time, wandering along an empty street, a ghastly-looking beggar approached me, covered in sores, mutilated & in filthy rags — and I laughed at him! I know the difference now between a real beggar & a fake. There is a beggars' town outside the city where, like actors, the able-bodied train & make themselves up but children are actually mutilated.

For an instant he looked sharply at me, puzzled, & then he laughed too & waving one of his crutches, danced off down the street, turning again & again to look back at me & laughing every time. He is the first Indian I have met with a sense of humour. He deserved some money.

Then, in another street, this one crowded & noisy, I heard the notes of a flute, sweet & clear above the tumult & I crossed the road & spoke to the flute-seller — & bought one. I rested on a seat in the park in front of the Fort for a little while & watched the death of 2 kites on the banks of the Hooghly. . .

Each day, when I returned to the monastery, I hurried to the shelter of its walls which seemed to keep the inside from the outside although I knew by this time that the outside was but the obverse of the inside and had to be accepted. And I wrote:

The soma juice which made the ancient Aryans drunk with religion has been so adulterated and kept so long that it has turned into a black brew of holism which has driven their descendants mad.

But madness & sanity, good & evil, filth & sweetness, the lingam & the Third Eye — the lotus flower with its roots in the mud — all have been created, sustained, destroyed & recreated — are one & must be worshipped.

On my last day, I was granted a ceremonial interview with the head monk, a sign that I had been approved, and I prepared myself.

In an upper room, in an atmosphere that was immaculate, he sat behind a table with books and manuscripts on shelves behind him and effortlessly and without pause, delivered a sermon which lasted for two hours. When he stopped I rose and in gratitude, bowed my head, put my palms together in the namashkar and then withdrew.

Belur Math is a sanctuary which lies upon the dark road through India and, like the tip of the wick, illumines it for the lost and despairing traveller. When I went on and reached the next circle, my guide was waiting for me. I wrote before I left:

I have begun to penetrate beneath the ghastly surface & to feel my way down to the essential India below. I have learnt not just to look, to listen & to criticise & shrink away in horror, but, with my whole being, am beginning to *know* — why these people are as they are.

I not only revere the long succession of saints & sages, their hymns & their philosophies but begin to *experience* the warmth & kindness, the artistry & creativeness which are there, half secreted — not just glimpse them but sometimes touch & even take them.

On the threshold of knowledge as I move to their rythym, their terrible rythym of oneness, to the dance of the opposites, sublimity & obscenity, I am beginning to love them — and to exalt their divine madness.

The World is Dance — and I am dancing.

7

I SENT ANOTHER cable to Peking and the next evening flew to Hong Kong. And wrote to my mother:

YMCA Hong Kong. February 18th 1957.

"I arrived here this morning. . . An abrupt transition — from Medieval India to this 20th century clean, well organised, prosperous, easy, understandable & dull-looking British colony. And tomorrow I venture into yet a 3rd world, a 3rd historical epoch — Red China.

"The YM, which appears to be bi-sexual, is a very well run establishment. A lovely, comfortable, clean room. A spring bed! I've been sleeping on charpoys & planks. . . I'm as decadent in a western way as India is in an eastern!"

"I've done nothing here — just slept the whole afternoon. The monastery, the setting-off for another country & the whole coming-to-an-end of the first, hardest & probably most important phase of my travels was exhausting. Nehru's sleeping achievement — 4 hours — is a common-place in India. I have never slept more than that myself, and often less — the winter climate & the tension — but at the end, in Calcutta, things seemed harder than ever & I felt the reaction when I arrived here. But now I am alright & looking forward to the next adventure. I have learnt to do so many things that I found difficult at first. I am hardened & liberated in so many ways."

"This is a muzzy-headed letter. I'm still drowsy & not certain what I'm writing & doing — or where I am! . . . A reading is being arranged for me when I return to Calcutta but I am getting bored with these performances. The whole work grows stale to me. So much has changed & moved on within me & without."

I took the train to the border, had my passport checked by the British border guard, walked across, was checked again by the Chinese guard & then transferred to the Chinese train. In Canton I was met by a woman representative of Intourist and taken to a

102

hotel on the waterfront where, from my window I could look down on the river life.

I only had my £100 British travel allowance which I knew wouldn't last me long and so, I hurried on. I went about with my guide the next day and caught the train for Peking that night. Two days later, I wrote to my mother:

Hankow. 22/2/57.

"I have got as far as this — right in the middle of China. When the train arrived this morning at Wuchang all the passengers were tumbled off & we bundled down some steep broken steps & boarded the ferry, an old paddle steamer, & crossed the great Yangste river — a marvellous sight — to catch the connecting train on the opposite side, at Hankow. When the new bridge is finished this year the trains will connect. I have had 6 hours here & used the time tramping all over the city with an Intourist guide."

"I also had a day in Canton . . . a wonderful spirit prevails — of energy hard work, hope & happiness. The contrast with India is significant. The people are as friendly, smiling & helpful as everyone reports. . . Unless I can find some means of living cheaply I shan't be able to stay long. The slow pace of India will be quite out of the question — which is a pity — because rushing things is not the way to know & understand a country."

"We have travelled through wild, rugged hills lost in cloud, wonderful rivers, gorges etc reminding me of Scotland, only softer & more richly coloured — not so grim. The weather, so far, much the same as England — raining, damp, foggy, a bit cold. . ."

On the 27th, from the Pei-Fang Hotel, Peking, I wrote again. A letter from her was there to greet me.

"I travelled hard-class from Canton, in a 6-berth compartment with vigorous, noisy, friendly Chinese men — the berths like 3 narrow wooden shelves each side, so close that one had to crawl into them — the top ones — my choice (to get out of the way) close to the roof & claustrophobic. I did this to save money & to feel & know the people, quickly & intensely. . . I arrived late at night in a snow storm & bitter cold. . ."

Perhaps because of the censor, this was not the whole story. The "friendly' men, all of the older generation, were at first very hostile when they learnt that I was English. They glared or pointedly ignored me. On the second day, however, they softened a little and by the time that we reached the Yangtse and changed trains, we were talking in sign language and they were smiling and laughing and bringing me cups of tea.

On the second stage, they were all students in the compartment, directed to work projects all over China and they, by contrast, were sweet and friendly from the start. They even knew a few words of English and when I left the train and they went on, we were sad to have to say good-bye.

Another Intourist guide met me and took me through the snow storm to one of the old hotels, now reserved for foreigners; for delegations, official visitors and salesmen. Individual tourists like myself were unknown. English was spoken at the reception desk and there were menu cards in English in the dining room. My room and bath were luxurious and the central heating and double glazing were good when entering out of the cold.

It was customary for foreigners to summon a tailor and have a padded suit made at once, but I could not spend money on anything like that and the macintosh which I had bought in England for the occasion, large enough to envelope everything else, served me well enough.

I had come with Sir C.P's letter of introduction to Dr Ma-Yin-Chu, the Vice Chancellor of Peking University, another to the Minister of Posts & Telegraphs from a prominent Communist friend in London and a third to the Chinese Peace Committee.

To each of these I attached a letter of my own explaining that my purpose in coming was to see something of the beauties and treasures of old China, to meet writers and to study the New China. And I told them that my time was short as my travel allowance would not support me for long. I despatched these letters by hand, expecting prompt replies.

I had come at a propitious time. At a recent meeting of leading scientists, writers and artists, Lu Ting-yi, the head of the propaganda department of the Party, had declared that China now felt strong enough to adopt a policy of freedom for independent thinking and debate — "freedom to express one's opinion, maintain one's opinion and reserve one's opinion and freedom to criticise" he said. "Those who propagate materialism and those who propagate idealism must be at liberty to debate. By open debate and not by administrative orders will materialist thinking gradually overcome idealist thinking, will ideological problems be solved and academic development be saved from stagnation." And he ended, "Let a hundred flowers of all seasons blossom together and let diverse schools of thought contend."

I wrote to my mother:

"In spite of all the cables & supposed arrangements, no one here knows anything about me!! I came armed with introductions but

so far no one has responded. While waiting for some recognition, I
tramp the streets & alleyways, palaces & temples, markets &
parks, studying the people — collecting all the strong impressions
which the eyes & senses give — measuring the impact of the first
most powerful days. . .''

In spite of the cold, so much of the life of the city was out of
doors. I wandered up and down the great open market where, on a
bookstall, I found a copy of T. E. Lawrence's 'Seven Pillars of
Wisdom'. I visited the Forbidden City and walked round the lake
in the park watching the children play. In a back street I came upon
a large open-air reading place. Under a canvas roof, small
platforms were erected upon which sat readers, all women, each
with an audience, on rows of benches, closely packed before her.

Each book was read for a prescribed time at the end of which the
listeners left, to return the next day for another instalment and
another audience took their place. These audiences were
composed of working-class people, probably illiterate, but
familiar with the oral tradition.

I went round the only large department store in which the
shelves and tables were stacked with pitifully rough, drab
consumer goods. I followed the sound of music down a muddy lane
where, inside a ring of canvas, a troop of entertainers were giving
a performance. At the entrance I held out some coins. I did this
wherever I went and felt sure that they never took too much.
Inside, jugglers, wrestlers and acrobats followed one another
before an appreciative audience sitting on benches round the
canvas walls.

Down another muddy lane, I came upon a man beating a
donkey. I shouted and went up to him and held his arm but I didn't
cow him as I did the travelling zoo man in Delhi. He looked at me
angrily as if he would like to beat me, too. I stopped him for a
moment — that was all. And all that I did in Delhi.

I bought some fruit from a street hawker, a young boy with a
lovely sensitive face who smiled so sweetly as he carefully picked
the right coins from my hand. I wandered into a street full of
pedlars selling old jewellery and trinkets. Like the people in the
Moscow pawnshops, they may have been members of the old
capitalist class selling what remained of their possessions, to
survive. And I bought some little saucers. They did not look happy.

Everywhere else, dressed in their blue denims — 'blue ants', as
Westeners called them, (appropriate in a time of heroic struggle
and shortage), the crowds looked well-fed, happy and confident.
Even behind the gauze masks which many wore over their mouths

and noses to protect them from germs and dust (about which they were fanatical), one could sense that they were smiling and hear when they were laughing. And they all had homes of some sort. Out in the streets of the little houses, early in the mornings, they could be seen doing their Tai Chi.

Although they admitted to me later, that there were still pockets of extreme poverty and depression in distant parts of the country, there were none to be seen in the imperial city nor in the other towns that I passed through.

In 1949, after the Long March and defeat of the Kuo-Min-Tang, the Communists came to power inheriting a legacy of disasters in a situation of chaos. For decades the country had been ravaged by civil wars, foreign wars, revolutions, famines and epidemics. The civil administration had broken down, lawlessness ran everywhere, corruption pervaded everything and destitution was general. Yet now, 7 years after, there was order, honesty, progress and relative prosperity.

When the British left India in 1947, they left democratic institutions, medical and educational services, roads and railways — the complete and efficient superstructure of a modern state. And agriculture and industry flourished. Yet now, 9 years after, everything was running down and there was more poverty, disease and corruption than ever before. These were the differences which I set myself to study.

At midday, I went into the little dark cabins, workmens' restaurants, and looking at the clients' plates, pointed to what I fancied. In one of them, I went into the kitchen where a row of huge cauldrons steamed and bubbled on tiny stoves and I peered into them all. And the cooks laughed and served me generously. Wherever I went I was taken for a Russian. The country was full of their technicians then.

After a few days, when I received no replies to my letters, Dr English, a New Zealander living permanently in the hotel and speaking Chinese, began telephoning several times a day, to each of my introductions, informing them of my presence. When still nothing happened I continued my solitary wanderings. And wrote to my mother.

"Soon, my assertive western character will begin a determined assault on the people whom I am so anxious to meet. I feel like a sadhu beholding the insistence & upsurge of my own nature. But time is against me. I calculate that I can only survive here a fortnight & so I have had to change hotels, move from a comfortable & quiet one to a cheap & noisy one on the far side of the city — but even this is no bad thing — everything enlarges one's experience. If the worst befalls & I fail, I shall not come away quite empty-handed. I could not be in Asia & not visit China & I shall carry something valuable away. All life is an adventure. Nothing is predictable — the unpredictable becomes the goal & the findings are great and the failures as important as the successes. India has taught me that."

"I have been several times to the theatre & I shall go out to see the Great Wall. On a clear day one can see the Western Hills. Although the landscape now is brown or snow covered, I can sense the beauty & loveliness of the country. . . I shall see all I can before I am driven away by shortage of currency & failure of friendship. But what will come — will come. I do not worry."

"The common people among whom I have moved, appear very responsive & friendly, humorous, fastidious & attractive — very understanding, intelligent & alive. Absolute honesty prevails."

"When I turn & depart from here I shall virtually be homeward bound. . . The thought is strange. I seem to have been away so long, to have moved so far in all respects, to have changed, to have grown attachments here in Asia — to have expanded until I belong here, belong everywhere — until I embrace the whole world."

After two days in the clean but shabby and very out of the way hotel, I realised my mistake, that I might be cutting myself off altogether from the communications I was waiting for and I moved back — by tramcar once again. And went on walking.

Several more days passed and then, enraged by the insult that was being shown, not to me who was of no consequence, but to my honourable sponsors, I decided to go into action. There was no head that I could hit and so, true to the historical traditions of my race, I adopted gun-boat tactics. If the Chinese would not speak to me I would bombard them into submission.

The HQ of the Chinese Peace Committee was located in one of the old ambassadorial residences, surrounded by a high wall. After reconnoitring the ground, I approached the huge wooden door and hammered on it and the sound reverberated wonderfully. When it did not open, I hammered again — and went on hammering. When it opened a crack and a man peeped through I pushed my way in. Taken by surprise, unable to push me out again, and fearing that I would advance upon the imperial palace he took me into his office in the gatehouse — and telephoned.

After a long conversation he put the receiver down, addressed me with an angry volley in Chinese and then fell silent. I sat on, apprehensive until, through the window, I saw a man coming down the long drive and I went out to meet him and, with an expression of extreme annoyance, he invited me to accompany him to the house.

He led me into a large, dignified room and we sat down, far apart, on long black lacquered seats adorned with brocade cushions, set at right angles to each other with a long low table before us — and I told my tale of neglect.

Expressing great surprise, in a cool tone, he assured me that he had not received any of my cables, my introductory letter or my telephone calls and that he had no idea that I was in Peking. When all that was over and a pretty pot of green tea and little cups were brought in, he got down to business and grew more friendly.

What did I want to do, who did I want to meet, where did I want to go and how long would I be staying? He knew all the answers but I repeated them, emphasising that I wanted to meet writers, theatre people and educationists and, reminding him of my currency problem and of the promises given me in Delhi, asked him to provide me with an interpreter and a car.

"Will you make your own programme" Mr Chi said at last, smiling now, "and we will call on you at once."

He took me down the drive to the big door which the gatekeeper opened, also smiling now — both of them smiling as I went out. But as I walked away I did not believe that anything would come from all those smiles and agreements.

The next morning, I set out as usual upon my perambulations but at midday a powerful feeling drove me back to the hotel. Five minutes later my telephone rang.

"We have arranged for you to meet some writers", a voice said, "the car will come for you in 10 minutes time."

I flung myself into better clothes and was downstairs at the door when my interpreter entered and we drove away together to the start of my dubious China conquest. And at once I laid my cards on the table.

I told them that I was not a Communist, that I did not believe that Marxism-Leninism was the right political system for Britain, with her long traditions of liberalism and individualism although, as a great ideal, I wished for its success in China. Having declared myself, I hoped that in the new sweet summer warmth with a hundred flowers bursting into bloom, that when their petals opened, with my help, some of them would talk.

A private room in a restaurant opposite the Forbidden City had been reserved and three smiling, unassuming writers of some sort had been hastily collected. This first conversation, as I remember it, was disappointing and what impressed me were the balconies and the timeless atmosphere of the famous old eating-house — and the meal. Peking duck and all the subtle and curious delicacies that went with it.

When I returned to the hotel, I was told that the Minister for Posts & telegraphs had called on me and would call again and that Dr Ma-Yin-Chu had sent a message asking me to visit him that same afternoon. The fuse had been lighted and everything at once exploded like a multiple Chinese fire cracker.

It was the 4th of March, ten days after my arrival — and I wrote:

Today is the first day of the meeting of the Peoples' Consultative Conference which Dr Ma is attending. It is made up of outstanding individuals & political groups. Most of my time with him was taken up with political slogans & pointless laughter... He was only doing his duty, seeing me. He was not interested in literature. He is first & foremost a politician — a commissar.

To my questions I got no real answers & to my statement that in Europe too much science & technology had been taught recently — the humanities neglected — with the result that western civilisation is deficient in moral & spiritual values & qualities, he replied that this could not happen in China because scientists worked for the people & therefore everything they did was right & good.

He was rather like the religious personalities in India who preach all the time, are not interested in the listener & just roll off their sermons, making no human contact. They live in an abstracted world of spiritual exaltation. Dr Ma lives in one of political exaltation.

Two important things came out.
1. That Peking University is beginning courses in comparative philosophy. Hegel, Kant, Whitehead, Keynes, Russell & Marshall are being studied. Russell has been invited to give a series of lectures on Idealism. All schools of thought — to learn from every-where. The first fruits of the new policy of 'a hundred blooms'...
2. That his daughter is being held in America. And for one instant, at the gate in the half dark when I was leaving, I saw his *real* face. The mask was off & I saw the face of China — a face of fury & hatred.

I gave him Sir C.P.'s friendly message and, aware of the suggestion in his letter of introduction, he said he would arrange for me to read my work in the University. Later that day, I talked to a British business man, an 'old China hand', who had arrived on a trade mission. And I wrote:

The Chinese hate all foreigners. When the Russians took over foreign property — they just took it. The Chinese expropriated nothing. But they created every sort of difficulty, imposed colossal taxes, high wages etc, making the business impossible to run. Then, when the owners asked for it to be taken over, they refused unless ... perhaps . . . after payment of a huge sum. And the foreigners themselves were held. No exit permits were given them. They could not run their firms, they could not pay to have them taken over & they could not leave.

One firm was asked to pay 2 million pounds to get one of their employees out. They had to decide whether to do this or leave him to go mad. He remained for 7 years. His own firm extricated themselves better than most — they paid to get out.

The British took a lot from China but they also served her well. They built Shanghai — & all the railways.

The first exhilarating years of a revolution give place to all sorts of difficulties & discontents. China's troubles are yet to come — during the next 10 years.

Some 'White Russians' that he knows have been living in Tientsin on the gradual sale of their property. They are not allowed to work. Now the property has run out & they are desperate. There is nothing they can do. Most 'White Russians' were sent back to Russia & to concentration camps.

My mother wrote again.

"It is spring weather here. Susie finds sunny corners & sleeps in the garden most mornings. I tried to mow the grass but it was too soggy We've had deluges of rain. Primrose Hill is simply squishy all over. . . I met such an attractive young couple with a boxer dog. They knew Susie & greeted me & asked about you in India. We said we'd all meet again on the Hill but although I've looked for them, I haven't seen them. . . I am very busy all day — there is never time to do half I want to — yet I have nothing to write about. . ."

But she knew that that didn't matter, that her letters were important however trivial their content. And I knew that she was lonely.

On March 7th I wrote again.

"All goes wonderfully well now! An individual straying alone into China with urgent & special demands is still something of a rarity & it took the Pekinese some time to get over the shock! But when they did they were fine. . . Yesterday I read my work to the 3rd year English literature students in the University. It was a strange but exciting experience. Their knowledge of spoken English was practically nil & they strained to understand;

expressions tense, eyes fixed, sitting on the edges of their chairs . . .
they were in such pain that I soon stopped & just talked & they
asked question after question (through the interpreter). They are
hungry for knowledge & for contacts with the outer world —
especially the West. They hate their isolation.

"They took me round the University, still talking. Their
libraries are immense & comprehensive. . . Bertrand Russell is
coming to lecture again. They never forget that he taught here
once & is one of the father's of their revolution. They are
confident, wide open, able & ready to welcome all the contending
ideas of the world, to learn from them while they create their own
new world on a broad & liberal basis."

"Two days ago, I was taken out to the mountains & I spent
nearly the whole day climbing & scrambling up & down the Great
Wall! From tower to tower, from peak to peak. It is not over-
rated. It is grand & awe-inspiring — truly, one of the wonders of
the world — & a fabulous experience. From the heights to which
we climbed, we could see range after range of mountains & mile
after mile of the Wall twisting along the ridges & down into the
gorges on its tortuous 1700 mile journey across China.
Astonishing! It was icy cold but brilliant sunshine — the wind
from Siberia — exhilarating. We clambered down eventually &
ate a sandwich meal in a hut in the pass & then drove to another
famous sight — the Ming Tombs. Today, I go to the Writers
Union & tonight I am dining with a Minister of the government."

"That young couple with the boxer dog live in Belsize Grove &
have a very nice-looking mother who would do for *you*! She also
looks after their dog when they go abroad. . . " I was attempting to
find her a friend.

At the Writers Union, I was taken into a large bleak room full of
tables and people sitting casually round them. At one of these
about a dozen writers were waiting for me and when some of us sat
down round it, the rest pulled up chairs and sat close behind,
forming a double circle. I wrote afterwards:

Shiao Yeh & Yeh Chun Chu — very pleasant & interesting men but
a scribe recording everything, as well as my interpreter, destroyed
any real conversation from the start. Real topics were avoided &
slogans repeated.

Behind me sat a writer whom I had met in Delhi and who spoke
English and bending forward, close to my ear, he kept up a
whispered commentary on the speeches as they rolled out.

"That's not true. . . It isn't like that at all. . . That's not true either. . . It's just the opposite. . . None of that is true. . ."

Where the flowers should have bloomed brighter and bolder than anywhere else — none did. The wind was still too cold and I came away bewildered and depressed, pitying the brave man who had leant out of line and whispered in my ear.

Mr Chu, the Minister, was a charming little man and because he had lived in England and talked so naturally and gaily about his life there, as we walked to the restaurant, I hoped for a real conversation at last. But my only note reads:

Dinner with Mr Chu — absolutely no talk out of him at all. So I talked.

I now requested to meet writers more personally and I was taken to a private flat and received by several very intelligent young men but when I saw that even here, the flowers would not open, I did not wait for the slogans — but talked myself. In a land where the people only smiled and giggled and repeated political texts, suddenly I found my role as lecturer. In India I had learnt to listen — and now I learnt to talk. And I stopped at nothing. Into the parched ground, like a torrent, I poured the free waters of the West. I did not see the flowers open but I knew that the roots were nourished. Everywhere, to these speechless prisoners, I set myself to talk. And the powers allowed it.

After this, I spent a morning with Dr Wei, the Minister for Education, whose purpose was not to leap over one of the walls, like mine, but to pull down the most ancient and sacrosanct of them all — the Chinese script.

It had already been simplified and now he wanted to abolish the picture characters altogether and substitute the Roman alphabet and so bring China out into the world. I did not need to talk to him but let him say it all with his charts and diagrams and study papers and cool campaigning passion. It was a purely specialist occasion.

After attending a performance in the theatre, I was taken to the China Opera School and I watched the students training. And took notes which I append (No. 4).

I paid a visit to the British, Australian and New Zealand community. There were about a dozen of them, all working in the language translation department of the Foreign Ministry and meeting every evening in Rewi Alley's flat.

They were completely isolated, never went into a Chinese house and had no Chinese friends and so were thrown in upon themselves, a little lonely cluster existing precariously upon the surface of a vast Red land. They were astonished when I told them that I had been into the big, bare, unheated ice-cold house of Dr Ma — and into the flat of a young writer.

I was taken out to a co-operative farm where hot-houses for winter growing were sunk in the earth to roof level, simply and cheaply constructed and, except for the electricity, primitive. But, to go down out of the snow into a lovely market garden, beautifully laid out and tended, green, rich and extensive was to behold another Chinese wonder.

I went in to one of their little houses. The long room, which had no furniture or floor covering, was raised about two feet at one end and under this concrete stage a fire was lit and the families slept on it at night and sat on it by day. Appendix no. 5.

My money ran out and on March 12th my interpreter called for me as usual and we set out for the last time. But when we returned in the afternoon she pulled something from her pocket and without any change in her expression or in the tone of her voice, handed it to me.

"We want you to stay one more week in China as our guest. We want you to see Shanghai and the ancient city of Hangchow. Here is a 1st class ticket to Shanghai. Will you give me your 3rd class ticket to Canton." And with that she drove away.

That night, Mr Chu gave a farewell dinner party for me. As well as Dr Ma, Dr Wei and his wife, Mr Chi and Mr Chu's wife and daughter-in-law — Dr Foong-Yu-Lan, the foremost Chinese philosopher and Buddhist scholar, a famous poet and a singer from the opera, were present.

We were received in a large, bare room with an enormous oval table in the middle and a sofa and some hard chairs in a corner — identical with Dr Ma's, and as cold.

At 5 o'clock the next morning, March 13th, I wrote:

I sat on the sofa with the philosopher, Dr Foong, the rest in a circle round us. He was very sympathetic & I'm sure we could have talked at once — but we didn't. With all the others silent, staring & laughing at nothing every other moment, only general remarks were possible. The poet looked heavy & unhappy. Dr Ma was the greatest laugher of them all. Then, very timorously, Dr F observed that he had visited India. I responded at once & tried to draw him on & when he added that he had stayed in Banaras University, I plunged in with my tales & when he went on to speak about the new temple that he saw being built there & we both agreed that there were enough temples in India already — a real conversation was set going.

Then, abruptly & deliberately, Mr Chu ended it, summoning us all to the table saying that we could talk so much better there. He placed me between himself & Dr Wei, like captors, and there were so many people in between that Dr F was almost out of sight. And we never talked again.

The dinner was not ready & we sat waiting. Mr Chu was very attentive & Dr Wei very sweet & I struggled to talk to them both. The rest remained silent, laughing or giggling — some banter passing — the atmosphere getting worse all the time. And when the dinner came it got no better. I threw out lead after lead but not one was taken up & any response at all — was just a slogan.

A conspiracy of silence has surrounded me from the day that I arrived until now when I am leaving. I do not understand it.

They say that they did not receive my cables & so did not know that I was coming — then admit that they did; they say that they did not receive my letters & telephone calls — then admit that they did. I ask to meet individuals — they say yes but no one materialises & the people whom I do meet just smile & talk in slogans or, like Dr Wei, in technicalities.

And finally this party. The philosopher & artists, the sort of people I have been clamouring to meet, gathered together on the last night but all communication cut or prevented by the physical arrangements, the ominous atmosphere & the determination of all present not to talk.

As for the Commonwealth community — they are exactly like the Chinese — clams — just small talk, banter, laughter or silence. Dr English preaches slogans incessantly, Rewi Alley says nothing. Nan Green is the most sympathetic & human but refuses to elucidate or explain or say anything of importance. A silent, smiling, inscrutable group but less attractive than the Chinese — less suave, gentle, aimiable & friendly-looking — all fanatical-looking.

What is really going on beneath & behind all this — the lies, the smiles & the silence? If I had nor forced that door open would they ever have opened it? And when I did & they received me but refused to talk — why did they allow me to talk? And why do they entertain me for another week? What game are they playing with me?

What I observe of the masses of the people is good. They look happy, are better dressed, fed, housed & treated than they have ever been but I imagine that they are docketed, recorded & organized — man, woman & child — & their movements controlled, everything controlled. But how long will this last? They have never had freedom but will they one day demand it? or is regimentation natural to them? does it fit them as it does the

Russians because they have been jumped out of feudalism without any democratic traditions in between?

After 3 weeks in Peking I have seen no flowers blooming — only rank weeds still suppressing them. I have no answers or near answers to any of my questions or any profits from my searchings. I feel that I have achieved little or nothing of understanding unless perhaps one thing — that I am in a police state.

I drove with my interpreter to the station and on the platform we embraced — and she wept. And her weeping broke the silence of Peking.

8

ON MARCH 16th I wrote to my mother from the King Kong Hotel, Shanghai.

"My plans changed dramatically just before I left Peking. Thanks to the kindness & generosity of the Chinese Peace Committee I am travelling more slowly to the border — spending 4 days here, a night in Hangchow & then another night in Canton. And I am travelling 'soft', a coupé to myself — less tiring but far less interesting. . . Here, I am being wonderfully looked after by the Dept for Cultural Exchanges . . . seeing things & meeting people & living in the lap of pre-revolutionary European luxury, in a delightful suite on the 7th floor of a skyscraper hotel, built by the British in the old inter-national settlement days. It is quite a jolt to be transported into such a world . . . so remote from the real one. . ."

"I have 1½ hours to myself before leaving for the opera & I am sitting at a desk in the wide window looking out over the great city. This afternoon I met a wonderful crowd of women in their simple homes & this morning, a family of 'reformed' capitalists. The conversations instructive & absorbing, the contacts warm & wonderful. . ."

I felt a difference in the atmosphere at once. Peking was the monastic heart where, in all its purity, the faith and the rules were preached and preserved in prescript and silence. Shanghai was where it grappled with reality. The smiles were more relaxed and the slogans sounded less like the words of God and, at the end, I saw a lovely bed of flowers burst into bloom.

After the many years of foreign domination, the people were passionately engaged in cleaning up what had been the most corrupt, vicious and crime-ridden city in the world. They showed no resentment towards me as a scion of the perpetrators but were happy to show me what they were doing and how much they had achieved in the 7 years since Liberation.

They took me to schools, clubs, clinics and playgrounds which had once been brothels, gambling dens and commercial offices and introduced me to 're-educated' criminals, prostitutes and more capitalists. My notes I append (Nos. 6, 7 & 8).

A most moving experience was my visit to the Children's Palace, established in what had once been a high office block. Above the gymnasiums, theatres and lecture halls on the ground floor were class-rooms, laboratories, workshops and studios providing every conceivable activity for children of all ages, with interests and aptitudes of every kind.

As I went from floor to floor and in and out of rooms I saw busy, happy, creative children in them all — many swept off the streets.

I went to meet some writers. Their silence was the more ironic for they had managed to turn the new freedom policy into another slogan.

> Chinese revolutionary policy was tolerant from the beginning, even before the Soviet 20th Congress. The spirit of letting many flowers blossom was always there, but not practised. Mistakes were made & writers were subject to strains & tensions — but not now. All views can be expressed now. The right course is being followed now.

On my last day, I was invited to go to the Futan University at 9 o'clock in the morning, to read my work. About 20 professors were waiting for me — smiling. Most were young and wore European dress and their manner was vigorous and hearty but a few were sensitive, beautiful old men with long wispy beards and long delicate hands, wearing traditional Chinese gowns. After my experience in Peking, I was not surprised when they told me that the students would not be able to understand and that I was to read to them — the English speaking members of the staff.

Before we settled down, they asked me if I would mind having my performance recorded, explaining that they would then have modern English verse, contemporary ideas and an authentic English accent to use for teaching. For a moment I feared this, but I couldn't refuse and later, when I got to know them, I was glad.

They placed me at the end of a long narrow table and they sat each side. All the morning and far into the afternoon, kept going by incessant cups of green tea, I read, stopped, discussed and read again. Yes — discussed; all the things in heaven and earth that I had so passionately longed to talk about. There were no slogans and the flowers opened, one after the other, and blazed before my eyes. It was the high point of my China journey.

Six months later when the flowers grew and opened everywhere and threatened to alter the colour and balance of the whole landscape, they were brutally stamped into the earth again and some of the brightest were pulled up by the roots and punished.

The next day I left for Hangchow.

. . . . .

"Above there is paradise and below are Soochow and Hangshow" is an old Chinese saying. In a land which is fragrant with poetry, where the works of nature and the works of man have coalesced in lyrical profusion. Hangchow has assembled them together in a glorification of beauty and ethical religion.

The West Lake is divided by two narrow causeways into three smaller lakes with islands in the middle. Willow and peach trees and rare flowers grow along the causeways, little arched stone bridges break the paths, temples and pavilions seem to float upon the water and goldfish ponds lie sunk among the trees. And soft hills ring them — some conical in shape.

I walked along a causeway through an arch called 'Orioles Singing in the Willows', to a beauty spot called 'Autumn Moon in the Calm Lake' where stands the 'Pavilion for Watching the Lake' and then on to the other side, to the pavilions of 'Literary Upsurge' and the 'Six Harmonies'. A dainty poetical ramble.

At the bottom of 'Solitary Hill' lived a poet of the Sung Dynasty who was known for his love of plum blossoms and cranes. He planted more than 300 plum trees and kept a crane and it was said that he had plum blossoms for a wife and a crane for a son. The Crane Pavilion stands today where he lived then.

In the 'Yellow Dragon Cave' at the foot of the 'Hill of Precious Stones', where a spring falls through the dragon's mouth, pavilions have been built and a temple for the worship of Lao Tzu, the founder of Taoism. There are hundreds of Taoist and Buddhist temples, pagodas and palaces round the lake and upon the hill tops. Even upon the sides of the hill called 'Peak Which Flew from Afar', Buddhist images are carved.

Whenever the Chinese come together in a group for work or worship they fall into single file — and trot. And little snaky lines of pilgrims trotted from one temple to another.

I climbed the path which circled round and round the 'Yu Huang Hill' to the Taoist temple at the top, called the 'Temple of the Lucky Star', with pilgrims overtaking me and others running down. The top was crowded and the view was superb.

"Religion is not persecuted in China' they told me here. Churches and temples are repaired and every consideration is given to religious opinions and conscience. "Any good idea from the past" they said, "can be incorporated into Marxism and carried forward into the present and used in the new way of living". The lovely new slogan.

Not only were these flowers soon destroyed but a few years later the Red Guards were let loose upon the whole land.

I spent two days in this enchanting place, grateful for a glimpse of the artist soul of China.

· · · · ·

On the journey to Canton I found myself sharing a coupé with a Hungarian woman and a child. When the revolution broke out in Hungary, many technicians working in China sent for their children and this woman had set out with a large party and travelled about delivering them. She was now on the last leg of her journey — with the last child.

She was an attractive woman and spoke English and we took to each other at once and, for the next two days — we talked. Staying with the technicians, in remote provinces, she had become possessed of an immense amount of inside information.

"The Chinese," she said, "have always been secretive by nature and they are more so now. Entertainments, smiles, laughter and professions of friendship mean nothing. They just serve their purpose and are their way of dealing with foreigners."

Some of her tales were horrifying and I grew disturbed that she should be entrusting them to me, for if it were known that she was going about revealing them, I was sure she could have landed in a Chinese prison.

With her life in my hands, as I thought, I was so moved that on the second day a loving, unthinking, incautious, wild desire rose up in me to reciprocate her trust, and give her my life in return. And I disclosed all my own experiences, doubts and critical conclusions.

We arrived in Canton in the evening, the family met her and clasped their child and as they took her away she said good-bye to me in a swift, cool manner as if nothing had occurred between us. She was completely changed.

When I reached my hotel and came to my senses, my thoughts

were disturbing. Why had she talked like that? How could she trust me as she did? Why had we been put together on that train? And as my imagination went to work my thoughts grew frightening. I had forced the door open and then talked for a month, unconstrained liberal talk and now I had talked again to her — even more subversively. Was she an agent provocateur and had I talked myself into a trap? And the face of Dr Ma at the gate appeared to me again.

I was expecting to leave for the border the next day and I longed for the night to pass. When the interpreter came in the morning and told me that there were no trains that day, I was sure that I had fallen into the jaws of the tiger.

She took me to see temples and beauty spots and monuments commemorating the revolution which had its roots and heroic beginnings in Canton. And the day and another night passed.

The next morning she came with the same story — no trains running to the border. And I didn't believe it. I would have gone to the station to find out for myself. But I couldn't. I was guarded all the time. She never left me and another busy but desperate day yawned before me.

We went first to talk to a street organiser in whose house advice was given and instructions issued and lectures and classes announced. The smiling zealous woman made all the communal activities sound so enlightened and humane.

In the afternoon we visited the boat people. The boats were crowded together on the river and we clambered from one to the other, ending in a school set up in a barge moored alongside the embankment. It was a very interesting experience and my notes I append (No. 9).

That night, I was entertained to dinner by a Women's Organization presided over by a highly intelligent but grim-looking person who didnt even trouble to smile. The others smiled the harder and the more toasts they drank to me, the more frightened I became. At 5 o'clock the next morning, still not sure if I would be allowed to leave that day, I wrote:

I am thankful to be escaping from China. Wonderful & remarkable things are being done here. I have been overwhelmed with beautiful gestures, entertainments, help & professions of friend-ship — but still I am desperate to get out. And I know why. There is complete regimentation of mind. In spite of the '100 flowers' & with one exception, the Futan university, no one thinks independently, all conversations consist of slogans & can be

fantastically unreal, with no continuity, no statement & answer —
set speeches regardless of what one is saying & asking. The leaders
could speak — but don't. The rest can't.

After being lavished with kindness here & loaded with
expressions of undying friendship, my last conversation was with a
writer & went like this:

He.   You are always welcome to China.

Me.   Thank you. I want to come again.

He.   I think you know all about the Chinese people now.

Me.   No. I know practically nothing about them. How could I in
      so short a time & living in hotels?

He.   A writer must study the people. I think you have studied the
      people in the streets.

Me.   Yes. But that is only superficial. I don't *know* the people.

He.   A writer should go out to the villages. All Chinese writers
      go out to the villages & to factories.

Me.   I should like to. Could I do that if I come back? Get off the
      beaten track?

He.   You are always welcome to China. We will do everything
      for you & we hope that you will bring your friends with you
      — other writers.

Me.   If I come back can I go out into the villages?

He.   A writer must write for the people. I spend much of my time
      in a village or in a factory. It is necessary for a writer to go
      out to the people.

Me.   Will you help me to do that if I come back?

He.   I don't think it would be possible.

Me.   Why not? You have just said that a writer *should* and that you
      would do everything for me.

He.   I don't think you would understand the language.

Me.   I would learn some Chinese & I could take an interpreter.

He.   I don't think the habits of the people would be the same as
      yours.

Me.   Of course they wouldn't. I would have to adapt myself.

He.   I take a job in a village or a factory & then I return & write a
      book. A writer must go out to the people & write for the
      people . . . etc

When I climbed into the train I thought I was free but, smiling
still, my interpreter got in, too, saying that she wanted to stay with
me and enjoy my company for as long as possible. But I didn't
believe her. I wasn't even sure if the train was going to the border
or whether, with that meaningless smile and those meaningless
words she was escorting me to my doom. When it got there and I
walked across and the British border guard smiled a real smile — I
could have hugged him.

I arrived in Hong Kong carrying the first germs picked up in all the months of germ-infested travel. Watching from my window, during those last days in Canton, some micro-organism in the putrid river air rose and lodged in my throat. I lost my voice and a fever troubled me.

On March 23rd 1957, I wrote to my mother:

"Well, I'm out of China & the whole extraordinary experience is now behind me. . . As soon as I arrived yesterday the press besieged me for news from the forbidden & mysterious land beyond the guarded border — the heaving giant of Red China. I spent the afternoon giving interviews & today, my little bits of information & ignorant opinions are headlines & fill columns in the local papers — English & Chinese language. With the political tension everywhere so acute & misrepresentation so common & almost unconscious, one is scared of giving wrong impressions . . . PS. The pressmen say that I must be the first writer to enter China alone & uninvited. . . That is news in itself it appears!"

On the 25th, from the YWCA in Calcutta, I wrote again.

"I am back in India & it feels like coming home. . . I arrived yesterday half dead. The China adventure was very nerve-racking, more exhausting than anything I've done so far & then Hong Kong just finished me off. . . When the articles appeared the telephone began ringing again. Requests to speak — a veritable avalanche of people & obligations.

"I agreed to address (!!) the United Nations Association & gave a random talk lasting nearly 2 hours (!!) on English poetic drama, Indian, Chinese & World theatre with a comic interlude on how *not* to produce a play in New York & with a peroration which pointed to the cultural & political resurgence of humanity (that's all !!) — translated by a wonderful man, the official interpreter for HK — Mr Ma Man Far. It was a fine audience & wonderful to be able to meet so many HK people — to feel & touch them & carry something of their hearts away with me. It was worth the effort. "

"It is getting pretty hot here but I don't really mind it — the local people seem more overcome than I. I am resting today — tomorrow I begin again. How many hundreds of people I must have met & got to know in the last 6 months. This rubbing shoulders with the world is a fabulous experience. "

Sir C.P's wealthy friends, the Sekhars, arranged for me to give a reading, then a talk on China and then invited me to stay.

Their bungalow consisted of two very large rooms — a grand sitting-room like those described by Nirad Chaudhuri, and a bedroom in which the whole extended family slept — not huddled but in tiny, individual curtained cubicles. I declined the invitation, preferring my drab lonely cell in the YW. Afterwards, they told me casually that one of the children lay ill, in a cubicle, with typhoid fever.

My throat got no better and my own fever persisted. I was sure that I would recover as soon as I got out of the heat and the foetid air of Calcutta but I could not leave until Sir C.P's money arrived and altho I went about, I lay for much of my time on my bed, pondering my China journey — and the circle which no one could square.

Nehru made a speech that very week saying that it would take 40 years to raise the general living standard in India by democratic means. China had done it in 7 — by force. Western observers said that 40 million people had been liquidated. The Chinese admitted to 15 million and a figure in between was probably the truth. In 40 years as many, if not more, would die in India of starvation. So which was the better way?

I knew the way that suited me. I felt that I had just jumped out of the jaws of the tiger into freedom, tolerance and diversity. Yet how could I choose — when I was related to neither? It was best for me to keep silent.

My plan was to return to Bangalore where I had been asked to give another reading and then go on to Ooty, but when the money came, R1000 (about £75 then) and I learnt that Sir C.P. had been called away to Madras by the death of a friend, I changed it.

I flew to Bangalore where the fever abated and my throat was cured the next day, met all my friends again, gave the reading and then flew on to Kerala. From there I wrote to my mother.

Mascot Hotel. Trivandrum. April 4th 1957.

"His plan was for me to go on up to Ooty & stay at a luxury hotel at his expense & wait for him. He thought that this would be a rest cure after China & an escape from the heat of the plains — very thoughtful & kind — but not my idea of the best way of filling my last weeks in Asia so, on the spur of the moment, I flew here this morning & arrived for lunch."

"The Malabar Coast, Cochin & Cape Comorin are places of great historic interest, teeming with ancient temples & monuments while Kerala itself is the world-shaking Indian state which has just elected a Communist government to power — through the ballot box! The first in the world to do this. And Kerala (the old Travancore) is the matriarchal state which, as Diwan, C.P. created... He expects to be back in Ooty on the 15th & I shall amuse myself looking at temples & Communists until then. . . I have had to postpone my air passage. . . You *must not* use the mower — get Charles to come in & cut the grass. . ."

I now understood Sir C.P's resistance to the inclusion of Kerala into the Indian union — and the jeopardising of all his achievements. It was not only educationally more advanced (hence the ironic election results) but economically & socially as well.

Trivandrum is a beautiful garden city with great trees everywhere and flowering plants and I saw no poverty, depression or pollution. It was another world. I soon found the local writers — and wrote:

In steamy, tropical, afternoon heat I gave a reading, organized by the Head of the Sanskrit College, to the Literary Workshop, composed of writers & students. It went down well. A meal followed in a tented hall where they placed me on a dais — alone & garlanded!

I also found my Communist friends from Delhi, P. K. Punoose and his wife. They were leaving for Cochin the same night and they asked me to come with them and at 3 am we set off by car together.

Here again, was an attractive prosperous town full of British and Portugese maritime monuments and museums. The Malabar coast was where all the sea-borne invaders of India had landed while from end to end its sandy shores were impregnated with mystical powers. "If you sit on the beach and meditate" Sir C.P. had told me, "you will have transcendental experiences."

I walked along it and watched the giant waves of the Arabian Sea crashing upon it but I did not sit down on the vibrating sand, draw power up into myself and try to break through into another dimension. I was earthbound again and too restless.

We stayed two days in Cochin, in the official guest-house, and then Mrs Punoose and I left for their village, about 70 miles away.

The four rooms of their little square wooden house were contiguous and openings led from one to the other. they had no windows, only heavy outer doors and when these were closed, of course, the rooms were pitch dark. when they were open they were darkened by overhanging trees. I did not have to adapt to the usual animal ways for a hole had been dug behind a bush. I wrote to my mother:

"Their house is in the middle of the hot, steamy tropical forest in hilly undulating country. One day, starting at 4 am we drove 100 miles up into the mountains to the tea & rubber estates — all in her constituency — where we visited a tea factory, talked to the workers & were entertained in various houses in the usual warm & primitive Indian style. From there we drove to a lake in the middle of a game sanctuary & in the evening, returning slowly in a boat, could see the wild animals coming down to drink — elephants in great number, many varieties of deer, black monkeys but, unfortunately no tiger. There were many about. A tribesman had been killed by one the week before while fishing.

"The whole expedition was vague, dreamy, planned yet unplanned — with much waiting about, time wasting, useless talking & irritation yet, it was a tremendous day — with much achieved. . ."

There was another more dramatic day which I did not write about. As before, we planned to start early and travel by bus to visit some relatives. Before leaving, I looked in my purse to see what money I had and was shocked to find a hundred rupee note (about £7 pounds 10 shillings then) was missing and I could only conclude that while I was asleep inside the mosquito net someone had crept in through the open door, found my handbag and taken it.

At first, I did not want to upset Mrs Punoose by telling her but in the bus, after thinking it over, I decided that she ought to know. It was her servant, of course — and she was furious.

We reached our destination, climbed a hill to a fine bungalow set in a clearing, with a small brown river winding below — and were enfolded by an excited family. After much talk and a specially prepared long-drawn-out meal, I bathed in the river with the children and in the afternoon we caught the return bus.

When we arrived, Mrs Punoose marched up the village street to the house of the chief of police, a close friend of hers — and I told my story. He made some wise remarks and then, losing interest, drifted to another subject and we sat on in his parlour talking pleasantly. We went home, at length, and in the evening he appeared.

The case was settled. The criminal had been apprehended, had confessed, been taken under guard to the hiding place, had restored the money and been released. And he handed me the note. But as the confession had probably been obtained after a beating, I was sorry now that I had spoken.

That night we had to bolt our doors and sleep hot and airless. Not long before, a servant in the village had been dismissed for stealing a fountain pen, had wandered about for several weeks and then come back and murdered his master.

On April 17th from the Travellers Bungalow, Ernakulam, I wrote again:

"I arrived here last night & today I fly to Coimbatore & then up the mountain by bus to Ooty & C.P. . . . . My Communist friends are very fine people & this trip has been a fascinating penultimate experience. . . They have asked me to attend the opening of the State Assembly on the 27th. If I do it will mean postponing my return again. I will decide when I get to Ooty."

I was so happy to be with Sir C.P. again. We walked the hills as before and at first, it was I who talked and he who listened. Then, he who talked once more — answering my questions, lifting me, restoring me and guiding me.

"You must go back to Kerala" he told me. "At the end of your great journey you cannot return to England until you have been down to Cape Comorin, a place more sacred even than Banaras where Rama crossed over to Ceylon helped by the monkey, Hanuman, to rescue his wife, Sita. And, on the way, you must stop at the old palace of Padmanabhapuram where the frescoes depict episodes in the life of Krishna."

"I will go," I said, "and afterwards attend the opening of the State Assembly."

On Easter Sunday, April 21st, from Ootacamund, I wrote again.

"For a long time I have felt that I was struggling to get home but had to surmount event after event, rather as in a dream. Like C.P, I can reject nothing — & the longer one does this the deeper one gets & the more opportunities rise up to hold one & prevent one from escaping. There is so much to be seen, so much to be learnt, years are needed to satisfy one's craving for knowledge & understanding — and yet, at the same time I crave to get away, crave to return home. Perhaps I am pursuing my aims in too intensive a way — because of the time factor — perhaps I have seen & learnt so much in such a short time that I am surfeited & weary & can absorb no more. I don't know. I only know that I long for the day when I shall board the plane for home."

I had written to Nehru from Calcutta, telling him that I was back from China and giving Sir C.P's address. When a letter came from the Prime Minister's Office, addressed to me, he must have wanted to know what was in it — and opened it. When I arrived he gave it to me, without an envelope, saying that it had been enclosed in one to him. But now, in India, I no longer thought this reprehensible, nor was I surprised to learn that Nehru still had no time for me, and not surprised that during all these months, Sir C.P. had done nothing about publishing the epic.

Before I left, he took me into his bedroom to show me once again the beautiful bronze figure of the Dancing Siva which stood on a table near his bed.

"You must write a history of India," he said.

"I couldn't", I exclaimed. "I am not a historian."

"You can."

"I only want to write plays. I haven't got a historian's mind. I like turning facts into poetic fantasies."

"You have a balanced mind and you span both east and west. Only you can do it."

I thought no more about it. Now, I wonder if the simple ragged story of a pilgrimage, composed of facts woven with experiences and raised by perceptions; begun with no intention of being history and not the sort of history that he wanted and asked for is, nontheless, the sort that is wanted in our time. Lived, unacademic, humanised and whole — feminine perhaps? And the only sort that I can write.

We parted lovingly but it was not a good-bye for he would soon be in England again and the old pattern of his comings and goings would be resumed.

Halfway from Trivandrum, I stopped the car at the little palace and saw the frescoes of the god Krishna making love to the gopies and to Radha, his wife. I was equally impressed by the ancient lavatory chutes constructed like modern drains, installed on each floor and flushed with pails of water.

I drove on and before reaching the tip of the Cape where three seas meet, I could hear the roar of the waves.

The State Rest-house stood alone about a quarter of a mile from the sea with a flat reddish-brown maidan in between, the straggling village to one side along the eastern shore and an infinity of beach and forest on the other.

I was surprised to see that the tip of the continent was not a tip, but a straight end — and I guessed the reason why. A pair of celestial scissors must have snipped it off so that the Christian and the Hindu gods had each their holy, undisputed spot and, with enough distance in between could not see or be seen by each other and so, could not quarrel. A Hindu temple sprawled in the eastern corner and a statue of the Virgin Mary, erected by the Portugese, stood in the other.

After settling in my upstair room which had an inspiring view over land and sea, I went downstairs again and opened the front door to find a multitude outside — of beggars. A foreigner had been sighted and the whole town had turned out.

I distributed my coins and then with a gesture, indicated that I had no more. But that had no effect at all. Whining, moaning and rubbing their stomachs they followed me and would not be shaken off, and helpless before them, I cut short my first walk and retreated to the Rest-House.

When I went out again later they were still there and pressing close and pawing me, they followed me again — and defeated me again. I took shelter until the morning when I rose at dawn and in the half light walked across the bare brown plain to the sea intending to bathe in the mystic waters and afterwards, meditate upon the mystic sands.

I reached the low cliff and looked down upon the waves rolling in fast and roaring like no other sea, like tigers in the jungle. Frightened but excited I scrambled down to the beach and then, and then — stopped dead. It was the town lavatory with no tide to clear and cleanse it. I walked on farther but it was just the same and so, finding some space, I undressed and picked my way into the water.

The sea was too dangerous to swim out but I played in the tumbling surf and felt the joy of it. When I came out I hurried over the desecrated sands and returned to the Rest-House where, already, the crowd was gathering.

Later, when I went to the village, or little town as it was, and they followed me again, instead of suffering them I shouted at them — and I found it took effect. Some dropped away. And I went to the temple where, I was told, 500 Brahmins were fed every day. Then, walking down the narrow street between dirty and degraded houses I came upon a little shop, clean and bright, selling pathetic little articles in aid of an Orphans Home. I wrote afterwards:

> The Home is in the ancient temple. Good people but hungry for money, devouring me like the beggars who follow me — yet sweet & friendly when I declined to do more than buy some little object. Well-intentioned yet inept & incompetent, struggling hopelessly & forlornly in this god-filled, god-forsaken spot — even here up against all the poverty & inertia of their continent.

In the afternoon, the waiting crowd was smaller and my horrible shouting reduced it still more. When I set off for the Virgin Mary only a handful were behind me and they soon tired and fell away.

The distance was about 3 miles, of desolate coast and forest with the going soft and difficult. Halfway, I came upon some fishermen dragging a net along the water's edge, but I hurried past them for I was frightened of the people here and when I reached the end, was glad to find no one living there at all. Surrounded by fallen buildings, colossal, She sat high upon Her throne abandoned and immaculate, an exile as I was, beside the Hindu seas. And I prayed to Her.

The next morning I went down to the beach early again and left my things in a hole in the bank. I had been frolicking about in the surf for some time when, happening to look round, I saw a tall, powerful man with a murderous face, standing in the shallows, watching me. When I moved along, he moved too, and making a dash out of the water I circled round him and as I ran to the bank he came after me, and as I scrambled to the top — he followed. I was in the open then, in view of the Rest-House, but I trusted no one there to aid me and I ran a long way before I dared to stop and get into my clothes. Whatever his intentions were — they were certainly not friendly. Afterwards, I wrote:

Strange, desolate, remote place of myth & legend & mysticism. The waves thundering in, line upon line, smashing against the rocks & swirling up the soft, multi-coloured sand, streaked black & red & white. Sand & barren dry red earth.

And beggars — the whole population turned out at sight of a stranger & a foreigner. They hung round the Rest-House, pursued me everywhere, even down to the beach & into the sea — the same determined, devouring spirit but more impudent & resentful — more dangerous — more suppressed violence here than anywhere else.

Beggary & excrement — everywhere, everywhere — all that is left of a great heroic myth. Supernatural sands and legendary seas — and excrement, excrement. . .

I returned to Trivandrum.

The boundaries had been re-drawn and Sir C.P's old state of Travancore/Cochin was now the new state of Kerala and the first session of the First Legislative Assembly was ceremonially opened by the Governor. He welcomed with joy "the peoples' long desire to have their own state" and outlined the programme of the first administration.

I sat in the Speaker's Gallery with my friend, Mrs Punoose, in the Speaker's Chair below and watched a consummate performance of the ritual of Westminster. And the next day I talked to the Chief Minister.

That grand western drama would have been the final event, the last opportunity upon my half-dream journey if yet another had not instantly arisen — the quixotic, eastern anti-thesis.

Vinoba Bhawe was in Kerala! I heard just in time! He might have been anywhere in India. I might have left. I had wanted to find and march with him and marvelling, I postponed my flight again, hired a taxi and chased him through the jungle, caught up with him — and joined his camp.

Sri Vinoba Bhawe was India's newest saint, generally regarded as Gandhi's successor. "The Indian peasantry can never be spiritualised until their material condition has been improved — and for this to happen they must be given land." he said. And dissatisfied, or despairing of the Land Reform measures promised by the government, he launched the Bhoodan, or Land Gift, Movement and for 7 years had been marching through the villages persuading the big landowners to give some of it to the landless. In all those years he had never slept two nights in the same place and many thousands of acres had changed hands.

About six disciples, one of them a woman, marched with him permanently but as he moved along others joined him as devotees or helpers and then left when their work was done.

He was old and frail and he wore a dhoti and carried a staff, like Gandhi. A jeep carried his camp bed, his chair a small table, special food and the personal belongings of his followers. It went ahead each night so that when he arrived in the morning, a room was ready and he could rest. Each village provided accomodation and food for the whole party. Disused buildings were taken over, offices and schools and tents were used, while the disciples often slept on the floor outside the master's room.

No one received me. There were no formalities. I found my way to a house where 3 women lolled on a dusty concrete floor. I dropped my bag and sat down among them — without a word being spoken. I had dreamed my way into Vinoba's dream.

A brass vessel containing drinking water stood in the middle of the room. Later, a thin grass mat was found for me to sleep on. We sat in silence or talked listlessly until 5 o'clock, the hour of the daily public meeting to which the landowners and peasants were called.

About 300 people gathered and, after the saint, I was the next attraction. They had never seen a white person before and they stared relentlessly — and the children swarmed round me.

He spoke, in Malayalam, for over an hour and most of it was a sermon. At the end, the landowners came forward, the crowd dissolved and the agreements were drawn up. After that, the disciples and followers were taken into a long low room where, sitting on the earthen floor, we were served with the traditional meal of rice, vegetables and dahl, on palm leaves. Later, we gathered once more for evening prayers.

A lamp lit up the white shirts of the devotees as they sat in rows chanting. Their loud harsh voices reached into me and lifted me as I sat at the side, listening. The fire-flies danced above our heads in sparkling waves and the whole scene filled me with the joy of the painter before a new revelation as I sat at the side, watching. And in the silence of the meditation that followed, as I sat at the side, all the months of ugly painful travel dissolved in the light of reality and truth.

Afterwards, I returned with the women to our room but whereas they dropped onto their mats and slept at once, like natural animals, I could not omit the inbred disciplines of undressing, washing and brushing my hair and teeth — by the light of a torch and with a mug of water. And when I lay down at last on the concrete floor I could not sleep, not because it was hard but because suddenly I knew that I must end it, reject the scenes that still lay waiting to lure me on and hold me — and break the spell that India had cast upon me.

I knew also that I could not continue in a half dream state, living largely by the light of my intuition; that I did not want to have a wholly Indian consciousness. I longed for the full restoration of my intellect and for the balance of the two within me. And I knew that I must find the new green life springing up within my own dissolving culture.

Excited by the prospect of a new adventure, I lay until we were roused at 3 o'clock. Silently then, we put our things into the jeep. A hurricane lamp was lit, the Master came forward and after a few whispered words, stepped out onto the road. About 12 miles was his nightly average, varying with the distances between the villages.

Like a serpent it wound through the darkness. The trees formed a perforated roof above our heads and the air was full of sounds. We made no noise ourselves and only the rays from the hurricane lamp marked our passage through the jungle.

He marched steadily, then stopped halfway for the drink which the disciple poured into a cup from the flask which she carried. He did not sit down. No one did. And no one spoke. The night's magic ruled us.

Before long, two people rose up out of the dark from the side of the road where a candle burned on the ground, with flowers placed round it — a little shrine. They stepped forward and when the Master stopped they fell on their knees and touched his feet. He blessed them and then marched on and they rose and came among us and marched, too.

Soon afterwards, a little group appeared and a more elaborate shrine. The same little ceremony took place and then they all fell in and followed. Shrines and people soon lined both sides of the road and when the Master reached the village at about 8 o'clock, a great concourse was behind him.

I went with the women to the room allotted us and the crowd which was to hang about all day, until the meeting, squatted round his room and, in equal numbers, round ours, pressing into the open doors and windows, the children even jumping in — to see the white woman. The devotees showed no concern for the starers and the noise they made and for me — there were harder things to come.

The hygiene arrangements were different in each village. Here, the women's lavatory consisted of a piece of canvas stretched round four poles and set out on the maidan. When, at length, I was driven to approach it, the crowd surged after me and when I entered, surrounded it, peeped over the top of the canvas while the children peeped through the slits.

On the fourth day I was told that the Master would see me and I was asked to write down my questions beforehand. I wrote down, one.

> The West has been overtaken by materialism and moves bisected, with one hemisphere suppressed and one ability discarded — lurching out of balance. Will the spirituality of India, preserved in the ancient books and kept alive in all its purity in the monasteries and ashrams and by lonely sages and, in a debased way, lived by the whole people — be taken up now and offered to the West? Will the religious genius of India heal the division in Western man — and heal the world?

He was sitting waiting for me with my question paper in his hand. I put my palms together and bowed my head and then sat down on the chair in front of him. Cold and detached, he gave me no greeting.

> No. The West has sunk very low and suffered very much but it must sink still lower and suffer more and out of the desolation it will find its own soul.

He preached for about twenty minutes and when he stopped, I rose, bowed and put my hands together again and, still cold and detached, he watched me go.

I knew that I could stay and serve him and march through a thousand magic nights and dream through a thousand days — but I had to go. I left the next morning and wrote my last note.

> The aim & purpose of humanity is to uncover the mystery of existence. Some believe in a collective search using institutions, organizations, systems, theories & experiments — others in individual & direct experience.
>
> Western science investigates & can describe everything but cannot answer the question, 'why'. India has known the answer for 4000 years.
>
> The Hindu prayer. 'I do not pray for wealth, possessions, success, service to the community, *anything* — only for a glimpse of Reality — God'.

By the time I reached Bombay, my passport had expired. India still tried to hold me — clung to me like the beggars and danced before me in the rich apparel of the gods, still wooing me and beckoning me on.

I had to wait several days for a new one and my Parsee friends came to me with affection and took me, unresisting, to observe an ancient Zoroastrian Ceremony. Fire, the purest element of all and ashes, aromatic substances and wine were the final enticements. When I left, at last, I had brought the opposites of India together but I had not squared the circle; not fitted the divine form into the human and perfected my own life — and the life of the world. I had to go on trying.

In the afternoon, when the taxi drew up before No. 10 Primrose Gardens and I got out and slammed the door and stood paying the driver, barks and screams came from inside the house. When my mother opened the door, Susie hurled herself out, kissing and leaping all over me.

"I told her this morning that you were coming home today" my mother said, "and she's been waiting at the door ever since."

PART II
9

I HAD LONGED for this moment. To see my mother and Susie again and to return to the civilised beauty and restfulness and safety of the home I had created but when, after greeting them, I looked round — I felt like a stranger. And in the days that followed when I settled back into my rooms and talked to my tenants and took up all the sweet accumulated gains and pleasures of the house and then, from across the road, gazed at my property, high and huge — 5 ponderous floors of it — as I had gazed so possessively and with such pride before — I loathed it.

We each had a lovely flat, the tenants were happy, the rents flowed in, there was money in the bank and for the first time in our lives we were financially secure and carefree, yet I felt crushed by the very weight of the bricks and mortar, depressed by the very feel of a houseful of grateful dependents and tormented by the phenomenon of a successful business. For me now, only one good thing had come out of all the effort to establish and maintain it — it had paid for my journey to Asia.

At once, letters began coming from Sir C.P. On May 2nd, 1957 he wrote.

"Your breathless' letter en route to Bombay reached me in Mysore. . . I am very glad that you saw the frescoes in the Padmanabhapuram Palace & spent enough time at the Cape to absorb its atmosphere. . . Vinobha Bhawe is a muddleheaded fanatic but a good man of the type of Peter the Hermit — a type which with the best intentions can be very destructive. . . It was wonderfully exhilarating to meet you and if I have succeeded in imparting some of the essentials of the ancient thought which is ever renewed & is constantly undergoing a renaissance in the light of modern science, I shall have discharged a most pleasant & necessary duty devolving on one who will always give you affection & love".

On May 13th he again touched on Vinobha.

"As for Vinobha Bhawe, my reactions are negative but then I

135

am not a typical Indian of the Ghandian persuasion. But there is a core of fact & reason at the centre of his movement — although it is essentially illogical & likely to break down in actual implementation. All wholly renuveratory gospels have a history of initial success in India. . ."

But I was not put off Vinobha for I was a wanderer like him, a nun and vagabond and a Peter the Hermit type of European.

I had successfully tested the Abdication epic in Asia with my readings but I knew that it could not be played or published in England, on libel grounds alone. For several months I read it to my friends, to groups and in schools and then, sure that it would have to wait and losing interest, I put it away. I wanted to get back onto the Path which I had lost since my return and write again and by this time we had decided to sell up the business and both live in the country. But until we did this, another cottage was what I needed, one cheap and quick to find — and my mother left for Aldeburgh on yet another house-hunting holiday.

With money in her pocket now, she went to a small but exclusive hotel — not, as in the past to a second-rate lodging, hiding her food in a suitcase. And the letters flowed again with all her vivid little tales.

Arriving on July 17th, she wrote at once.

"The hotel is run beautifully & all the people in it are 'our sort' . . . Dinner is at 7.30 when I shall wear my 'Perfect Lady's' clothes! . . . We are only a minute or two from Benjamin Britten . . . a homely little outlook from my room — flowers & vegetables, little trees & a green bank, so fresh & countrified & lovely air. We are crazy to live in London. . ."

I had friends there and she was soon being entertained and, when a bus strike began, walking miles and miles every day to empty houses. She wrote again.

"The food is v. good & v. generous. Dinner never less than 5 courses & I wade through them all. . . Well — to begin my diary. An agent gave me an impossible house but instead of going to see it, decided to call on your friend Mrs C. I seemed to walk miles till I came to her mucky, dirty home, neglected garden — but lovely flowers. She is most kind but most distracting. Put about a gallon of water on to make 2 cups of Nescafe, fussing about while I sat resting peacefully waiting for it to boil. It took so long that when it was ready I had to go or I would have been late for my lovely lunch. . . If I had not the interest of househunting & could not tramp the countryside — I should be bored.

I replied:

"You write wonderful letters. You *did* do a lot the first few days. You must feel very braced. You don't mention the 'ladies & gentlemen' in the hotel? Is it that you have failed to impress them or, have they failed to impress you? You really should get some high society for your money as well as just board & lodging. I shall be very disappointed if you spend your whole holiday in traditional Burrell style — house hunting! But perhaps you are so conditioned to it that you just can't do anything else — it's second nature now! . . ."

There were no cheap cottages. And she wrote:

"I'm not going to househunt any more. . . I am now amusing myself looking for artistic junk to paint. . . I went to the Antique shop & saw a jolly old man cleaning brasses. He did not talk but bawled at me & haw hawed at everything. His shop was too superior for me & he told me to go to Ing's & Beaston's, on the corner. I went to both & then back to Haw Haw to show him the dirty treasures I had bought at Ings. "I told you to go to Beaston's too" he bawled. "I did but no good, no good" I bawled back. Then, someone came into the shop & Haw Haw hawed so loudly that all the trinkets shook. "It's 'im! It's 'im! Mr Beaston 'isself! Haw! Haw! Haw!" Mr Beaston was a tall, fine looking man & seeing the junk in my hand, thought silently a moment & then said, "I believe I can help you. I will look out a few things — so come again". . .

"Now that I have got over the glamour of paying enormously &, in consequence, thinking I was getting so much, I have come down to Earth & realise the Artificiality of it all. First a programme shoved under one's nose — dishes with such lovely names — the titles alone make one's mouth water — but poor quality meat camouflaged & tasteless, sauces sounding so wonderful but which make one choke. All money, money money & Bunkum. . . I am afraid I look so distinguished & awe-inspiring & wealthy in my new clothes that most of the visitors avoid me — but I have made a few friends. Having got under the surface of things I realise that the majority of them are well-to-do risen up lower classes. . ."

Sir C.P's son, Sundaram and his wife, were coming to England now and because they were short of foreign currency, he asked me to give them £40 and put them up and they stayed in my mother's flat. And I wrote:

"The Indians arrived yesterday & were thrilled & delighted & grateful. The son has nothing of his father's intellect, dignity & personality but they are warm & affectionate & simple & I like them — even more than when they entertained me in Bangalore. They rush about being entertained by grand people & then come tumbling back here like two excited children to tell me all about it, feeling at home & happy. . ."

When they left she returned and soon after that I went back to Yorkshire, taking Susie — and stayed with Nan again. On August 20th I wrote on a postcard:

"I arrived here to a wonderful welcome & felt elated to be back. The Scar Top people may be willing to sell & there are other empty houses — so things are starting well. . ."

On another postcard the next day:

"I have been up to Scar Top. The windows are all broken & it is more derelict than ever & I have written to the Halls. The air is so health-giving & I have friends everywhere. My Asian postcards were passed all round the village. Susie is very happy & very good, so far. . ."

When the Indians left my mother's flat they travelled on the Continent and then returned to a London hotel. On August 21st, my mother wrote:

"I do hope you get Scar Top. . . The Indians lost no time. As soon as they arrived back he telephoned to say that he was bringing his wife at 10 o'clock the next day & picking her up at 4. I had a fit but tried to seem delighted. I hung about waiting for them until about 12 when *he* turned up, saying his wife was tired but he would bring her in the afternoon — with a friend. I invited them to tea. At 4 o'clock he dropped them both on the doorstep & went off somewhere else & we waited for him to return. When the doorbell rang at last, *she* hurried to open it but came back alone — while he did some telephoning in the hall. He was ages but we sat down to tea eventually."

"When I had filled all the cups she somehow shook the table & filled all the saucers. The mess & muddle she made then! — But after that we settled down fairly happily. Then, she was keen on washing up & taking her friend to the kitchen to show how 'at home' she was. I told her not to as the water was cold & went away for a minute to give him the taxi number. When I returned I found them in the kitchen both taps full on, the remains of the cakes among the wet things on the sink board which was one big slop, a pool of water on the floor & the friend drying up with my bath towel! 'Au revoir but not good-bye' she said ominously, giving me a fat hug — meaning nothing. If they ask to come again I will not make excuses, not let them know how anxious I am to see the last of them — because of C.P. . ."

I replied.

"I *am* sorry about my Indians. Don't endure that irritation again — say you are ill, say anything. It will not affect C.P. We have done our duty by them & satisfied him. . . A rumour is going round that Scar Top is up for sale at £400. An agent came, looked up & said, 'I'm not going up there' & drove away. . . All the village people are keen that I should buy it — & sure that no one else will. . Susie is having a lovely time but she doesn't really appreciate visiting. She sits in the middle of all the turbulence (2 boistrous children, Nan pretty boistrous too, Vera the wonderful maid & David when he is home) with a pained expression — but she is very long suffering & forbearing & good. . ."

A few days later on a postcard.

"I am in Skipton waiting for a bus after going to Leeds to find the Halls & I traced them from their old address & found her *in*. She was friendly & we laughed over all our quarrels but the house was never up for sale. That was just some stupid confusion & they can't make up their minds. . ."

And the next day, in a long letter:

"A month ago his mother died & they will get a 5th share of her fortune (£20,000) but there are death duties & family wrangles all of which will take months to resolve. I believe they will sell in the end but now is not the time to press. . . They are dreaming of all the things they are going to do with this fortune — & repair & live in Scar Top is one of them. . . I have looked at all the empty houses here & Nan has driven me about but none are possible & I am thinking of buying a caravan — & waiting. . . The Hebden farmers have offered me land to build on, a new & exciting design perhaps — but the old Scar Top house still draws me — it has an atmosphere & a grandeur. . ."

On August 30th she replied.

"Try offering her a *lot*. A quiet house that you love in a place that you know is worth anything to you. Try £500. I'd give even more — £1000. Have another talk if it does not worry you to death pressing her. . . She is crazy. Her letters & her ways long ago were never normal. However great their fortune they would never live there & she will let the house fall to pieces before she makes up her mind. . . The Indians telephoned. I shall leave my wife at your flat on the mornings of the 30th & 31st. I said I would be delighted to have her on the 30th but would be out on the 31st. I have been waiting all day for her. Aren't Indian ways comic! I am going to be very firm if they try to come tomorrow. I painted while I waited so did not really mind. . . Later. The doorbell rang at 7 o'clock this evening. She felt too poorly to come this morning. They rang me at 10 o'clock (they *said*) but got no answer. Anyway, I have successfully prevented them coming tomorrow. But again we said, 'au revoir but not good-bye' — & they are not sailing until November 15th!'"

Two days later, on September 1st, I wrote.

"I am going to Skipton tomorrow to see the RDC about caravans & building regulations — and moving to the Longthorne's. Nan & David are so kind but this house is impossible to stay in for long. . . I get no sleep & just can't think & make decisions. Like Susie, I hate visiting. . . There are many advantages about caravan life yet I fear it, fear exposure to the weather, fear noise & the feeling of being out of doors when I am used to working half buried in thick-walled houses. . ."

On September 4th she wrote:

"A caravan seems the best thing at the moment. One can always move it & get out of it quickly if she does sell. . . When the Indians came that evening, it was humbug her 'having a headache & feeling poorly'. They had obviously come from a party. She was all decked out in her best — diamonds in her ears & one in her nose — if I had a nose like hers I would not draw attention to it! She came again yesterday but in future I shall only allow him to drop her on the doorstep for Tea — never another whole day. And always they leave saying, 'au revoir but not good-bye! . . .'"

I arranged to meet the Halls again but when the day came and she sent a telegram to say that she had flu, I made up my mind to buy a second-hand caravan.

It was delivered to Nan's house where, in the yard with the hens running about and Susie watching them, like a chained huntress, knowing that she must not chase them, I cleaned and repainted it and my mother came from London to sew curtains and help. When I discovered that every raindrop on the aluminum roof was like a drum beat, I ordered heavy canvas to be glued all over it — and for this I had to wait. When she left, I saw her onto a crowded train at Skipton, concerned about her journey. And she wrote on her arrival:

"You do too much for me & think too much when you have far too much to do & think for yourself. I am perfectly capable in every way — only muzzy headed. Wait till I am 94 — I am only 84 — & then I will have a companion-help & a bath chair & all the rest! . . ."

Our twice-weekly cleaner, an ebullient Welshwoman whose tragi-comic life we were deeply involved in had, after many agonizing delays, married again. Her new husband, Charles, was a handsome lay-about, pleased to live upon her earnings and enjoy her cooking. My mother ended her letter:

"Doris was brimming over with excitement about Wales when she came this morning. She went to bury the father of her first husband's half brother — taking Charles with her. But they arrived too late — he was already buried — nevertheless they all seemed to have had a lovely time & they all admired Charles very much! . . ."

On September 11th, Sir C.P. wrote:

"What a silent person you are. You have not answered my letter & my son tells me that you are in Yorkshire hard at work on your literary enterprises. . . The more I observe developments here, the more keen I am to spend a long holiday in England to get rid of my mental cobwebs & find my (psychological) feet. . ."

And again on the 28th.

"Yours was literally a 'breathless' letter. House & caravan hunting. . . I wonder how I shall fit into a caravan! . . ."

I went on waiting for the canvas to arrive and in November returned to London, too — but not for long. On the 21st I wrote again from Hebden.

"I found everything in the van dry & in order — even the matches could be struck — so different from all my houses! The canvas has come, they will do the work in 2 days & I shall then have it towed up to the site — in the meantime, coal & oil & calor gas will be taken up & stacked in advance. I am at ease now, feeling that I am near to being settled. . . I watched you walking down the platform at St Pancras yesterday — station partings are always sad & painful. Susie wasn't particularly pleased to be back although she has such a lovely life here. She was far more excited & delighted when she returned to London. She ran all the way from the bus to No 10, rushed up the steps, pushed at the door, then dashed downstairs to you. She is more keen on us & her home — even than rabbits! . . ."

Then, the first shock came and I wrote distractedly.

"I have had to change all my plans. After I had had ½ ton of coal dumped in bags at the gate of the field, Mrs Longthorne calmly said that I'd better not leave it there for long as I might lose it! It transpired that in the slummy-looking farmhouse about ¼ of a mile beyond, lives a notorious thief! And they never thought of warning me! Within 24 hours a quarter was taken. John has brought down what is left. They say now that nothing is safe from him. When I went away he might even have broken into the van.

Added to that, old Dixon (supposed to be mad but the most sensible of them all) has told me that the snow always piles up in that field & the van would be buried. . . I can't take it up to Scar Top because it would not get round the sharp, narrow turning off the road onto the track. I have been away up the Pately Road this morning looking all over the Metcalf's land (Vera's family). I doubt if I do any serious work this winter — the difficulties are so great. . . Also, the ventilation is worrying me. The stove is set too high — over the wheel. All the heat rises to one's head with a belt of cold around one's feet & legs & hips. I have to open a window to get my head cool — & then I am cold all over. . . I am back in Nan's rowdy house. I am fed up with the Longthornes — they are so stupid & self-righteous & humbuggy when they know they have done something silly. . ."

And a letter flew back.

"Your letter this morning is simply staggering — inconceivable how those half-baked villagers could stand by & look on & not utter a word of advice or warning . . . a notorious thief! . . . I long to run away from them all — what a treasure Nan is — in the midst of it all she gives you a home. . . O dear, my letters are so balmy & you are going through such misery & worry. I believe some day you *will* find a permanent place to write in & have a car & be near congenial people & all this will be simply a past bad dream. . ."

On the 28th I wrote again.

"I move up to the lower side of the Metcalf's land tomorrow — 300 yards from the farmhouse, behind a wall with a few small trees for protection & a stream close by — letters & parcels will be left in a box on the road & Mr Bond delivers once a week — all very comfortable & pleasant & good enough for now. . . I am being cautious until I get used to the caravan & the worst of the snow is over, then I shall move it onto the moor, higher than Scar Top with glorious views, a good rough road & a babbling brook. . . The Metcalf's are a very nice family & Arthur is most sympathetic, repeating that they will try not to disturb me — John will follow with a trailer load of coal & my trunk. . . Susie did a terrible thing yesterday — killed one of Arthur's hens! I was so shocked & frightened that she would do it again, get the habit, that I hit her and still feel miserable — & it may have been unintentional. She may just have pounced on whatever was moving in the long couch grass. And the hens are the same colour as the grouse. When I owned up today & paid for it he was very pleased. He thought a fox had killed it. He is very tolerant about her & hopes she will catch the moles. . ."

To this she replied:

"What a relief. I was in dread of what the next news might be. .
You could buy some very warm boots to sit in & have a blanket
round your knees. . . I am in & out of shops now trying to find
boxes & jimcracks. No success yet. I went down to Camden Town
yesterday & shall try the Portobello Road. . . If you ever have a
moment, do draw me a map of where you are & where the caravan
will stand. . ."

On December 1st I wrote on a postcard:

"The move was rather hair-raising. We got up to the farm
alright but because of the uneven ground, the van tipped slightly,
we detached the tractor & manhandled it through the narrow
stone gateposts, scraping one side. when we got it through it ran
away down the hill & only stopped when it sank in some mud —
the tractor then pulled it out 50 yards from the house — & there I
still am. There is no possibility of getting to the place I chose & I
shall move onto the moor. I do hate not having my own land &
being dependent on farmers & not feeling safe — lots of minor
troubles as well, but they'll all pass & I'll get settled one day. . ."

The next day, walking down to the village, we had to pass a
farm where hundreds, literally hundreds, of chickens were
pecking about the open moor. When we reached it, Susie tore into
the middle of them, seized one, raced on and then brought it to me
and dropped it at my feet where it lay as dead. Again, I was
frightened and furious — and hit her. Then, to my astonishment
and relief, the hen opened one eye, then lifted its head, jumped up
and ran away. She had sinned again — but at least not killed again.

"Today, in a thick mist, the caravan was towed onto the moor
— a wonderful place, much better than the low damp hollow I
first chose — the mud & narrow gates were blessings in disguise.
Tom Longthorne has redeemed himself — dashed up with John &
the tractor to bring the coal & today, uprooted the heavy stone
gate post on the moor & knocked down several feet of wall to let
the van through — then stayed up all day settling me in. Four men,
plus a fifth shepherding nearby, have been helping me & after
every sort of difficulty & delay I am settled at last. . . When it is
hard physical work or simple things like delivering milk & parcels
& putting me up, the Longthornes are kind & loyal & wonderful —
when they have to think they are hopeless — & they are all the
same, these inbred remote hill farmers, left behind by the world &
I must not let myself get impatient & irritable. . . I am having
screens built on the weatherside. . ."

And she replied:

"I have a horror of snowdrifts. I shall never forget Boston when we waked to pitch darkness — snow up to the 2nd storey in one night! Do have terrifically strong windscreens built. . . It is not just the inbred people where you are — human beings are like that everywhere. . ."

I returned to London at Christmas and left Susie. We had decided to let her mate again. Her maternal instincts were as strong as her hunting ones and I did not think it would be a difficult thing for my mother to arrange. On her walks about Hampstead and on Primrose Hill she knew all the local dogs and often talked to their owners. She would only have to select an aristocratic bridegroom and obtain the co-operation of its owner, perhaps offering payment in kind — a puppy.

On January 9th 1958 I wrote from Hebden again.

"This carvan seems ill-fated. In spite of their solemn promises, I returned to find that the builders had not put up the screens. . . Today, the noble English are as unreliable & ignoble as everybody else & I planned to buy the wood so that Tom & I could do the job ourselves. Then, he suggested that it would be better to move it more into the wall corner & rashly, I agreed. Up they both came in a squall & John lugged it forward with the tractor but, manoeuvring it into the corner, got one wheel stuck in the mud & it tipped — then, trying to right it, he overstrained the retractable legs & they both began to buckle! We rushed about with rocks, shoving them under the wheels & girders but finally had to give it up. I shall have to wait until the frost comes & we can pull it out. . . A terrific storm blew up soon after they left & all night long I was battered & towards morning, felt myself rolling out of bed! When I got up & went out I found that it had sunk another 6 inches. I spent half the morning trying to hold it from sinking any more. . . I was once more in despair & began to detest it but it is my own fault for bringing such a flimsy flamsy stupid thing to a place like this & at this time of the year. But I am feeling better now & must reconcile myself to it for the next few months & then, somehow get a house somewhere. . . I've just been listening to the storm news — more gales are predicted. If there is any damage to No 10 — tiles? Do ring up the builder. Although stuck in the mud & tipped & in disorder, I am more sheltered than I was & it could well have been worse last night — 100 mph, they say. A ventilator blew open & the rain poured in but it warmed up quickly — none of the mildew & vaultish cold of the old damp houses. One must be thankful for that. . . I do miss Susie. But when I get settled & absorbed in my work I shall be self-sufficient. It is hard enough keeping oneself alive & going here — let alone an animal. . ."

On the 11th day my mother replied:

"It seems unending, the worry of that blasted caravan. . .
Yesterday, Susie was married. She had been quite placid until two
days ago when, on the way back from the shops, she went wild
over a retriever & he over her. Had I not been near home I would
have had to call for help. They were quite uncontrollable. I
fumbled for the latch key on the doorstep, a tangle of wild dogs at
my feet. I managed to push Susie through a crack & squeezed
myself after her, jabbing at the retriever with your long stick. O
dear, the insanity of Creation! The next day, I rushed for the
waiting lover. First, they tore about my sitting room, banging
against everything, hugging each other round the neck. No early
Victorian modesty about Susie. She was all over her grimy
unwashed lover. Then, too comic the whole situation was. I had
knotted up the net curtain to be able to look through the window
occasionally and suddenly from outside, came furious growls &
barks & slobbers of angry foam ran down the pane — Butch, from
round the corner madly jealous, watching his rival! Then, the
lover rushed at him — growls & barks from inside. I thought
between them they would break the glass. Susie, the cause of it all,
sat serenly on her tail, quite unperturbed, like a perfect little lady,
waiting for it to be over. I dropped the curtain & they subsided &
the whole business followed. . ."

On the 13th I wrote:

"Two absolutely glorious days — frost & brilliant sunshine —
mountain weather. This is a wonderful spot. I would never find a
ready-made house in such a place. It has its compensations —
caravan life. And today, wonder of wonders, the builders turned
up, drove their lorry over the frozen ground & heather & erected
the screens in a few hours. Tom & John followed & with great
effort, pulled the van out of the hole & into position. I am settled at
last!

On the 18th I wrote again.

"Well, the screens came only just in time — a tremendous gale
has been blowing since early morning & I hardly feel it — just a
trembling & occasional lurch. . . I still can't give my whole mind to
my work — I feel more as if I were engaged in a climbing
expedition with Hillary & Fuchs, than a literary endeavour &
spiritual quest. I sometimes wonder how I have got here — and
question why? I haven't got over my astonishment although I
know I shall know in the end. Perched upon this remarkable spot,
one feels in another world — one cannot even see the civilised

world in the valley below — just range upon range of desolate hills
— in bad weather grim but grand, in good — very heaven. . .
There are snow warnings tonight so probably what I have been
preparing for, fearing & waiting for, is upon me. But I fear it no
more — the caravan cannot blow over & I have stocks of food to
last me for weeks. If you don't hear from me, don't worry. I shall
be eating like a fighting cock & dashing about helping the farmers
dig out their sheep. The land about me is parcelled out among 6 old
farming families who have lived up here for generations — the
fine rough men & their dogs walk the moor after their sheep. . . My
old bedroom shoes are in my wardrobe. I ought to have given them
to Susie when I went away."

And the reply came:

"I gave Susie your old slippers & she took one of them to her bed
& lies curled up, hugging it. . ."

10

IT WAS some time before I could write on a postcard, "All these great blind, efforts that I make are acts of faith & feeling and such acts (the only ones worth making in life) never really fail even if they seem to sometimes — & sooner or later & ultimately, they succeed far beyond themselves"; and before I knew that the high hills of England were my Himalayas and I could say, "I love this caravan". Perhaps Europeans always have to struggle physically when they climb their mountains.

When I returned to England my dream state was soon broken as my intuitive side lost its supremacy and although it was painful to be back in a western, wholly rational, atmosphere, it was a relief not to be floating in an eastern sea, alive with psychic images and instances. And now, striving for balance in myself and refusing to accept the either-or situation, I wrote and at the same time turned inwards and repeating the Hindu prayer, longed for and hoped for, 'a glimpse of Reality — God'. But as soon as I did this, I lost interest in the world, failing at once to square the circle.

On March 5thm 1958 Sir C.P. wrote:

"When you were in India I realised that you were on the eve of a 'vita nuova'. Not only had your horizons widened with your travels & experiences but there was a new spiritual ferment which was bound profoundly to modify your outlook. What you need now is not so much new reading & thinking but what the Indian yogis style, 'Dharana & Pratyahara' — selections of mental processes & concentration. . . I still think that in your drama you have expressed yourself effectively but the limitations of dramatic situations & dialogue may not contain all your freshly acquired psychological treasures. Something like Cardinal Newman's "Apologia pro vita sua" — an essay or assay portraying your 'cyclic unrest fulfilled with solemn equipoise', may well be your next literary adventure. "For all the past, read true, is prophecy". And so, what you term an autobiography may also be the biography of a world in crisis. . . Like you, I often feel desperate about the existing 'way of the world' but still I am hopeful for humanity. It needs the shock of new catastrophes & new revelations but the divine in us will never utterly perish. . . It may be a good idea to pay another visit to India, with which you are truly more akin than, perhaps, you are aware."

The autobiographical work which I began then is, after a long gap, what I am finishing now. I can only hope that it will turn out to be both the history of India he first asked for — and the 'biography of a world in crisis' which he asked for now.

The snow fell heavily, the caravan was partly buried and I dug out my coal and cut a path to the spring and, trying to 'select my mental processes', worked on. Only one thing disturbed the long serenity of the winter. On March 14th at 10 am, I wrote to my mother:

"About one o'clock this morning — I was just going off to sleep, half asleep I think I was, when I heard a bark — one clear, soft bark — & when, after some seconds, I became fully conscious, I thought with a start, 'no dog could have barked *here* — that was Susie's bark, gentle as when she talks, asking for something'. And I became suddenly terribly anxious & forlorn, I thought that something must have happened. . . I grew more & more agitated & all the sorrows of birth & life & death swept over me & through me & it was hours before I slept again. . . It was more than a dream — it was reality. Either she had travelled here or I was there. Perhaps the puppies were being born & she was waking you as each time in the past she has waked me — & telling me now? I will walk down to the village this morning & try to find out. . . It snows on & off all the time but when the sun comes out in between, the air vibrates with life & health & hopefulness. . ."

On the same day, the 14th, in a letter crossing mine and before she got my wire, she wrote:

"At about 4 o'clock this morning, Susie woke me with a loud & tragic bark which frightened me & I leapt out of bed. . ."

And the next day, after receiving my wire, she wrote again:

"She must have called you first softly, then 3 hours later, waked me with that loud, wild bark. Her eyes looked so tragic & appealing then. She adores you. . ."

I rushed to London and was there when the puppies were born — not in the lovely bed my mother had arranged for her in her bedroom but on the floor beside my chair, as we sat talking in her sitting room.

I returned to Yorkshire and the letters flowed again.

On March 27th, she wrote:

"Susie kicked out my book & slept in the broken chair last night so evidently she wants to be cooler & away from her 6 little hot water bottles. . . She eats her porridge, drinks her Lactol, her friend the butcher gives her lovely meat & the tenants give her chicken — & the puppies thrive. . . The laundry man has been & we will go for our walk now although I'm sure she will not allow me to sit on my favourite seat for long. (Later.) She gave me about 5 minutes 'sit', then put her nose in my lap, meaning — 'Home James'! . . . Poor Seddon is ill — on the verge of a nervous breakdown through overwork at the SPCK, cries at the least thing & doesn't know how she is going to go on standing it. Then, last night, on top of it all, Taylor stole (!) her milk & she rushed down to me in a terrible state because her NERVES depend on a glass of hot milk on going to bed. Bennet away, so I stole one of *his* bottles! & took it up to her — she almost shed more tears in gratitude. She really is in a most hysterical state. No wonder she nearly killed Bennet with wild driving when she gave him a lift! . . ."

On April 1st I wrote:

"I have no news worth writing about. I stay here in complete isolation & the days glide by — I am hardly conscious of time & this withdrawal is essential to me — the quietness is phenomenal, only the sound of the wind & the curlews — sounds which I love . . ."

Every time I returned I loathed the house and when I finally returned in May — loathed it even more. And my mother understood.

I telephoned the agent, it was valued with all its furnishings & fittings and put onto the market and two parties were soon contending for it. A pleasant, straightforward commercial gentleman and a country clergyman and his wife, out to acquire a little London business to augment his stipend. Out of sympathy for the 'cloth' I chose them and soon regretted it. It was a long-drawn-out and acrimonious sale.

All the tenants left when they heard the news and I had to advertise for new ones to keep the income going. Contracts were to have been exchanged in July, then in August. My mother took a furnished flat in Hythe to give us both a holiday and she and Susie left. I stayed behind for yet another hold-up and slept on the floor for our personal possessions had all been taken into store.

On August 10th she wrote:

"I do wish you were here — the sea looks so inviting. Susie was very subdued on arrival but when I took her on the beach, bucked up & never stopped rolling — she found so many smelly things &

has made the flat stink of fish. . . We will take turns if we have to stay on long at No 10. I shall be quite comfortable with a box for a bed or a deck chair borrowed from next door. . . The crowd was terrific at Victoria but I had a very nice porter. . . You did help me to get off, Love — straps for my bag & lovely food & so thoughtful to write the address that I was going to — I'd quite forgotten it. . . It was lovely walking along the beach this morning to buy the Observer in a *minute* little shop — no lead on Susie & today, she is a new dog. . . It is a very nice flat, the sun pouring in, sea view in front & view of the old church behind — but it's a bit mucky ! . . . "

And the next day:

"This flat will be a great rest — it is so airey. In London we suffer from lack of air & pure air. Thank God we are leaving. Here, Susie & I live in a hurricane. She is not quite sure if she likes it — doors & windows wide open, curtains whirling & flapping — the lovely sea almost on the doorstep. . . I hate to think of you all alone surrounded by that exhausting crowd — solicitors, agents, buyers & even *in* the house, unwholesome people. . . The neighbours took a fancy to Susie at once & asked if she liked bones. When I was asleep on the sofa yesterday I was just conscious of a bang on the floor — when I waked I saw a parcel in the middle of the carpet — a big meaty knuckle bone ! They had shied it through the window ! . . . "

Then, from domestic comedy to heroic drama. On the 13th she wrote:

"Your pc this morning is good news. You will be able to leave London at last. . . I wish Susie were a lap dog. . . Yesterday I had a never-to-be-forgotten day with her. I took the flower walk to the town to save her from being on the lead. Halfway, I sat down on one of the inviting seats — not half a minute were my eyes off her but she was gone. Rabbits, mice, moles, rats — she was gone. My calls got louder, my shrieks penetrated all Hythe. At last she came, covered in earth & a lump of mud for a nose. Luckily I had started early & there was still time to do my shopping. Then, on the way home, wandering along the beach watching the bathers I dreamingly passed our flat & went on beyond the houses to some waste land, thick with weeds, an absolute maze. When I realised where I was & turned to go — no Susie. I daren't leave her. . . Over an hour passed. I got so anxious, thinking perhaps she had got into a bog. . . At last a man & a dog came by. He said he had seen her, trying to get up the bank but the growth was too thick. He said it was a veritable rabbit warren. I am sure the rabbits were hindering her more than the growth. "

"The sky was black in the distance. . . Another hour passed & the cloud was on us. At last she came from out the jungle — but too late — hail was pelting down & hurting her & she tugged in the opposite direction. Truly, the thunder was incessant, the crackles sounded & felt as if literally *on* my head, while the lightening kept striking the ground a yard ahead of us. At last we came to the big hotel & dashed up the steps & a guest opened the door. I was drenched but they have big mats & I dripped onto them & a man brought me a steel chair. We sat for ½ an hour until a break in the storm came & I hurried home. . ."

After much mean haggling over the contents, the Hancocks signed the contract and I left for Hythe. When we talked about the storm and her ordeal, all she said was, "Hunting is Susie's talent and she has the same passion for it as the artist for his work". As she had had for hers and been so frustrated. As I had for mine.

We were homeless and the plan now was for my mother to live in a country town or village and I, in an isolated cottage near. But because I had already found the 'new green life springing up" — the New Age movement — and had begun to chase the gurus, travel to teaching centres and attach myself to esoteric groups. Yorkshire seemed too far and my mother did not really want to live in the north. And so, starting the search where we were, we took a furnished house on the Kent Downs and leaving her there, I returned to Yorkshire, to bring the caravan down.

On September 5th, I wrote:

"It is so lovely being here on the top of the moor again & I feel sad to be leaving it altogether. The remoteness & purity are soothing & restful to the spirit. Kent is overcrowded, noisy & sordid & I still hanker after living farther from London, in a grander place. . . But what pleases me is the idea of having a real working home — I've longed for that for years. . ."

On the 11th, I wrote from a 'Discussion Camp' near Lowestoft.

"It took us 2 hours to get the caravan off the moor. The towing man was most skilful & I stopped worrying as soon as he took charge. I spent the night in the van, in the middle of a crowd of vans & awful shacks & shanties outside Leeds. In the morning, I came on here & left him to deliver the van to you. . ."

And from the Camp again, on the 15th.

"Completion day has come & the Hancocks have not paid up. I hear they gave the tenants a weeks notice, turned off the hot water, then ripped the house to pieces. I've told the solicitor to press for a settlement. . . No planes & real rural country here & wild beach. . ."

On the 17th, my mother replied:

"I wish now that we had gone straight to Suffolk. If we move we cannot let Mrs M down. I believe our rent is a godsend to her. Miss M thinks it was a Higher Power which brought you together. I think the Power was more on her side than yours for the house is damp & the chimney smokes — but I like her. She is strung up with nervous energy & fills the room with high voltage power as soon as she enters. Miss M just the opposite. Her writing work is far above my intelligence — all accuracy & knowledge & deadly dull. She had not discovered how vacant my brain is & was keen to have my opinion. My head was in a whirl not to disappoint her. I said something non-committal & then, fortunately, the electric lady came swishing in & saved me. . . I am dying to begin house-hunting but where shall we start? Canterbury is in a hollow & anyway, I will not look for a cottage all among the Holy! . . ."

On the 21st I wrote on a postcard:

"If I have made a mistake in going to Kent & wasted money & time, it can't be helped. . . I shall search the Downs & the country-side below . . . if we find nothing or don't like it — we'll move. . ."

We didn't like it and in November, moved to Suffolk, making Halesworth our base. My mother went into lodgings and Susie and I lived in the caravan, parked on a farm near. The town was in a hollow, her room was damp & she soon developed aches & pains & began to roll about. When the Hancocks paid up at last, £3500, I rushed to Southwold, which we had once known so well, and loved — and bought her a little house.

During those months of post-India turmoil when I was trying to change myself and at the same time, change my world, I stopped writing to Sir C.P. and let him draw away. Once before, in my youth, I had revolted against my situation and fought my way out of it through humiliating darkness into the light of a new beginning. Now, when I left the PEN Club and the Peace movement and all my complacent friends and stopped giving readings of the Epic and pulled up my only root — London; when I was running from the ugliness and hatefulness of my environment and, once again, floundering in the gloom as I searched for an alternative society — I rejected his help. I seemed to have to run and fall and run again — alone. But in the New Year I wrote to him and on January 3rd 1959, he replied from Madras.

"A thousand thanks for your comforting letter. I was greatly worried over your long silence. You are literally a 'Wandering Jew' and feel restless in almost every environment, but I am like you in temperament & deeply sympathise. . . I do hope your Sea play gets produced. It will certainly create an impression."

And again on the 12th.

"What a breathlessly worried letter was yours of the 5th. And how deeply I feel for you & for the loss of time & energy in the course of your 'Wanderjahr'. . . Your letter reminded me of the saying in one of our Upanishads सै॒ञ्जु॒ञ्ते॒ञ्त्रो॒श्री॒टी॑ः (Meaning that you really enjoy yourself best after renouncing things). . ."

I brought beautiful wall papers from London and when the little house was redecorated and my mother arranged her furniture and ornaments and I hung her pictures, it reflected all the charm & beauty of the old culture. And she was happy creating another home and her health improved. "I am cured of my tipsy ways!"

I went on searching for a cottage for myself and, in my frustration, went constantly to London to stay with my kind little typist friend in Primrose Gardens, reporting back little bits of news from those crowded tragi-comic houses.

On April 20th 1959, I wrote on a postcard:

"Poor old Mrs Thomason died this week-end & I have just watched her being taken away. No friends — no flowers — just her business-like son dashing jauntily about. No one had looked after her. She never ate anything & twice recently set the house on fire. But for the other tenants she would have been dead long ago. They did their best. She was a dear old thing. All the heads hanging out of the squalid bed-sit windows watching her go — including mine! . . ."

And on another:

They've installed a coin geyser in the bathroom of No. 10 — and doubled the rents. The Man of God even more mean & nasty than his stupid avaricious wife. . ."

When Susie was first taken to the sea, as a puppy, and she saw me walk into the water and all but disappear, she had screamed with anxiety and then plunged into the waves and swum out to save me.

When a thief came one night to steal coal, in Appledore, she had driven him away. And now, she defended me again.

When I bathed every day, she always sat at the water's edge watching until I came out and was safe and then, went off to her rabbit bank.

One day, when I was dressing on the beach, a crowd of rough little boys appeared and, shouting obscenities, surrounded me and one of them grabbed my long stick. I caught the other end and a tug-of-war ensued. Leaving her bank at once, Susie sat on a rock — and watched.

For a long time I was friendly, trying to persuade the child to drop the stick, but as soon as I lost patience and spoke severely, at the same time wondering how, clad only in a towel, I could get rid of them, Susie came down from the rock and walked slowly, quietly and resolutely towards them and such was her tiny canine power, that they all fled before her.

On May 5th Sir C.P. wrote again.

"Talk of telepathy! It is wonderful how we react on & to each other. I was just wondering if my letter would reach you — & now here comes your answering one . . . & it indicates more restfulness & zest than I have observed in you for years. God bless you! . . . As for Tibet, China (like Stalinist Russia) is simply following the age-old territorial aggressive policy of the Manchu Emperors. "Plus ça change, plus c'est le meme chose". . .

If I had lost my restlessness — it was not for long. The search seemed hopeless and, in addition, I found that the east coast air was *too* bracing and made me livery and, with a rucksac on my back, I set off for the high hills once again on yet another crazy, self-destructive hunt for a working home. And my mother was not altogether happy. She found the Southwold people snobbish and unfriendly and the spirit of the town, cold.

On September 17th I wrote from Derbyshire.

"Arrived 2 hours ago. I've got into a very nice house & kind helpful people. I've been to all the agents & already feel a different spirit here. . . I know this climate suits me — but does it suit you? . . the climate must suit you as well. . ."

And she replied.

"*Any* bracing climate anywhere will suit me. Peace of mind is what will suit me — I am always depressed here — fuming internally — all this comfort for me — & all wrong for you. I shall sell this house & leave it with the greatest joy when you have found a quiet house. . . What bliss life could be. . ."

Everywhere, people were now buying up the old cottages as second homes and finding nothing, I moved on to Nidderdale, in Yorkshire, where I found a temporary site for the caravan to which, a month later, I had it towed. On October 13th, wrote:

"These people are remarkable — all wanting to help. I've made so many friends & feel as if I had come home. . ."

On October 15th, Sir C.P. wrote from Ooty.

"In a few days I shall be completing 80 years of my life & I am proceeding to Madras as my sons & friends are making a function of the occurrence & have overborne my reluctance to be forcibly reminded of my age! The Annamali University is opening a Library constructed in my name & erecting a bust. . . I go out to you in spirit as to one who has been the truest of comrades and the most discerning of friends. God bless you. . ."

He had chosen the way of the advocates and the governors, the way of the wanted men, the insiders, and had risen from one forum to another until his brilliance took him to the top.

I had chosen the way of the poets and playmakers, the way of the unwanted and the few, the constant outsiders and, more than half-way through life, I still writhed like a worm in the earth, like a worm under the feet of the king. The year before I had written on the back of a discarded letter:

"This year I am 50 — for nearly 30 years I have been writing — & still only for myself, it seems. I don't blame the world. My odd course was inevitable & I have got used to my obscurity — I expect nothing else & have come to think that there is good in it. One's art is put to every test — & this is the best perhaps??

I still don't know if my work will live — whether it is good, bad or indifferent. I am certain that it *will* — but I don't *know* — no one has ever told me. I have no external proof that I am not just another passionate mediocrity.

The final test of an authentic artist is dedication — the vows of an artist — abstention from the world & all its pleasures — I have not known of any passionate mediocrity going so far in his arduor as to give up his whole life for his passion.

This I have certainly done — but still that is no proof that my work is good. Perhaps I have done this for an illusion. If so — then I must be mad! but such madness I think is better than the conventional life in which happiness is the main purpose & success the main show. A crazy, seemingly futile life spent following a will-o-the-wisp is more rich in experience & wisdom than the other — more ultimately sane."

When I read his letter now I believed that I had another 30 years to rise out of the ground and stand where he stood and so I felt no jealousy — only joy to see him crowned. And soon, I would turn in the ground where I lay and lose all desire for a crown.

On the 18th I wrote to my mother:

"I have advertised & tramped up Nidderdale — there are no suitable houses but I like the dale . . . a fine, resourceful builder tells me that he could build me a 2-room house for £1300. In the meantime, he has introduced me to some awfully nice farmers — the man is rough, probably illiterate but the wife was a teacher & the house is full of quite good furniture & books & they will let me take the caravan onto their land. The only disadvantage is that they are high on the moor with only one bus a week & a 2½ mile walk down (& up) a very steep hill to the main road. . . I am having a rest today, staying at home in the caravan — feeling peaceful & content to be back in these parts and, assured that I can build, haven't got that hopeless feeling any more. . . After Southwold, Harrogate is like a metropolis — perhaps you will think it too towny?

"I wish you were not alone", she replied. "I wish I were still young enough to help you like old times. . ."

On November 1st, I wrote:

"My advertisement brought forth 8 houses & I have now seen them all — each took a whole day — the distances are so great . . . all noisy or in windless hollows. I shall have to have a car in the end but daren't buy one yet, not knowing what I may have suddenly to pay out. . . My plan is to find a good place for the caravan for the winter & move it now, stock it with coal & then come back to S for a rest. . . The caravan is not cheerless, as you seem to think, but very cosy to return to every night — it is the hopeless hunting that is tiring & dispiriting. . . How are your boxes going & have the sun rays stopped your hair falling out? . . ."

And she replied.

"What an effort it all is. . . Do buy a car — not a second-hand one — they are always such a trouble. I could give you £50 towards it or plank down the £100 when it comes from the Artists Benevolent & live on dribblets afterwards. . . My 'passionate keeness' for painting cigar boxes & junk has cooled off! — such inspired Genius can only work in fits & starts! Also, as the days draw in, I've been taking Susie for *morning* walks. Yesterday, we called at the butcher's on the way back. She knows that the meat I buy is for her & when I reached the door with a big parcel & the man took it out of my arms while I got down the steep step, she

grew most excited & kept leaping up at him — frantically trying
to reach & snatch it away. If she had been a biter she would have
bitten him. She didn't calm down until he gave it back to me... My
hair is better but not cured. If I get as bald as a convict I must
invent something becoming and, at least later, I can wear a
Heavenly Crown!..."

On November 6th I wrote:

"Suspecting that the builder was too sanguine, I travelled miles
& miles to see the County Planning Officer & learnt that as this is a
National Park, no individual, isolated building is allowed only
small buildings with farming obligations. I shall probably have to
settle down in the caravan until a house turns up. The C.P.O. said
that if I put it somewhere high, off the beaten track, they would
turn a blind eye & not order me to move it... This is a terrible
money squandering life — 5 to 10 shillings a day I spend on buses
alone — but I've got my Rebate & am not short, so don't give me
any more but use what comes to buy yourself a new winter
dressing gown..."

And in her next letter:

"I am *not giving* you money — only paying back a little of all that
you have spent on this house..."

On November 8th I wrote:

"I have decided to move to the inaccessible farm. I feel drawn
to those people. It is more important to be with real friends than on
a bus route. They have even offered to lend me their car — but I
wouldn't accept it — I might have an accident & damage it — but
they will drive me into H when they go to do their shopping & for
the rest — I shall walk, hitch-hike & put up with it... I think I shall
end by living in the caravan forever!... You don't realise it but we
have dropped once again to the level of the working class, not the
top layer — but lower. The top ones own motor cars & week-end
cottages & I'm having to compete with them... If I could walk
into an agent & put £5000 down on the table, I'd get the house I
want tomorrow & be working at once. I've not had a real working
home of my own since West Wratting — 22 years ago. I've moved
from one awful house to another & spent months & months & years
& years either with no house at all or tramping about the country
looking for one. If I had had a settled home I would have
accomplished so much more & reviewing my situation now, it all
looks mad — I am mad to go on putting up with it. How valuable
the sheer experience is, I am not sure — how it will end I do not
know. At the moment I am too tired to do any more... I am not
only competing with the working class but forever hobnobbing

with them & dependent on them. I have never before felt quite so declassé. I am received into their lives as one of them & I am grateful, but the friendships are always on the 'nice cuppa tea' level — warm & consoling for the moment but so limited, inadequate & hence tiring in the long run. . . What a state of chaos our lives are in! If Southwold were a friendlier place I should feel like saying to you, 'Stay'. You have a nice little house, so why root yourself up with the awful effort of moving & more house hunting — for you as well. The whole prospect appals me. But S is a most unfriendly & horrid place & I'm sure you would be better here. . ."

On the 12th she replied:

"Today you are moving. . . Don't forget that since leaving West Wratting you have written a Masterpiece, recognized by the finest brains all over the world. You could never have written it there. That was a tame little place. You have suffered so much frustration that you are seething with suppressed Force & Fury. Whatever you write now will be like fireworks. . ."

Or, I would be worn out. The ironic fact was, that when I got my house and wrote again, the 'Force & Fury' were tempered and directed somewhere else and I wrote just to fill the denying days of winter.

On the 15th, on a postcard.

"Move successful — I am now finding my way about my new territory — hitch hiking is the way to get about. I am writing this in Pately P.O. No letter boxes on High Moor!"

And in her last letter before I returned to Southwold for Christmas and a rest, she wrote:

"It will not be an 'awful effort' for me to move. My few sticks of furniture are nothing. I am very keen indeed on coming to Harrogate. I shall go to a cheap hotel & look for a flat. . . The greengrocer woman, for such a gentle little thing — is rabid about S'wold. She hates it & whispered the other day (apropos of nothing) that the whole town ought to be washed into the sea! I was curious to know why — but a customer came in. . ."

11

WE PUT my mother's house onto the market and, after Christmas,
I returned to High North farm. And wrote:

"I arrived with loads of luggage & when I got off the bus at the
bottom of the mountain — instead of the taxi which I had ordered
— there was Mrs Russell! When we reached the farm a marvellous
tea was waiting for me, a fire in the caravan which had been kept
burning for 3 days, all my bedding strewn about airing, water,
coal, milk & eggs & later in the evening — a wonderful supper in
the farmhouse. I am being doted on. . . My instinct served me well
when it drew me here. . ."

Nan befriended me in Hebden — now, in another distant dale, I
was befriended again and I set about my task with renewed energy
and hope. And my mother wrote:

"I did enjoy your letter — & it was so unexpected. I imagined
you battling with the snow, lighting the stove, bringing in water. . .
What a relief & what lovely people. . . Susie has taken up football!
On Saturday, during the usual match, we were walking round the
field & had reached one of the goals when the players came rushing
towards it. Susie went wild with excitement, got through the
wire, pranced onto the field & joined them. She tore down among
them to the other goal but fortunately, came back to me when I
yelled. . ."

I now learnt from the Ministry of Agriculture that the
obligations relating to small holdings had been abolished and I
applied for a permit to build a house on land offered me by the
Russells. At the same time, scouring my new territory, I came
upon a small empty farmhouse, half derelict, high on the moor
above Pateley Bridge. I walked on to the nearest farm and asked if
they would sell it and said I would come again when they had had
time to think.

On a postcard I wrote later:

"We met again today. The man proved very shrewd & difficult
& asked for more time to think. These weird, primitive dalesmen

are maddening to deal with. I offered him £500 — far more than it is worth. They loathe parting with their property & will let it fall to pieces rather than sell. . ."

On January 19th, 1960 after discussing all the difficulties of the Southwold sale, I went on:

"This evening I shall be completely out of fuel. When I was away Mr Russell ordered *coal* — because he thought it would 'make a nice flame for me' — when I particularly asked him to order coalite. Coal would block the flue. I've had to walk miles today to the coal merchant. . . And I grow more & more worried about aircraft. The aerodrome assured me when I went there that no planes would fly this way & the Russells told me there were none. They are incessant. Oh, the stupidity & awfulness of all these people. I am going into Harrogate to call on the Bomanjis just to meet & talk to someone intelligent & of my own kind. . ."

My mother commented:

"The Bomanjis will be a relief from all the Blockheaded peasants. . ."

Sir Chatterji Bomanji came from a wealthy Parsee family and having served the Raj well, was knighted and received into the highest imperial circles, dividing his time between his mansions in Bombay, Sunningdale and Harrogate. When he died, his widow and daughter and adopted son settled permanently in England.

Lady Bomanji was an outstanding figure in the social and charity life of Harrogate, an Anglo-Indian grandee of impressive appearance, enormous energy and enthusiasm and considerable intelligence and when I was stationed there during the war, I pursued her and won her friendship. And to be entertained in that glittering mansion and waited on by exotic servants, was a pleasant change from army life.

When, in course of time, I left for India, it was Lady Bomanji who gave me introductions to her family in Bombay and her niece who helped me through the Customs. Now, not only was she president of half the charities in Harrogate, but she had found a vocation. Attended by Mehroo, her daughter cum lady-in-waiting and her son Phili, the Controller of her Household, she drove about Yorkshire in her Rolls Royce, giving talks to Women's Institutes, Rotary Clubs, societies and guilds and was much in demand. She regaled me with one of these talks, word for word, and I thought it rather good — especially the element of Zororastian teaching.

On the 24th January, I wrote:

"The little farmhouse is off! It is bang on a training route —

they stream over me here & then on. The RAF now calmly send me another map with this route marked on it, saying that it was a misunderstanding — *my stupidity* — when I actually *have* the first map with this route not marked. You just can't trust anyone. I shall have to move the caravan about until I find a safe quiet spot. I feel like emigrating. . ."

"I spent a weird day with the Bomanjis. They invited me to a grand luncheon party — all the aristocracy of Yorkshire there. It was like walking into a world that I haven't glimpsed for years — the conversation brainless & the whole atmosphere artificial. As for Lady B & Mehroo — they are infatuated with themselves, their grandeur & their sweetness — the whole house oozes with conceit, complacency & sentimentality. I suppose I didn't see that side of them before — it was not so blatently displayed or time has filled the pot & now the saccharine runs over. . . After lunch, we were entertained to a film show, in colour. It started with shots of the various Bomanji mansions together with their liveried servants, uniformed chauffeurs & fleet of motor cars, featuring close-ups of Lady B & M (occasionally Phili who shot the film) posing before the camera like film stars! The naievity was unbelievable. I wanted to burst with laughter! Next came scenes showing M performing an Indian dance! all got up in radiant white galumphing about the stage like a great fat cow!! with an excessively glum 'spiritual' look on her face! A cow would have been more graceful — & spiritual! After that, mother & daughter clasping each other lovingly beneath rose arbours, beside swans on a lake, herbaceous borders, beneath arches or posing on marble staircases looking queenly etc etc. Then, with scores of notable guests seated at a banquet — all *chewing*. And lastly, receiving royalty on various occasions, one of which was the garden party during the war, when the P Royal honoured them & in which *I* figure — in uniform — with a fat silly smile, looking not at the camera, of which I appeared to be unaware but at the world. But that sequence shifted quickly & continued with me cut in half! They are such snobs, yet they encourage *me*! with no understanding of what I am & do. But in spite of themselves I believe they are fond of me — & in spite of their silliness I am fond of them. What a family! What an extraordinary mixture of the profound & the ridiculous. . ."

The aircraft changed their route again and I wrote on a postcard:

"I have half bought the little crumbling farmhouse (Laverock Hall it is called — 'lark' Hall — isn't it a lovely name) & the architect is coming up today to see it, when everything should be settled — if they don't change their minds? . . ."

Two days later, on the 10th March, I wrote again.

"They *have* changed their minds! so that's off again — but I'm not sorry — I don't really like it. . . Things went better yesterday when I made another application for a building permit & was told that I stood a good chance as my site was so high & not likely to attract others! . . ."

On the 14th, I wrote again.

"I would like to return to S'wold to help you with the selling but feel I ought to do as much lobbying as I can here before the various Council meetings when my case will be decided. I walked 7 miles last night to go to a meeting at which Lady B was in the Chair — hoping to meet some of the local gentry & make influential friends. This building plan depends so much on these petty local people — so powerful & important on all their little committees. But I met no one. The B's, in a better atmosphere, were much more sensible & they are very very kind — when told what to do. . ."

After the meeting, the Bomanjis drove me to the bottom of my hill — and left me. It was misty in the dale and as I climbed it got thicker and before long was so dense that it was hard to keep on the road.

At the top where the road turned sharply and circled widely round to the farm, I decided to take the short cut that I knew so well. I found the gate and set off across the field to the next one — but I never reached it. I walked and walked, completely lost, fearing that I would be out all night in the freezing fog. Then, still walking in circles, I came to a wall and climbed over it. The next moment, I fell into a ditch and knew that I was back on the road — and I followed it, thankfully.

At the beginning of April. I wrote:

"One has to go very warily with these building bureaucrats. I found I was in the middle of an awful lot of fiddling & petty corruption & getting so tied up that I went to an architect to steer me through & he has put in yet another application. In the meantime, I go on hunting & I'm still hanging on to Laverock Hall. . ."

A woman was now elected mayor of Southwold and on April 3rd my mother wrote, 'you told me to congratulate Fanny Foster & she was so pleased that she invited me to tea'. She liked her and the attraction was mutual and she went on to describe this cultured, sensitive person and her pleasing home. And ended, 'she is sorry we are going'."

On the 8th I replied:

"Your letter made me most uneasy again, made me feel that it might be a great mistake to sell your house, make you homeless again perhaps for months & then settle you down in yet another place — particularly as I am still in such a hopeless situation myself. You have made a friend & would soon make others & S'wold is so villagy, easy & attractive. You always throw up everything — never think of yourself &, whether wise or foolish, rush after me on whatever crazy, perhaps mistaken move I make... My affairs go from bad to worse. The architect has told me that the builder's estimate is far too low & that the County Surveyor has done nothing about my application. It hasn't even reached the Planning Authorities . . . builders, officials, Councillors seem one & all a lot of horrible brutish cads — no gentry anywhere & I begin to hate the place. And the architect agrees & says the graft & corruption everywhere are sickening. At least *he* is outside the stewing racket... I've been in a state of crisis all the week & am seriously thinking of buying a car & starting all over again somewhere else. . . The Russells are sympathetic & allow me to use their telephone now but I still feel trapped in this maddeningly inaccessible place & less & less able to go on walking & hitch-hiking & waiting for buses. . . The utter impossibility of living in this country, strewn with obstacles, is making me desperate as year after year my work goes to pot — & I don't want you to land where I am. . ."

On April 11th she replied:

"Your house hunting is an absolute nightmare. Yes. It is England. As long ago as when I returned from S. Africa, before you were born, I noticed the frustration — the complications of life and, I can't describe it, the spirit — the mean, unhelping spirit in everyone. All suffering from Nerves? And after California, it was just the same — then it may have been the war but you, as a child, noticed it & the school horrified you. In England one has to fight all the time against Lord knows what? an old overcrowded island cut off from the world? . . . I *want* to leave S'wold. I do not *like* S'wold ("villagy, easy & attractive) It is rheumaticky & potty... I don't mind how or where I live when I am flat hunting — I'll go to one of those "Girls Friendly" places — bed & breakfast. . . With the outside repainted this house looks lovely. I do wish it would sell. . ."

On Good Friday, I wrote:

"The architect has received no answer to the very good letter which he wrote to the County Surveyor & so he is now going to

make a *fresh* application. Isn't it awful — the power these petty
officials have — & one can do nothing. . . In the meantime, I have
advertised again & written to agents all over Yorkshire — but not
a thing. For every small house there are 100 applicants & people are
paying up to £700 for derelict cottages & then another £3000 to
restore them. . ."

On the 20th she replied:

"Your Good Friday letter has come — those ignorant,
brainless, callous men. . . I am very disappointed today. Some
people came & seemed so keen & were coming again, but have
decided against it. I was so sure it was sold & you would know
what capital you had & your struggle might be easier. . ."

On the 26th I replied:

"You needn't feel so desperate to sell the house. The sale will
not affect what I spend here — there is no connection. The only
hurry is for you to get re-settled. So don't get fussed & worried but
let things take their course. . ."

That I could still exercise my intellect and commune with my
teacher, in spite of the frustrations of England, emerges in a letter
from Sir C.P., dated April 13th 1960.

"Your most welcome letter was like a breath of fresh air
blowing over the high moors. . . I have accepted the chairmanship
of what is called a 'high power commission' to investigate the
present condition & future development of all 'Religious Endowments in India' (temples, muths, monasteries etc) & to make
proposals for their proper management & the utilisation of their
resources, estimated to be about 800 crores of rupees (600 million
pounds). I shall have to travel from the Himalayas to Cape
Comorin & the work will keep me occupied for a year. . . Yes, we
are constantly communing with each other & very telepathic. . .
What an adventure — waiting in a caravan to build a house nearer
the high Heavens, but you are nothing if not a crusader & one with
a wry sense of humour. It is well that you are having the time to
read & reflect. . . As to vivisection, I am entirely with you as to the
misuse of this practice by all & sundry in the name of science &
India, as you say, is incriminated — the world is very imitative. As
Oscar Wilde put it whimsically, — '*Most* people are *other* people.
Their thoughts are other peoples' opinions; their lives a mimicry
& even their passions a quotation'. India has not yet regained her
essential self. God bless you, my dear, dear friend & comrade."

On April 30th, I wrote again to my mother:

"My affairs are coming to a climax. In 2 days time I shall know
the result of the building application & on the same day I have yet

another meeting with the Laverock farmer, Mr Wardman, when I shall offer him £1000. He has changed his mind 4 times so there is no saying if he will now be finally tempted? . . ."

And on May 5th, on another postcard:

"I am down in Pateley. I have bought Laverock Hall — paid the deposit & clinched it & tomorrow will see a solicitor."

And she replied:

"At last! ever since your first pc came I have been watching for the post. Susie knew that something was up & sat halfway up the stairs every day where she could see the gate & the postman through the fanlight over the door. When the second pc came she gave up her watch & curled up in her corner. The 'little old crumbling farmhouse', as you call it, will be better than building. You will make it lovely — knock it about — plan the garden — plant trees — it will be thrilling. . ."

I returned to Southwold to beautify the house and garden still more and to try to speed up the sale.

It was one of a row of Victorian houses, with mellowed bricks and pleasant rooms, but it was not 'period' and not in a fashionable part. We had made it into a 'gentleman's house' and when the gentry came, they admired it but were put off by the 'Bed & Breakfast' signs and bad-taste curtains in the neighbour's windows. The others admired it, too, but their dream was of a neat semi-detached — and they did not return either. When I left a month later, it was still not sold.

On the 18th June, on a postcard, I wrote:

"I am in Harrogate stirring up the solicitor & architect. The latter is going out tomorrow to determine the boundaries & measure & plan the repairs. I was so elated when I left them that I went off & bought myself a macintosh. . . Mrs R met me with the car when I arrived last night & brought me back to a wonderful welcoming supper & smiling faces. The hills are so grand! . . ."

And she replied:

"Your pc makes me elated too! but I will not go out & buy a macintosh!! I will wait till I get to Harrogate — & then I will let myself go. There are no end of things I mean to buy. Grand Mountain scenery will pass me by. Plate glass windows will draw me like a magnet! . . . Swarms of trippers have begun here — the roads are crowded with cars & the coaches turn out hundreds by the 'Gentlemen & Ladies'! . . ."

On June 22nd I wrote again:

"The boundaries & water sources are settled, the plans are being prepared & I hope the contract will be ready for signing next week. I have set them all to work & now I have nothing more to do — which is good, for haytime has come & I can return a little of the kindness by the giving of my labour. Every day & all day I am out driving one of the tractors — & I enjoy it! It is something new & novel & very satisfying, to roar & rattle round a big field at top speed, cutting, turning & raking. Then, a hired baling machine comes & tears round picking up the lines & pressing them into bales which are tossed out behind it. In about ½ an hour it has cleared the field. Marvellous really. After that, I drive the tractor slowly round, dragging a cart, the men fling the bales onto it & we bring them in for stacking. One feels very clever & powerful manipulating these machines — which is what everyone feels but which, of course, is a complete illusion. Any child can work them... The beans are beginning to climb — will you help them to catch onto the strings... I miss the bathing but love this mountain climate in the summer — hot sunshine, cool breezes & cold nights..."

She replied on the 24th.

"How thrilling your tractor driving sounds! When your life is written what a lot there will be to put into it. What adventures & experiences. What other writer has lived so brilliantly & strenuously... Yes, I will train the beans. I may get someone expert to do a bit to the creeper round the front door. It is a foolish thing — it does not seem able to help itself..."

On July 2nd I received a telegram from the agent informing me that an offer of £2250 had been made for the house and I authorised her to accept it. And on the 4th, my mother wrote:

"The sisters have come again & brought a friend & are in raptures. They love the garden, noticed your seat, the clusters of roses & those lovely blue fluffy things — it really looks exotic now — & I thought, "Why the devil don't they offer more?" When the lawyers & agents take their commissions, you won't get much... Our neighbour was looking her dirtiest this morning — I hope she didn't show herself — & 'Bed & Breakfast' was full in view... until the surveyor has been & not found any dry rot in the roof & everything is signed & sealed, I shall be nervous... Funny little Susie enjoys her powdering — she gets into the positions she thinks I want! she really is a clever little thing — & afterwards it seems to soothe her. I give her pills as well & the rash is getting better..."

The contracts for Laverock were exchanged, I moved the caravan & then returned to Southwold. We packed up the house and I brought them both to Harrogate. Susie came out to the caravan and my mother stayed in comfortable lodgings and within a week, we had found her a flat — inexpensive, convenient for the shops, bright and pleasing, suitable for the creation of yet another home and 'inspiring' her to go on with her boxes.

We both had a home now but not much income. I used most of the capital aggrandizing my hermitage.

12

IN MY LETTERS, I had agonized in my usual way about my work although that long struggle to reach the high hills was not to find, as in the past, the solitude and quiet in which simply to write, but to go beyond art to the Source itself where, not the artifact, but the artist becomes the subject of the endeavour. But I still did not realise this, did not realise that I was no longer art-filled but wholly god-filled as I resumed this journey.

Laverock Hall stood 1000 ft above sea level where the hill folded back, in a similar position to Scar Top. It was a typical north country long-house with the dwelling quarters in the middle and barns and byres extending on each side.

Green sward, which ran into the heather, surrounded it and the land sloped gently upwards to the road where the Wardman's farm stood on the edge of infinity and, with a ¼ of an acre of walled pasture, it was now a little island in the Wardman wilderness.

To enlarge the house and the dark, pokey rooms, I incorporated one of the barns, knocked down walls and ceilings and knocked out windows on the west, the weather side, bringing in the moor and opening up a distant view of Great Whernside, even more spectacular than the view from Scar Top.

The front door, in the centre, then opened into a large hall with a wide, imposing staircase turning up to a gallery, or gantry, out of which led the upper rooms. And the place looked more like a small baronial hall — than a hall of singing larks.

But when I moved the caravan into the shelter of a wall and prepared for the winter, the house was half a ruin, the boundary walls were down and all this was only a vision and a set of plans.

When the workmen arrived, after much waiting, my hard labour began. Mr Wardman had told me that the track down to the house was firm but as soon as the lorries left the road, they churned it up and the autumn rains would have made it impassable.

Three hundred yards of road had to be built and the estimate was £1000. Goaded then by his wife, who felt pity for me and some

168

guilt, he came to the rescue. Together, we dug two parallel trenches and then with the tractor and trailer, scoured the moor for rock which we tipped into them and then filled up with quarry waste. Working against time, section by section, the lorries like impatient monsters creeping up behind us, we finished it and gave them a hard run through just before the weather finally broke.

Soon afterwards, I had my first quarrel with him. He had kept calves in the barn and when he took them out, left over a foot of liquid dung behind, in which they had been standing, and one of his conditions was that he could collect it. When he didn't, urgent requests were made for its removal. When it still remained and the men stood idle, I lost my temper.

It was shearing time and the farmers were gathered from all round, helping. I tore into the middle of them and shouted something silly, "If you don't move that dung today I'll never speak to you again". But it wasn't the words that mattered, but the shaming and humiliation before his friends. In the afternoon it was gone and I learnt that only by bullying could I, as a woman, get my way with this rough race — but not always with impunity.

He knew that Susie ran about last thing and that night he set out with his gun to get her. But his little daughter saw him go and, knowing what he meant to do, ran after him and stopped him. I learnt all this much later.

I had found my hermitage and I waited in the van contentedly beside it, but before I could enter it, I was thrown violently back into the world.

I had always known about vivisection but India had extended my sensibilities and since my return this knowledge had sharpened until suddenly I saw that in the body of my own society an abuse had lodged and grown over the centuries until it lay concealed like a vast, obscene cancer.

The conscious, responsible and deliberate infliction of pain upon laboratory animals was far worse than the unconscious cruelty and callousness that I had seen and condemned upon my travels and until I had made my witness, my inner journey had to wait. From the caravan I now launched my campaign.

There was a branch, completely dormant, of one of the Anti-Vivisection Societies in Harrogate. I roused the members, we formed a committee and went from house to house recruiting more. And we met every week in my mother's flat.

Fortunately it was an open winter. The snow did not prevent me from getting down to the bus and going into Harrogate, nor prevent the lorries from getting up and when the work was finished and the day came when I could move into my house — I did not want to. By then, I had consciously renounced the arts and my own creativity and I knew that I had come away to the high hills, not to live in a baronial hall, but in a nun's cell. I should have stayed in the caravan. But I could not undo what I had done.

The anti-viv campaign gathered momentum. We started a correspondence in the columns of the local press; we wrote articles ourselves which the press were persuaded to print; we called on the Bishop of Ripon and other clergy and when, soon afterwards, he preached a sermon, taking as his text the verses relating to 'man's dominion over the animal kingdom', we got up in the middle of it and marched out in a body; every week we attended Doncaster market, notorious for its vivisection trade, and outbid the dealers for the cats and dogs; we marched and demonstrated outside a local laboratory; we organized jumble sales; we held small meetings regularly and one monster meeting when speakers came from London. The committee of women, with one staunch man who kept some kennels, worked passionately.

When the spring came I worked still harder, digging up the virgin ground to make a garden and rebuilding the wall to keep the sheep out and, afraid to face me with yet another appeal, my mother wrote this letter.

"On Sunday, June 11th, 1961 — Harrogate"

"As a child my one idea was to paint but my mother always frustrated me. Then when I grew up I was keen to marry & have children & when I married I believed my ambition would be gratified — a generous hearted husband & rich enough to pay for servants & give me my freedom. Then, soon after you were born, I was left a widow with very little money . . . & no likelihood of painting the way I wanted to. When, at last, I had a little money . . . *I could not* paint! my talent had left me — completely! Why? What *did* it? overstrain? tired heart? what did it? I was just as keen, in fact more so — but my strength had gone out of me."

"I promise I will forever hold my peace & not criticise when you overstrain your heart & nerves — I know that I drive you into a frenzy of fury when I do. But don't you see my point? You are so gifted & I dread your risking killing your talent, too. I dread your force & power leaving you."

She stopped there, without a signature — just a few dashes. It was her last attempt to save me from myself. It was the last cry of an artist whose talent had been destroyed by the world; of a woman of genius who had sacrificed herself — for me.

All I did in response was to buy an old car which, at least, saved me the climb up and down the mountain. After 2½ years when I resigned from the committee and resumed my journey, no one in Harrogate was unaware of what Gandhi called, "the worst of all humanity's crimes".

I now spent my days in meditation, yoga, reading and rebuilding the dry-stone wall — and the wall soon became my teacher and most powerful guide.

In the silence and solitude of the moor, choosing, discarding and choosing again; often cutting and reshaping, then lifting and fitting the living stones into an irregular but perfect order; soft, yet hard and heavy; grey, yet shot with colour; blind lumps that ring and breathe; impossible to hurry and with no desire to, a few feet raised each day; pinioned and powerful, the wall unites with the mind and holds it in deep meditation and at the same time — heals.

At one end of the long-house there was a small paddock, surrounded by an inner wall which I rebuilt first and then within its shelter, dug and sowed my vegetables. And the plants grew and were full of promise when, suddenly, the rows heaved up and they began to droop and die. The moles had come.

I pressed the soil down and nursed my seedlings back to life — not once, but several times a day. I tried smoking out the runs and sinking wire round the walls. I tried everything except traps and poison. I did not know that I could talk to them.

Then, one morning, when I looked once again upon the havoc of the night, I cried out in despair, "Oh Susie, what shall I do? What shall I do? I shall never have a garden here." I tended the survivors and went into breakfast. But she did not follow and soon afterwards, laid a dead mole at the front door. Then another — and another.

For three weeks she sat every day beside the runs, listening and pouncing, until she had rid me of those charming little creatures and my garden was allowed to grow. And keep me fed all through the year, for the great fat mother potatoes, giving their lives, became empty shrivelled bags while their young, on the ends of their umbilical cords, swelled in their turn. Before the drama of sacrifice and immortality I wept every time I dug them up.

About a quarter of a mile away to the east were my only other neighbours, the Swires, dairy farmers from whom I got my milk and eggs. He was another Wardman and she, another refined intelligent wife. So often, superior women from the towns married these brutish hillmen.

She hated the moor and was often ill but he showed no concern and expected her to slave on without complaining. The house was damp and draughty, the roof leaked and the walls oozed, the paper was peeling and the plaster was dropping off. The only means of heating and cooking was an inefficient open fire with a hook over the flames, broken hobs and a cracked oven in the wall at the side. On wash-days, an ancient stove in the scullery was lit, which smoked when the east wind blew.

The furniture was rough and sparse and the curtains no better than rags. It was a miserable home in which I used to sit, listening to her troubles, learning more about the people of the hills and exhorting her to stand up to her husband. And I pointed out tactfully to him, that the house was in need of some repairs. He had plenty of money — but he wouldn't spend it. And he gave her none.

During the bad winter of 1962/63, we were snowed up for 9 weeks. The helicopters flew out fodder to the distant farms; the telephone lines were down and my house was half buried and I had to dig myself out; the postman struggled up through the drifts, walking on the wall tops, often bringing food parcels sent by my mother for Susie (she didn't know that we found hares and rabbits, half eaten by the hawks, lying frozen every day); the milk was got out on sledges — and I wrote again; wrote because I could not get to my wall and to the god within it. And while all this was going on, Mrs Swires took to her bed in agonizing pain and prayed that she might die.

Spring came and a sudden thaw when the snow cascaded down the hill-side, swamping the houses at the bottom. And the walls reappeared and I was able to go on with my building, able to observe once more every office of my Rule, in my longing to transcend myself — until I was disturbed again.

My mother had been finding the steps to her flat difficult to climb, she disliked her landlady who lived below — and she wanted a place of her own. And she found it. An old stone house, in a desirable position which would convert into two fine flats, she said, one for herself on the ground floor and an upper one which could be let.

I was appalled. But I had a house of my own so how could I deny her? Her need was genuine and the plan so sensible and the house so cheap — £1400. Six months were now squandered upon agents, surveyors, solicitors — and raising a mortgage. She moved into it at last, very happy and I retreated again — and wrote to Sir C.P.

He replied from Annamali University.

Delegation of British women to Auschwitz (1955)

Dinner in honour of
Dr Sir C. P. Ramaswami Aiyar, K.C.S.I., K.C.I.E., D.LITT., LL.D.
Vijayanagaram Bhawan, Banaras (1956)

Party given by the Nepalese delegation at the Writers Conference in Delhi (1956). The author and Carlo Levi seated on the left, and on right, an Egyptian delegate

Asian Writers Conference. Vigyan Bahwan – Delhi. December 1956. The author and Monica Felton in back row. Mulk Raj Anand in foreground.

Mosque and palaces on the Ganges at Banares (1957)

Bathing ghats at Banares (1957)

Pir Vilayat Inayat Khan. Head of the Sufi Order in Europe

A Chinese Monastery (Labrang)

Laverock Hall, Pateley Bridge, Yorkshire

My mother, aged 92, at Laverock Hall

Sir George Trevelyan, Bt.

Angela Pleasance in "The Journey". Round House, London (1976)

"I have accepted the Vice-Chancellorship of this university once again, after having functioned during the last 3 years as Chairman of the Hindu Religious Endowments Commission & various committees, including one to re-organize University education in India. . . I have been constantly on the move & unable therefore to be as closely in touch with you as I have always desired to be & always have been. But if my conduct is inexcusable, yours is even more unpardonable and, in view of your protracted silence, I should by rights have forgotten your existence. Anyway, all's well that ends well & I am glad to learn that you are not only keeping well now but that you are back on your 'mountain top' & you have completed Part I of your book which I hope to read when I am in England. And this brings me to the great news that I shall be in London from the 12th July for the jubilee meeting of the Commonwealth Universities. I shall stay on afterwards & hope it will be possible for you to be in London when I am. . . Owing to the present exchange position I shall not be able to live in the style that I used to do & so, I have reserved accommodation at the National Liberal Club. . ."

I followed my Rule upon the moor until the time came to meet my beloved teacher again. He did not go to the Club because a wealthy Indian friend lent him a convenience flat in the Bayswater Road, consisting of two enormous bedrooms and an even more enormous reception room, all facing the Park, on the ground floor.

I had to occupy a tiny, windowless room wedged in the middle, no better than a box-room, which led out of the kitchen and was intended for a servant. The kitchen itself looked out into a well at the bottom of the building and was airless and dark. He was keeping the other grand bedroom for his grandson, Karthik — training in management in a car firm in Coventry — and for his wife, Uma, and their child.

For five days he attended the Commonwealth sessions. Then, we went to Oxford for a week-end conference, where I was to stay at a hotel, but when we arrived and he found that he had been given a student's room he walked out, insulted, and we drove straight back to London.

He woke me every morning at 5 o'clock to serve him with a glass of boiling water but he didn't want to go to expensive restaurants any more, for which I was thankful. It may have been the exchange rate, or the intriguing situation, but he chose to eat at home and I cooked and did the shopping and all the chores. When Karthik and Uma and the child arrived, I became servant to them all. Uma never lifted a finger.

There must have been good moments but all I remember of that visit is the horrible flat and the bizarre role I played. But he loved it all, the flat and our family oneness — and casting me as their slave. I did not show him the book.

Afterwards, on July 29th 1963, he wrote from Madras.

"It was a wonderful holiday that we spent together in London. We came very near to each other & comprehended each other's outlook intuitively & thoroughly. I felt heartened & refreshed & felt that you too felt quite at home & at peace. God bless you. Au revoir till next year. With loving regards & my heartfelt greetings. . ."

And the next day, from Annamali:

"I have returned to the University which is a true haven of peace & leisured culture. But I *do* miss you badly — more than I anticipated. . ."

A few more quiet months passed before my mother's neighbours told me that twice she had fallen down outside the house and they had had to help her up. She was 90 and I knew that she could no longer live alone. And she knew it, too, and said cheerfully that she would go into a Home. But when we drove round and looked at some, we were both appalled and I asked her then if she would come and live with me on the moor — not together, but in a flat of her own. And she agreed — with her usual enthusiasm. She had to. She had no choice. She moved at once. And we let her flat.

Adjoining the house was the cowshed, divided into stalls, where I kept my coal. I now planned to knock out windows and doors and turn it into an open-space flat with a sitting-room, bedroom, dining room and kitchen in each corner, separated by the old posts and bars, rubbed smoothe and glowing by the cows. Four lovely living pens — with a bathroom built on. And its own front door.

The same builder was too busy to come and I settled on another and soon found myself contending with a gang of crooks and incompetents. I was several weeks getting rid of them and when I fetched my milk I regaled Mrs Swires with the latest stories of their awfulness. And the tales inspired her to versify.

> About a mile from Pateley Bridge
> High on the horizon's ridge,
> Lives a versatile lady at Laverack Hall
> Who can write a play or build a wall,
> Even lay a concrete floor
> Or fix new jambs to an old door.
> Necessity's the Mother of Invention so they say
> She has learned this is true in the hardest way

For the 'workers' don't care if they come or go
Their motto seems to be 'let's all go slow'.
They do a bit of this and a bit of that
Then sit around for a good old chat.
Manana! Manana! the Mexicans cry
As from siesta they open one eye
But up here this lady can't live on that chance
And the workmen have led her a merry dance.
A haughty one arrived last week
And with colossal cheek
Looked down his nose and made it quite plain
That he viewed the job with the utmost disdain
Saying "Anyway it's time now for tea!
Will you mash a cup for Malcolm and me?"

When I was mashing tea for the workmen and pouring out my woes to Mrs Swires, I must have vented them in bad temper on my mother and then gone out early one morning and left her a letter of remorse. And this is her reply:

"Philippa — Susie was on the gallery yapping at your door — when I had let her out I found your clever letter — I realise every word of it. But apart from my being "sweet & soft", I am Balmy — my brain is half gone which is maddening to myself & to anyone who lives with me. By nature I am far from being a gentle nice character. I am critical & I *don't* love my fellow men. . . Your great fault is *generosity* — you have a big generous heart & want to make this cowshed all so nice for me & only devilish men to deal with. . ."

When the new builders came the work progressed, but our relief and pleasure were cut short — when Susie died.

In the afternoon she was racing about the moor and the next morning I found her half paralysed. I drove her into Harrogate to the vet and he diagnosed a stroke. During the five days that she lay, or hobbled about, while the clot moved towards her heart, her misery was written on her face. It was January 1964 and she was 13½ years old.

I buried her in a corner of the garden in which she had sat so faithfully. Soon afterwards, I was woken in the night by her bark, just as she had woken me before her puppies were born. I still grieve for all my dogs — and she I had the longest.

My mother moved into her cowshed flat; her pictures were hung on the rough stone walls and her treasures set out in the lovely pens and she seemed very happy. But as she sat by the window and that marvellous view, she never looked out at it. She had once written, 'grand mountain scenery will pass me by' and when we drove into Harrogate once a week, she jumped out of the car and, literally, ran to the shops, 'to the plate glass windows like magnets', to look for junk that she could paint, to look at things on display, at things everywhere — to look and look and then just potter about the streets looking at people. She was a townswoman and now, she was stranded on the moor.

It was not just groceries that I went in to buy. I was selling again — bits of our remaining silver, porcelain, anything of value, to pay for the latest building orgy.

That summer of 1964, Sir C.P. came to England again. He attended all his usual conferences and then buried himself in the British Library, for at the age of 84 he had begun writing a history of India. "My mind has never been so lucid or my powers so great", he said. My history was not enough — he had to write one, too.

When he had finished his research he said he would like to have a medical check-up and a week of absolute rest before going on to the Soviet Union and I suggested a Nature Cure Clinic. He liked the idea but would only go, he said, if I went with him.

"But I don't need a check-up and a rest" I protested. "I understand my ailments and can deal with them myself". But when he insisted, we both set off for Champneys.

When examined, he was passed as 100% fit. I was pronounced a wreck! Nothing less than a fortnight, they said, would be of any benefit at all and he agreed to pay for another week and leave me there. I fasted while he enjoyed the delectable meals.

At the end of the week, he expected me to accompany him to London and see him off at the airport the next day, but the doctor forbade it. Then, an hour before he left, when we were talking in his room, he said:

"I will keep enough money to get away tomorrow and leave you the rest", and he counted out £150 and laid the notes on the bed. "I shan't need this". I told him how much I did and how grateful I was but when I began picking them up, he stopped me.

"I think I may need more", and he took back £50. I began again but he stopped me again. In the end he left £50 upon the bed.

"That will pay your fees here", he said, returning the rest to his wallet. I thought he had paid them. It was just enough for another week.

While I was away, I arranged for one of the Swires boys to bring my mother milk every day and keep an eye on her and the Russells were glad to drive over and visit her.

I had been thinking of selling some furniture, to raise money, and had talked about the pieces and the prices in an undecided way. When the Russells came, thinking to please me, my mother showed them what we had to sell and they bought the lot and returned with the tractor and trailer the next day. A wardrobe had then to be moved up to the gantry and they did this before they left.

When I returned, I was angry to find the furniture gone, practically given away, and angrier still when she told me what had happened. They had put the stand of the wardrobe upside down and when she opened it, later, it toppled onto her and lodged on the balustrade and she had to crawl out. Had it fallen flat she would have been trapped inside it.

She seemed quite well as she told the tale but the next day I found her lying upon her bed, to all appearances — dead. When the doctor came he diagnosed delayed shock and left some medicine, making it plain that he would not come up the hill again and, plainer still, that he believed she should be dead and that I was wasting my life caring for her.

Standing by her bed not knowing if she was hearing, I assailed him. Afterwards, when I gave her the medicine and it made her worse, I looked upon him as a criminal.

She lay unchanged and after several days I went into Harrogate to look for a homeopath and called at the herbalist shop, believing that the friendly little man would tell me of one. Instead, after learning what had happened, he went behind his screen and after a few minutes, came back and handed me a bottle. I forgot about the homeopath and drove away.

The first dose was effective and the next day she was sitting up and talking. I sent her to a Nature Cure clinic in Norfolk for a combined convalescence and holiday and she wrote from there, describing the place and people in her usual amusing way. When she returned, feeling well and happy — I was sick myself.

Yes. The doctor was a criminal and I was right to be so shocked and angry, for I was the devoted daughter for whom the crime of matricide was detestable in history, detestable in others now and, in me — unthinkable. But as the days and weeks passed, I began to wonder if I was the daughter that I thought I was; if I really liked the mothering that I was still getting; if, in truth, I felt that it had gone on too long and that I wasn't free — and needed to be. I was thinking — the unthinkable.

My mother was not possessive and demanding, her love was

selfless, always a free gift and sactificial, yet I wanted no more gifts and sacrifices, no links of any kind upon this planet, no companions on the journey — for all the Paths to cosmic consciousness were single and aloneness was the traveller's stern condition.

The actual caring I did not consider but when she came out to the moor, she changed it. We had our own compartments yet we rotated in a capsule lapped by solitude and space and the cord tightened, my Rule was disturbed and I kept losing what I had gained.

I had been feeling all this, consciously, with Susie for she was very possessive and held me tightly to my condition, to my humanity, and my love had become painfully ambivalent. When she died I missed her and I wept and felt more lonely — but more free.

I had inherited the heart and mind of Cain and now I was repeatedly committing the same, yet ever changing, crime and when I confessed it to myself and understood that I could not square the circle and that only through the murder of the beings I loved could I escape and reach the Ocean of Awareness, beyond the field and grip of a cruel confirming force — I wept as I ran.

Sir C.P's visit to the Soviet Union was a great success. As an elder statesman and leading educationist, he met all the important people and went to all the important places and he returned to India, thrilled.

On October 14th 1964, he wrote from Annamali:

"The progress made in the matter of intensive training in technology and science & of wide-spread general education, particularly the marvellous development of adult education is phenomenal . . . & the pace fairly took my breath away. Their building programme is also spectacular. . . It is true that Russia is greatly handicapped by not having even a marginal supply of luxury goods; & their shoes & boots are inferior in quality & the menus in their hotels are not as varied or tasty as in the rest of Europe. What, however, matters is the tremendous enthusiasm that pervades the country & especially the student population. They work for 10 & 12 hours a day without intermission in Higher Secondary Schools & Universities. No lecturer or Professor lectures for more than thirty minutes, the rest of the period being devoted to seminars & questions. Their concentration on science is truly marvellous. A person is not allowed to take a Doctorate

before he completes a first rate thesis & three years of hard work
. . . every person aspiring for a Ph.D has to face twelve examiners.
Unless all the 12 agree, a Doctorate is not granted. . . Out of the
35000 students in the Moscow University, about 30,000 are
devoting themselves to scientific & abstruse technological
topics. . ." And pages more of this report.

After her second winter on the moor I noticed a change in my
mother. She had stopped painting boxes and lost her liveliness. Her
face had lengthened and her expression was stoney and I knew that
the moor would kill her — not old age. I went into her from time
to time every day but, in between, she lived in silence with
nowhere to walk and no life around her. And I was under still more
strain.

I had finished another section of my book but not achieved what
I had come for. No sweet manna had fallen from above and no
vibrations, no rich sustenance, was coming up from below and I
felt suspended between heaven and earth — suffering from astral
and terrestrial starvation. After 6 years, I too, had had enough. We
both needed to return, if not to the life of the world — at least to
the fine confusion of it's streets.

I put my baronial hall on the market and dashed to London and
was lucky to find a beautiful ground floor flat in Hampstead, at a
rent that we could afford.

Before we left, Mr Swires had the farmhouse repaired and redecorated and a Rayburn cooker installed — not because of any
words of mine and to please his wife, but because his elder son had
revolted and left the moor and he was afraid that the other boy
would go, too.

And before we left, after a friendly period, I had my last quarrel
with Mr Wardman. After inspecting his sheep, one day, he
decided to go down to the pub before going home and he tied his
dog in a ruined barn on the way. But he didn't go back for it. He
was offered a lift up to his farm and left it there — and there I
discovered it. Never thinking that it could be his, I fed and watered
it for two days and then telephoned the RSPCA. After they had
come and gone, he swept down on me like a moorland storm —
and we never spoke again.

And before we left, I had my last sad night.

I was walking along a lane between pastures owned by the
Swires and over the high wall I could see a cow grazing peacefully
with her calf beside her. When I reached the gate and she could see
me, she rushed in front of it, her forelegs stiff, on the defensive and

her eyes wild with terror. She knew the system and thought I had come to take it. I hurried past, as anguished as she.

Lorries went from farm to farm, on a fixed day every week, when all the calves born during the week, right up to the day before, were collected — most going for slaughter. And the cows moaned for days. That is the system by which we get our milk.

13

FROM the Penine Hills, my Himalayas, down to a London suburb.

The massive Edwardian houses in Wedderburn Road, were converted into flats, occupied by high professional people. We had landed among the gentry once again and my mother slipped back among them and responded to the familiar vibrations of the world.

Her pictures looked so much finer hung on the white plaster walls and her ornaments were so much more suited to the marble mantlepiece in her beautiful room with its high ceiling and ornate cornice, pannelled doors and parquet floor.

Through the wide bay window the sun poured in and she looked outwards now, at flowering shrubs and the Hampstead aesthetes passing by. Not only looked out but walked out to the second-hand shops on Rosslyn Hill and to see the cars and buses — and she talked to the neighbours. Restored in spirit, at the age of 92, she lived and painted again — for she had come home.

As for myself, after those years of solitary struggle without a glimpse of Reality, I had come away dried-up and in despair, needing a teacher at whose feet I could sit again. And, 'when the pupil is ready the guru appears'. Not just one appeared — but many.

Britain, with her traders and her soldiers had conquered and aroused the East and now the movement was in reverse and the East was invading and arousing the West. The gurus had come, bringing with them the fusion I had longed for — and the West was ready. And when I found them now, my desire to hold in my hand the Pearl of Great Price flamed more intensely than before and my belief in the immediate coming of the New Age became a certitude. The power would come down to meet the human spirit leaping up.

In the opening paragraphs of an article entitled 'The Fire that we Passed Through', published in a New Age journal in 1980 when I was nearer to those frenzies years, I described what was happening better than I could do now.

After the war, the spiritual renaissance moved slowly at first like a deep incoming force, quietly waiting, and then suddenly exploded; the heavens opened and hundreds of middle-class women, chiefly middle-aged and elderly, were swept off their feet. Men were in a minority and the young were caught up later. And what an explosion it was!

People threw up their jobs and pension rights, moved to new areas to be near the spiritual centres, stopped reading the newspapers and lurched ecstatically into another world. And I stopped writing.

The gurus arrived from the east and the native teachers rose like divinities among us; esoteric books poured into the shops and libraries, everywhere classes formed and fed the hungry every night and, for those heavenly week-end courses, one had to book a place months in advance; and the long hard trek to the ashrams of India soon followed.

How beautiful it was! Bending to touch the feet of the gurus, sitting in the front row gazing up at the masters on the platforms; devouring all those marvellous books; waiting for the messages from discarnate beings brought to us through the open channels of the mediums; meditating in the lotus posture; doing Yoga in our sky blue leotards — so much sensitivity and oneness and kissing, presaging a new exalted age! It was so good to have been born then, to be one of the fore-runners — one of the Chosen! And what beautiful people they all seemed — the Chosen!

Turned upside down and inside out, aglow with excitement and happiness, what were we all wanting and learning and really doing? . . .

On the one hand, I saw the renaissance as a mental shift which would lead to the practical re-ordering of the world which I had dreamed of but never thought to see in my own time; as an alternative to the ugly, materialistic society which seemed so clamped upon us, and the purely political solutions we were offered; another way out of the staleness and stagnation, an escape way which had miraculously appeared and which, for modern man, feeling betrayed by his god and struggling with absurdity, unloved and unwanted in this world — would be a leap.

On the other, I saw the 'new green life' springing up in England and found that the Ancient Wisdom taught me all and more than I already knew and that I must set off again on the journey which, if I had the strength and determination this time, would bring me trembling to the edges of a veil which I could tear apart and see and know what lay beyond. And, looking and longing for mystical experience, I was pleased to pick the psychic fruits by the wayside which quenched my raging thirst a little. And conscious change was essential — the fascinating probability of self-transformation.

I had my first dramatic change when I was young, overnight, and I had changed so many times since, had so many births and deaths, but now I had to climb and climb until I reached the summit for only then could I really claim to be reborn. And how I longed to do this, to cast away my ego and return wearing the garments of a saint!

Fifteen years later, when I wrote that article, I could laugh a little and laugh when I write this now, but the New Age Movement *was* exciting, so many of the people *were* beautiful, and the teaching was inspired as we stopped at the vibrating power points, saw into the ancient mysteries, saw the advancing waves of the new psychologies and sciences, practised the liberation arts and experienced each other. I will pick some fragments from the jewelled talks and set them down.

Pir Vilayat Khan, Head of the Sufi Order in Europe, opening a congress on Meditation.

"This Congress is a joint venture between Sir George (Trevelyan) my spiritual brother and myself. It seems to be an encounter of two worlds, east and west, as at the time when Parcifal met his half-brother from the east. It was only through this encounter that the Grail was found. Through our unity we can accomplish great things. . . Some would like to move ahead at a very fast rate and form what has been called an overchurch or the one religion but to try to overrule or supercede the ideologies of the different religions is not our objective . . . maybe in another century there will be one religion and some of us can forsee this because it does not seem congruous that men of different faiths should pray, worship and meditate separately. . . I realise the tremendous resistances and difficulties which have their roots deeply embedded in the documents, dogmas and scriptures of the past and if we try to reconcile the irreconcilables in these texts we will find that they hold us in watertight compartments. . . Yet these are all views of the mind and the basic thing is the experience of God . . . the word God has been used far too anthropomorphically in the past and we might speak about a basic intuition that we are part of a total reality, aware of a deeper area of consciousness. . . There are moments when we are carried beyond the frontiers of our ordinary consciousness, when we may suddenly feel the pulse beat of life, feel part of the process of evolution and becoming, and know that the forces of life are driving us towards some great apotheosis at the end of time. . . At this Congress, the different speakers will show us how it is possible to encourage this state of awareness and lucidity in the middle of everyday life and how to use the great laws governing our existence for the achievement of that which God has placed in our safe-keeping at the moment of our birth. . ."

He went on from there and the teachers of east and west followed, each reiterating that meditation is the key that will unlock the door to this awareness; each describing, not meditation itself — which is indescribable — but a different method and a different path; each emphasising its power to heal, to change the life of the individual and to spiritualise society; each stressing the need to experience the dichotomy of the world, warning that if we don't the inner and the outer life may be split; and confirming that the householder and the mystic can, and must, be one. And I knew that if the circle could not be squared, then the opposites must dance together, transcend the split and heal the world.

Sir George spoke last. For his and other talks see appendix 10.

There were 16 speakers. Most lived permanently in Britain and one could follow them about. And there were many more. They were legion for these were the years of the great explosion when the New Age seemed suddenly at hand.

While I rode to the music of the spheres on this spiritual merry-go-round, my mother lived her own peaceful painting life — and we were both happy. I cooked the midday dinner and, in an improvised kitchen in a corner of her room, she got her own breakfast and supper. I engaged a woman to take her for a daily walk and to do little things for her. And we were well off again for the Artists Benevolent Institution had increased her grant.

In November of that year, 1965, Sir C.P. wrote again. He was dashing about India in his usual mercurial way and, at the same time, his 'History of India' was progressing. He was 86 now with his energies and faculties undiminished. And my book was progressing, too, and he 'looked forward eagerly to its completion'.

The winter passed and in March 1966, he wrote again. He had resigned the Vice-Chancellorship of Annamali University, the Presidency of the Indian Universities Board and all his chairmanships — to concentrate upon his book. All this was startling and signified how important it was to him and the urgency which had now overtaken its writing.

"The materials are immense", he wrote, "and I propose to stay continuously in Ooty until, with you, I am able to declare that it is finished — at last! Hearty congratulations on your strenuousness and drive ".

"I met the Prime Minister, Indira Gandhi, in Delhi. India is under terrible strain. Assam (asking for separation). China indulging in an 'encore' attempt evidently. Pakistan openly recoiling from the Tashkent agreement. But she is 'game'. . . I have just sent to the publishers a volume of biographical sketches dealing with over 50 personalities that I have known during 60 years. . ."

A month later, on April 28th, came the high point of the year for my mother — her birthday party.

She liked the idea of a party when I proposed it but fearing that her frequent need to leave the room would be embarrassing, had turned it down. Yet, to be defeated by something so trivial and ridiculous seemed a pity and when I suggested that she sit in her armchair upon a bedpan, she saw the beauty of the plan — and jumped at it!

I bought an old screen and covered it with a lovely rich wallpaper to hide her kitchen, polished up everything, made a cake and invited the neighbours and my friends.

When the day came, dressed up in all her best, confident and dignified, she mounted her throne. One by one, as by a queen, her guests sat beside her and for several hours, sparkling with merriment and charm, she reigned. The real triumph came afterwards when she found that the throne had not been needed!

On June 22nd, Sir C.P. wrote:

"I have just received a pressing invitation to address the Oxford Majliss (Indian Students Union) during the Michaelmas Term. The British Council has also repeated its offer to finance my researches in London (completing my book). Therefore, subject to the difficulties arising out of the devaluation of the rupee, it may be possible for me to spend the greater part of September & the first half of October in England.

"I am giving you early intimation & would ask you to let me know your programme then. It would be delightful if we can spend as much time as possible together. . . Things are getting very confused in India but the Prime Minister is managing the situation very bravely. . . She has developed great statesmanship. . ."

He could not refuse that 'pressing invitation'. I offered him £50 towards his expenses and on July 9th, he wrote again.

"I have received a communication from the British Council

that about £200 still remains to my credit. I spent just over £50 of
their grant last year — so, you can spend *your* £50 on Hilton dinners
for us both.

"In addition to addressing the Oxford students on some aspects
of Indian art & philosophy, I may have some other fixtures. Your
programme of courses sounds awe-striking in their variety &
profundity. I hope that you will spare some time for your admiring
& loving friend. . . England seems to be undergoing a sort of sea
change & I look forward to an entrancing time. . ."

On August 8th he wrote:

"It is good news that you are straining every nerve to finish
your book. My book of biographies will be published in November
by the Asia Publishing House of Bombay. I think you will like it. . .
The Royal Commonwealth Society has elected me an Honorary
Fellow & the Athenaeum an Honorary member. So there are two
more 'dignified' resorts available to us if we get tired of the
Hilton, the Spanish Restaurant et hoc genus omnes. . . I shall have
only 3 or 4 hours of note-taking every day — at the most. The
afternoons & evenings will be yours & I want, during this visit, to
enjoy as much of you as I possibly can. . ."

Again I was going to be subjected to those awful meals which I
would have to swallow to make him happy, to help him live again
the golden years of the Round Table Conferences when he sat at
the tables of the high-born and the high-in-office. By pretending
to enjoy them, have to help him to forget that the great houses
were no longer open, that his hosts were dead and that I was the
only friend that he had left, his last close link with the England that
he loved so, with the Empire that he fought and loved through
every minute of the battle.

On August 20th he wrote again.

"I hasten to felicitate you on the completion of your work & its
delivery to the publishers. . . My publishers are enthusiastic about
my book of biographies & the likely public response. May I also
wish & pray for a real public 'acclaim' for your magnum opus ! . . .
In Oxford they want me to inaugurate the Festival of Indian Art as
well as speak to the students, and I have been invited to Cambridge
as well. You will, of course, accompany me to both. . . We shall
have many days of delightful communion & mutual enjoyment of
worthwhile things (food, theatres, excursions etc). Au revoir then
& with all love & exciting anticipations".

The completion of what he called my 'magnum opus' brought
me neither felicity nor acclaim. Begun as a serious work,
relinquished, picked up again and finished — I was bored with it.

My lovely writing passion had left me altogether and I didn't care, for I did not want to be impeded on the climb. I did not try any more to square the circle, or even bother about balance, for the Mountain was now my single passion. I sent it to a publisher and when it was returned, put it away.

He arrived in the middle of September excited and more forceful than ever. He had had a medical check-up before leaving Madras. We plunged into an orgy of London enjoyments and gourmandizing.

"I want to go to some of the places in England that I've never seen", he announced at once. "I'd like to start with the Isle of Wight. Why shouldn't we go there next week-end?" And I booked hotel rooms.

We set off on the Friday and made the crossing on the hover-craft, then a new invention and for him, an essential experience. The hotel was attractive, the manager most friendly and the beautiful room, facing the sea, with its own balcony, he found in every way satisfactory. We settled down happily and the next day he hired a car and we drove all over the island.

In the evening, after dinner, we sat on the balcony and talked as we had never talked before. That is to say, we talked about ourselves. No high falutin' subjects — just confidences, sweet recollections and intimate assurances and, among the last, some very practical ones. He told me that he had influence with one of the leading London publishers and that he would take my Ms and recommend it himself and, too, in spite of the currency difficulties, he would find a way through his international financial contacts, of making me a regular allowance.

All this astounded me. He had promised to get the epic published in India and done nothing and his concern for my welfare in the past had always been so unreal, his gifts so vacillating and uncertain but now, for the first time, I saw that he *could* feel, that he really wanted to help me — and would.

In the warm September air we sat late on the balcony, the only light coming from the room inside. It was the evening of 'communion' that he had been looking forward to — perhaps the ultimate 'fixture' that had brought him.

The next morning, when I went to his room after breakfast, I found him unwell and still not dressed — suffering from diahorrea. He scorned the idea of a doctor.

"I shall fast", he said. "There is nothing that cannot be cured by fasting. All I want is some tonic water." And I went to the telephone.

"No", he shouted angrily. 'Go down and fetch it." I took no notice, ordered it and then left him to bath and dress.

At lunch-time he came into the dining room and sat at the table moodily, watching me eat and afterwards returned to his room. When I went to him later, a stench hit me when I opened the door. He had soiled the carpet everywhere and now, for a shirt, was wearing his pyjama top. And he wanted to leave.

He was silent on the journey and at the club, I left him at the lift and then told the manager that he was not well.

Early the next morning he telephoned me. "I've been awake all night", was all he said and, "I'll come at once", was all I said.

I still didn't think it serious. It was the first time in his whole life that he'd been ill and I just thought he was shocked and taking it badly. I got through to the manager and told him to send the club doctor up to him at once — and then left in a taxi.

When I reached him he was sitting in an armchair and the doctor had not been. I sat beside him, waiting, and we talked. He was calm and loving but I was anxious now and soon went to the telephone to hurry the doctor. When the door opened, not the doctor, but the head porter came in.

Together then, we carried him back to his bed but he was frightened now and resistant and immediately sprang out of it and rushed back to the chair and we wrapped a blanket round him. A few moments later, he flung his arms up, his head went back and, both clutching him, we heard the death rattle.

When the Indian High Commissioner arrived with members of his staff I recounted what had happened and then left him to be attended by his own. The next day, the press all carried long obituary notices.

Very soon, by every post came letters from his family asking for an account of his death and I replied to each of them, giving every detail. When the demands multiplied and I asked them to pass my letters round, they wrote the more. When, at last, I had satisfied them and I asked them to send me something by which to remember him — I got no reply.

After a simple vegetarian diet and the disciplined life of a yogi, I am sure it was the meat, the rich sophisticated dishes and the childish abandon — the longing for England and his Englishness that killed him, long before he need have died with his work unfinished. The serpent of discord lies between the bodies of the lovers in even the most successful marriage — in the union of east and west, in the fusion of the opposites.

After 16 years my father-teacher-lover had left me and gone on and, after the shock had passed, I let him go. I did not mourn him. It was a strange, wonderful relationship — a karmic engagement which, in this life, had now been fulfilled.

Another year passed and as my path grew steeper but clearer, my mother's fell and became confused. She was 94 now and although she was mentally perfectly sensible she became, not just muddly in her ways, but chaotic and uncontrollable. She still went for walks but stopped walking to the bathroom, using a little basin and bucket — and spilling them. When I got her a commode, she would not use it.

She lost all sense of time and became morbidly nervous. When I went out in the evening, she soon believed it was after midnight and that I had been kidnapped or run over, and telephoned the police. A dreaded Home seemed the only solution.

However, an admirable middle-course appeared when I heard about the Abbeyfield Association which provides the machinery and advice for individual people to set up homes for the elderly themselves and with the help of my highly social neighbour in the flat above, I formed a committee of influential Hampstead women.

I found a suitable house in Highgate, we applied for the 100% mortgage under the scheme and the conversion work began.

A Borough Councillor, a formidable woman, dominated the committee. They were all very keen but not workers like the anti-vivisection people. Our meetings every week were fashionable tea parties at which the Councillor held forth and, inspired by her statesmanship, the rest threw out innumerable ideas, good, bad and ridiculous and went happily away, leaving me to carry them out.

And I did. For a year I slaved. A beautiful Home was opened, with 9 lovely rooms and my mother was given the best; large and sunny, with french doors leading out into the garden. Only when it came to the choosing of the warden did the woman upstairs volunteer to help.

We interviewed several and chose a pleasant, capable-looking single woman with good references — and a mother of her own. And soon they all moved in, the tenants with their furniture — and the warden with her mother.

Calamity portended in the first week when my mother reported that the food was poor and I sampled a meal and agreed. Discovering then, that she was buying all the provisions from a shoddy little shop in Kentish Town (which no doubt offered her the highest discount) I asked her to transfer our custom to a reputable grocer in Highgate. But she didn't.

Then, waiting until she was out one day, I inspected the store cupboard and found the shelves stacked with convenience foods (even potatoes in tins) which she heated up and served, cooking nothing with her own hands — because she couldn't.

I carried the revelation to the committee, believing that they would be as shocked as I was. But they weren't. Perhaps they all bought tins and packets (of superior quality, no doubt), regardless of the additives and spurious, inadequate components, enriching and inflating them with expensive supplements. And the other tenants seemed quite satisfied.

I brought nutritious extras for my mother and said no more. But the war was on. Sensing that I was her enemy, threatening her mother's and her own existence, her adoration for me changed to hatred and she was now determined to get rid of me. She complained about me to the Councillor and when, at the next meeting, the Councillor upheld her and ruled the whole committee, the truth rose to the surface. I was the one man out and always had been — and the warden was one of *them*.

As time went on, I saw that she was lazy and dirty and slopped about the smart house in a dressing gown and bedroom slippers half the morning and, worst of all, cared nothing about the tenants — only her own mother claimed her interest and solicitude and in a way that was quite insane. She wanted her to be helpless and had made her so, turning her into the baby that she had never had herself — petting her, kissing her, hugging her and suppressing her. The poor old thing confided to me once that she had no freedom and no power over herself.

When I reported all this to the committee the Councillor attacked me, vilifying me personally and shouting her disparagement of all that I had ever done. And no one spoke up in my defense. Only a man who was at the meeting, our solicitor, showed some sympathy afterwards.

It was the end. While I was making the arrangements for my mother to come home (I had to get rid of the lodgers who were in her room), the warden still got at me by persecuting her.

She could have been happy. She behaved normally again, made friends and loved her room and the house, but I went wrong at the beginning. I should never have entrusted my labours and her future to that monstrous woman, that Councillor (she was a devil), and to the weak ones who fluttered round her.

Afterwards, I learnt that the good references which the warden had collected, were written by people determined to get rid of her and careless — how! She had gone from place to place with her mother and by the time she reached Highgate, she was a desperate woman.

Victorious and left without any supervision, she made the house her own. One by one the tenants left, others came, left and came and when, at last, the committee admitted their mistake, it took them two years to get her out, by which time the house was so run down and so in debt that they had to sell it. And thus, a good thing ended.

My mother settled back into her room, hating the warden with a characteristic hate, not because of what she herself had suffered but because of my defeat — and the pity of it all. She could not know that worse would come.

When the basin and bucket returned, I was tormented. When the policemen met me on the doorstep, I was vexed. And when I had to cut her nails and brush her hair, I recoiled. I still had feeling but I walled it up — and froze.

"You have become so cold" she said. And I hated what I had become.

One day, she fell down but she did not call out. She was afraid to. When I found her and struggled to get her back into her chair, I hated touching her. Pluckily she got onto her arthritic knees and tried to help me raise her. She was a dead weight. Inside, I was torn by love and pity — outside, I was hard and hateful.

When she was in her chair, at last, she smiled and seemed exhilarated by the struggle. I ran from her exhausted. Soon, I could not read, think, meditate, pursue my journey — and my health began to go. And she watched and understood.

"You can't go on like this", she said. "You must find me a Home."

I obtained lists and went to look at them, settling finally on one in Littlehampton. It was a long way from London but the sea air was good and I had a friend there who would visit her.

I moved her with her furniture, her pictures and her ornaments (she wanted them all) and, in spite of the hideous curtains, carpet and alien atmosphere, made her room into something of a little home. And every week I spent a night with my friend and two days with her, taking her for walks along the sea front in a wheelchair. And I could talk to her again, smile, laugh with her — and touch her.

She took her meals in the dining room but she made no friends and when she began doing peculiar things in her room (she had brought her little basin) — they didn't like it.

One day, I found her in bed. She was not ill but just unhappy and she got up when I came. They didn't like that either and I began looking for another place. Soon afterwards, the matron telephoned and, complaining of something else outrageous, asked me to remove her at once.

I took her then to a bright little house near Farnham and hung the pictures against a violent wallpaper and this time, things seemed more propitious. She took to the matron, a jolly friendly woman, and although she did not unpack her paints, I brought her books to read — and she conformed.

I kept the flat on in case she had to come home again but when the Artists' Benevolent money went to pay the nursing home fees, I could not pay the rent and so I let it to some Americans for three months and lived rough myself in an empty room in Kilburn. When she seemed happily settled I gave it up and moved into two unfurnished rooms at the top of a house in Tufnell Park, with my landlady at the bottom, a working class family in the middle and a shared lavatory and bath two floors down. It was a slum district and a slummy house but I liked it, liked the people in it and was glad to be out of that mansion in that wealthy quarter. It was cheap — and I was free.

Yes. Free to attend to my soul and run after the gurus again. At the end of her days I had turned my mother out among strangers because I could not bear the burden for a few more years. Perhaps, just because she had always put me first, herself last, it was bound to end like this. My ego, created large — then irreparably encouraged.

The journey of the western soul can be an inner or an outer experience. I longed to climb at once and had tried and tried, but before I could hope to reach the Light I had to go down into the darkness of the world again and encounter the all-too-solid monsters and demons waiting for me there. Highgate was the prelude to a new descent.

14

ANNA MORDUCH was head of the Sufi Order in England and I regularly attended the meetings in her Wimbledon cottage. She was a scholar, author and a 'shepherd' along the road.

We climbed a ladder to the loft where she had created a tiny chapel dedicated to all the religions and where she led us in meditation before giving her talk in her sitting room downstairs. Here are fragments of one to which she gave the title, "The Golden Thread of Gnosis".

> If therefore ye are intent on wisdom
> a lamp will not be wanting and a shepherd
> will not fail, and the fountain will not dry up. Anon.

> There is a record of gnosis, of deeper knowledge, which connects all teachings through the ages like a golden thread. It is known by different names in various schools. Some call it the homeward path, some the royal road, others the quest of the Grail. The methods vary, but the aim is the same. In ancient times these truths were confined to the Mystery Schools in the inner temples and death was the punishment for those who betrayed them. In our time . . . they are being shouted from the rooftops wherever we go. However, that Ariadne thread can be followed into our own period of changing values and easy words and it might be a good thing to probe into the problem of this hidden thread and the coherence of the ancient wisdom teachings. . .

Not only did these truths have to be preserved in all their purity but they were dangerous to follow without long training. She went on to describe the process of initiation into the temple mysteries of Egypt and Greece when the veil was removed and the candidate became an epopte; one who knew that man was indeed the image of God, that the whole cosmos was reflected in him, according to the formula, 'as above so below'. Then, after leading us through the Kabbalah and the suppression of the ancient wisdom by the Inquisition in the 13th century, she went on:

This teaching appeared again in the Grail romances, the stone of God . . . in the adventures from castle to castle . . . in inner plane experiences showing the way from animal man to human and then to man of Light, symbolised by the life and death of the Christ. . .

And on:

There is a little lotus flower in a little space wherein are lodged both heaven and earth, sun and moon, lightening and stars. It is the Self free from evil, ageless, deathless, hungerless, thirstless, real of desire, real of purpose. . .

And

We have called this golden thread, the thread of Ariadne, which links us with the king's daughter who helped Theseus to find his way out of the labyrinth at Knossos. . . This is the point at which we find ourselves historically and personally. If we want to find our way out of the labyrinth we must be guided by the thread of love and wisdom. The symbol for this reversal is the Shepherd's Crook. See Appendix 11.

She was another great teacher. I stayed the night with her once and the next day, after walking on the Common, we sat in the Calerie Garden and I talked about my work and life and as she listened, she took my hand and moved close to me. I loved her but I could not stay with her again.

Early in 1969 a new teacher appeared at the College of Psychic Studies in South Kensington, John Ross, and a course of six weekly lectures was announced.

He was about 40, short, good looking, with black hair and dark penetrating eyes and a still, controlled manner, emanating qualities both benevolent and frightening. With a clear arresting voice, he expounded the science of Yoga, not just with the cool intellectualism of all the western teachers, or the detachment of the gurus, but with a direct and burning power which was novel and exciting.

He did not want us to take notes or read books. "My teaching", he said, "cannot be found in books". And I obeyed. One should absorb such teaching. . . At the end of 6 weeks he had made such a mark that he was asked to extend the course and we all met again after Easter.

He had established himself and was even more confident and compelling — and I was even keener. When he led us into the monasteries of India and Zen, into the holy places of the Sufis and the Mystery Schools of Egypt and revealed the truths passed from one initiate to another — I disobeyed and wrote some of them down.

Before long, out of the large number attending, about twelve drew unconsciously together to form the 'inner group' which stayed behind and went with him to a café, the Hayloft, where he went on talking — all wanting to be near him, listening avidly, gazing and adoring, mesmerized. Mostly women.

I was one of them and Anna was another. I was drawn to him like the rest yet I was always on my guard, nursing a faint reserve. Occasionally, I contrived to walk with him to the station and travel with him in the train. Sometimes he was kind and sometimes cruel — or both together — and it was on one of these journeys that he told me sharply to stop writing. I had already done this but now I understood how imperative it was to abjure the thing I loved, believed I was born to do and for which I had given my whole life. Only by the 'naughting' of my talent could I be free to go higher.

Here is the first fragment from my illicit notebook. I have had to sort them out and make them coherent for he jumped and ran about as he led us over bridges into heaven and through rifts and caverns to the gates of hell, stopping at every stage and station in between — at one verity after another.

Maya. It is our way of viewing the world which makes it an illusion — false, uncontrolled seeing, false concepts which have no bearing on the real world. We are trained & attuned to only one wave length & blind to all the others. We must look afresh at everything & learn to see things as they really are, savour every minute of life — that is real living, all else illusion — Maya.

It is mind that creates reality, that controls intellect & brain & body. But it hops about like a grasshopper. We have to master it & look down at the body, at God & out at people & things without emotion & attachment. Uncontrolled mind makes you a hungry ghost — and a desire-body.

Never think with the brain. (He gave a loud shout). You heard that not in the brain but in the solar plexus. There are large areas of the body that remain dead all through life & which feel & understand. The feeling in your foot is as important as the feeling in your head or heart. Primitive people do not worry but exist as 'the lilies in the field'. Plants & trees have mind & emotions but do not think. Mind is in the most primitive cell. The stigmata results from the force of the mind dwelling upon a certain feature. Mind, not brain, is the centre of mentation, controlling all the other centres — including sleep. The Egyptians said that man is a cosmos — so must he function as a cosmos. When you realise this & obtain control over the mind — you will experience Satori. While the mind rushes about like mice on a treadmill it gets you nowhere. " Be still and know that I am God ".

In the evolutionary struggle the eyes developed. Sight allows you to see the shapes of objects. Form is important to Western man. The French Impressionists showed us the quality of light. When you throw the eyes at something, focus like the rifle, this is the process of mentation — but when you look with sightless eyes, eyes out of focus, inside eyes, eyes that are not mentation; when you see the world with the eyes of a child — you will attain Satori.

And again.

Fools of God — the troubadors, motley etc came into Europe with the Sufi 'fools of god'. Fools are children — who see through things — get through logicality into the heart of things — into the mind of God — which is akin to madness. Part of the mystical process is to recover the pre-puberty feelings before these changed & became less powerful.

Man looks everywhere for God except in himself. The education system creates fallacious ideas — I and It — not wholeness but separation. Mentation, intellectuality, is not concerned with the inward journey. In Egypt that was the whole concern of religion. Christianity & Judaism destroyed the illogical, beyond-time teaching of Jesus, formalising it. Metaphysics, theology, intellectual concepts lead only into cul-d-sacs. The head is the worst enemy, the Sufi masters say, and much learning is a weariness. The Eastern schools teach by experience — verifiable & practical — no logic, only cause & effect. Wake up! Stop dreaming! clean out the Augean stables of the mind — education & conditioning. Obtain control over evolution & gain the Cave of Treasures.

"Never think with the brain" but with every part of the mind. I did that in India and loved it until I came to feel unbalanced but when I returned to England and the intellect displaced the intuitive mind — I was unbalanced again. Hearing it taught now, in this cogent way, I longed to get it back.

On May 22nd, the group entered the House of Sorrows — and his arrogance increased.

Better it is to go to the House of Sorrows than to the House of Rejoicing — for there is more to be learnt in it.

Mystical experience is very real, a matter of feeling, pain &

suffering — not a cloudy thing. The development of group work is all-important. Teachers are only catalysts. The group should bind together strong in love and service. You can never serve God until you love each other — 'lay down your life'. Christianity has taught us this. Some causes are brought into effect slowly & Buddhism & Christianity are only just beginning to make an impact. Teaching techniques stimulate intuition but the teacher only turns the key — the pupil pushes open the door. The teacher must be someone who has undertaken the inner journey & knows the way. *I* know the way.

He then taught us the exercises.

1.   *Objective concentration.* Instead of letting the mind flow out — concentrate all vital forces within yourself. Observe yourself — every action all the time.
2.   *Ear wagging* — to get control at the back of the neck — to make the mind conscious of an area you are not normally conscious of. And a preliminary to control by the mind of the anal area.
3.   *Frog exercise.* Lie in bed & go to sleep on your back with knees bent & legs wide apart. To energise vital centres at base of the spine. Faculties there have to be roused when dealing with real meditation. Loosening of the sacral area. The thinking mind must begin to be concerned with areas usually mechanical & unconscious. The coccyx (tail) must be related to a sensing mechanism in the mid brain.
4.   *Deep breathing.* 3 or 4 weeks after opening of the pelvic area — the U-pu-wet. Easy rythym — in through the nose then out in blowing action — say U-pu-wet between each breath as many times as possible.
     Also — focussing upon the moving finger.
     Anubis, the Opener of the Ways — also known as U-pu-wet. The last U-pu-wet is a slight strain — the sound goes through & out of the anus. Object to strengthen the muscles & affect the anus. Twitch tail muscles & wag buttocks in same way as ears. Twitch thighs — eventually you will gain control & develop tactile sense in the tail — gain nerve sensation in controlled empathy — train the mind to take part in a muscular exercise. Greater knowledge of our being — awareness of a new force — result — the personality will change. Dreams, reveries, interior experiences & phenomena will enter the mind during meditation.
     Like the lotus with its roots in the mud, we must accept & gain knowledge of, & talk about, the lower regions of the body. These techniques are slow & gentle with small affects at first. But this is only a beginning & none of it can be found in books.

He did not tell us what these exercises were and we did not dare to ask for now, with bursts of anger, he suppressed all questions. I suspected that they were Kundalini Yoga and I soon stopped doing them.

> By spiritual training you can build a bridge to God. In the west it is thought that will is the driving force — in the east, it is imagination. Freud & the psycho-analysts & their theories have damaged the west. Primal energy is the force that drives things — the blind force that is in each of us & which training teaches us to control. Force & form are the magnetic basis of the world. . ."

Deeper and deeper he went, showing us the blinded initiate in velvety darkness, the Great Lord of Midnight, the green face of the Risen One, the evil of Kali, the darkness of the Underworld and the blackness of the Void, the black negative aspects of white, both divine — Earth as divine as Heaven.

> The pyramids were built to show that Egyptian civilisation was in tune with the Cosmos. Today, our civilisation is crying out for this — but the only temple in which man can square the circle is within his own body. . .
>
> I gave you some exercises. Are you doing them? I can tell from your faces. If you do them exactly as I've taught you, the jackal-headed god and Opener-of-the-Ways, will give you control over your body & the experiences for which you thirst.

And soon the faces changed. People came looking strained, some shrank away and others made scenes, cast themselves upon him in anger, or adoration, or despair; some confided their experiences, some gave him cheques, and when he set us tests and trials and chose a woman for himself, hysteria raged and the group became a band of bewildered stragglers. Yet still I stayed to listen — and to watch.

> I am the Fool of God! God's madman! walking among people who call themselves sane — but what I teach you is your destiny. Mystical experience and super-normal powers are built into the blue-print of evolution and only waiting for men to reach up & claim them. The Mysteries of today will be the open knowledge of tomorrow.
>
> Wake up! you eat too much & sleep too much & your houses are too comfortable — you are digging your own graves with your teeth — you must learn to fill yourselves with the food of heaven — with love. . . .

At the end of June I attended a week-end course in Surrey and when I arrived I found that one of the Vice-Presidents of the college in South Kensington was also there.

Bill Blewett was an old man of great wisdom and sweetness — and he was a spiritual healer. I decided that this was my chance to express my anxiety about all that was going on in his college.

As we walked in the park between lectures, he listened with astonishment and disquiet. He told me, at once, that it was Kundalini Yoga that Ross was teaching which, even for the group was unwise and for the crowd dropping in haphazardly, positively dangerous.

Soon afterwards, in the Hayloft, Ross talked about the group and in a letter sent later to the President, I described what happened.

> "... about welding us into a close all-loving group, as near to each other as brother & sister, mother & father, helping each other, ministering to each other, responsible for each other. And at the end when I was leaving and he took my hand and looked into my eyes, all my doubts and fears and dislike vanished and love rushed up. I loved him, loved everyone in the group, everyone in the train and in the streets as I walked home — I loved the world. "This is it" I felt. "He is my Master". And I was transported with joy.
>
> This lasted three days. Then just as suddenly, it all went into reverse. A violent distrust and dislike of him overcame me. When I sat before him in the class I was conscious only of the evil in him. The harsh voice, the arrogant gestures, the intolerant expression, the sarcastic remarks, the uncontrolled anger and aggression. . ."

It was like that experience of evil, of the dark underside of the world and of man, in the station in Berlin, the same sudden seeing — and escape.

Not long after that, he spent a whole session, 2 hours, repeating the exercises. He showed us pictures of rows of men in the frog position and he lay on the floor demonstrating it. And a new one. Standing with his back to us, he lifted up his coat, placed his hands on his buttocks and showed us how to exercise the muscles round the anus. It was then that I left, before the term ended. I hated, not only the obscenities and dangers of the teaching but — the 'vehicle'. I still could not learn to accept the devil in the angel. But before I was free of the affair there were other dark encounters.

My mother had settled down in Farnham. She grumbled about the nurses and little irritating things and I sympathised, hating to think that she should have to suffer the pains and humiliation of exile. But, on the whole, she was content.

She had never been religious. She had always laughed at the Church, nor had she been introspective and she said that she did not like her fellow men. But even if she didn't, she had always been interested in the ones she met and gone out of her way to help the ones who needed help. And she believed in an after-life. Now, we not only talked about the past, about her early life and about the journeys that we had taken together but I began passing on to her some of the teaching that I was now receiving and I told her about the new journey, I was on.

As she listened, week by week, her eyes gradually opened until she saw the Way and rose and joined me and with the break in our life's relationship mended, we travelled together once again — until she soared ahead of me. I had redeemed my sin of coldness but my other sin, turning her out among strangers, I could never put right and now, as she lay among them, the angel of mercy became the dark deceiver.

The matron, her friend, told me that she needed a larger office and as my mother's room, by the front door, was very suitable she wanted to move her to another, just as nice. The news shocked me for she was so settled and I begged her to wait awhile — it might not be for long. And she said she would.

Several weeks passed. Then, when I arrived one day, I was surprised not to see her watching for me through her window and waving when I came. I thought she must be ill but when the door opened and a nurse led me down a corridor to the back of the house, I found her sitting in a long narrow room, her furniture ill-arranged and her pictures piled in a corner.

They had put her into the bath one morning and left her while they moved her things and then led her out to view the fait accomplis. My anger and my anguish and the matron's excuses could not undo the devilish act.

I found another Home in the same district, with a pleasant room leading out into the garden and a matron as characterless as the other was powerful and once more I hung the pictures — and waited to see if she would settle.

And while I waited I read a newly published book, "Experiment in Depth", by P. W. Martin, a disciple and friend of C. G. Jung, and it so impressed and helped me that I wrote to thank him for it. To my surprise and delight he invited me to come and see him.

I arrived at Oxted after lunch on a hot summer's day and a woman, one of his disciples, met me and drove me to the large

country house standing in the middle of a beautiful park — the
Centre in which he lived and taught.

With another woman disciple standing beside him, he greeted
me at the door. He was a tall handsome man. We all walked out
into the garden and crossed the lawn to where four chairs had been
placed in the shade of a tree. I now take up the notes which I made
afterwards.

> Visit to P. W. Martin at Tallboys on July 21st 1969.
> Three of the chairs were close together, the 4th, to which I was
> directed, was by itself, facing them — like a court of judgment.
> Mrs M had been to the British Museum and looked up my play,
> 'The Continent'. She must have made notes for they all seemed to
> know what it was about — a Morality play. And they had all read
> the epic (the shortened version which I had sent him). They called
> it a great fantasy worked out over 16 years — a work of fiction,
> they said, not history — the Megalithic Age ending in the Queen —
> a kind of Saviour symbol.
>
> P.W.M. Edward was a simp. The play will never be played or
> known but it was useful in your development.
>
> Talked about John Ross & the Maharishi's School of Meditation
> — then more questions.
>
> P.W.M. Have you ever been told where you are centred?
> Me.   No.
> P.W.M. I have been watching you. You are throat centred — but
> it never moves up to the head or down to the heart. Static.
> Very strange. The only other person I have known like
> this was a Korean girl — & she was bone-headed. But you
> seem to be quite intelligent.
>
> (To be throat centred is to be a communicator — which I am)
> P.W.M. Do you strike out at people? (Animus or Shadow).
> Me.   I don't think so.
> P.W.M. No. Perhaps you don't. I've been watching for it.
> (Thinking about this — I think I do — but not at once —
> afterwards by writing — couldn't bear any more of the solemnity
> & judging — reacted unconsciously by talking — telling stories &
> acting them — told them about the swami in Delhi — disciples
> enjoyed them & laughed at the amusing ones — but after every
> tale, he called me a crackpot.)
> (Went into tea & met Mrs M, a sweet little woman but completely
> crushed.)
> P.W.M. Tea's late because you've talked so much — entertained
> us so much.
> (Sitting round the tea table they began discussing me.)
> P.W.M. What can we do with her? She would make a good group
> leader — but she has no content.

Disciple.(timidly) Yes. She's very compelling.

P.W.M. She's a crackpot.

Disciple.(to me) Have you ever taught?

P.W.M. She's a crackpot.

Disciple.(bravely) You would make a good teacher.

P.W.M. (ferociously) You would be no good in a group. You would break up any group you joined. You would prima donna it. (To his wife) What do you think of her?

Mrs M. (very timidly — in a whisper) I think she's nice.

Me. Thank you — after all these insults I can come to you for comfort.

P.W.M. You're just a crackpot — seeking all over the place but always on the surface — never going deep.

Disciple. (more bravely still) But she has good ideas.

P.W.M. Yes — but no content. (Then, to me) You don't go to church. You don't pray.

Me. I do pray.

P.W.M. I was just dropping a brick for you to pick up — the first time you've done it. How do you pray? Who do you pray to?

Me. I don't petition God.

P.W.M. Then what do you do?

Me. I pray to be lifted up.

P.W.M. To be lifted up? that's alright. But you don't dream.

Disciple. She *does* dream.

P.W.M. She's just a crackpot. You're trying to write for the theatre.

Me. A new kind of theatre is needed.

Disciple. Religious drama?

Me. Yes — something like that.

P.W.M. You're not a spiritual person. You're not capable of spiritual advancement. You're just a prima donna.

Disciple. During the war — were you in danger? did you feel fear?

Me. Physical danger did not make me afraid. The only time I have felt fear was in a psychic experience. (Told story of the Nazis in the station in Berlin)

P.W.M. You're just a crackpot.

Disciple. Well, at least she has courage.

Other disciple. And she has humour. She can laugh at herself.

P.W.M. Well, you *are* in a hopeless state, aren't you? (looking at his watch) I don't think there is anything more to be discussed so you had better catch the 6.30 train. Christine, take her to the station.

(A few minutes later — when I was in the car)
Au revoir.

Disciple. Thank you for entertaining us.

(Mrs M smiled & waved.)

(Next morning — woke feeling as if I had been run over — aching all over & dead tired — when I got out of bed saw that I was covered with bruises — down to the waist — wore off & faded by lunch-time.)

He had punched me with words that came from his mind and their power had marked my flesh — stigmata. I did not strike back then nor when the Highgate Councillor attacked me, but just stood before them, too amazed for anger. Now, long after the marks have gone and the man is dead, I am striking back.

It may be that when he received my fan letter, he perceived another pliant woman worshipper, another likely disciple, but when he met me, knew at once that he had made a mistake. And he was disappointed and angry with himself, with his intuition in which, as an occultist, he took such pride and which had let him down. That may explain the state of his mind. It does not explain how a man can write a book about the spiritual life and put down his pen and pick up a club. Another faulty vehicle!

My mother did not settle. She was pleased with everything at first but after a few weeks began hating, shouting, misusing her bed and spilling the basin and when the matron, not unkind but weak and silly, complained about her tantrums and pointed to the carpet, I defended everything and, in my turn, accused. In the valley of loneliness and unhappiness I would not have her treated like a naughty child — and judged. Until I could remove her, a reign of violence hung over her days and nights.

In the next place, and the next, the pattern was repeated; first liking and being liked followed by a storm of awkwardness — rejection and coercion. I had no home to bring her back to and each move made her worse. The teaching which had begun to lift and bring her some measure of acceptance was now completely lost and her life seemed to be going down in chaos.

The very mechanics of the moves became a nightmare. The quantity and the packing up. Each time I left something in the van to be transported later to my already overcrowded rooms. And she did not miss it.

This went on until the end of that awful year, 1969, when she reached High Barnet and a little Irish matron and where, at last, she settled and our talks began again. But not for long. When I arrived at the door, one day, the matron herself opened it.

"She's got to leave! They've all got to leave!" she cried wildly. "They never told me and I've only just heard. They've been given a week to get out! A week!"

Over her head, negotiations had been going on for the sale of the house to a group of doctors planning to convert it into an abortion clinic.

As I was the first to know, I was the first to run round Barnet, ahead of all the other desperate relatives, and find the only nursing home vacancy — a shared room. She didn't like it but the crisis situation amused and distracted her and when a single one came empty, she settled again — and this time, for good.

15

WHEN Bill Blewett told the President of the College what John Ross was teaching he showed no concern and the rest of my information he dismissed as malicious.

However, if he was not concerned, Bill and I were. I still went to the college every week and when the class ended and the crowd streamed out of the room, I waylaid members of the group to gather news. Some would not speak to me, others couldn't. Anna, whose attentions I had been avoiding for months, was pleased to.

Ross had been to Wimbledon and stayed for seven hours, talking all the time. She, who was such a talker herself, could not get a word in. I wrote afterwards:

> One of the topics was the concentration camps. He shook all over & then broke down & wept. Then, pulling himself together, apologised.
>
> "Do not apologise" she said. "I am honoured, for you have shown me a depth of compassion & a greatness that I would not otherwise have known about."
>
> When they talked about my leaving his class he became very aggressive. "I don't care who leaves my class. I don't care if *you* do." Then added, "She may come back".
>
> "But he *should* care". I interposed, "especially one such as you, whom he loves so dearly."
>
> "Yes. He should" Anna replied (a little surprised).
>
> He told her that she must leave Pir Vilayat. And he followed up the visit with a long, loving & beautiful letter.

Then, during the holidays, when I was searching in the college library for books on Kundalini, I ran into Kitty and we went on to the Hayloft.

> K. When I asked you in the library why you left J.R's classes, I was testing you. I didn't mean to speak to you. But I changed my mind. It is a relief to be able to talk to someone. I can only do so now because I am free.

P. When & how did you get free?

K. It began with an experience in the frog position. It was like a sexual experience only far far more wonderful & it lasted for 3 days. Then it was followed by a vision of a book. The loose pages were lifted upwards (not turned from side to side) & they contained his teaching. I saw where it came from &, for the first time, understood it. And I was free.

P. And now you can see him as he really is?

K. Yes.

P. From the beginning I had doubts about him but I was hypnotised, too. For weeks I tried to suppress my dislike & fear & then, do you remember that night here when he talked of welding us into a close, all-loving group? . . .

In the words set down in a letter on an earlier page, I recalled how that incident had finally freed me.

K. When you experienced that rush of love — everyone did. But, as with you, it didn't last. The group has fallen apart and is all at sixes and sevens.

P. Everything must have boiled up since I left.

K. Yes. It has. And that week-end!

P. At Rachel's house. Tell me about that. He said that he would carry us all 'up'.

K. It was awful. We were not carried 'up'. We all returned desperately depressed & feeling hopelessly inadequate spiritually. We recited mantras on the lawn in the early morning. It was while I was walking with him in the grounds that he said to me, "I can hurt you". "Oh no you can't", I replied. He didn't — and he can't. Even when I was hypnotised I could stand up to him. There were things going on that week-end that I can't speak of. Rachel's parents were away & she had got rid of the servants. There was no one to see.

P. Sometimes I feel that he was acting — unconsciously perhaps but putting on a performance. Did you ever feel that?

K. He told me that he had once wanted to be an actor. "An actor!" I replied, laughing at him, "You'd be a ham actor." He brought photographs. One was of himself during the war in the uniform of a colonel in the air force. "What Air Force?" Many were of villas, mansions & penthouses.

P. He told us, one night, that several millionairesses had wanted to marry him, implying that he was above money & women. He is always saying that he is a poor man. He is proud of it.

K. "Are you really poor — or only relatively poor?" I asked him once. "I am really poor. I am on my beam ends", he replied. "I could get you a good job as principal of the Spiritualist Society in Belgrave Square at a very good salary. I have influence there ". They turned him down. It was looking for a job that brought him to the college. They advertised for an assistant principal. When they turned him down, too, he was furious. But that is how he got in as a lecturer.

P. Did they know anything about him when they took him on?

K. No. Nobody knows where he comes from, what his real name is & how he has spent his life. We think he was born in South Africa. He told us that he was a professional medium at 9 years old. But one can't really believe anything he says. Yet his lies are not really lies. He is living in another way. He is like a man from another planet.

P. Do you know why his hands and head shake so, at the slightest upset? Like a man with a palsy?

K. I asked him that. He first told me that it was caused by the cruel beatings he received as a child. Another time, that it was intense concentration. Another, a dislocated bone in his neck.

You know that I had an accident & I have a bad back & am always in pain? Well, I asked him for a healing. He said he would have to have me stripped & in the frog position. " Why do you look shocked " he asked. " Well, the idea does take a bit of getting used to ". But I agreed.

He is married, you know. He says he is going to divorce his wife & marry Rachel. She was a beautiful woman with luminous eyes before all this began. Now she has changed. She is coarsened. "

Rachel was a wealthy woman, in her thirties, refined & attractive yet immature & spinsterish. She adored him from the start & now felt she had been chosen and possessed by a god.

P. As you describe all the private meetings, the intimate relationships & all the emotions being stirred up, it all sounds absolutely turgid.

K. Yes. Turgid. That is the word.

P. Not spiritual teaching, true guidance along the Path. Surely it can't go on?

K. No. It will explode & he will return to Africa.

P. How can you be so sure?

K. I have been told.

P. Will you go on until then?

K. Yes. I must go through with it. My only fear is that I shall be hypnotised again.

(And the next day she was. And a month later she was 'hurt'.)

She asked me not to repeat anything that she had said and to keep our meeting secret and the next morning, when I spoke to Bill on the telephone, I did not mention it.

Two days later, however, she came up to me in the library and before several people, shouted angrily, "I swallow everything I said to you in the Hayloft the other night". After that, since there was no more need for secrecy, I told Bill and he asked to see my notes.

When he had read them he pressed me to let him show them to the President, "the importance of the College being saved from exposure (re, the naked healing suggestion) which could be disastrous", he wrote. And, in the light of this new danger, I again agreed.

When the new term started I walked away from the college one night with Elizabeth, another member of the group, in an agitated state, and we sat on a seat outside one of the museums while she recounted all her frightening experiences. When I told her that Bill Blewett could help her, she agreed to see him. After that, I became the agent for his rescue operations and every week I pulled our someone for him to exorcise and heal.

When he went away for a short time, he asked me to look after her as her condition still made him anxious and my way of doing this was to write her what I thought would be an amusing and invigorating letter.

The week-end conference at Haywards Heath at which Ross spoke on Sunday morning, was so illuminating & interesting that my involvement & distasteful actions seem more than ever justified...
He arrived (with Rachel) about 10 minutes before his lecture having travelled down from London by an early train, slipped into the hall looking like a frightened Mephistopheles and dived into a seat by the door. His face was white & strained & he shook the whole time. When he was called to the platform — in a slow, sonorous, dramatic tone he delivered a string of beautiful platitudes, constantly looking at his watch. He spun it out for an hour. All the dear old things adored him & some saw white auras round him, but the more astute were uneasy & one woman called him a 'red devil'.

Throughout the week-end, Anna seemed wretched... She told me that Ross had told you at the very beginning that you should not join his classes. Is this true? I think they are trying to smear all those who have dropped out or seem uncertain. Kitty, I was told had been in a concentration camp, implying that she is queer & unreliable. By the same token Ross, who is said to have been in a Russian prison camp, should be a bit mad, too! which he certainly is! But more of this hateful but fascinating drama when we meet..."

I had now produced two damaging and confidential documents which were soon in circulation. The President showed my notes to a member of the Council and then — to Ross. Elizabeth showed my letter to Anna and also — to Ross. And a storm broke over my head.

Kitty vilified me, then, in an anonymous letter to the President, vilified Ross, then, after receiving a psychic attack (agonizing stomach pains) wrote to him again denying what she'd said.

Elizabeth accused me of something I had not done and, at the same time wrote abusive letters to Ross and created scenes in his classes. Ross, himself, warned me that he could use his psychic powers to 'hurt' me physically and his civil ones to take me to court while the President charged me with having committed a breach of confidence when, at the same time, he was taking private lessons from Ross. (This came out later). And Anna, who had resigned from the Sufi Order on account of her differences with Pir Vilayat was now re-instated with all her titles and power to initiate and, flushed with victory and feeling strong in her posture as a spiritual leader, scourged me in a deluded, holier-than-thou letter. See appendix 12.

Craziness and confusion were total for they were all in the power of Kundalini.

The work of the College was equally divided between the practical and the intellectual. In numbered rooms throughout the day, mediums gave sittings or held classes in mediumship and extra sensory perception while every evening people eminent in the field of psychic and spiritual studies lectured on such subjects as clairvoyance, telepathy, astrology, spiritual healing, Christian mysticism and so on. All the activities were conventional and highly respectable, the participants were invariably earnest and dignified and the atmosphere throughout was impressively calm.

Into this dull western academy of enlightenment came John Ross, magnetic and forceful, with his esoteric acrobatics; first opening our ignorant minds to the mysteries taught in ancient schools, and then our inert neglected bodies to the serpent power of the cosmos. No wonder we were excited when he came, intoxicated when he stayed and driven mad before he left.

But now, if the madness was to be stopped before it spread and killed and before the newsmen came listening at the door and peeping through the windows, something more had to be done. Private notes and letters and rescue operations, the shifting, unreliable evidence of the victims and being knocked about oneself — were not enough.

In the College library I had found the treatise, 'Serpent Power' by Arthur Avalon (Sir John Woodroffe), 'A description and explanation in full detail of Kundalini Shakti and the yoga effected through it, a subject occupying a pre-eminent place in the Tantra Shastra', and taken extracts which, although only fragments of the huge volume, were enough to provide evidence that was absolutely damning — and I sent them off to Bill. It was on this level and with this material that Ross had to be fought. Here are some.

"The bases of this Yoga are of a highly metaphysical and scientific character. For its understanding there is required a full acquaintance with Indian philosophy, religious doctrine and ritual ... those who wish to put this Yoga into actual practise must first satisfy themselves of the value and suitability of it and then learn directly of a guru who had himself been through it. His experience alone will say whether the aspirant is capable of success. page 25.

"...The Serpent Fire, which the Hindus call Kundalini is in the lowest centre, the Muladhara ... the object of the rousing of this force . . . is to exalt the physical consciousness through the ascending planes to the 'heaven world' ... the ultimate union with the Supreme Self. . . Apart from the necessity for the possession of health and strength, the thought, will and morality, which it is proposed to subject to its influence, must be first purified and strengthened. . . page 11.

"The Sadhaka (pupil) must be competent. . . The mere dabbler in the pseudo-occult will only degrade his intellect with the puerilities of psychism, become the prey of the evil influences of the phantasmal world, or ruin his soul by the foul practises of phallic sorcery. . . People who arouse Kundalini in the Muladhara to satisfy their desire for worldly enjoyment and do not attempt to lead Her upwards to the Highest centre ... super worldly bliss are 'the true prostitutes'. page 12.

"... proper place, time and food ... no distractions, no anxieties ... pure vegetarian food ... no long walks or violent exercise ... in the case of beginners no sexual intercourse. The stomach should never be more than half filled ... but no outright fasting... Sexual force ... instead of allowing it to descend into gross seminal fluid, is conserved as a form of subtle energy and rises to Shiva ... made a source of spiritual life instead of one of the causes of physical death ... sexual desire becomes extinct... As one forces open a door with a key, so the Yogi should force open the door of Liberation by rousing Kundalini. pages 217 & 224.

"If the Kundalini is worshipped in the Muladhara only, not taken higher . . . this is black magic . . . common in the western schools . . . to gain temporal objects and enjoy . . . but not

Liberation. . . The highest and most difficult form of Yoga is Raja Yoga . . . the practitioner gradually attains purity and becomes fit for Savikalpa Samadhi. pages 251 & 254.

I added. I have not been able to find any reference to the frog or ear-wagging exercises (of course I have not been able to read this huge volume very thoroughly). But, since Ross taught the frog with the aid of Egyptian pictures, I would hazard a guess that this is a method developed there and not by the Indians.

Soon after this, in the middle of a talk on meditation, at Friends House, Pir Vilayat turned suddenly to the subject of Kundalini. "It is alright for people living in caves in the Himalayas " he said, " but unsuitable for those living in society. The Sufis did not teach it. " And later, in an answer to a question, " In ancient times, aspirants were most carefully selected and given long purification training before they were considered fit to be given powers. But now, occult teaching is thrown wide open to everyone and powers are obtained by people who are not ready for them. "

Anna was there. I did not know if this was a special message for her but it was just the confirmation that I was wanting. And I wrote afterwards to Bill.

Do they, or do they not, wish to have the Kundalini taught under their roof? Many societies, centres and groups look to the College for guidance and its teachers and teaching automatically acquire the stamp of probity.

If the answer is *yes* — then strong action will have to be taken whatever the short-term consequences. If *no*, then you and I can stop wasting our time and energy and be saved from any more knocking about. But the Council *must* do something, they cannot drift any longer. Ross will soon be invited everywhere. They will have launched an unknown man without references and a clearly stated teaching programme upon the trusting world of seekers. Soon it will be too late to stop his advance and the damage which will undoubtedly accompany him. "

He showed the extracts to the Council and on November 6th, he and several members had a meeting with John Ross which he reported to me afterwards. And I commented:

That he admitted that he is teaching Kundalini is of first importance and since, in his defence (!) he stated that he was not teaching it in full, not carrying it to its high religious end, then he has condemned himself as a 'black magician' — and our case is proved.

On this level, Bill carried on the struggle single-handed. I still did not understand why there was so much resistance.

In the meantime, a bizarre occurrence was reported to Kitty, by Anna, who had been having tea the day before with the wife of the Dean of Westminster.

The Dean was in the Abbey when a woman rushed up to him and flung herself at his feet and clutched his legs, crying out, "save me, save me from that monster." He tried to calm her but couldn't and so fetched his wife and Anna. And Anna did — and they took her to the Deanery.

She said she had been a nurse in Westminster Hospital until a man persuaded her to leave and become his secretary. And she went to a big house and lived with him — was hypnotised and the most terrible things were done. She had escaped but she was still terrified of him. . . When they asked her who this man was, she said — John Ross.

Then, there was another closer, frightening incident. Bill woke one morning paralysed and unable to speak and the doctor diagnosed a stroke. With his chief adversary removed I thought Ross would come out the victor. However, after three days, he recovered. It had only been a psychic attack. He returned to the battle and when the term ended Ross received his dismissal.

But this was not the end of the affair — it rumbled on for months. I soon received a letter from the President, addressed to all those (40 people, Bill told me) who had appealed for his reinstatement and explaining why this was not possible.

The dangers of the exercises, devised to lead to the raising of Kundalini: Mr Ross's belief that in the school which he represented presented these could be overcome; the other schools which stressed need for long preliminary training; the conflict of opinion which had arisen; Mr Ross's wish not to adopt any other method; the open classes exposing untrained people perhaps with characters not firm enough, to awakened forces with which they could not deal; and so the deadlock — and the choice; the President's responsibility and regret; his gratitude for the general esoteric material which Mr Ross had taught and the interest he had aroused . . . the goodwill with which he was leaving.

As my name was down on the petition I replied at once, protesting and setting out in full my experiences from the begining and, at the end, I took up one of his points, pushing it as far as I could.

In your letter you speak of 'the school of teaching which Mr Ross represents'. Did you ever find out just *what* this school is? It is not Indian, for he several times revealed ignorance of Indian philosophy and habitually mispronounced Indian names and words. On the other hand, he always associated the Egyptian name, Anubis — the Opener of the Ways — with the exercises.

He is thought to have been born in South Africa and he told us that he had experienced several African tribal initiations. I would guess that his 'school' is Africa with a gilding of the gods of Egypt.

You will now understand why I am shocked to find my name on your list of Mr Ross's supporters (and if my name is there, one wonders just how authentic all the others are?) and I must ask you to do two things; have my name deleted and then inserted in the records as Mr Ross's first active critic and useful participant in the long-drawn-out struggle to expose and remove him from the College."

And he replied:

Mr Ross, of course, has not been 'exposed'. On the contrary I have great respect for the reality of his teaching. To speak of him as having been 'removed from the College' does not in the least accord with the friendly relation I have with him. . .

After Christmas the classes were resumed in the home of one of the devotees and the President, I then learnt, was continuing as a private pupil-possessed like them all! The force at the top with which, unknowing, Bill and I had been contending.

In January 1970, I received a 6-page letter, barely legible, from Anna. She thanked me for my Christmas message and referring to my remarks about the cleansing of the temple, pointed out that in all Christian initiations, it is both an outer and an inner process. She went on:

Perhaps you have already heard that my way and John's have finally parted . . . he never forgave me for the things I was supposed to have said about him and after I gave you that message I was aware of great pressure upon him, of a spiritual crisis — that is why I stood by him although I was unhappy. ... I was expecting him to tell me where his classes would be held — instead I heard from Kitty that I would not be welcome back. After the first shock I felt a sense of relief. It had to come to an end and I remember only the good things that I received at the beginning . . . and I pray for him and hold him in the Light. He needs it. Dear Bill embraced me when I told him I had been 'emptied'. . . . So now, dear, there is no

barrier between us and our love is restored to its true level. When
you feel that the moment has come, my arms are open to welcome
you back. . . Pray for him if you can.

She still would not believe that her arms repelled me.

Kitty became the agent and, as late as June 1970, was producing
cases of breakdown, schizophrenia, psychic attack, change of
character, bewilderment and confusion and Bill, assisted by an
osteopath, continued with his healing work.

At the end of the Easter term, Ross returned to Africa, as Kitty
had predicted, taking Rachel with him. It was for her that I
prayed. I could not forgive the 'vehicle' his crimes.

Before he left the college, I read another remarkable book, 'The
Testimony of Light', published during that same convulsive year,
1969. It consisted of a series of connected messages, received over a
period of a year and a half by a medium, Helen Greaves, from her
friend, Frances Banks, who was dead.

I had never been interested in the work of mediums but this
beautifully drawn tale of life after death, with a rich dramatic
element running through it, I found both moving and convincing
and I knew, at once, that I must adapt it for the stage.

I did not know Helen Greaves or where she was to be found but
when I arrived at a conference in Brighton a few days later, I
walked up the stairs beside her. She was very surprised when I
asked her permission to do this but after thinking it over, agreed.

As a young woman, Frances Banks, went to South Africa as a
nun in the Anglican Community of the Resurrection and for most
of her time there she was principal of a Teacher Training College,
teaching psychology, English and art, loved by generations of
students and respected throughout the colony for her services to
education. Then, at the height of her powers and influence, she left
the Order and returned to England. This was the reason, as
communicated to her friend, after her death.

> As you know, I dedicated myself to the religious life, repeating the
> creeds and forms with my lips, my will stretched and exerted to
> keep me honourably performing to the best of my ability those
> vows which I had so solemnly made until, after 25 years of such
> devotion, I found myself unable to go on any longer.
>
> It was not that I no longer believed in God, or did not care to
> follow the pattern of Jesus, or doubted that Christ was the Light of
> the World, but because, into my experience and thoughts had
> seeped a new explanation of these mysteries and doubts of the
> veracity of so many tenets of the Faith. . .

In England, she became Tutor-Organizer at Maidstone Prison and from this experience wrote her first book, 'Teach them to Live'. This was followed by several text books on psychology, an account of her researches into psychical and mystical phenomena, 'Frontiers of Revelation' and, lastly, published posthumously, 'Four Studies in Mysticism'.

In addition to this, she lectured widely and founded, together with Helen Greaves, Bill Blewett and others, a group for the study and practise of meditation which expanded and continued after her death.

Seeking and service characterized her life. She inspired the young and sat with murderers, and taught them how to live — and lived passionately herself; in perpetual longing for mystical experience, in perpetual striving for the break-through to Reality and in certain knowledge of the continuity of life.

She and Helen Greaves were intimate friends. It was said that they both loved and envied each other — for the 'open channel' of the one and the intellect of the other. "Frances was the brains and organizer in our partnership. I was able, humbly, to supply at times the counsel of the 'Inner Voice'", Helen wrote.

These disparate, warring yet complementary gifts enabled them to work together psychically and spiritually, experimenting in telepathy and exploring the deep levels of meditation until the time came when Frances was able to use Helen's 'open channel' to send back a description of the last undiscovered country, a message that there is no death, that "the last enemy that shall be destroyed is Death" — and to reveal herself in a great confessional passage. See Appendix 13.

That was the background to the project and on Saturday, November 29th 1969, I wrote to Helen:

I started work on 'The Testimony' last Tuesday and I am in a state of permanent intoxication! The words which at first were of no intrinsic interest to me, have now taken possession of me. I cut and prune and transpose and act and recite the lines to myself, loving them as if they were my own. . . I can see and feel now how the drama should be staged and the vision grows daily more tremendous. That this work should have come to me fills me with awe and gratitude while the responsibility of it all, I carry with a kind of trembling confidence. . .

The communications, or scripts, consisted of narrative which combined both description and reflection and which had to be converted into dialogue, and colourful stories, already half in dialogue, which had to be tightened and completed.

The narrative portions, although overwritten and a little dense, were always constrained and intellectually profound and acceptable, while the little dramas tended to be naieve and sentimental, their endings occasionally improbable and inconclusive. Although, even in my euphoric state, I recognised their weaknesses (perhaps confusion in the 'channel') I looked upon the text as sacrosanct. Only one scene, a drug story, which I considered dangerously unsound, did I dare to question and although Helen was upset, she gave me permission to alter it, saying that no one else had noticed it. A week later, I wrote again.

> I am reaching the end of the first gruelling stage; the detailed study of every word and line, deciding which passages to keep in their entirety and which to reduce and extract the essence of; reshaping the lines, where necessary, for the ear instead of for the eye etc etc. when all that is finished I can turn to the imagining stage, shaping the scenes, entrances and exits etc.
>
> I must tell you that some of the scripts, the marvellous confession lines, for example, transpose into dramatic passages as grand as any to be found in the great classical dramas. I would like to declaim some of them onto tape so that you may hear and thrill to their sound and meaning.
>
> I am sorry I upset you. I drove home my point too vigorously. Forgive me. I didn't notice the difficulty myself at my first ecstatic reading — it jumped out at the second critical one! I know how to deal with the problem now. "Such small errors as there have been will be adjusted, or will be of little matter..." as Frances writes on page 122. I shall work all through Christmas and I hope to have the first draft for you to see soon after. I work as one possessed and the bliss of such possession is my way of worship. With love... PS. The book is a rapturous mystical outpouring — the play will be a great mystical-religious drama.

Half hidden in the shadow of all this bright ebullience there was one disquieting thing of which I did not speak. After I had been working — for awhile, I became aware, with my inner eyes, of someone looking at me with a severe and disapproving expression. I thought it was Frances for she seemed to be wearing a habit, although she did not look like the photograph in the frontispiece. But she worried me. I did not understand her, for had she not written:

People living on earth, the erudite, the cultured and clever minds, the devotional and religious minds, the uneducated, the illiterate and the closed minds, must all be reached. All need this knowledge.

Was I not taking her voice beyond the book that she might speak directly to the world? I worked on disregarding her and when the draft was finished, she went.

My only respite was my weekly visit to my mother. Her armchair, a small table and the pictures hanging on the walls were all that she had left of her own. But they seemed enough for she was happy now. She liked her little room. "You are not a sharer" the Matron had said understandingly, when she gave it her.

She had her discontents but they were not serious for the Home was wellnigh perfect; the nurses not the flighty young agency girls who came and went but older women who had been there for years and with whom she could form relationships. And the matron was a friend to us both.

My discontent was her deafness. Her hearing-aid was no longer effective and shouting was so tiring and so, I began scribbling down what I wanted to say and these scribbles became a regular form of communication, with the inestimable advantage that she could keep them and study them, when I had gone — and pick up and continue the talking points when I returned. And they became a book.

On January 12th 1970, I wrote to Helen again.

It is finished! It *is* a play. A stupendous drama. I am sure of it. This is what I now plan to do. Give two readings — to friends yes, of course, but more especially to influential & professional persons who will make suggestions and even *help* in the launching stage. Such readings will make it known to a large number of people at one go & do away with the slow passing round of scripts. Also, many people cannot read playscripts comfortably. . . I will get an actor to help me. . . I would prefer you to *hear* it first — read & study it after. Shall I come to you? . . . I am so excited about this now. I can't wait to be driving on with it. . .

But she wanted the script. On the 16th she replied, from Sussex.

Herewith your excellent script! And thank you for all the work and care you have put into it. . . After talking on the phone with you this morning I realise more than ever that we are both 'under compulsion'! this could be a new break-through in drama technique and in New Age teaching! *What* responsibility we have

— it almost frightens me! However I know we shall be given strength, courage and inspiration. . .

She attached her comments.

Wonderful religious drama. Quite correct. Suitable for performing in a church (Southwark Cathedral) — or in Theatre-in-the-Round in Chichester. . . PB has done a remarkable job — hardly any thing of the original script has been altered. Excellent and careful piece of work. With some alterations and corrections should make a most uplifting drama & spectacle. . .

And I scribbled all this to my mother. We had never talked of death — now it became an open and regular topic.

The play is about life after death, a cosmic drama, based on messages 'sent back' by a woman who died, to her friend — a description of the world that she has gone to — the beautiful & fantastic world that you will soon go to . . . the friend says that I am the 'next link in the chain' — 'under compulsion' to turn these messages into a play which will be seen by thousands — a play in which there will be music, dancing, film, sound & light — a play which will not only teach & help people, take away the fear of death, show them how marvellous life is — going on & on — but which will change the theatre itself — start a new trend, away from sex and violence & cruelty — the sort of theatre that I have looked for & struggled for all my life & have failed to find or promote . . . & which will open up possibilities for my old plays. . .

A week later.

I have been working on the script again & on February 4th & 10th I give readings with an actor. . . In the meantime, the Bishop of Southwark has offered his Cathedral for the first performances.
    Matron is pleased that I have moved your chair. She is going to tie a string to the bell & bring it near you but until she does they can't hear your shouts when they are in the kitchen. Shall I bring you a lot of missiles to throw out of the door when you want them!!!!

As she read these scribbles every week, she considered her own prospects with interest but it was mine which excited her. She saw me, the great writer, at last acknowledged by a stupid world — her belief in me proven and her dream come true.
    Before I went to Equity to find an actor, a Sufi friend suggested her out-of-work nephew and when I heard that Peter Polak would

help me I arranged to run through the script with him the night before the reading. When he came to my seedy house and I opened the door, even before I knew that he was not only a fine actor but an experienced director — I knew that he was *our* man.

On February 6th, two days after the first reading, I scribbled:

About 30 people crowded into the drawing room, some having to stand, among them the Vice Chancellor of Surrey University, a cousin & niece of Malcolm Muggeridge, eminent clergymen, scientists, doctors etc — a lovely audience — all absolutely held & enthusiastic about the play. The V-C offered £1000 there & then towards its production. . . Peter was wonderful. We acted to each other as we read. He is dead keen on the play & they *all* fell for him so I shall not have to run round looking for anyone else for the key man is found. . .

The worst is over — presenting the script for the first time & getting the support of all those critical people. Now the responsibility is not all on me. . . There is still work to be done. I don't worry any more — & yet I do. I am so used to feeling anxious — so used to doing everything alone — that I can't take things easily — trust others, helpers on other planes & artists here — & not worry. . .

I like bringing you cakes — they are *not* a fag to make but a relaxing activity, especially yesterday, the day after the ordeal. . . There is a comic old woman here — a magpie — who picks up things wherever she goes & hides them in her locker! Matron found one of your books in it!!!

The second reading was even more successful. Afterwards, a few displeased Cassandra voices rose from the group. The text, like revelation was too subline to touch, they said, and to spread the message from a vulgar, unconsecrated stage would be sacrilege. But these purists were not listened to.

The group, founded by Frances ten years before, was now like an exclusive club. Membership was by invitation and the chosen were expected to be well advanced along the spiritual path. The meetings at which Helen brought exalted teaching down through her ' open channel ' — her ' celestial telephone ' as Frances called it — were the high points in their private lives.

After a few days rest in a Quaker Retreat House, I was scribbling to my mother again.

All through the Boer War, when he was fighting, Philip carried 2 books in his knapsack — ' Pickwick Papers ' & Macaulay's ' Essays & Lays of Ancient Rome '. I have not brought you these today but

Ibsen's 'doll's House'. When you have had enough of the Bennett family & the lovely illustrations, you can turn to Nora. She was a *new* woman when women were just beginning to revolt against their servile position — as men's dolls — playthings — kept in doll's houses. . . Grandma was a Nora, giving up her great gift just to breed & look after her selfish husband — but she did not revolt.

You did not marry that rich banker in Cape Town because you knew you would become his possession — he had to *own* everything — and you would not be his or anybody's doll . . . but most women *were*. They had no rights — no money of their own — they belonged to a man as soon as they married — & *most* men just looked upon them as playthings, breeders of their children & keepers of their homes — not their intellectual equals. Even today, women are second-class citizens — because we live in a man-made world — a civilisation determined by man's philosophy & outlook — a materialistic world of brain & intellect — & not of feeling & sympathy and intuition.

Even if I had wanted to marry, I never met a man who would have allowed me to write & be myself — not expected me to sacrifice my talent for his & for his comfort. . . A woman is often *apparently* dominant & confident but the doll & servility are always there — deep down below the surface. . .

You were always a *new* woman. You went to Africa to find the father of your children & a man who would let you paint. That was a clever remark of Matron's — 'you went for the man rush — the others for the gold rush'! But he was never put to the test.

If you had gone to him & said, Darling, I've had my babies, the nurses can look after them & now I am going to paint again. When we married you promised me I should. I want to go to Italy. The servants can run the house, you can entertain the guests, put up with an empty bed & give me plenty of money. How would he have taken it?

Remember, he was going into politics & would have been an M.P. — perhaps a Minister, with a significant social as well as political life. Would he have let you go? *Was* he the perfect man? It would be lovely to think so, yet sad to think what you lost when he died — love, security & freedom — not that long lonely struggle. . .

She was silent — but she had her answer a week later. "It was best that he died and that we had to knock about the world together."

And I scribbled:

So that you were free to paint, then trapped again — by me. You adored your art until I came — then you adored me & put me first. If you had not had me you would have gone abroad & lived among artists & developed your art & become a well known painter. You were as great a genius as any man — but all your prime years you gave to portraits, turned them out like a machine, just making money — or failing to & wearing yourself out as a lodging house keeper.

The great painters you once knew & talk about now were *men* — with women round them. It is almost always true that great artists have been helped to their success by the women who sacrificed themselves. Men don't do this for women. But *you* did it for me.

First you painted to bring me up, then to give me my freedom to be a writer then, worn out, you stopped painting & became my servant. You would not be a Nora to any husband but you became one — to me. Love was your undoing.

"I wanted you before I had you" she said, "and when I had you I never stopped adoring you."

I know. I know. That is the eternal tragedy of woman. And perhaps this quality of selfless love surpasses genius and crowns all.

"I shall paint in the next life."

Yes. Yes, you will. You will carry your talent on with you and bring it to fulfilment.

"Shall we meet again?"

Of course. Great loves, great friendships &, I suppose great enmities, go on from life to life. There is no division between life & what we call death — only the dense atmosphere & slower vibrations of the earth plane separate us. Mystics can break through the density & actually live in the next world, a world of mind & spirit, while they are still here.

Thought is a great power here — it will be one of the powers by which we shall live there — by which we shall project ourselves, create what we desire & know what we want to know. We could do all this here if we developed our latent powers. . .

On February 21st when I was with her again, I scribbled:

I started work again yesterday — with Peter — the final knocking of the script into a play — shaping it, strengthening it, building up the characters etc. He is a most imaginative & experienced man & I am learning a lot from him.

I read bits of it to the Quakers & all the other tired, worn out people fleeing from the noise & stresses of London — they were thrilled & talked of nothing else.

You gave me my freedom & I wrote as I wanted to write but I failed in the world because I was writing what was not the fashion — not wanted. This play will revolutionise the theatre, start a new trend . . . and my time is now coming. I am happy & confident for the years of obscurity &, often depression, are over. . .

I found the door locked when I arrived today. There is an old woman downstairs who keeps escaping. Her relatives dumped her here & have never come back. She got away again yesterday & Matron & all the nurses were flying about in all directions looking for her. She is so dotty now that she thinks she must get home to cook the dinner. She was so exhausted when they found her that they had to put her to bed. Poor old thing.

A week later.

I'm so glad you are working on your memoirs again. I've never heard that bull story — your father sitting contentedly in a field painting the cows when among them, unbeknown to him, was a bull! Why didn't the bull climb up into the tree too? Can't you imagine them both sitting in the tree together! If only you could draw that scene! Daddy, Bull, Tree — & Mother looking anxious from the safe side of the fence! What a comic picture! What with bears & bulls your memoirs will make exciting reading.

It *is* my work — & yet is *isn't*. I have only carried on the work of Frances — made her messages into a stupendous drama for the teaching & healing of humanity. . . You were always interested in people — you were compassionate & good to anyone who grieved or any animal that suffered — that is the personal form of love for humanity — mine is the general.

Peter and I met every week and worked on the play scene by scene — in between I did the re-writing. I kept in touch with Helen, telling her all that we were doing and asking for her suggestions.

On March 5th she wrote:

I was very thrilled by your talk on the telephone last night, and I do wish you every success with the play. I am much looking forward to reading the second version. You are so dedicated & sincere & have delved so deeply into the meanings & implications . . . & brought them into a form where the 'theatre-goer' & man in the street, as well as the more enlightened souls will be able to understand them. It will be wonderful one day perhaps, to sit back & 'see', the whole book unfolded by actors & actresses. Bless you for all your work. . .

When I went to see my mother that week, I found her in bed with a recurrence of her dysentry trouble.

It is *not* something new. You've forgotten that you were constantly having it in the other Homes. Excitement brings it on. It was some annoyance or a move — now, it is *me* & all that is happening. But you mustn't worry, for it will stop as it always has before.

This room is icy! No wonder Matron soon decided that you were not a 'sharer'. You like your window open when it's snowing — your companion would want it tight shut in a heat wave! That must be why I am so hardy — born into a howling draught!

I like the last story that you've written. How fastidious grandma must have been! Wouldn't buy her clothes in a shop — however grand — because she wouldn't try on anything that someone might have tried before her! So she had her things made by a dressmaker. I used to hate those grand shops — not because I cared how many people had tried the dresses on, but because the serving women were so snobbish — they made me feel like a rag-picker which, of course, I was! And still am!

On March 14th.

Have you forgotten that this is my Baptismal Day! when, dressed in a long beautiful, Indian embroidered robe and you, all in black, still mourning, but looking so soigné & so beautiful — I still have the photographs — we set off together in a carriage for St James's where the tender-hearted bishop added my second name because I was going to be such a joy to you!!! That was the first journey that we took together.

How different from my birth day when you only just got home in time! I was intelligent even then! I didn't want to come naked into the fog, onto a cold hard pavement, but waited for a warm room & a comfortable bed!!!

No — not brain or intellect, but sensitivity can break through the veil — *it is only a veil* — between us & the powers & people on other planes — between the living & the dead — for there is no death — life is continuous, we just pass from one experience to the next. . .

The next week she was up and in her chair but still worrying — not about herself now but about the nurses — and the trouble she gave.

Nurses are trained to do unpleasant things. . . In hospitals it is worse. . . It is because you have hardly ever been really ill all your life that it comes as a shock — having to have everything done for you.

I can't give you an immediate answer to your problem of how to get up from your chair & get to the commode quickly. . . If I could instal a special attendant for you, I would — but how bored she would be just sitting about all day waiting to lift you up & down. . . It is very difficult to organize things right for the old — and as you have just said, this little Home is *so nice* & Matron is *such* a dear — & you are so pleased to feel how fond she is of you.

But don't worry I will try to do something to make things better — & Matron will too — & try to understand that these nurses are here to help you & that you don't need a *special* one as well — you're real trouble is what it has always been — you think too much of others — and criticise yourself too much. . .

The next week she had her own solution. She remembered her birthday party.

It was alright to sit on the bedpan for one afternoon but if you sat on it permanently you would get sores. That is why Matron is reluctant to give you one even if it would make you 'live happy ever after'! She's not so sure that it would!

Your jotting down style was very good for a magazine, the first idea, but now that you have written more of your reminiscences & we are going to make a book of them, it seems to me, when I study them carefully, that they need a little cutting & polishing & some linking up. I have been doing this & I am now afraid that you may not like it???

It is going to be quite a sizeable book — about 40 pages. Amusing in parts, sad in parts — interesting throughout. It should have illustrations — reproductions of your work and photographs of *you*!

No high thoughts — or low ones today! Only chapter I of "The Memoirs of an Elderly Woman of 97" — which I am taking away to work on & keep safe.

The next week.

You have tried the one here — not even someone young & light could sit on it all day & now the only solution to the problem is to *ring the bell* — every half hour if need be. Matron *wants* you to do this. It annoys her when you don't. So you mustn't mind doing this. . . She is as anxious as I am to stop you worrying — which only makes the trouble worse.

I will bring your own bedpan next week & you can try it and prove to us that you *can* sit on it forever & ever. But if that one, too, gets painful — then I shall win my bet!

Peter and I work & work & work on the script — act by act — & then go back all over it again. In the end it will be a tremendous play — so it is worth all this toil & sweat. We work together so well — we trust each other. He is sure that it is going to make a great impact on the public & go all round the world — & live on.

And the next.

I am very pleased that you had that little vision of the photograph. If you can 'open yourself' — make yourself receptive, you may have many more such visions — guidances — experiences — which you will find helpful & comforting.

I am going to see a film showing psychic surgery being performed. No instrument. All done by MIND alone. Internal organs or diseased pieces of the body just float up & out — forced out by Mind power alone! What do you think of that?! Can you bring the power of *your* mind to bear upon your body & its problems? I believe you can — and *will*.

On April 12th, Helen wrote:

Thank you for your letter. It all sounds so exciting. . . I am sure 'They' could not have found a more sincere & dedicated person than yourself. All strength & inspiration & encouragement to you.

So delighted to hear that Sir George Trevelyan has invited you & Peter to read scenes from the play at the Attingham Summer School That should be a lovely week & should attract an erudite crowd. Yes. I would love to be there with you. . .

I was very interested in your ideas about TIME, and the play. . . You are quite right, it did not intrude into the book . . . but the play is different. It must be a difficult problem but I feel it will work out. . . And the Religion and Science theme! I am more and more astonished, (indeed I marvel) at the depths in 'Testimony' . . . which you are discovering! Which I think shows more than ever that I was a Channel only, and not the Source!

Rosamund Lehmann might be helpful . . . and if you have made Mother Florence into a strong part, her sister might be interested in acting it??? Actually, those who heard you read the part, thought your interpretation was most sensitive and beautiful. . .

Well, my dear, I look forward so much to receiving the second draft, and digesting it. Do hope I won't be quibbling about anything!! . . . I'm a queer soul! . . . But I do realise that this play is being 'directed' from another Level of consciousness, through you and Peter. Bless you both.

On April 21st, I scribbled:

I will pay up my bet! Even if you can sit on it for *part* of each day —
that will be something. . .

Peter & I worked together for the last time & I feel so tired &
stale that I am going away tomorrow to stay with a friend in Essex
— & finish the writing there. She lives in a big historic house with
gardens & farm land & she is collecting all her friends & I am going
to read the play to them in the great beamed room, with the ingle-
nook fireplace at one end.

After my return, on May 2nd, I scribbled again:

You have finished writing your memoirs & stopped reading & you
are bored again — & because the awful bath affair was last
Christmas & your trouble has stopped & the chair agony is over,
you are finding new annoyances & getting restless & wanting to
move again. . . But being annoyed is only an attitude. I know it is
hard to become impervious to the people round us — but even the
annoyances of life in a Home are better than nothing — better to be
annoyed — than a cabbage! And there are so many *good* things here
— & we should have to go a long way to find anyone as kind &
genuine as Matron. You know all this.

The friend I stayed with has 4 children. The eldest has left his
wife & children, the 2nd one is drifting, the 3rd has married a most
peculiar American & gone off to live there, & the youngest has
spent 5 years in & out of mental hospitals.

Now he is at home steadily destroying the property with his
'schemes'. The latest is to create a lake beside the house, flooding a
field & making the old house damper than ever. He has rooted up
the flowers, let the horses & cattle into the orchard, built a new
entrance drive & blocked all the ditches & drains, pulled down the
garage, chopped down all the hedges etc etc. And she is frantic.
This is what a full family life *can* be like. My poor friend. She is
treated by them all like a buffoon, she says. I have told you her
story to make you laugh — and cry.

Why don't you sit at the window with a string attached to a tree
outside — & knock top hats off?! I used to enjoy throwing water
onto peoples' heads — & I had the police onto me — a woman
threatened to sue you for a new fur coat!! Do you remember?

I walked along the bottom of Campden Hill Square the other day
& I had a good look at the top hat place. It is just the same — the
mound, the bushes & the trees — & I could see your brothers, Noel
& Harry, hiding there, jerking down the branches & the top hats
whirling off the bald heads & the hairy heads into the road — under
the horse-drawn omnibuses!!! You are seeing them now &
laughing. You are still frivolous enough to enjoy the scene!

We must make money from our plays & books — then we can
buy houses, engage special nurses, live as we want to live & be

independent of all life's torments!! In the meantime, why don't you entertain yourself by keeping a day-to-day diary of all the comic, tragic, amusing & annoying things that go on here! Title could be — "What it's like living for 100 years"!

On May 6th, I wrote to Helen.

Here it is at last — the final version! I have told Peter that I can do no more for the present. . . He is satisfied & the next phase can now start.

He understands & respects the teaching although he is not interested in the intellectual themes & problems which the minor characters personify. It is character, dialogue & action which concern him. A theatrically effective play is what he *must* have in order to get really excited about it.

And we *all* want that — a play that will 'come over' to ordinary theatre audiences — the 'uneducated, the illiterate and closed minds' — as well as the others. And the characters & scenes which I have now developed at last satisfy him. He feels he has a play now with which 'to go to town'.

When I broke out of the strict form of the book & dared to do all this developing & expanding, I was sure all the time that I was not betraying the spirit & teaching, that every word I was writing, every character I was enlarging was *coming out of the book — was of the book*. And I felt that you & Frances were with me — that we were all working together, striving to make of this great book an equally great play.

Love to you and blessings be upon you as you read. How marvellous is it all! PS. I have put back that last line that you expugned. Peter & I still feel that it is said or implied throughout the book, that it is the message of the book, that it ties up the whole play.

On May 8th I was with my mother again.

Your 'psychic people' showed you the right photograph for your book. . . No. It is too soon to get myself photographed for the play.

And I can't spare the time or money. But if one *is* wanted when the time comes, I am hoping that you will have another vision, that 'they' will tell you which old one I ought to choose? Would one of those fat infant ones be impressive? 'Portrait of the Playwright'

The 'psychic people' are your friends, with you all the time & looking after you. Thinking very deeply helps to bring them into your sight.

About those pills. I have just torn up my words of wisdom. I will shut up now & leave it to the 'psychic people'. If they think you ought to take them they must come & drop them into your mouth!

That poor old thing escaped again. She used a belt to pull the high bolt on the front door back & got away. She didn't know where she was going when they caught her. How awful to be flung into a place & left, not know where you are & feel desperate to get away — get home.

I am waiting to hear from Helen.

16

ON May 9th Helen replied, attaching a report to her letter.

The play received and I have spent the last two days going through it very carefully. I do appreciate all the work you have put into it, and the careful manner in which you have tried to keep to Frances' script. It must have been a most difficult task and one I confess I would not have liked to have taken on.

This version is a great improvement on the first, as you have broken up long chunks of monologue, and the scenes, on the whole are more dramatic. I congratulate you on much of it. . . *But, I cannot allow anything that was not actually in the book or implicit in it.* And I must admit that in parts you have rather let your imagination run riot in your very commendable effort to bring in dramatic scenes. . .

She gives examples — and then goes on:

I am so sorry that I have to insist on the changing of these scenes. . . This book was a sacred trust from Frances. . . What right has either of us to change it?

There are some smaller corrections . . . and I would like to help you by *suggesting* the new wording. . . Could we not work this together?

My dear, I know you will be disappointed but I must be true to myself and my trust. . . I knew when you suggested scripting it, that it would be a terrific task, as this play is like nothing done before . . . but you wanted to try, did you not? If we can come to an understanding and you feel that you can change the scenes I have criticised, then I feel that there is a good play and that Frances will be with us. . . If, however you do not wish to alter this version, then I'm afraid we will have to shelve the whole idea. I could not let it go out with the errors and discrepancies that have crept into it. . .

About next Saturday . . . I will come if you decide to go on with it my way. I suggest, if you still feel like reading them. . .

She suggests the scenes she would like read — and goes on:

229

Sir George has invited me as his guest for the week-end, if you do read the play in August. . . Anyway, all this is now dependent on whether we can be in harmony over these alterations. I for one would be terribly sorry to see the break-up of what prospected to be a unique challenge in the theatre, and to feel that by keeping to my principles, I had renounced your friendship . . . and I hope this does not happen. We are indeed being tested on this . . . how big are we both . . . and how much are we willing to forego our emotional reactions, and to keep to the truth of what my friend wrote in her scripts?

Bess you and thank you for all you have done. Love and blessing on you.

And she opened her report:

This is a sensitive and imaginative rendering of the book 'Testimony of Light' . . . though in some places a little *too* imaginative! It is, however, a big improvement on the first draft and, I should think, would act better. Some of the scenes are very well done and only minor alterations are needed — a word here or there. With most of what you have extended I can agree. But, I must be quite honest, and disagree strongly with some of your innovations which are not even *implied* in the original script, and which would give a totally wrong impression. These must be cut in a way I have indicated before I can agree to any further dramatisation. . .

She then states her objections, in detail, and ends the report:

The rest of the play is very much as before and should be very impressive. I will concede the last line that you want to keep. Prologue good. Now that you have not made me sit in the corner writing, I do not object to my name being in it, as the friend and author of the book.

She kept the script.

That the changes and the one extension, to 5 out of the 18 little dramas, virtually a fraction of the whole book, should produce such a dire reaction — her talk of 'shelving' the whole thing — shocked me, especially as they were not totally new to her, for I had always telephoned her after Peter and I had been working to tell her what we had done — and she had listened, understood and acquiesced.

However, as she had praised and accepted the rest of the play and shown a readiness to work with me, we only had to meet when Peter and I would explain things, if need be alter things — and 'come to an understanding'. But would we? I already sensed the approaching storm.

When I selected, pruned and shaped the narrative passages, my object was to make them actable and more easily understood. When Peter and I 'let our imaginations run riot', our aim was to make the dramas clear where they were confused and credible where they were obtuse. We had to elicit and restore what we believed Frances had intended but which had got lost on the way or when being committed to paper, by long hand. Only later did I learn that the friend who had typed the original scripts had, without saying anything, already edited away a lot of the verbosity and confusion.

On May 12th I telephoned her — and was hit by a blast. Shouting accusation and abuse, she raged for half an hour. I shook before the onslaught and my attempts to speak were drowned. Afterwards, I telephoned Bill and the next day, the 13th, wrote to her.

Last night, after the very painful telephone conversation — or tirade one could better call it — I made up my mind to end the whole business, and felt a sense of relief at being free.

This morning, I hear from Bill that you are prepared to meet and discuss the alterations that you want in a fortnight's time. So, I am drawn back, in the interests of the work.

Your letter and report of May 9th were as friendly as always and reasonable and the way to understanding and agreement was wide open. Yesterday and today you have changed, you seem to want to hurt and humiliate me, to close the way and disappoint everyone else.

I said last night that we must meet and explain things and I told you that we would alter things that you object to, but although there are plenty of scenes unaffected by your strictures which we could read next Saturday, you now cancel the reading altogether. I have submitted to your directive (as conveyed by Bill) to read the book and not the play — in order not to let down completely the people to whom I gave my word. And I have given an undertaking not to carry the script in my handbag or conceal it about my person!

In your letter and report of May 9th you praise the new version and your criticisms affect only a small portion of it. I cannot understand why this storm has blown up — distorting and destroying as it rages.

Yours rather sorrowfully and wearily,

The next day, the 14th, she replied.

Your letter to hand this morning. I agree that I was in a great state of upset and disappointment on the telephone, about the travesty of the play, 'Testimony of Light'. If I lost my temper . . . I feel that there was sufficient provocation. However I beg your pardon if I was over-brusque.

She then enumerates 'variations of the truth' in my letter — repetitions of my telephone assurances which, no doubt, she did not hear and my assertion that only a small portion of the play was in dispute. Then, going over the 5 scenes again, she accuses me of over-sentimentalising, over dramatising and negating the message of Frances. And continues:

I did not cancel the reading on Saturday until I had taken advice from an authoritative source. You say you could read scenes already passed, but my advice was that *nothing* must be allowed out to the public until the *whole version* has been approved and agreed by me and by the publishers. I can assure you that members of the board (including clergymen) would never approve such scenes. And Attingham agreed and the suggestion to read from the book came from there. As for the entertainment of a few selected people being stopped it would be far worse if we let down the thousands who have read the book and have been uplifted by it! It was also pointed out to me that I would be bombarded by letters expressing disappointment and disapproval of the play as having cheapened the book!

It was also emphasised that, by letting you read scenes at a public function, I was tacitly accepting you as the script-writer of the play; and this I cannot be sure of doing. Since you have already broken your promise not to introduce *any* material not in the book, I cannot feel much reliance and trust in your work, for you have flagrantly inserted pure inventions of your own!

Therefore, I advise you, for your own sake, not to mention or discuss the play at all, as this would save you embarrassment later on, if I shelved the whole project, which I assure you is very possible. I believe that one day the play will go out to the public, but it may not be *your* script version! So try not to get yourself into more embarrassment! If you recall, you persuaded me to let you have a try, but there was no binding agreement about this; and after this very sorry performance we will have to be very careful and very assured before making any of it public.

She finally accused me of 'rushing into the reading' without her consent and ended:

It was also emphasised by some advisers that this was a lovely book, a 'pearl of great price', and one which I have never claimed as my own . . . and yet you have the temerity to alter it for commercial reasons. I must make these points clear to you as they are clear to wiser thinkers, and they are not my 'strictures' as you so rudely term them, at all. This is not a storm that has 'blown up' but the verdict of wise and experienced people! I venture to suggest that you moderate your ideas about my trying to humiliate you, which are not true.

I showed these letters to Peter and gave copies to Bill, and the same day, the 15th, he wrote to Helen saying that I 'deserved better treatment than words like 'temerity', 'flagrant' and 'commercial reasons'; that Peter and I had never said that we would not make alterations and were ready to discuss them; that 'she would have to go a long way to find two other experienced people to give their services and work so hard'; and, he was 'sorry to be mixed up in this and hoped that he could now drop out'.

It was a mild but brave letter, for Helen was his old friend and guru and the Group was at the centre of his life.

The meeting the next day, at which she had forbidden me to read the play, saying that if she came and found me reading it she would stop me, was the AGM of the World Spiritual Council.

Many people were coming to it especially to hear the play and although I was in no mood to go myself, it was imperative to read them something — read the book, explaining discreetly that the final version was not ready — and to make a statement.

I avoided the people when I arrived and sat on the staircase out of sight, feeling mortified and bitter and, until Bill came and sat beside me, utterly alone. When my turn came, I began with my prepared piece.

Some people are still saying that this book, 'Testimony of Light' is too sublime to be transferred to the theatre because, reflecting our sick society, it is so corrupt and vile.

Yet the theatre has come out of the temples and the churches and some of the highest thought and teaching and language have come to us in dramatic form. Temple ceremony and ritual and plays.

It should not reflect the darkness by which it is surrounded but provide a light and, if translated to the stage, the book will do just that — set a new trend away from the kitchen sink, which will lift the theatre back to its original high place where it may blaze and guide.

And through the book there runs a strong dramatic element as if the knowledge which Frances Banks was so anxious to see disseminated and which she returned to unfold, as if her great message was intended for the theatre.

"People living on earth, the cultured and clever minds, the devotional and religious minds, the uneducated, the illiterate and the closed minds must all be reached. All need this knowledge. . ." Those are her words.

The world is ready, we have the play, the theatre will proclaim the knowledge — and all will be reached.

I then read my cut copy of the book and the audience responded warmly. Afterwards, a sensitive friend told me that when I began she saw me in darkness which gradually cleared until, when I came to the end, I was surrounded by light — healed of the blackness inside me by Frances and her book.

Ten days later, Peter and I arrived with our scripts at the flat where Helen was staying, expecting to discuss the five controversial scenes of the play and come to an understanding.

When she opened the door her manner towards me was hostile. A script lay on a table beside her chair in the sitting room, but it was not the same as ours — it was her *own*! She was writing the play herself! And she told us, at once, that my play would not be discussed, for it was 'out' and hers was the one that was going to be produced — in Guildford Cathedral. It was all arranged.

She was being helped by a great dramatist 'on the other side', she said, and when I asked who, she was not allowed to reveal the name but hinted that it was Shakespeare. And she read us the scenes that she had finished.

They were mine. The play was mine. She had selected the same scenes and passages, made the same cuts and developed the same characters. Only the dialogue was not mine — nor was it Frances'. When she stopped, she looked at Peter.

"Will you direct *my* play? she asked him.

"Yes". He replied without a moment's hesitation. She then turned to me.

"And will you assist him?"

"I am not a director.

"You read rather well" she went on, patronisingly. "Will you read *my* play at the Summer School next month?

"Yes", I replied, "if I think it good."

I was as ready to work for a good play, her play, as for my own which, after all, was not really my own.

She then offered to pay me compensation. I rejected this with contempt — and we left. Out in the street, I could hardly speak to Peter. I had just agreed to work for Helen's play myself and was trying to be detached, yet his instant acquiescence had seemed like a betrayal — an unreasonable emotion yet the bitterest of all.

On May 31st, with my inveterate habit of picking up a pen after everything, I wrote to confirm what had been said and decided at the meeting. Some of the points are compressed into this paragraph.

> You acknowledged that I had given you the idea of turning the book into a play and you said you were very sorry to disappoint me and you offered to compensate me financially for all my work and expenses . . . and you asked me to tell you what you could do for me. . .

On June 4th, this brought a sharp reply.

> I cannot agree that the statements in your letter are an entirely correct report of the meeting.
>
> You repudiated any offer of help made compassionately by me. . . Since there was no contract, nor signed agreement between us, you must realise that I am under no obligation to you for any work done by you on a dramatic version of the book, Testimony of Light, which was written entirely at your suggestion and of your own free will and desire. I hope that this whole sad affair and misunderstanding can now be closed. Yours.

I learnt from Bill that the Vice-Chancellor of Surrey University, Dr Peter Leggett, had arranged for the production of the play in Guildford. He was the latest recruit to the Group, a mathematician — and her blue-eyed boy.

I waited, we all waited, for her and the 'great dramatist' to write their play. And I laughed at the conceit and did not believe that Helen, once a minor journalist and author of an obscure book on psychical phenomena but with no literary qualifications or knowledge of the theatre, could produce a better version of the play than mine. My feelings were equivocal and frightening. We both seemed threatened with damnation.

.   .   .   .

All through that month of turmoil I visited my mother and watched her life changing. Her 'psychic people' were closer and appeared more often, helping her to get away from the irritations of the Home and the limitations of her body. And I scribbled:

Yes, you will find that beautiful house & live in it. They have shown you a vision of the future — & you will go on seeing it until you know it so well that you will know where that house is & how to find it. And you will never lose me. I shall always turn up when you call. I think Polly is a new friend whom you will get to know when you reach the house.

You are gaining the power now to go wherever you want to. It doesn't matter how helpless you are — & stuck in your bed — you can take yourself away & go to places & meet people & lead an exciting, independent life, not caring what this Home is like. You have become free of it. Your mind can travel. I shall go to that house too & be with you.

I sat on the grass the other day beside the Round Pond & ate a picnic lunch & looked across to Kensington Palace & thought about the past — about Campden Hill & you — & my own infancy. Kensington Gardens, the Round Pond & the Broad Walk are just the same — perhaps more crowded on fine days. The masses have invaded them & their purity has declined with the decline of privilege.

I have begun working on your book again. Why did those daughters have to mind you? I thought you had nurses & governesses galore. Your brother, Frank, married one of them — Florence — & when he abandoned her she took to the bottle & slowly drank herself to death, leaving a poor little baby behind. Her father, Henry Moore, was a great painter. I didn't know that he died after falling off the top of a knife-board bus.

There is an old woman downstairs who loves treacle tart, like you — so I have given her some. She gets very depressed because no one comes to see her. Perhaps a piece of tart will cheer her up.

On another day.

I went to Dulwich to have tea with my dear friend, Trixie — the psychic person. After tea we sat together & messages poured through her for me & for you. At one moment *you* were there. And Philip came with his love for you. And I was told to stick to my course, use the gifts I have been given — & never to despair. . . I came away feeling so happy & I wanted to tell you so that you might feel happy & at peace with so much love & interest round you — waiting for you. Do you yourself *feel* Philip near you? Is he one of your 'psychic people'?

I was also told that I would soon be moving. I am longing to move & I have been looking for a cottage.

No. Not to another *land* — yet! *You* will go to another land first & I will join you when I have finished my work here. . .

That poor old woman is still escaping — at all hours of the day & night. Matron is quite worn out with anxiety. . .

Moving, was always in her mind — and places were the substance of her visions. A week or so later.

The 'psychic peoples' idea of your moving to a tent under a lovely tree with flowers all round, is beautiful. I would like that, too. You will move there & very soon. . . You can move yourself. Yes, that is why they do not come to me . . . move with *their* help. They can arrange everything in a way that I can't. You don't need me any longer.

No. There is nothing wrong with your brain — but you are living in two worlds now — here and with the psychic people — & that is good because they will help you to go wherever & whenever you want to. . .

Do you remember when we camped in tents in Canada and, during a storm, our tent blew down & your head went through a hole in the canvas. You looked so funny & when they came to rescue us, they all laughed?

No. Your memoirs are not a book yet. I am still looking for the right publisher — this is the difficult part. I am going to bring typed copies for you to read & to give to the nurses to read.

And soon after that.

You can make another life *now* . . . with the 'psychic people'. . . You have become one of them & can do things *yourself* . . . you will soon learn how to *take yourself* away.

Do you talk to them? Try talking to them. Ask them to direct you to that tent in the lovely grassy field. The more you talk to them the more they will answer & help you.

I think Philip is one of them — and he is trying all the time to help you — but you must help him to help you — think of him — talk to him & to them — *feel* yourself going to the place that you want to move to.

With the power of your mind you can go anywhere — do anything. The people who annoy you here are not important — ignore them — only your psychic people are important — concentrate on them.

I will pack up your things & that will help you to get away.

She was wanting so much to go and I was sure that I was keeping her. She had looked after me, all my life, and she still felt that I needed her and she must not leave me alone.

Later.

I have brought you a little book of messages sent back by two women who died young∫ . . . I may not be able to receive messages but you will be able to come back and help me. You will not leave me alone. You will help me more from there than you can by staying on here. . . And you will paint again & drop your old worn-out body & take on a new & finer one. . .

    ∫By Rosalind Lehmann & Lady Sandys.

But still she did not go.

On July 4th, Helen wrote to tell me that the 'dramatization' was nearly finished but as her typist friend was in Australia, it would not be ready in time for a reading at the Summer School.

"So if you are still interested, it is quite in order for you to read passages from the book". And she asked me to tell Peter.

We read from the book and then I waited to receive the typed script. When it did not come, I relied on reading Peter's for, as her director, he was bound to get one. But he didn't and on September 8th, I wrote:

Your play is finished and typed and ready for production and so the time has come for me to write to you again . . . because I do not think you are aware of what you have done to me and why I feel as I do.

    You have a dramatic sense, as I once told you, but you have no knowledge of playwriting and without the groundwork that was given you, the long studying of the text (you admitted many times that I was finding things in the book which you never knew were there), the gradual solving of all . . . the problems, the writing of version after version, the readings . . . the work with Peter, the stage-by-stage creation of a viable play and pattern for you to use — you could not even have started. And without the enthusiasm which was aroused in all those who heard it read, or heard about it, you would not have been stirred to go into playwriting yourself and production facilities would not have been so readily forthcoming.

    The scenes which you read to us and talked about provided quite sufficient evidence of your close adherence to the pattern of my play and from them it can be inferred that the remainder of your play contains similar plagiaristic material.

    Is it fair then that you should launch your play and claim it as entirely your own? It is not. And so, I am going to ask you to do two things.

    First, that upon the title page and wherever your play is advertised or otherwise mentioned, you include an acknowledge-ment of my work. And second, that whatever money you receive from the playing, filming or televising of the play, a half share (my share) should go to a fund (already being considered by some of our friends) for the establishing of that University of the Spirit which

Frances dreamed of during her life-time and afterwards recorded so movingly in her book.

No author should make money from the play of this book nor obtain any personal glamour from it. I had decided, had my play been produced, to present it anonymously and to devote all monies earned from it, to the University.

Much time has passed and now that I have made my viewpoint absolutely plain I do hope that you will understand at last and respond sympathetically, so that our friendship may be resumed and the dark affecting hindrance which lies in the lighted path of 'The Testimony', and in *your* path and mine, may be cleared and its mischief finally forgotten. Yours.

PS. You asked Peter to direct the play for you. Even if you have gone back on this now, it would be a friendly gesture to let us read the script.

She did not reply. Then, quite by chance (or was it chance?) I read in a newspaper that a new and remarkable play, 'The Testimony of Light' by Helen Greaves, was soon to be performed in Guildford Cathedral. And I rushed into action. I telephoned the Cathedral to get more information and then wrote to Dr Leggett.

September 21st 1970. Personal and confidential.
Dear Dr Leggett,

It would be so much easier to do nothing — just to walk away from the unpleasant scene. But I cannot. Principles have to be fought for and the principle with which I am now concerned is justice, or fair play.

After rejecting my adaption (the final version) of 'The Testimony of Light' without a hearing (refusing all explanation, discussion and willingness to alter things to please her) Helen Greaves wrote another play herself (which you know about) and now, after throwing over Peter Polak, whom she had asked to direct it, we hear that her play is to be staged in Guildford Cathedral.

The letter which I wrote to her on September 8th, she does not answer. And so I appeal to you. Can a play inspired by such a splendid book, be produced inside a church accompanied by so much animosity and injustice?

I enclose a copy of the letter which explains it all. I so hope you will use your influence to right these wrongs in the simple ways that I have asked for.

On the 27th he acknowledged this letter and said that he would write again after making some enquiries. On October 1st, I wrote again.

Thank you very much for your letter. Is there anything I could do now to help the situation?

Can we not all work together for the play — *whose* play does not matter — the *best* play . . . a joint play anonymously presented. . . ? and then for the University of the Spirit which could be such a Light in our midst? In haste.

On the same day I wrote again to Helen.

I hoped for your understanding, a response and a reconciliation. . . Is there anything more that I can do now to help us both out of this unhappy situation — to straighten and set things right?

Dr Leggett telephoned suggesting that we meet at the Royal Commonwealth Society on the 16th at 6.30 pm. Helen replied that the matter was now in the hands of the Vice-Chancellor of Surrey University.

17

I ARRIVED early, as I always do for appointments and, coming all the way from Guildford, he was punctual to the moment.

He knew me, of course, from that triumphant first reading and I recognised the little man standing in the crowd at the side of the room, quietly offering a thousand pounds.

His manner was easy and confident and he seemed delighted to be meeting. In the lift we talked familiarly at once and when he led us to two comfortable arm chairs and we sat down, I was surprised that such a busy man, dealing in weighty matters, could be so concerned and unhurried. It was a good start and this is my record of how it continued.

P.L.   Well, how do you think the world is going?

My notes do not give my answer to this vast opening question. They begin when he got down to business.

I am no judge of plays but there will be no need to read & compare scripts and that sort of thing. This must be decided on a much higher level.

I will put my cards on the table. Helen acknowledged that the idea of a play was yours but she has told me that her play has been written by a dramatist 'on the other side'. She wrote it in two weeks and was told that it is *this* play that is to be produced. My intuition and insights convince me that this is true.

(He expected this information to bowl me over . . . to silence me and settle the matter)

P.B.   Yes. Helen told us this and when I asked her *who* was writing it, she said that the name must remain a secret.

(He seemed surprised)

I am afraid that my intuition and spiritual insights are not developed so highly that I can take this claim on faith. I am still on the level where I must read the script in order to

241

decide whether it is a totally new play written by a great dramatist — or whether it is based on mine.

(He was, I think, a little shaken by this.)

P.L.   My idea is to have a meeting — the 3 of us — in Margaret's flat.

(I objected to this & he agreed to a neutral place — the Royal Commonwealth Society) And although I am Helen's friend, I would act as a sort of chairman.

P.B.   What would be the purpose of this meeting?

P.L.   A reconciliation.

P.B.   But I must read the script & Helen refuses to give it me. She says she could not trust it to me. I might copy it or run away with it. She must know that she only has to put a copy in the bank to copyright it.

P.L.   Oh no. We don't want anything like that — copyrights! This must be kept on a high level. At this meeting she could hand the script to you — with me as witness . . . etc.

P.B.   Alright. If she will give me the script in that way I will come to such a meeting. . .

P.L.   I don't want to read any of the correspondence — or know anything more about the matter. That is not necessary. We can keep it on a high level etc etc.

(Although he did not want to hear my story I forced a little of it on him, the months when I was working with Peter & keeping Helen informed.)

P.B.   . . . and she was full of blessing & love & encouragement. When she finally received the script she criticised certain scenes & words in a crude & tactless way, but praised it as a play & said it would act well. Then 3 days later, she suddenly changed. She raged at me over the telephone & then wrote me a horrible letter, contradicting what she first wrote. She had decided to write it herself & that was her way of getting me & my play out of the way.

(He listened — a little surprised I thought.)

P.L.   Of course you will keep that correspondence. It might be needed at a later date.

(He said this in a tone that sounded as if he wished I hadn't got it & he would prefer me *not* to keep it.)

He was in no hurry to go and, after a pause in the notes, they continue:

(I told him the story of John Ross & Paul Beard, the President).

P.B.   I am very concerned about that crowd of young people.

P.L.   It is Paul Beard that I am concerned about. How is it that he couldn't judge the man in the first place? What is that college like? Are they always having storms there?

P.B.   I don't think so, but I only came into it last year.

(We then got onto the subject of teachers — 'vehicles' as I have learnt to call them — who can never apply the teaching to themselves. Only a handful on this planet ever have. The Buddhas & the Jesus Christs)

P.L.   Joan Grant writes marvellous books. I have read them all & loved them. But when I met her I was disappointed & one of her sons told me that she was a most difficult woman to live with. Great composers have been two-sided also.

P.B.   Yes. Many artists of all sorts have been despicable characters — but they have not made such big claims as do these mediums.

(By that time he had lost all interest in the play & he went off shocked & shattered)

P.L.   You have given me a problem far worse & far more important than the other one, to reflect on, were his last words.

My notes end with these comments:

I found him pedantic & fussy & very confident & didactic. What he said he expected me to 'take'. "This is a very important matter — it must be settled on the highest level & I know that I am the one to be the mediator". He seemed to enjoy being dragged into it.

I felt that his life experience had been narrow. He seemed naieve — in both a worldly & a spiritual way.

He acknowledges that the idea of a play was mine. How could 'the other side' allow me to work night & day for 6 months only to take my idea, cast me away & do it themselves? I think this is utterly immoral behaviour — the 'other side' no better than 'this side'.

I could not believe that his simple plan to obtain the script could succeed but I underestimated his job, class and masculine power; stronger than the power of the persons on 'the other side'.

A date was fixed and although Helen refused to come to London, she agreed to see us in her house in Sussex. I went to Guildford where he met me at the station and we were driven off together in his official car. The journey took an hour. This was my chance to consolidate *my* power over *him*! — to undermine still more the efficacy of his intuition and his insights and to restore his common sense. He was a good liostener and by the time we arrived I had related quite a number of my life's adventures and recurring storms.

"You are a catalyst." was all he said.

"I am a protester."

Helen opened the door, unsmiling — grim. I still could not believe that she would meekly hand her script to me and when we gathered in her sitting room and the uncomfortable small talk went on and on and the air didn't lighten, I grew still more apprehensive. Then, suddenly he stopped it and brought us to the point. And I admired him then.

It seemed to have been planned. I was to hand my script to him — for him to read. But before I did this she demanded to see it and she went slowly through it to make sure that I had not altered anything to which she had objected. She then handed it back and I handed it to him. Then she handed hers to him. And, after a decent pause, he handed it to me. When this sombre ceremony was completed he rose — and we left. I was amazed to find that I was holding it.

Thanks to Dr Leggett, I won the first round in the struggle. But there was more agony than gladness in my victory that night. As I travelled home it burned in my bag.

If, after all my scepticism and near-blasphemous remarks, it *was* an original and better play than mine, I would have to fall upon my knees and, worm that I was, work humbly to promote this miraculous addition to the Shakespeare canon. I did not look at it in the train nor when I got home. I did not have the courage. But in the morning, feeling stronger, I picked it up, read — and exulted! But not for long.

The structure of the play was mine but every scene had been altered, the characters changed, a love affair been introduced for Frances and the dialogue was, largely, Helen's. If ever there was a travesty of the book — this was it. And I was determined that this play should never reach a stage and be given to the world.

When she handed it over, she told me that I must only keep it for three days and must not show it to anyone. I did not show it but I read bits to a friend. "Peg's Companion stuff" was all she said. And I kept it for a month to analyse and prove to Dr Leggett and the Group that their goddess had fallen; that like so many western teachers without temple training, she had used and then abused her gift.

In a two-part document, comparing the scripts line by line, I sought to prove two things — plagiarism and unfitness. In the first, I showed that the selection and reduction of passages were mine, in the second, the improper alterations and vulgarities.

I sent it to Dr Leggett. He studied it, accepted it and read it to the Group. Helen was not present. And, shocked and bewildered, they accepted it, too.

On December 11th I wrote to him. This extract starts with Point 3.

> This is to confirm the main points of our telephone talk yesterday and to add two more.
>
> 3.   For a better explanation of the sudden change on May 12th, I hope you will consult Bill once again whose opinion always seems unerring.
>
> 4.   When I finished that document and sent it off to you, it was as if the slate had been rubbed clean, as if the shock and hurt, the sense of bewilderment and isolation, were all swept finally away and, about a week later, a most powerful feeling came to me that my next action must be to approach Helen myself.
>
> When the right moment comes — after you and others have prepared the way by carrying down to her the message that will shock and heal at one and the same time — then I must go alone to her with love and, truly, a most deep desire for renewed friendship — for reconciliation.
>
> 5.   It pleased me to hear that the Group accepts the idea that the book must be carried forward into the theatre. And after the reconciliation, I want the whole Group to hear, discuss, judge and help to shape the final version of the play. (From now on I am going to stop calling it *my* play.)
>
> 6.   On May 16th, at the height of the storm, when I read the book at the World Spiritual Council AGM, I gave a short preliminary talk on the theatre and on the play of The Testimony. Here are my rough speaking notes. They will help you and the Group to understand how I view the theatre (and have viewed it all my life) — as a temple, for which I have been writing — that does not yet exist.
>
> 7.   About a fortnight ago, I happened to be seeing Lord Harewood. He is not only a very busy man but, as you may know, a very strung-up and agitated man. I asked him to give me an hour to read a unique and remarkable play and I went again the next day and read to him alone. Lady Harewood was unable to be there.
>
> For the first half he jumped about in his chair, lit cigarettes and stubbed them out, rattled the ash tray on the table and jingled keys in his pocket and, finally, jumped out of the chair and perched himself on the arm!
>
> I thought he was going to bolt from the room at any moment! Then, when I got to Frances' monologue, those wonderful passages — her confession of failure, finding her spiritual body, making her own new garment etc, he quietened down and by the end, was absolutely still. Healed.

Afterwards, he said, "This is not my sort of thing, not my subject — but it is a *very* interesting play". And he asked many questions and we talked about it for quite a long time — overrunning the hour which was to have been my limit.

If the play can carry Frances' message and heal such a man (who would never read the book), surely that is just what she wants?...

On December 17th, Helen wrote:

I am withdrawing completely, my play on the book, Testimony of Light. There will be no dramatized version of the book at all.

The Publishers (Churches Fellowship) have informed me also that no public reading from the book is allowed without their permission or my consent.

No play or dramatised version of the book can be published or performed without their permission or that of the author. The subject, therefore, is closed.

On the 20th I wrote to Dr Leggett.

She has withdrawn her play. I am afraid there has been a leak. That will make things harder... You said there would be an explosion if my document was divulged to her too soon. Shall we get it now? I attach a note giving Bill's explanation of the sudden change on May 12th... In haste and wishing you some rest and peace during these Christmas days.

Bill's interpretation

When Helen received the final version on May 8th she saw that it had come out effectively and would be a success in the theater. She was half pleased & half not. She criticised some parts but was prepared, in an ambivalent way, to continue the collaboration & advance the play.

Then, between the time that she spoke to Bill & the evening that I telephoned her, she became fully conscious of her *real* attitude & she decided to write her own play & get all the glamour. To justify this she had then to damn mine altogether — and me with it.

During the last weeks of work on the play, she was always saying, "You & Peter are going to be *made* by this". Glamour was on her mind. She had already received so much from the success of the book & it had gone to her head. She had to have it all. She did not know that I meant to present my play anonymously.

He replied:

No, there has been no leak; not, anyway, of the kind you suspected. . . But I did, of course, say a little, but only very little, when I spoke to her on the phone. And in a letter to me afterwards, she said:

"Forgive me if I was sharp on the telephone. . . Since then I have been thinking over the whole matter and have had a deep spiritual experience.

I am now resolved to withdraw the play and to leave the situation in higher hands and to await Direction. From now on I am letting go and letting God resolve this matter and shall not discuss it again."

What are required of us now are patience, forbearance and prayer. Greetings and best wishes for 1971.

The holiday season passed quietly. Then, Helen was shown my documents. Much later, I described what happened.

Dr L took up my case with the Group in a fair & splendid way & they accepted it & hoped for a reconciliation & settlement. But when the contrary happened, when a storm of unprecedented violence & viciousness broke on them all and the Group was disrupted, their goddess exposed as fallible, the 'great dramatist' laughed at; when their own spiritual progress was in jeopardy *then*, they hated *me*. I was 'the cause of it all' — 'the fly in the ointment'.

It did not matter that I was the injured party, that they had accepted that the book should be carried forward into the theatre — they wanted me, the outsider, pushed out of the way, silenced, forgotten, so that they could restore their tarnished idol & resume their cosy little corporate journey along the Path, their souls on the march again.

I was almost as much shocked by the behaviour of the Group as by that of Helen.

They were right. If I had not come with my vision of the theatre, with art, and forced them to acknowledge it, all this would not have happened. But since it had, they suffered all the pains of the addict when the drug is withdrawn — for they were addictions. The endless round of meetings and chasing and sitting at the feet of teachers.

In a scientific, mechanized, male civilisation in which the intellect has been enthroned and intuition and feeling repressed, people crave for sensation, excitement and escape and look for them in adventure, sport, sex, war and even crime and on the mountain slopes of spirituality, the New Age people, when I was one of them, strained for peak experiences.

But because their spirituality was so intellectual (they could not change their western skins) the peaks were seldom reached; the listening and the running and the reading were as far as they could get and these, in themselves, were beautiful and charged with the substance of the finest drugs.

On a lower level, too, the New Age movement was attractive. For the upper-class adherents, survivors of obsolete social patterns and mostly women, the groups were the equivalent of the old exclusive social circles, the meetings every night took the place of the dinner parties and the week-end courses, often in relinquished country mansions, were like faded repetitions of the once grand visits. When, unwittingly, I broke up that high powered group, I broke up a whole concatenation of forces.

Knights of the spiritual renaissance, as Sir George Trevelyan called it, they were noble, their passionate seeking far preferable to so much that went before, but they were not reborn immaculate.

. . . .

I bought a derelict cottage in the village of Castle Camps, near Saffron Walden and, on July 24th 1971, I scribbled to my mother:

> When I heard yesterday that the cottage was mine, I took a one-day holiday & went to Brighton. I had 2 lovely bathes & then slept on the beach. The sun came out & burnt my face. Don't you notice it?
>
> I have no special view — just fields at the back & old & pretty cottages in front — some with thatched roofs. There are 2 trees in the garden — an apple & a plum — & lots of weeds. Perhaps if I mow them down they will become a lawn! I love nettles — they are better than spinach. I am always pleased to see them in a garden. I will draw you a picture of the cottage.

I paid £1000 for it, obtained a Council grant and embarked, once again, upon building operations. It was so near London that I could travel down for the day to oversee the work and I visualised the time when I would travel up every week to see my mother.

The vision of her own move to the tent in the lovely grassy field had faded and her 'psychic people' had gone away and she was unhappy and discontented again. I scribbled:

> Couldn't you put up with this until I get into my cottage? then I will move you somewhere near me where I can see you every day.
> You are lonely — and bored. You cannot really make friends

here — just nurses — and you cannot paint any more... When you were young you never grumbled about anything — you were the most enduring, unselfish & heroic person I have ever known. Can't you use your deep & splendid stamina, your will, to overcome these little things & hold on until I can arrange something else.

Perhaps it is all this seething discontent that keeps your 'psychic people' away — can't you think about them & the lovely visions which they bring you? Let them take care of you. I will take care of you, too. I promise you that I will find somewhere that will calm & satisfy you. I will never abandon you.

At the culmination of her life and love she was caught in this dilemma. She was ready to go and wanted to but because of me, wanted to stay and, confused myself, I tried to help her to do both. I exhorted her to bring her 'psychic people' back, knowing that they could take her and at the same time, because her state was so piteous, promised that I would move her myself and begged her to be strong and patient. I didn't know how I ought to act — except as her double-talking advocate.

The unhappiness continued. Bedpans, commodes and wet sheets again filled her mind and blocked her way. Even money worries held her.

On September 10th (1970) I scribbled:

You *tried* sitting on a bedpan. We had a bet on it, don't you remember? and Matron struggled to help you but you had to give it up & I won my bet. But I still haven't received my sixpence!

No. *I* don't pay for this Home — the Artists Benevolent organization pays for it — as for leaving me your capital — you haven't any — I took it long ago! And blewed it in America!

I will bring some pads to lie on — and then at least you won't wake in the morning swimming in the ocean!

When you get to heaven you will not be helpless any more — you will walk & run & fly — & there aren't any bedpans there!

Her sense of humour was as lively as ever. I could still make her laugh and cheer her up. But the scripts got fewer. She could not always read them. On September 23rd, I wrote:

I bought these n-gowns at Marks & Spencer. The cheaper they are — the more lace! We couldn't afford plain ones! Grand & gaudy you are now! I shall bring my mending & sew while we talk.

When you sat on that bedpan at your birthday party I watched your face for the agony I was expecting & wondered what we

would do when you couldn't bear it another minute! I would have
had to clear the room while you rose!

I will find you somewhere to go — I promise you — I have lots of
ideas — but I must move first — try to forget your irritations &
think of something else — something funny — like knocking off
top hats!

The 'psychic people' will turn up at the critical moment & see
that you get through the gates of heaven!

And they turned up *now* — three months before the 'critical
moment' and talked to her and showed her the tent in the grassy
field again and, although she did not move at once and still
grumbled, she was concerned about the practicalities of life, when
she did. And on October 19th, I wrote:

Why bother about food? Just live on pills! made from seaweed out
of the ocean — one pill per meal — quite enough — & I'll bring you
treacle tart & bananas. What more will you want?!!! And there
may be some nettles growing round the tent door. They are very
nutritious — especially chewed up raw!!

And still I joked and still she laughed. That was the last thing I
wrote. She moved to her half-way home, the irritations of the
here-and-now ceased and I sat beside the tent talking to her as she
came and went, as she held me and then let me go.

On January 16th 1971, I wrote in my diary, 'found her much
feebler & near the end'. Three days later she recovered a little but,
after that, she was unconscious. I wanted so much to say good-bye
but I was afraid to speak in case, even now, I brought her back.

On the 22nd, I asked Matron if I should stay the night. "No" she
said firmly. "She might go on like this for days. I will telephone
you if there is any change."

At 3.40 the next morning, she let go of me and of herself. And I
felt that I should dress in white, like the Japanese, and wave as to a
soul released. About a week later, I woke in the night hearing her
call out my name and many times she has come back to me in
dreams, giving me strength and guidance.

.   .   .   .

Dr Martin Israel was Senior Lecturer in Pathology at one of the
teaching hospitals and later took Holy Orders. He was also a
mystic of great humility and integrity of character, leading a life
of detachment on the one hand, and active ministration on the

other. He seemed like a vehicle without a fault and as a star among the New Age lecturers, I followed him about.

At a week-end course on Mysticism, speaking hour after hour rapidly and in a monotonous tone, the teaching poured out of him and we listened, never bored, not hypnotised, but lit up and drawn up, in ravishment.

He was a member of the Group and, after several bitter and unhappy weeks, it was to him that they turned and, under his direction, met again. Catalysts can be useful to the righteous as well as to the graceless. But although the Group settled down again, my hammering went on. They never forgave me the downfall of their goddess and the spoiling of their lives.

And then a champion arose. I had met him once on the spiritual merry-go-round. He was a healer — and now I wrote to him.

Helen has grown even more disputatious and difficult and those surrounding her feel that she is quite unapproachable at present.

But, this does not mean that someone outside her Group — perhaps with a different power and approach — should not attempt to help her — and the situation. . . It is very fine of you to offer yourself in this very sad affair; agonising for Helen herself and sad that the play is blocked and cannot yet help the many who are in need. "People living on earth, the erudite, the cultured and clever minds, the devotional and religious minds, the uneducated, illiterate and closed minds, must all be reached. All need this knowledge."

Only the theatre will do this. Those words of Frances' were her mandate to me . . . and I pray and strive and wait now for the reconciliation which will release everything & see them realised.

And he replied:

I've given the matter much thought. . . It seems to me that there are 3 possible causes for Helen's blocking your play:

Cupidity — she would like to have the TV etc royalties. She did exhibit a sign of this when she asked the Churches Fellowship for royalties higher than she was already getting under agreement.

Spiritual pride — She might want to see her name attached to the play and not anyone else's.

Influence of the forces of evil. They would, of course, use either, or both, of the above.

If one of these is the cause — or all of them . . . then the only way to reach her is via the spirit, and this takes time to become effective. . .

I was never aware that the exercise of his healing power over Helen was effective but I was glad to have a new friend who wanted to help, not only Helen — but the play. No one else cared about it. Now that Dr Leggett had seen justice done, he was indifferent and Bill hated it, and always had. As I wrote later, "He took up a fair & objective attitude at the beginning but when Helen's play was written, he did not want me to challenge it. He wanted the whole thing to die down even if it meant that her play would be produced. But when I did, he bravely supported me — and held out the longest".

The publishers were the next to strike. They wrote to say that they 'gathered' that readings of my script had been given: that I must not give any more; that my play had been adapted from the book without their permission and that all copies must be 'destroyed' or 'kept completely confidential'. And I struck back:

Two readings of the first version were given at a special meeting in London in February 1970. . . No readings of the final version have been given *whatsoever — anywhere*.

Helen Greaves gave me permission to adapt the book. She told me . . . that she had settled the matter of the publishers' permission and the fact that the General Secretary was present at the first reading, approved the whole project and telephoned me afterwards about religious broadcasting — surely proved this?

You demand that I 'destroy all copies' of the play or, 'keep them completely confidential'. The former course has about it the rather nasty odour of book-burning associated with Hitler's Germany. The latter is just non-sensical. How do you know that you are not ordering the destruction of a masterpiece and future vehicle of the spirit?

You invite me to come and discuss the matter. But your letter leaves nothing to discuss. What I do ask, however, is that I may meet the person who has conveyed the false information. . .

The bishops and other notables, their names massed on your notepaper, are ill served, first by such an error and then by such ignorance and blindness.

I ignored the feeble, senseless answer.

Soon afterwards, Bill and I attended another conference in the country and during the week-end, we met a Mrs Pettit, the woman who had typed the first script of the book and then Helen's play. When Bill told her the full story of what had happened since, she listened eagerly.

I had asked Bill to give a healing to a friend of mine who lived in the same district and at the end of the course, Edith sent her car and we left together for her house.

It was a good week-end — the lectures and the healing. But the aftermath was appalling. A few days later, Bill wrote:

I do want to tell you what a lot of trouble I have had about the conference, the Churches Fellowship and Iona.

Mrs Pettit has apparently told Helen that I was always with you, 'in your pocket', that we left hurriedly during a lecture & went off in a taxi! I have refuted these statements but mud once thrown sticks or at least smears.

The effect on the Group has been bad & somehow I must save the situation because the Group is *invaluable* to all of us.

Also, Helen has been told that you had said that she was on the 'dark side' and that I had been supporting you... I must do all in my power to get her back happily into the Group & therefore it is important that no one should report on our meeting each other. She says that 'many people' have been ringing her up to tell her that I was with you at the conference... So, don't be surprised if for awhile you get no invitation to come to us — or to meet in town.

I hope we shall soon be able to forget all this trouble . . . you know me well enough to know I have not said anything to let you down. With my love.

Mrs Pettit had betrayed us. I was now separated from my venerable and staunch companion, the invitation to read from the book in Iona had been cancelled, the Churches Fellowship had proscribed me, the Group was against me and countless unseen, unknown tellers of vindictive tales surrounded me. Even Peter had been dragged into the dance of hate.

On April 10th, I wrote to him.

This nasty affair goes on. Just when I think it has subsided & I am able to forget it, I receive another knock on the head. . .

Accusations, demands, even scandals — all distorted & inaccurate are flung round viciously & hurtfully. Human nature as seen in these so-called spiritual circles seems no better — & is perhaps worse — than in more ordinary places.

My only relief is to have withdrawn to the country where I am among simple, unpretentious people. The air I breathe is purer in every way.

I know that you continue to have your difficulties too. (He was still out of work). I should not grumble. But whatever you may have been told — I have *not* been talking round.

Time passed and when I heard that Bill had visited my friend, Edith, I wrote a letter which I never sent.

I have been waiting & waiting for you to write & tell me that you can see me again — that Helen & the Group are now satisfied with this further turn of the screw upon the sacrificial victim, that the private detectives have been withdrawn & that your vision has cleared & you are once again master in your own house.

It is not pleasant to be cast suddenly away from the friend whom one trusted, & called 'the fly in the ointment'. And now comes the shock of hearing that you have called upon & been entertained by my friend, Edith. She, whose visiting you made one of your reasons for breaking with me.

There seems no end to the double-crossing & unkindness emanating from the Group. . . Am I to be finally disillusioned by you, too — who likewise 'tread the Path' & claim high spirituality?

Instead, on August 5th, I wrote to him and to his wife, Pat.

It is many months since I last heard from you and all the time I have been labouring on this cottage . . . & I am beginning to enjoy the fruits, the pleasure of inviting people to stay and — the fruits & vegetables springing up in the garden.

You were once keen to come here. I hope you still are & that you will both come & stay now? I hear that you both visited my friend, Edith.

Is it true that you — Bill — are not too well? I hope the rumour has reached me wrongly.

They did not reply but, Mrs Pettit reappeared with a long chatty letter and I realised that she had been impulsive and unwise after that week-end, but not a deliberate betrayer. And I travelled down to the country to see her.

After I had shown her Bill's letter containing the distortions and blown-up charges concerning her and us, and told her of the consequences, she naturally wanted to write to him. I hoped that when she did she would put in a word for me.

She sent me a copy of her letter.

I have only JUST learnt of the havoc I caused when, rather naievely but with good intent, I rang Helen. . .

After such an uplifting week-end I thought, when I got home, now 'what would Frances wish me to do'? And I picked up the telephone. I hoped Helen would *welcome* a reconciliation. I

suggested that she wrote to P to wish her joy in her new home and
to offer condolences on her bereavement.

I was shocked and disappointed at the reaction, for I believe that
those who talk and write about the LIGHT should make some
attempt to LIVE in it! What a pity it is that wonderful truths get
sullied at the human and personal level. . .

A few days later, she wrote to me.

Mr and Mrs Blewett have been on the phone — overwhelmed. . .
He said, 'reconciliation is the most wonderful, beautiful thing in
the world'. They have been through hell . . . and he says he'll never
be the same again in this world.

Did you know he has cancer of the jaw . . . please send healing
thoughts to both of them. I know you will. As for that other one . . .
words fail me . . . she'll pay . . . someday.

And I replied:

I am pleased that you wrote to Bill. . . But I am disappointed & I
will tell you quite bluntly why.

You, the erstwhile betrayer, have put yourself right with them.
You have had your reconciliation — 'the most wonderful,
beautiful thing in the world'. But you didn't do anything to help
me. They poured out their sufferings to you and you were
moved. . . If any consideration had been given to mine, to what
they, in addition to Helen & so many others, have done to me they
would have telephoned me as well & we would have had the
reconciliation which, as I told you, I have so wanted all these
months, tried for, but had refused. I am still 'the fly in the ointment', my hurt ignored.

I ended:

I am what I am, the hated, the outsider, 'the cause of it all' — just
because I fell in love with Frances' book, saw its value to the world
as a play & dedicated my whole self to it.

Because you are anxious only to help & heal I have given you my
point of view, however egotistical. But in doing so, at least I make
no claims to high spirituality at one and the same time!!!

Her reply was wise — but stinging.

I see your point of view only too clearly — but it all reads like
Dennis Wheatley!!

I had hoped you would have had compassion for a dying old
gentleman. They were rushing off to the hospital when they

phoned me . . . even now you may find there is a letter on the mat. If not — cannot you rise above it? . . .

If only you COULD, you could find the whole affair had had an ennobling effect upon you — lifting you in a tremendous leap, higher on the Path. For it is through *people* that God works, and it is not our experiences that matter — but what we DO with them.

Mr Blewett said on the phone "I wouldn't have been without the experience of these last months — despite the pain". Cannot you look upon it in the same way. Even H may have had her own persona (mask) shown to her — everyone may have had important lessons to learn.

Don't feel hurt and shut out STILL — for this is very immature — you have the depth of character that should be able to sift, keep — and reject the rest as unworthy and *finished*. . .

I wasn't trying to put myself 'right with anyone'. I've spent a lifetime trying to overcome the slights & insults heaped upon me. . . We all have a blueprint before birth — we know our mission, but forget it until it comes like this — in intuitive flashes. Use it, Philippa, gold in the fire. You CAN — many wouldn't or couldn't.

I was too "immature" to make the 'leap' and in no state to be stung any more, when I replied.

You said that you wanted to teach wherever you could find a pupil. Now that you have found a sinner, or backslider, you can preach — which is better. As a detached critic I can praise your sermon, but as the recipient I find serious flaws in it.

First, the Dennis Wheatley opening. I have never read anything of this writer's work but I sense that the comparison is unflattering and in a sermon I am sure that it goes beyond the accepted canon of what can be juxtaposed with theological material.

Because you are impulsive by nature with a tendency to rush in too quickly, without enough thought & knowledge of the subject, the sermon is full of false charges & platitudinous, school-teachery admonitions & exhortations . . . and the tone as much as the contents provokes an extreme reaction. Therefore, instead of healing & helping, you make things worse, so that now I have to rise above the sermon, too! What a load of failings I have to throw off before I can 'take off'!!!

You say you understood my point of view 'only too clearly'. I am glad. I meant you to . . . my disappointment was that you ignored it. . . It would have been so easy for you to act as a mediator & I thought I had good reason for assuming that you would.

I was told that Bill had *had* cancer of the jaw. but that it was cured — and I rejoiced. How can you, how dare you, accuse me of lack of compassion when I have had him & his illness in my thoughts and prayers ever since the day that we were so brusquely parted.

And now that I know that he is dying — isn't my desire for a reconciliation even more urgent? "No." you will say again. "You must rise above the desire". This is high talk, indeed, and a holier-than-thou attitude is one of the worst dangers along the Path. . .

And so, rising above all this (!) I end and sign my name most warmly.

Soon afterwards, I wrote to Bill again.

First, let me say how grieved I am to hear that the cancer is not yet cured. This is a new blow . . . which I know you will have accepted with your usual calm. . . You have treated so many cancer patients and now the healer has to heal himself.

I referred to Mrs Pettit's innocence and reconciliation with him — and went on:

The months of estrangement and silence have caused me great pain. Are you still so menaced that a friendly word or gesture is still impossible? It all seems so senseless & wrong, beyond all rational understanding. The experiences of the last two years are valuable, of course — but shocking.

I do not know how much your general health is affected and what your life is like now, but if enough water has passed under the bridge for some sort of reconciliation to be possible — I would be so happy.

I have accepted my role as scapegoat. It is an archetypal and not ignoble one. . .

Pat replied, telling me that Bill's jaw was again clear of the cancer but that the treatments had affected his general health. And went on:

Bill wants me to say that he feels no ill-will towards you but when you said that Helen was on the dark side and then it became clear to him that you were against the whole Group as if it were *evil*, he had to decide whether to leave the Group or give up your friendship.

I replied saying how thankful I was that he had been pronounced clear of the cancer again — and went on:

The new shock of your letter makes me feel so hopeless & weary and my first reaction was to be silent — to just ignore this fresh accusation & reason for our estrangement . . . but I suppose I must defend myself once more.

I have only been 'against the Group' because the Group was

against me — and not against *all* of them, for some are fine, like Bill himself and Martin and Peter Leggett. But if that is what he came to think — why didn't he have it out with me? Not condemn me unheard? So unlike him.

Nor did I ever say that H was 'on the dark side'. I do not like and never use occult language of that sort . . . to have still more injustice heaped upon me by Bill & you, once my best friends (& still most dear to me) is the hardest thing of all. Et tu Brute.

Soon after that, he died. I wrote expressing sorrow and then telephoned to ask about the funeral. An angry, tragic voice came through. If I had not dragged him into the John Ross affair and then into the preposterous business of my play, he would be alive and well today. *I* had caused Bill's death, I heard her say.

Helen's hate had spread to nearly everyone I knew, reached into everything I touched and every place I went to and it was time that I did something to end it.

I waited for an opportunity to speak to Dr Martin Israel. And it soon came. I was taken, unexpectedly, to a private meeting and after his talk, when the devotees crowding round him had, one by one, melted away, I remained.

"What can I do", I asked him, "to break out of the darkness in which for months I have been living? Shall I go to her in the country, go with my love — and ask for hers — plead with her for the reconciliation which will heal us both?"

"No", he answered. "*We* are trying to heal her. It would be no use your going. And she would not see you." He was a shy man and he always looked on the floor when speaking, but at that moment he looked up — straight at me.

"Helen is a wonderful person but she has gone very wrong over this. But I am supporting you". And a wave of healing power came to me and encompassed me, the darkness lifted and as I rose above it all, the whole amassment of hurt and unhappiness dissolved and left me. He did what I couldn't do for myself.

A year later I wrote to Helen, and quoting Bill's words, 'a reconciliation is the most beautiful, wonderful thing in the world', asked "dear Helen, are we not together capable of willing such a thing?"

She replied saying that she no longer felt any animosity towards me. The tone of the letter was cold and she would not see me but — it was enough. I was out in the light, happy in my cottage and working on a new play.

I had met three vehicles upon the road and seen each carry forward some beautiful teaching — and then collapse.

18

OF THE MANY hundreds of New Age communities, centres, groups and organizations, only three that I knew of at this time showed any concern for, or even awareness of, the dimension of art in society.

The Findhorn Community in Scotland, awarded an importance to the drama which was unique; under Sir George Trevelyan at Attingham College, poetry and play readings were regularly included in the esoteric courses; and the World Spiritual Council, with Sir Adrian Boult as president of the British Sec tion, wrote, in clause 3 of their official pronouncement: "The WSC recognises that the creative artist or thinker is as much a channel for divine inspiration as the seer or mystic".

Apart from these, the New Age people were as philistine as the rest of the population. In fact, their passionate spirituality seemed to enfeeble and disbalance their other sensibilities, as I learnt so painfully when I dared to turn one of their holy books into a play.

Although my reading of 'The Testimony' at Findhorn had been stopped by Helen, I went there on a 10-day course during the summer of 1972 and found a talented drama company, already planning to build a theatre, and I was so impressed by their work that I left them a script of my epic drama and they had since been working on some of the scenes.

Here, in deep spiritual soil the seeds of art had been planted and watered and were springing up and when my new play was finished, it was here that I sent it, with a letter to the American director — dated February 16th 1973.

> If you like it and would like to produce it, then this could be the beginning of really ambitious New Age drama — there is time to prepare it for the Edinburgh Fringe in August. . .
> But, there is a question. *Should* it be launched by a New Age Centre — the Alternative Theatre — or forced straight into the existing theatre to be battered and bludgeoned, succeed or fail?

259

Guidance will decide for you and I wait to hear. . . And so, as the writing pressure is lifted, the pressure to launch it takes its place! There is no rest — nor do we want it. . .

That was my first move, but I was nervous of amateurs and it was not my intention to present it only to the converted, clapping and kissing in agreable suburbs but, at a time of national decline and darkness, to fling it, like a celestial rocket, into the dirt and poverty of the market place. Findhorn would just have been the easy way of edging it out into position. But it was not to be easy like that as the director soon informed me.

Congratulations on 'The Journey'. It's a monumental piece of work of which you should be proud. Such a massive theme, and yet treated with so much concrete clarity & imagination. . . But as far as Findhorn is concerned, it doesn't look as if *anything* more is going to be produced here. . . All the attention is being removed from form level & we are being forced to turn within & examine ourselves & our spiritual purpose in the universal plan. . . This is right for too much emphasis has been put into 'showing off' Findhorn. . .

In any event, we should never be able to produce your play at our present level of development . . . not enough actors (even doubling roles) , the cost would be immense to do the play justice. . . I have a vision of it being produced in a *very big way* — full-scale elaborate production with magnificent sets & lighting & costumes — those mountain scenes. . . I can even see it as a film — perhaps even more so. Maybe I will be involved in a production of it somewhere — but not at Findhorn. I may not be at Findhorn much longer. Many of the Americans are moving out. There will be centres formed & much work to do in America.

I hope this letter does not depress you. In spite of the changes I feel very positive about everything, & this includes your play.

It was all gone! all the lovely growing plants trampled back into the ground, their first blooms condemned as 'showing off'.

I began sending it to managements and agents. I had done this twice before so uselessly but now I was hardened and I had friends and followers — and a play with an apocalyptic message.

'The Journey', re-written in contemporary terms, is the old old allegorical journey of myth, literature and religion which has been variously described as the journey of the soul through Matter and its return to the Source; as the journey down into the dark of the Unconscious and then up into the Light; as the search for the Treasure, for the Higher Self — God.

If the tales and images of the past are manifold and the travellers have all been men, now, as western civilisation breaks up in discord and bewilderment and the ground is cleared for renewal, a girl sets out.

From scene to scene, through outer turmoil and inner darkness, facing tests and trials, failing, falling, but seeing what she has to see and knowing what she has to know, she goes on and on until the journey ends where it began — at the source of Light and Love and with a vision of the New Age.

With the fusion and extension of inner and outer experience the action of the play moves upon a level at once real and surreal, at once here and now — beyond and always. It is my journey — and the journey of us all.

I had failed before but now I believed that things had changed, that the world had reached the threshold of the new age, that the cultural sector of society should be the first to sense this and that my work would, at last be understood and wanted. But I was wrong again.

Whether within the confines of one's own mind or within those of a minority movement, one always feels one's visions to be universal and the movement bigger than it really is and one misreads, or is completely blind, to the realities of the world outside, naievely flinging out ideas and ideals which have not yet arrived.

The play was read and analysed, always 'with great interest', compared (not always flatteringly) with 'The Pilgrim's Progress' and 'Peer Gynt', even praised sometimes in a bemused way but with no sense of its significance. The readers were so aimiable and well-wishing but it was social realism that they still wanted. And the fringe theatres were too small.

Only one agent was *not* so interested and aimiable and our telephone exchanges were so comic that I wrote them down afterwards and sent them to the New Age friend, a professional, who had recommended her.

Me.   I would like to send you a new play.
Agent. (With a roar) I only take professional authors.
Me.   I am a professional.
Agent. (Roaring still louder) Well, I have 60 top authors on my books already, more than any other agent — and I can't take on any more. *They* are all *looking* for authors — *I* am trying to get rid of them. The only script I could consider now would be a masterpiece. What plays have you had

	produced . . . where . . . when . . . Watergate! That was ten years ago. . . ? What have you done since?
Me.	I stopped writing for fifteen years to try to lift the level of my work.
	(Ominous silence)
Agent.	Commercialism means nothing to me. It is the quality of the play that counts with me. How many characters are in your play?
Me.	There are three principal characters and. . .
Agent.	Principal characters don't mean a thing. The smallest part actor gets £30 a week today and a play costs £10,000 to put on. No one will even look at it if it isn't economic. It would be an absolute waste of time to send me your script.
Me.	I don't mean to. But I could send you a synopsis or come to see you.
Agent.	(Still roaring) I can't see anyone or read anything. I went to an opening at Brighton last night. I am going to another tonight. I am busier than anybody else. It is unfair to a play to see the author first and as for a synopsis — that is even worse.
Me.	Then if you don't want to read the script or a synopsis and you don't even want to hear about it — how are you ever going to know if it is a masterpiece. . . ?
Agent.	(Nearly exploding) Well, what is it about?
Me.	It is a journey play — a Peer Gynt type of play.
Agent.	My God! You'd better buy 'Contact' and look for another agent.

And I commented to my friend:

Poor thing! How much does she reflect the contemporary theatre?
What a test of the climate! I was sometime recovering from her
aggressiveness, sheer rudeness — & her voice. She is obviously a
very successful agent. But even if she ever stooped to take me on
her books, I would be terrified to get into her clutches!

I didn't know how important that awful conversation would
one day be to me. In a long letter, my friend replied:

Yes. She is a successful agent but more like the American ones —
aggressive, noisy & rude. Over there, playwrights & actors believe
in the 'hard sell' & personal contact. . . It is a marvel to me that
they still manage to remain kind & warm-hearted people . . . they
have trained their emotional bodies to withstand these rough
assaults on their sensitivity. . . Try not to let yourself be hurt by this

— nothing can touch the real you, it is only the personality that feels the hurt. . .

I was not hurt — only made finally aware that nothing had changed and that the new play was as alien to its time and place as the others and I was more determined than ever to challenge the cultural bans and overcome the commercial ones — and launch it upon London. And an ally arrived, thundering every week in the Observer, powerless to help me but wonderful to listen to.

Robert Brustein, Dean of the Drama School at Yale University, spent nine months in England at this time, as guest critic. In a full-page article he wrote:

> Mainstream English drama is still anchored, to a greater or less extent, in social-realistic and even naturalistic, techniques . . . the new plays reek with sentimentality about the working class, excessive literalism, over insistence on the grime and squalor of industrial cities — and stale didacticism . . . the most interesting playwrights in other parts of the world have long since abandoned realism as a viable form of serious theatrical writing . . . by contrast English playwrights, with certain exceptions, are virtually indifferent to interior journeys and metaphysical investigations. . . If the theatre is to survive it will not be by throwing back a photographic reality at the spectator. . .

And in another, before he left:

> From all outward appearances the London theatre would seem to be in a state of flourishing health. Plays continue to pour into the theatres . . . and audiences flock to them with eagerness and anticipation. . . But after 9 months, I am gnawed by a suspicion that everything is not . . . as it appears on the surface. Ultimately a nation's art is judged not quantitatively but qualitatively and . . . to entertain the spectator becomes of less moment than to stretch his mind, engage his emotions & challenge his imagination. . .
>
> Is the British theatre really serious? Does it aspire not only to amuse but to create seminal works of art? To judge from the past season . . . transvestite revues, over-produced American musicals, superficial sex comedies, star-studded revivals and arthritic soap operas . . . no amount of critical cheerleading can conceal the fact that something is wrong . . . the serious play has virtually disappeared.
>
> The best modern theatres of Europe . . . have always functioned not as mirrors, reflecting the taste of the audience but as lamps lighting the way to new directions. . .

The play had now been read at Attingham, and found 'gripping' and Sir George's secretary wrote to propose a date for me to read it there but when she went on to express her views on the crisis at Findhorn (the two centres were closely linked) and to criticise the director, I rushed to his defence and into more polemics.

You say 'it is important not to condemn'. But who has condemned Findhorn? Eddie has not — and nor have I. He is a most loyal member of the community, supporting all the changes. . . In defending him, I now feel obliged to take up the whole subject of art and spirituality, with you. . .

You are so wise, yet you seem to be committing the old old sin of reducing art to a secondary category. You assume that 'turning within' and 'significant work' can only be done apart from art, when the artist has been pushed aside (crucified) to wait 'until the community expands again.' You separate and then dispose, in an arbitrarily chosen order, the two divine ways. . . Yet the artist is a priest, Truth seeking, and when this is truly understood there will be no need to set him aside until the self-elected 'higher' priests are ready to call him back.

Findhorn has talked about developing the arts for a long time & splendid beginnings were made and, as recently as last winter they were told, "the performing arts will play the most significant role in the new programme". And artists were attracted. Is it surprising then, that with the sudden reversal of all this, they are disappointed? And so when you say, ". . . poor Eddie . . . he minds too much . . . bless him . . . the fruits . . . we must all learn. . ." I find it painful.

Religion and art were once *one* — a whole — and the New Age will restore them to each other. In the meantime, we, who understand this, must work towards it, not go on tearing them asunder.

As for me, all my life the world has rejected me as an artist and now Findhorn does, too. Where, oh where, can I lay my head? . . .
PS. The play is now going out into the dark cruel world! . . .

In April, 1973, I gave the first reading at a conference of the World Spiritual Council and it was well received. Afterwards, I was told that a woman who had come in a near-suicidal state had gone away healed by the power of the drama and the recurring words — 'go on'.

Then, revelation came — and propulsion.

In the three years since I had bought the cottage I had worked on the garden and made it very attractive and I loved the place, but I did not cling to it, in fact, when the play was finished, I was bored with it and as I needed to be in London and could not afford two homes, I didn't know what to do. Then, waking early one morning, I did. Like an order, the answer came.

"Sell the cottage and you will have the money to produce the play yourself." When I telephoned the agent, I knew that house prices had risen, but I didn't know by how much.

"If you decide to sell" he said, "we will start by asking £11,500 but you must be satisfied if you only receive £10,000".

The very sum that that awful woman had told me would be needed! And three days later it was sold at the full asking price. The gods wanted it — and had opened the way!

I sold my old car, my last pieces of good furniture, even books that I didn't really need — and stored what was left. I stripped myself for the ultimate contest, and put £12,000 into the bank. I moved to a room in London and now approached the theatre as a backer, with big money — and a heaven-favoured play.

I soon learnt all about the hire of theatres and within a few weeks, the one I wanted most, the Round House, accepted the play and offered me alternative bookings. But, at the same time, Sir George wrote, suggesting that I send it to Coventry Cathedral.

When the new Cathedral opened in 1962, E. Martin Browne became the first drama director, producing the work of T. S. Eliot and other poets and establishing a reputation there for great religious drama. And when my script was accepted and the Round House advised me to open the play there, I moved to Coventry.

Sadly, when I arrived in 1974, Cathedral drama had declined and the director was young and inexperienced. We worked together on the script but, as we overcame the technical and local problems, others appeared and when the time came for casting the play, the difficulties seemed finally insuperable.

"I can't do it" he cried despairingly. "You must find another company. There are lots of good ones in Warwickshire. Let one of them do it and bring it into the Cathedral."

I went straight to the Criterion, a very good Coventry company with an experienced director, who agreed to do it — but not in the Cathedral. He hated it and wanted to take it to the Edinburgh Festival and I went there, booked a hall and returned with the good news. But when he put it to his company, not enough of them could be persuaded to commit themselves to three weeks away during the summer holidays. Their children came first and I returned to London, after more than a year wasted, and booked a 4-week run at the Round House for April 1976. This gave me 6 months to organize the production.

I lodged with a friend in Kingston, catered for myself and paid her £5 a week for my room. I was living on my annuity of £2 a week, the mortgage payments from the sale of my mother's house in Harrogate, and half a state pension (I had never been able to pay the full contributions). I had not touched the cottage money which, out at interest, now amounted to nearly £15,000. My finances seemed altogether sound and I went to a solicitor to discuss the formation of a company.

I sent scripts to top directors and their agents — not as a beggar but as a benefactor which, in my naievety, I believed I was. As before, it was read 'with interest', even praised and the agents sometimes held out hopes. One famous figure found the play 'interesting and demanding' but said his work now was all in the political field. A veteran of the Shakespearean stage liked it 'tremendously' but said it would be beyond his powers to do.

I went through them all, booked up and riding high and learnt that this golden group moved within a closed circle, no larger than the current trend, from which they could not break out — and they did not want to; young and old chasing the smash-hit, the spectacular, the pathological or straining for new interpretations. And the folly fed upon itself. I was not a benefactor! I was trying to buy and benefit where my gift and my money were not wanted. Peter Polak had left the luckless scene to sell insurance.

I advertised. The unknown, the untried, the out-of-work tramping the streets, applied. They did not understand the play, or like it particularly, but they were desperate to do it. I was so inexperienced myself that I could not, and dare not, choose and the Round House would not give me a contract until I did. And then, I found someone, in the small fringe theatre in Islington — the King's Head. He was experienced, successful with a sympathetic personality and appreciation of the New Age teaching. But, he was rehearsing then and could not say when he would be free.

I had to go on searching and when a young man wrote from Bristol, fresh out of the Old Vic School, with good reports, I sent him the script. When he returned it, a few days later, plotted out as he would direct it and he came to London and we talked, I was impressed by his abilities and told him that I would give him a definite answer as soon possible. I interviewed several others and then when he put pressure on me and the Round House did, too, I telephoned to Bristol — and engaged him. An hour later, the man from the King's Head rang to say that he was free.

I could have telephoned to Bristol again, there was nothing in writing and, in that short time, I could not have damaged him. I was sure that the King's Head director was better and I liked him better, but I could not do it. And from that moment everything went wrong.

A man would have done it, thought only of the play and thrown him over. I thought of him. At the other end of the telephone, I could see and feel his disappointment, if I had.

It was not feminine intuition, *that* was pulling hard the other way, but a feminine quality — feeling for the *other* — which paralysed me. And which was right at that moment? Both? The question is unanswerable.

Should the bold, often ruthless and cruel, but inventive and achieving character of man persist uncurbed? Should the tender, often enfeebling, sensibility of woman persist unchanged? Or, in a working marriage, should they stiffen and moderate each other and thereby lose, in each, a degree of what is basic and essential? Are their two natures absolutes and opposites which may only be reconciled or, could they dance unchanged and be transcended? If I did then what was right and good — it was weak and foolish.

At the beginning of December (1975), at a solemn, rather frightening little ceremony, with my solicitor beside me, on behalf of Aphelion Productions Ltd, I signed the Round House contract. I was now London management!

Afterwards, I wrote to Ann Todd, the film star, who had asked to read the play — and was herself a 'seeker'.

> For several years I have been discussing with Sir George Trevelyan and others, the possibility of forming a centre for the production of New Age drama and it is hoped that this company may become just such a focal point when, the ground cleared for renewal, a great flowering of the arts upon a new level may be expected.
>
> 'The Journey' is only a beginning. We hope that it's showing will bring out submerged work and inspire the new.

When he became director, John Baliol (his stage name) had mastered the structure of the play and the technicalities and decided on the method he would employ to produce it, but he did not understand its inner meaning — and I did not expect him to. I had to teach him and Sir George came to London for the week-end to help instruct him.

I had already engaged a production manager, Nigel Wilson, who had worked at the Royal Court Theatre, and a designer, Anne-Marie Schone, a talented German girl who had worked for the English National Opera Company, both recommended — and my team was now complete.

It is the job of a production manager to order, engage, over-see and co-ordinate everything technical and, above all, to control spending. When I engaged Nigel, he assured me that the backing was amply sufficient (I always talked about a mysterious 'backer', my disembodied partner!) but, due to inflation, between the time of booking the Round House and the time that the contract was signed, the rent went up from £1800 a week to £2100. We looked for a cheaper theatre but soon gave up the search as fruitless and although he still assured me that his budget could contain the increase, I cut the run from four weeks to three. That was the first financial set-back and disappointment.

The next came with the casting. For humanitarian and financial reasons I wanted to engage young, unknown actors at minimum salaries. But just as I had found it so hard to choose an unknown director, so John could not choose actors from auditions — and he did not want to. He demanded stars. Star performances and glamour for himself — and star salaries. Nigel's budget jumped — but he still showed no concern.

At the same time, the composer, a dear friend of mine, auditioned a young clarinettist but finding him not good enough for her music, dismissed him. He went away believing that he had been engaged and when he found he wasn't, the Musicians Union came down on me. That was the first row. She chose a well-known musician at double the salary. And the budget jumped again.

By January the casting was completed and contracts were signed — 14 actors and 2 juveniles, with Angela Pleasance in the leading role. And John moved to London.

A few weeks later, finding the play so onerous, he demanded an assistant and Nigel supported him. When I resisted, he threatened to walk out and although I knew this was only bluff, and illegal, I was afraid to thwart him — and gave way.

Soon after that, Anne-Marie complained that she was over-whelmed by the number of costumes needed for the many doubling parts, and must also have an assistant. Again, Nigel agreed. When I stood firm, this time, her manner changed. She did not want to show me her model of the set and when I insisted and went to her flat, I found them all there, ranged round her, hostile — and she got her assistant.

And lastly, Nigel found himself so over-stretched that he had to bring his girl-friend in to help him.

"But what about the budget?" I protested every time. "When they signed their contracts they knew what they had to do. They were told about our situation. They know we're not big-time management."

"You asked for a first-class production — and we're giving it you. It's a big play and we can't take any risks", he came back at me every time. And when we met every week at the accountants, his figures always appeared satisfactory — the future always seemed alright.

So why did I fight them? Their demands, the heavy spending on props and costumes, construction and expenses were understandable. They were artists wanting perfection for their work. And I wanted it, too. The money was there — so what was wrong? Why did they so upset me?

I came from another world and another class; I was a woman, inexperienced and easy, with money to hand out and they were grabbing all they could — not to exalt the play but to get glamour for themselves and give jobs to their friends. Yet they were only doing what came natural. They were what they ate and drank, what they loved and breathed — clever, qualified and able children of a pernicious system.

As John reached for artistic autonomy, Nigel for administrative power and Anne-Marie for unlimited scope and freedom, I was in their way, the enemy, and I felt that I had delivered my money and my play, not into the hands of lovely brother-sister artists, but into evil ones. And this production struggle was an extra scene, the prologue to the play. I was the 'Girl' in the drama, travelling through yet another blazing room of hell.

Before we went into rehearsal, the enmity grew so intense that I called John and Nigel to a meeting in the office of the junior solicitor, into whose hands my affairs had now been passed.

They were there before me and sat surly when I entered. The solicitor was bright but useless, if anything, leaning to their side and I knew that unless I could lift us out of the abyss — the play would never open.

"We have talked but settled nothing", I said at last. "Are we going to go away just as we came, to work on a journey play, containing themes of one-ness and 'a new way' and next week face the actors — hating each other?" I remember stopping then, to screw up my courage. "Can't we do what we are doing, in a better way — can't we *love* each other?"

I said it, heard myself saying it — the word they thought pious and ridiculous and I looked at their blank faces. I stayed behind to speak to the solicitor. They left in silence. And that outrageous appeal saved us — and saved the play. Their stubborn front broke and the air improved around me.

"Why the hell did you engage that bastard?" Nigel shouted down the telephone, in a friendly talk, a few days later. And John could smile at me and be polite. The actors assembled in a rehearsal room in Pimlico and the pressures carried us along until the next crisis.

And now the gods intervened again. The trustees wrote to say that I was now the last beneficiary of the Burrell Trust and to save themselves any more trouble they would like to buy me out with a payment of £800. At the same time, the purchasers of my mother's house informed me that they were now in a position to pay off the last £500 of the mortgage. And I flung these monies from heaven into the maelstrom.

My income was reduced to half a state pension. I couldn't take the train from Kingston to London but, with a free pass, spent three hours a day travelling on the bus, plus a long walk from the bus-stop to the house.

I carried sandwiches about and when I had to eat with others, chose a bowl of soup. It made me laugh to see myself living on £3 a week (after I had paid my rent), while writing cheques for hundreds every day and supporting in affluence, all the people round me!

Peter Brook's production of 'The IK', brought from Paris, was now running at the Round House but, in spite of the extragavant publicity and all the money lavished on it, was failing and we heard that the last fortnight of the run had been cancelled. This meant that the theatre would be 'dark' before we opened, which was a pity as one show always helps to publicise the next.

John at once asked if he could have 3 extra days for 'getting in' and rehearsing on the set and realising the enormous advantages of this, I cheerfully paid the extra £1000 — provided so fortuitously by the cashing of my assets.

"Getting in" to a theatre always starts at midnight when the last show has 'got out', or when the hiring legally begins. We 'got in' at midnight on March 25th (1976) and the next morning I received a bill for more than £1000, the all-night, double-time labour charge for the Round House stage hands. Nigel had over-looked this item in his budget which had to be paid before we opened.

John and Nigel had received their fees in instalments but on the weekly pay-roll, since rehearsals started a month before, were their 2 assistants, 14 actors, 2 juveniles, a musician, an assistant designer and a press agent. And now, a wardrobe mistress, a chaperone for the children and 2 stage managers. John had refused to do with one.

In addition, a lighting designer, a sound expert, a poster designer, a mime coach (to teach the travellers how to walk) and a photographer for the first-night Photo-call had been, or were still, attending with their services and now putting in for their fees. Over-time was being claimed by the actors and the children were travelling to and fro in taxis. The whole thing had run away — become a big-time show!

The last week of the actor's salaries and the rent were secured by monies deposited with Equity and with the Round House. There was enough money left to pay the actors until then — but not enough to pay the Round House, the day-to-day expenses and all the bills now pouring in.

Everything depended on the box.office and I went several times a day to see how the advance bookings were going. For the first-night they were good, better than usual they told me. But after that, they were worse than usual. I had to find more money.

The friend with whom I was living was a rich woman and a director of the company and, excited by it all and sure that she would get it back — happily threw in £1000. When the opening night came everyone was sanguine, everyone was happy — except me. I was terrified.

The event had been well publicised among the New Age groups and much talked about and it was they who had booked in advance and who filled the Round House on the first night. Sir George brought a contingent from Shropshire and mini-bus loads came from Coventry and other parts of the country and at the party afterwards, in the caverns of the Round House, the wine flowed, the congratulations flowed, the kissing followed and success was predicted — even by the hard-headed directors of the theatre.

People said afterwards that John had failed to bring out the nuances and deeper meaning of the play but, notwithstanding, it was technically a good production. It moved fast and effectively and the actors, one and all, were splendid. I was pleased and grateful and, for a few hours, I came up out of the darkness and the looming horrors, into the light of what seemed like a great beginning — and undeniable achievement. The next morning, I hurried to the newsagent. Five critics reported and did their best to kill the play.

Ned Chaillet, of The Times, was the least odious. Showing off his own cleverness, he skated over the scenes flippantly but politely. Keith Nurse, of The Telegraph, conceded that some of the scenes were 'unusually rewarding and funny' although the rest was 'heavy going' and, halfway, he wondered if the journey was 'worth completing'. Michael Coveney, of the Financial Times, described the Eastern religions as 'mangy creeds' and, after referring to Rudi Shanker and Herman Hesse, 'really thought that this sort of junk had had its day', 'this phoney backtracking', and that the audience didn't boo because, 'he suspected that they thought all the talk about karma was to do with mild curries and weird love positions'. The Hampstead & Highgate Express dismissed it in a few lines as 'a swamp of philosophical clichés'. And Milton Shulman, of the Evening News, wrote, 'Alas, when the eternal truth is revealed it is as profound as a homily in a Christmas cracker. Find the answer to existence . . . in searching within yourself. Well, I ask you!'

They were no better than a troop of Calibans lurching into a temple sniggering, blaspheming and defiling it.

The bookings did not pick up. 100 to 150 was the daily average, with more on Saturday nights and fewer at the matinees. In that great Roman amphitheatre, they were depressing — both for the actors and the audiences.

I could not stay away. Every day, after I had seen the bookings for the night and the takings for the night before, I ate my lunch on Primrose Hill, then walked about, then came back and sat in the restaurant with a cup of tea until the actors came bounding in at 6 o'clock, first to crowd the bar and then to queue at the serving counters and carry away loaded trays to the same long table where they fortified themselves with food, wine and togetherness before going out to perform to the frozen handfuls scattered about the empty wastes. The usherettes took to urging the sad isolated little groups to coalesce, moving the cheap seats to the dear ones, while I stood in the foyer watching them arrive, always hoping for more and then, when the bell rang, went and sat among them. I always had to leave at the interval to catch the last connecting bus to Kingston and reach the house by midnight.

It was the time of the parcel bombs and bombs in cars and one evening, all the parked cars round the theatre were moved and the traffic was diverted for the Mayor and Mayoress of Camden. They arrived in their Daimler, wearing their chains of office, and were received in the foyer like royalty.

I was not told of their coming and only by chance, as an after-thought, was I introduced to them.

"We've come to see if the play is really as bad as the notices", they said, smiling in a friendly and forthcoming way.

I sat with them during the interval and we got on well, talking about everything except the play. At the end, I stood where they would have to pass me, hoping that they would give me something — one generous word, but their smiles were different now and, as they hurried by, I knew that they would have liked to slip away without seeing me.

The rent was paid weekly in advance, but at the end of the first week, I did not pay it. I couldn't. They had the deposit, designated for the last week and *something* from the box-office and I hoped I could let it slide — and it did. Then in the middle of the last week, their accountant pursued me into the restaurant and, like a bailiff, handed me a letter and stood over me while I opened it. It was a bill for the unpaid rent and with it, an ultimatum. Unless I gave him a cheque there and then, the show would be closed that night.

They wanted their money. At the same time, they may have wanted to close the show, for without good takings in the box-office, the rent alone was not enough to keep the theatre running and, at a certain point, it became more economic to keep it 'dark'. When I admitted that I hadn't got the money, he looked startled and left me to consult the directors, returning later with a compromise proposal. £1000 would keep the show going.

I asked for time to consider this. I would have been glad to see it close. It all seemed futile now and every day, the agony was greater. But I couldn't let it. I had to keep it running to the end. An hour before the threatened closure, I wrote the cheque which not only emptied the company's account but put it deep into the red. And when Nigel then stood over me I wrote another, for £20, to pay for the children's taxis and the petrol for his van. With three more running days to go, London management was penniless — and heavily in debt.

John kept away. I never saw him again and my relations with Nigel were once more stoney. The old animosities revived and he wound up the production indifferent to what was happening. He was alright himself. He had done well. The engagement had given him experience and prestige and he already had another job.

The coolness and condescension spread to the Round House staff. The people in the box-office became off-hand and the usherettes smiled pityingly. I was now presiding over failure which nobody respects. Only the actors did not change. They alone rewarded me.

"We are old hands in the theatre" one of them said, "and whenever we have come together for productions in the past there have always been jealousies and resentments and quarrels. This is the first play in which there has been no disharmony. Although John told us nothing about it when we started, we have come to understand it for ourselves — and come to love each other."

On the last Friday, Equity sent someone in to give them their cheques. But worse than this humiliation, was the blow which came the next day when they refused to do the matinée.

The bookings were better and a large crowd of annoyed and disappointed people were turned away. Could they not have managed just one more? Was this the mean decision of them all after the march-in of Equity? or only of the shop steward? I never understood how they could do this to me at the end?

And the bookings on that last night were greater, perhaps portents of what might have been — given time? A man came up to me afterwards. "This is the third time that I've come. Why can't it go on?"

Yes. Why couldn't it? When I tried to 'stretch the minds of Londoners' — why did I fail? Blaming is the last act of failing — and as bitter. Everyone blamed different things. I blamed the over-spending, over charging and over-manning and bad relationships. I felt that the system had killed the play and was killing the theatre of the future. I called the critics barbarians and said the public was not ready.

The actors balmed the poor publicity of the Round House press agent and the notices which panned the play and ignored the players. Others blamed inflation and the bomb while Nigel shouted from the roof-tops that the play was bad and Sir George, my friend, whispered that he thought so, too.

All my plays had failed — the 'Testimony' before it even reached a stage — and in the limbo where they lay I did not know whether they were good or bad, whether the one was merely a scapegoat for spirituality become demonic, and the rest were victims of rampant materialism and debased policies and fashions in the arts. I only knew that in both worlds my work seemed useless and unwanted and, "I had nowhere to lay my head".

Hölderlin said, "In a spiritless age — why be a poet?" I might have said, "In a barbarous age why write verse plays and epics, upholding the Great Tradition?" Yet failure is not an abstraction but the other aspect of success — an uneasy pair but equal in value and in virtue.

The total cost of the production came to £21,000. I was £5000 in debt and the creditors closed in.

It was then that my little Jewish accountant, friend and lover of the theatre, who from the start had not charged me a penny, rose to defend me. Persuading them all that proceedings and bankruptcy would gain them nothing, the big scaffolding firm withdrew, the hiring firm, whose charges were exorbitant, took back their goods and the solicitor did not press his final claim. I sold the props and costumes, several friends came to my aid and after I had paid the bank and the small firms and individuals, only one bill was left, the largest — £4000 owed to the Ministry on account of the employer's unpaid contributions to NHI.

For months they were kept at bay, seemingly intractable until a woman official pursued me to my London lodging and, over a cup of tea, I told her the whole story.

"This sort of thing is happening everywhere" was all she said. We shook hands and she left and soon afterwards I heard that the liability had been written off.

A modern play, one stark set — a steel erection, simple lighting and the actors wearing, for the most part, jeans — cost all that money! How many rejected or neglected masterpieces it might have launched! I did not regret losing it. Money must be used for great causes and someone must always be the first, the pioneer to show and prove and wait, however long, to be followed. I was only sorry that it had been squandered.

I soon left Kingston. A rather grand New Age friend had just lost her husband and when her son moved into the manor house and she moved away, she left an old aunt living in the dower house. And now, out of compassion for my desperate straits and concern for her aunt, she offered me a rent-free cottage on the estate in return for housework. And this mutual-aid arrangement seemed wonderful. After three wandering years, I was longing for my own home again.

The aunt lived like a recluse in a beautiful Elizabethan house, standing alone upon a hill. No cars were allowed up the long winding drive, farm-hands brought her milk and eggs and poultry, villagers brought her groceries and a gardener grew her vegetables and gathered fruit from her orchards.

And no servants had been inside the house for years. Every room was thick in dust, cobwebs hung festooned from wall to wall, the books were stuck together and eaten up by worm, the windows wouldn't open, smouldering ash filled the great fire-place and heavy heraldic silver, black for want of cleaning, stood ranged upon the oaken side-board. It was like a fairy-story house.

At first she was nervous when, accoutred in cap and overall and gloves, I broke into each room armed with antique brooms and brushes which I found inside a black, mouse-infested cupboard. I was interfering with her way of life and her niece's solicitude, in absentia, was not altogether welcome.

However, as she watched her mournful house being restored, room by room, to its former glory, she was rather pleased and grew to like my comings — and to like me. And I liked her. But I soon lost my illusions about the mutual aid. I had been poor all my life but always kept my independence and now, I found myself in a tied-cottage, dark and damp, with feudal obligations towards an ancient dame and, after a few months when the dame fell ill, expected to nurse her.

Much as I liked her I would not do that and when I was told that my spiritual advance and creativity as a writer would suffer and I defied this spiritual blackmail and still refused, I had to go; store my furniture again and find a London lodging. Yet those fairy-tale and feudal months were all-important for they enabled me to get to my trunks again; to the one filled with my manuscripts and to the old Saratoga, crammed to the brim with my mother's unframed pictures. Ever since her death that trunk had worried me and now, when I looked at her lovely work again — it obsessed me.

I re-read the first part of what Sir C.P. had called a 'biography of a world in crisis', and thought it good enough to publish and when I moved to London, a literary agent accepted it. Agents had always been unapproachable or unreachable — gorgons or ethereal beings.

At the same time, I learnt that I could claim Supplementary Benefit which made me better off although it did not help me to buy another cottage (and few could be rented). When I heard that the British Legion were building sheltered homes for retired ex-service people, I applied for a flat in N.E. Derbyshire, hoping that if I lived close to the high hills which I loved so and where so much of my work had been done, I might find a cottage on the moors which I could rent.

It was 1977, the year when I looked back calmly at my seeking self and wrote the article, 'The Fire that we Passed Through'. The first paragraphs I have already quoted and I now set down the concluding ones.

The divine passion lasted many years. . . . Although I strained and struggled, the distance between me and my sublime desires remained the same. The break-through for which I longed still eluded me, and when a series of encounters overtook me, I was shocked to see the teaching fly out of the window every time and negative emotions erupt as destructively as ever out of the undiscarded egos of my spiritual superiors. I realised then that we all adored the teaching with our intellects but that few could *become* what they were taught. I saw how much unspiritual ambition and pride still flowed through our seeking.

When I finally acknowledged to myself that I was too poor and feeble to reach any of the peaks, that I had fallen in the spiritual race and was back in the wretched tenement from which I had started, I felt all the misery of failure and betrayal.

As time passed, however, so did my despair, and I saw that all the striving and straining after spiritual wealth, the conquering of peaks and running up and down exotic Paths twisting through the jungles of ancient cultures were so often self-deceits and unneeded; that I was back where I had started because within me and beneath my feet all the time was the Path that I must follow — my own Path. The art which I served, I knew would give me the insights that I craved.

All this was like a guilty secret when I turned back to the world, no longer feeling too high and pure to touch all its obscenities but, on the contrary, happy to live and work for common changes, knowing that a multitude of saints and mystics, backed by the celestial hosts, could not lift and regulate the planet without the aid of practical people conscious only of their contract of service and unmindful of themselves.

When this became my Way and I began to write again, the guilt dissolved and I no longer felt like an outsider, fallen between every world, but like a proud citizen of Earth, belonging and rejoicing.

Now, looking back, I feel that I passed through a white fire, beautiful, painful and cleansing which, if it did not make me into a saint or mystic, gave me a new consciousness, made me a new person, fitted in my own way for the task which lies upon us all — that of establishing, if not a heaven upon earth, at least a new and finer Age.

I have not squared the circle but I have reconciled the opposites and, in my own way, the Way of the artist, been able, at creative moments, to transcend them. A year later, I reached the age of 70, and looked back again — this time at my writing self.

When I was eight years old, playing in the garden of the bungalow in Los Angeles, I experienced the vision which set me on a horse above my fellows searching for the thing I had to do and when, fifteen years later, I found it in another vision and my power was confirmed, the high course of my life was settled.

From my first follies I was saved by my golden thread. My later aberrations and adventures were the rich, rash material needed for my art. When success did not come, only failure after failure, neither my confidence in my genius (as I was pleased to call it) nor my hold upon my purpose were ever shaken.

Now, suddenly at 70, they were. After all these years of life, nearly all of them engaged in struggle, why was I where I was and what I was — unknown, poor and living in an institution? Why had my plays failed, not one, but all of them? Was the reason which I gave every time — the unfavourable cultural climate — just an excuse to myself? The climate of the English theatre could not be totally unfavourable. When my grandfather failed, he sat in his studio blaming, not himself, but the world. Were my plays not the works of unrecognized genius, but of a second-rate scribbler — a passionate mediocrity? Were those early visions just hallucinations? Had I denied myself the natural pleasures and good things of life, lived in poverty and loneliness and sacrificed my mother — for a fantasy and monstrous conceit? Had I experienced, year after year, the pain and ecstasy of creation — only to give birth to idiot works? If so, then I was mad myself — and a mad begetter. After 70 years, I was ending as I began without having paused in the race — just a mad desiring runner, eyes fixed upon illusion, with a crown of nothingness to be won.

Haunted by depression I waited for the publication of my book.

The British Legion build their flats, often on cheap land, for people who like snug boxes with shops round the corner, all amenities and bingo twice a week and I found myself in the middle of a Council estate, in a village inhabited by barking dogs and lawless people, rent by the roar of motor bikes and the jingling tunes of ice cream vans, in the land of chemical and coking plants and collieries with motorways, pylons and high tension wires added to the ancient sprawl. Chesterfield was the nearest town, rough, mono-class and alarming. I felt overborne and effaced by the surging power and rasping voices of the risen masses — and I tried to get away.

The house agents could not help me and my pathetic pleas in the county newspapers brought no response and to tramp the hills as I did in the past, seemed useless now. After a year, I stopped struggling to escape and stopped waiting for my book.

Three publishers had had it. When I went to see the agent, he picked up a typescript lying on his desk and held it out towards me.

"This has been to 20 publishers and tomorrow it will go out to the 21st," he said proudly, expecting me to admire his devotion to his author and perseverance.

I reckoned that it must have been going round for seven years and, despising his complacency and being impatient, I took mine away and gave it to a small New Age publisher, specialising in the esoteric. He had read it and liked it and, if helped with a small subsidy, would bring it out at once. And an exciting joint event was planned.

I booked the National Book League gallery, then in Albemarle Street, for a week in May 1979, for an exhibition of my mother's pictures. The publisher worked to the same date for as the book contained the artist's story, a combined launching and private view was appropriate and novel.

The rent of the gallery was £250 — payable afterwards. I borrowed money for the framing by a local man and ran up bills for the rest. The total came to £900 and I relied on selling.

The opening party was enjoyable and by the end of the week when I closed the show, I had taken £1400, but sold too many — as I soon learnt.

I knew that I must go on yet I felt awkward. It seemed unnatural for a daughter to be doing what I was doing, motivated perhaps by filial piety and guilt. Then, Germaine Greer's great book, 'The Obstacle Race' was published, in which she wrote, "women must begin to sift the archives of their own districts, turn out their attics, search their cellars and haunt the salerooms . . . for lost women painters."

I had opened and emptied the Saratoga trunk and, writing and speaking with a new confidence, I went on.

Caught and driven by overwhelming forces, she scattered little gems about the world until her powers were broken and, in the end, living on charity, she died unknown.

That was her story. I stopped selling. More exhibitions followed. One of her miniatures was accepted by the V&A and is on permanent display and three more have gone to the National Gallery of Canada. Recognized as a great water-colourist and portraitist, she is no longer lost and the collection of her paintings is unique.

My book, 'The Golden Thread', went into the leading bookshops and a few libraries but it was not distributed abroad, not even in the United States and Canada where so much of the tale is set. The small publisher could not compete with the big firms in their grand offices which now market literature like merchandise, using the techniques of big business — the best-seller, the star system and mass production. Nor could he break through the barriers set up by the reviewers.

It did not fail, like the plays, because no one could any longer read it. It is very readable. It just sank beneath the weight of junk and dollar bills.

In 1981, with the money from the pictures, the book and subscriptions, I published the epic drama, 'The Isle, the Sea and the Crown — printing 500 paperback copies. I made no attempt to find a publisher but, after 27 years in trunks and cupboards, like the buried pictures, the buried plays, the buried everything — I had to bring it out into the light.

It received one short but good review (by a woman) and in a personal letter, Colin Wilson praised it. As I went from shop to shop, in London and elsewhere, the booksellers were friendly and bought a few copies but in the literary market-place it was an irrelevance — sixteen years of love and labour.

My flat was like a fall-out shelter in which I tried to keep myself immune from the dangerous radiation swirling round outside while keeping myself busy, inside. Each time I published a book or mounted an exhibition I escaped and each time I returned, I hurried from the station trying not to see the ugliness, hear the raucous sounds and breathe in the noxious air. And, as the years passed, I exchanged one depression for another. I no longer looked back at my life and felt that I had failed, no longer believed that my work was bad, and I was mad. But, just as I, myself, felt overwhelmed by my surroundings, so did I feel that all that I had given my life to, was obsolete — that both I and my work had been swept away. I did not blame the system any longer, with all its petty evils — but history.

These are extracts from a lecture which I gave to an adult education class, some time later.

In the Middle Ages the English were known as the songbirds of Europe — excelling in music and poetry. And Shakespeare, writing on many different levels, was enjoyed by the groundlings. Up to the 17th century there was a unified culture — embracing all classes.

After that, with the invention of the machine and the coming of the Industrial Revolution, an abrupt separation came between sophisticated and popular culture. In the 18th and 19th centuries the great bourgeois culture arose and with science and empire shared the corridors of power and the arts were the crowning glory of civilisation.

The national culture was lost and a high class culture reigned. . . Today, with the rise of a huge frenetic pop culture, this class, upholding a great literary tradition has shrunk into a corner and its culture has become the antithesis of civilisation.

Our image of civilisation is one of cars and planes and washing machines, of television sets, package tours, health services and supermarkets — crowned not by the great arts and high culture, but by pop art, commerce and technology. The achievements and traditions of centuries are being buried beneath a rushing, raucous stratum, by the weight of the mass society.

At the beginning of the century, the Spanish philosopher, Ortega y Gasset, in his book, 'The Revolt of the Masses', predicted and criticised the rise of the mass-man, ". . . his self-satisfaction, his will to intervene . . . and impose his own vulgar views, his deplorable ignorance. . . As the mass-man rises all values and qualities fall. . ."

But he goes on to say that there is a favourable aspect to the rule of the mass-man, "Inasmuch as it signifies an *all-round* rise in the historical level and reveals that the *average* existence today moves on a higher plane than that of yesterday."

The present period will have to be lived through until mass-man is educated and integrated into a new unified culture. And F. R. Leavis, writing later, says, "It is a commonplace that culture is at a crisis . . . mass production, standardisation, American salesmanship, efficiency — the machine. There are so many distractions that people can no longer read and if they try to, no longer understand what they are reading. . ."

And I. A. Richards, writing at the same time, ". . . It is vain to resist the triumph of the machine. Equally vain to console ourselves with the promise of a 'mass culture' that shall be utterly new and perhaps better than the one we are losing. This century is in a cultural trough rather than upon a crest and the situation is likely to get worse before it gets better. . . Once the basic level has been reached a slow climb back may be possible . . . a hope that looks very desperate in face of the accelerated downward pace. . . High culture has always been in the keeping of a minority. Now this minority is conscious not merely of an uncongenial but of a hostile environment. . ."

After speaking of my experiences in this 'uncongenial and hostile' environment, I went on:

I am now going to look at the plays which the trends call up reflecting, not lighting up, society — and at man, the maker of society.

In the great dramas of antiquity, the characters were gods and heroes, endowed with monstrous qualities and engaging in sublime moral contests, brutalities and foibles. In the 19th century, Tolstoy maintained that art should express the spiritual perceptions of a people.

In this century, after two great wars, the image of man shrank and he strode, or crawled, across the stages of the theatre and the world, not as a hero struck down by fate or by the jealousy of the gods, not as a spiritual being, but as a machine, as an insect, as a madman, devoid of divinity, in a world without moral order.

And after that, the curtains rose upon a frustrated, futile, absurd and desperate creature until the creature revolted and reappeared as the mass-man, angry, self-pitying, consumed by petty personal and class animosities, perversions, obscenities and violence — bent on destroying the Old Order.

Today, he grabs and smashes, shoots and runs, terrorises and tortures, exploits and degrades and, at the same times, whines and clamours for higher wages and more benefits or pushes for power and high position. In a world which he himself has overcrowded, polluted and reduced to anarchy, some nurse the subconscious wish for the mass death of a hopeless species in a flawed world, for another breath upon the waters and a new Creation; while others know that the work is not yet finished and Transcendence is still the Way.

A century of powerful plays depicting fallen man, a doomed society, an absurd world, have set a trend and imposed a style which have the theatre in their grip and have already reduced it to a pathological state.

And Bernard Levin writes: "Are the themes with which writers are obsessively concerned — violence, injustice, disappointed hopes, the darker side of life — true reflections of Britain in the throes of post-colonial decline or do they point to something rotten in the state of the UK? or are they merely psychopathic fantasies of a group of gifted neurotics?"

Britain aroused the world from centuries of slumber and stagnation and brought it into history, and now all go down in chaos together while a new world struggles to be born. Those themes . . . reflecting a fin d'epoch society, clutter the stages and channels and allow no chance for the visionary to spring up out of the noise and hysteria — and kill the unborn theatre of the future.

And Bernard Levin again: "It seems already true that social themes are inadequate in themselves to sustain and nourish audiences and artists. Perhaps the time is ripe for playwrights to explore new subjects and new styles. . ."

And the drama critic, John Barber, writes of the fringe theatre: "... The small off-centre theatres are obsessed by violent themes. Writers tear them out of the morning headlines. Actors learn to simulate the manners of the thieves kitchen. Their plays are compiled like living newspapers to expose the misery in our factories, our schools, our housing estates. Their aim is to rub our noses in the squalor around us. . .

These playhouses have been set up, and subsidised, to explore new ideas but social concern is driving these objectives out of sight. No one is interested any longer in looking beyond the headlines into the comedy and tragedy of the human condition. . . Only a handful of playwrights know that we are souls as well as citizens. . ."

Now, in order not to leave you any longer lying in the trough or staring at the kitchen sink, deploring the culture we have lost, I am going to pull you out and away into the future where new exciting scenes are appearing and ways to reach them and survive can be discerned.

In 1971, the American historian, Alvin Toffler, published 'Future Shock' and in 1980, 'Third Wave'. Both books present a visionary and practical programme for climbing out of the trough and riding upon the crest of the tidal wave upon which mankind is now advancing. He writes:

"Never before have so many people in so many countries . . . been so intellectually helpless, drowning, as it were, in a maelstrom of confusing and conflicting ideas. Colliding visions rock our universe. . . On a personal level we are being blitzed by fragments of imagery . . . that shake up our old ideas and come shooting at us in the form of broken or disembodied blips. We live in a blip culture. . . But the mass media which has created the mass mind is now coming under attack. . . Instead of masses of people all receiving the same message, smaller de-massified groups receive and send their own imagery to each other. . . There is a shift towards diversity. . . Consensus is being shattered. . ."

"The theorists of the 'mass society', obsessed by a reality that has already begun to pass, who hate technology and predict an ant-heap future, the death of individualism, diversity and choice . . . have been superceded. . . The super-industrialism of the future will require not identical mass-men, not robots, but richly different individuals. . ."

"Human intelligence, imagination and intuition will continue to be more important than the machine, although computers will deepen our view of causality, heighten our understanding of the inter-relatedness of things and help us to make meaningful 'wholes' out of the disconnected data whirling round us. The computer is one antidote to blip culture. . ."

"Enormous energies will be released. . . New religions will be born, new forms of art, great scientific advances and above all, new social and political institutions. And much is already happening. . . We are on the edge of a new millenium, on the brink of a new stage of human development, racing blindly into the future. But where do we want to go? . . ."

And I concluded:

If we can survive the advent of leisure, profit from the miracle and leap into the New Age, and putting on the new higher consciousness, build small de-massified communities, rescue and personalise the mass-man, restore creativeness, lift the arts to a new level of perception, into the region of mystery, and re-unify our culture — if we can do all this — where shall we then decide to go?

I shall not be here but my plays will be and I believe that they were written to help give an answer to that question. I have hoped, despaired — and now I hope again.

The fall-out shelter did not preserve me from the pervasion of the sub-culture. Such shelters never do and I walked out of mine into the alien streets and talked to the workers, the workless, the yobos, the vandalising children and to the women who are their mothers, their tarts and their wives. And the mass-man smiled at me and told me his story. He does not want my plays — but someday he will.

And the flat that was a shelter has now become a cell in which the nun, the bride of art — born slave to a task, herself a nothing, a finger moving as a pen — sits cloistered from the world recording the joys and hardships of the journey and, as she writes, thinks upon the strange and wonderful design that fixed and shaped it. The dark that leads to light and the journey that begins when it has ended, the failure that succeeds, the faulty vehicle that carries on the Treasure, the obscene that lies beside perfection, the one-ness that crowns and crucifies, the gap that is the primal sin and death that is not death — the opposites that dance in ecstasy and the circle that cannot be squared. The balance that may not be lost, the paradigm to be adored, suffered and transcended. And kneeling at the foor of the Tree of Life which reaches upwards and outwards, her service not yet finished, she holds the world in her orisons and herself where the artist can see beyond the general and bring back what she has seen.

POSTSCRIPT

ART IN A NEW AGE

How new is the New Age? Throughout recorded history, with every advance in thought and technology, there have been changes in consciousness — and new ages. But the perennial philosophy and the perennial activity of art have never changed in their essence — only in style.

The Marxists, with their utopian conjectures concerning the nature of life in the classless society, 'on the other side of history', are vague and perfunctory. But they do make several categorical pronouncements and ask a number of fundamental, often contradictory, questions concerning literature.

Will there be a need for it at all? Is it rooted in the imperfection of historical being? Will fiction be needed any longer to satisfy the desires and dreams of men? won't the *real* satisfy them?

Trotsky affirmed that art will last beyond victory. That 'the poet of the new epoch will re-think in a new way the thoughts of mankind and re-feel its feelings'. Pisarev declared that art would and should become obsolete. Ernst Fischer found such an idea intolerable and passionately defended the continuing validity of Goethe, Stendhal, Pushkin — and Mozart. But, would they still exist as in a museum? However, it is the western people who envisage and strive for a new age more radical and more absolute than the Marxist or any other that has gone before.

They believe that we have reached the end of an epoch that began with the expulsion from Eden and then advanced into the era of individual consciousness and are now about to see the individual integrated once more into the whole, but on another level, without loss of the essential individuality gained in between — only the loss of the inessential personality which arose during the struggle for consciousness and which can be cast away with the gaining of not just social, but cosmic one-ness.

Such a leap may take centuries to accomplish when the perennial philosophy will be reified — and art will change. The new age, or epoch, still too strange for us to imagine fully, will beget a New Man, not just the selfless man of the Marxist Society, but the egoless man of a spiritualised society.

The art which arose and has been nourished upon conflict,

suffering and protest, sharpened by hope and a bright unfailing vision — will disappear and the supreme work of art will be Man himself.

The images produced by the passionate artist seers of the past and received by desiring audiences will no longer be needed for the ultimate divinised form, beyond the word, the tune, the pigment and the expression, will grace and cover the earth.

In the meantime, art the teacher points the Way, and many paths into God or Wholeness, over-arching the via negativa and, transcending the opposites — the present sublimity and depravity of man — sustain and prepare him for the hard and perilous leap.

APPENDIX I

Sir C. P. Ramaswami Aiyar

Two essential ideas or ideals have been energising this country through the millenia. . . the first of these and India's contribution to the world — is fearlessness. . . Very little has escaped the investigation & analysis of the Indian thinker. Foreigners have criticised the lack of unity of Indian life & the apparently incongruous speculation. . . The country of the Buddha whose philosophy did not demand a Supreme Being, the Vedanta which does not postulate the existence of a Personal God & the devotee's complete submission of the self to a Supreme in a personal form. . . Contradictory varieties of thought which, nonetheless, analyse the Ultimate. . .

The second idea is that of rhythm, called dharma in some of our books & what the Vedas called rta, the science of harmony & of supreme order. . . Nothing is accidental or due to any human or divine intervention but happens in ordered simultaneity, according to a law existing from before time Rta, the idea of the continuity of existence is India's second contribution to world thought.

Life does not end with what we call death or begin with birth, nor co-exist with the turmoil & struggles & perplexities of existence. Life is regarded as a great harmony which, in the language of music, involves discords, swells into heights & depths but continues forever. . . Later, this became the doctrine of evolution. . .

These are India's main contributions to the world — continuity of life, a perceived order in everything & fearlessness as to the consequences of thought wherever it may lead. . . Indian thought has been like a subterranean river fertilising many countries although often not acknowledged. Zoroastrianism in Persia, Egypt, Mexico & Peru & Islam. And Christianity is not essentially different from Buddhism. Humanity is travelling in a spiral. . . Our ancient teachings tell us that when the process is completed & perfect man arises & vanishes into the Supreme, there comes again a cometary influence & the world is destroyed. Some have called this a prefiguration of the evolutionary doctrine.

Some of us were dreamers when working for political emancipation.

Gandhi was the greatest, the consummate dreamer — but a practical idealist, too. He dreamt of making a new world but now we are in the midst of reaction & disillusion. We expected too much, too quickly. We are not getting results & so feel hurt & angry, disgusted with our surroundings, with our unfortunate governments called upon to handle well-nigh insuperable problems & with philosophers unable to find the ultimate solution to them. . .

People in America have said to me, "We are suffering from lack of leadership. We are suffering from a lack of poise & mental balance. There is such a tremendous hurry to do things, get things done, achieve things that there is no room for thought. We are craving for something, we do not know what."

The malaise is due to the forgetting of the great fundamental truths which irrigated the cultures of the world — the first of which is a loss of consciousness of the world as one. The oneness of humanity has not yet become a real factor in the general consciousness. But even if we have not lived up to it & are torn by factions now, the complete oneness, not only of humanity but of all animate & inanimate life has been one of the fundamental bases of Indian thought through the ages & because of this ever present consciousness, India can give that rest & poise that the world needs. And the spectacle of Gandhi, as a man who had achieved poise & mental balance conveyed a message of calm & contentment. He was a healing presence in the world.

If India can retain its heritage of ideals — which once prevailed & which made it possible for us to understand the apparent diversity of Divinity & if that sense of unity & calm can not only be felt by us but communicated to others — that would be India's greatest contribution to the world.

The Universe is typified as a tree whose roots are above in the Infinity of the Supreme — the branches spreading downwards in the world below. That seems to me the true illustration of culture & what it connotes. One root, Humanity — striving, struggling, dreaming, aspiring & achieving — the branches, the results of that striving, the various manifestations of human genius — the literature, the art & the culture of the world springing from the same source.

The original meaning of the word 'idios' in Greek was the man who lived for himself, who regarded himself as the centre of the universe. The nineteenth century European thinkers &

economists at the turn of the century were largely 'idiots' . . . concerned with a very narrow aspect of humanity — the economic struggle & survival of the fittest. A man could put down all competitors if he lived according to the weakest going to the wall. 'Devil take the hindmost'. A cramping, antisocial system of thought.

Today, there is great danger of such idiocy spreading throughout the world — industrial techniques & their lop-sidedness, specialisation & cramping effects which take the mind away from the ideal & inspiring influence of craftsmen producing things of beauty.

In India, in the past, there were no industrial techniques, nor in China which reposed in the quietness of Confucian & Lao Tzean philosophy & where one of them said, "He who stands on tiptoe does not stand firm". When you are constantly looking ahead & anxious to move forward there is likelihood of physical collapse. And he added, "He who takes the longest strides does not always walk the fastest or for the longest time." We cannot prevent the advent of industrialism but we should remember these sayings when considering our achievements.

Zoroastrianism, the doctrine of the struggle between good & evil . . . which have been brought into existence for a mysterious purpose.

Our intellectual fabric today is shot through with European ideals & modes of expression . . . I could not talk to you like this — or to Indians — except in English.

The Europeans conquered us but they were not conquered by us — they kept their soldiers & their culture outside, separated. The world is maintained by currents of air & by ocean currents. The thoughts & noble dreams in any culture translated into literature, painting, sculpture & architecture are universal in character. India can best play its part by being a lender & a borrower.

APPENDIX II

Nirad C. Chaudhuri

Hindu family life is a dull dreary affair.

The mansions of the wealthy have drawing rooms & dining rooms in the European style, with chandeliers, wall brackets, Venetian mirrors, overmantles without fireplaces, some furniture & often a piano. But there is no brilliant entertaining, no conversation in these grand rooms for there are no women. They keep themselves in the zenana & the men only loll about in them in a languid gregarious way, going out to the brothels for their social life. And so, these big houses are silent. Not even the children disturb the quietness, playing — for they do not play.

The houses of the middle class are human hives & although built of brick, resemble more the mud huts of the working class, small in size with only a kitchen & bedrooms with bare cement floors & whitewashed walls smeared with the stain of betel nut. Wiping the soiled fingers on the nearest wall is a general practice everywhere.

In the kitchen is a stove created from a few bricks & no chimney. The smoke rising to the ceiling & then coming down again to find its way out of the windows. They meet in the bedrooms & sit talking on the beds. All gaiety is frowned on, all initiative discouraged & the generations do not mix. It is improper for fathers & sons to be seen together — the result is that the young sow their wild oats outside the family in violent, dangerous & degraded ways.

Nationalism is not a recent thing — & the Hindu must hate. He hated the British & before them the Muslims. The Muslims brought their civilising gifts, stability & great benefits to the masses. They were the salvation of the poor & so one fifth of the population became converts to Islam. So long as they were strong they were not challenged but served & fawned upon by the Hindu who felt subconsciously that his worm-like patience would outlast their strength & that without risking his life & possessions, he would win in the end. And he did. His nationalism surged up & he stamped on the head of his exhausted enemy. But after that, there was no one to hate until the British came, just in time, to avert a spiritual crisis. When they left, once again he was deprived of his passion & so he unloaded it on the Muslim convert, left behind.

I believe that hatred becomes a habit with a life of its own & when one object disappears, another must be invented. The Hindu is not tolerant. That is one of the myths. He hates all who are not fellow Hindus. Not rival dogmas, as in the west — but men are his prey.

Dante wrote of the teeth that bite a man & of the mystical realisation of charity & love. The teeth with which love of his country bite the Indian show no ascent from the plane of worldly love to that of just or divine love, but to a descent to an underworld of hatred, of cold ferocity. And the teeth are the venom infected fangs of the reptile, or of a prehistoric fossilised monster.

Ram Mohun Roy, the religious reformer of the last century & Vivekananda both nursed the same congenital hatred for the British until they went to England. They returned changed & charged with love.

There is no redemption for man except in charity & without it — the Indian has no hope.

Out of 400 million there are perhaps 10 million intelligent and capable people in India. Until now, there has been movement — the very weight of the mass has turned the wheel. But soon, this mass will become so overwhelmingly heavy that all will be swamped by it & all movement will cease.

APPENDIX III

Gist of My Speech on the Conference Theme

'A Crisis in Culture and the Writer's role'

In a period filled with physical & moral conflict, tragic, inspiring and dramatic, we would expect to see another Shakespeare, a Milton a Blake, a Byron or a Shelley arise together with a host of lesser men & women. We have the host but not the giants.

The host is divided into two groups. A small one composed of Communist writers on the one hand & a very large anti-Communist but progressive group on the other who have contemptuously ignored the Right but, at the same time, have recoiled from the Left and, thrown back into a decadent, stagnating atmosphere, trapped & isolated, in a void between two impossible courses, have been unable to identify & link hands with the revolutionary movements & countries of our time — and so, like England herself, have given no lead. They have occupied themselves by describing what they saw & felt around them or by writing for each other or, have withdrawn into private worlds of their own.

There is another peculiarly English factor which has contributed to their isolated situation — the historical, Protestant fear, conscious & unconscious in the English mind — of Rome. And of what in our time has been called the 3rd Rome.

But today, all this has changed. The recent demonstration of the madness of a dying colonialism, the liberalizing of the Communist regimes, the recognition that countries may advance towards socialism in their own way have together cut the knot of the dilemma.

This new spiritual independence has set going a new kind of nationalism which may transcend nationalism itself, for when Rome is no longer a menace within the gates friendship becomes possible, the world society may be perceived upon the horizon and the writer, emerging from his lonely & inactive prison & pledging his allegiance to humanity at large may at last play the lofty & tremendous role which is expected of him.

APPENDIX IV

China Opera School

They receive 15 yuans per month for food & allowances. They live in & their parents supply their clothes if they can afford to — if not, the State.

There are 440 students. 328 teachers & 3 departments.

1. Peking Opera. Children taken from 10 to 12 years (after primary school) by examination. 10 years training.
2. Local Opera. Taken from 15 to 17 (after middle school). 5 years training.
3. Music School. (Did not visit this).

About 60 to 70 new students taken every year. Examinations in 5 cities. 3000 applications last year. A 3 year trial. 30% of the time is devoted to general education. The level in literature & history is higher than other schools but lower in the sciences.

Before liberation, the star system operated. A few very highly paid — the rest almost starving. Now, all are paid more or less equally & the salaries are higher than for workers or government employees. A very honoured position both in the eyes of the people & of the government. They can be compared with scientists. Some artists may take private pupils but they must go through the school as well.

The provincial cities have their own schools for local singing training. Before Liberation there were no State-owned theatres at all.

A very happy atmosphere — the teachers kind-looking. Before there was much cruelty. Students were beaten mercilessly by teachers working for private profit.

APPENDIX V

Co-operative Farm

Started 4 years ago with 11 families.
1377 families have now joined.
1600 full-time workers, including women.
1400 mou of land.

They are paid according to output or work done by a points system. The average family income is 601 yuans monthly. Average individual income 571 — the highest 800 approx.

All meals from the canteen cost 12 to 20 yuans monthly. Meals taken at home are cheaper. Average rents not more than 1 yuan monthly.

At first, 30% was paid out in rents for the land brought into the co-op & 70% in wages. Now they hardly trouble about rents as the land brought in is so little.

Agricultural output is increasing all the time.

Democratic organization. One representative from every 10 families & these form a Co-operative Assembly which elects the manager & other officers — about 20 in all who administer everything & do manual work half time.

There are Primary & Higher Primary Schools to which 99% of the children go. The teachers are paid by the government.

There are members' & veterinary clinics with full-time doctor; & vets. Paid also by a points system but *more* than the labourers There is a store & the profits go to the Co-op.

They build their own 2-room, semi-detached houses, schools & farm buildings. The houses cost 700 yuans to build & 800 have been built in 4 years. They have underground hothouses for winter growing.

APPENDIX VI
Shanghai

Residents organizations cover every street. In the one I visited there are 446 families — 2100 people altogether of which 544 are housewives only, 488 the wives of workers & 56 the wives of industrialists & business men.

From the organization, 20 groups of housewives have been elected who organize the cleaning up of houses & streets, the introduction of new hygenic measures, child & maternity welfare, vaccinations & inoculations, newspaper reading & discussion groups & propaganda for new government policies. After their long subjection, these women are proud to come out & take part in things. They have status now.

Production Groups within each Residents organization. In this one, 103 women are working at home — knitting, embroidery etc.

Total population of Shanghai is $6\frac{1}{2}$ million of which 3 million are women & children. 350,000 are women workers. Last year 40,000 women got jobs for the first time. They want to go out & earn like men & be independent & *now* all doors are open to them — in spite of the difficulties. In 1949, the year of the revolution, there were only 180,000 women workers.

In 1953 the new *Marriage Laws* were published. Mothers-in-law are no longer allowed to ill-treat their daughters-in-law. Husbands are no longer dominant but must consult their wives. Women had been taught to obey everyone. Now they feel powerful for the first time. Husbands used to look down on women, said they fed & kept them alive, that only *they* were important. Now, women are recognised as being of equal value.

Housewives duties now. They must do 5 things *well*.
1. Bring about unity in the family & with neighbours.
2. Do their housework well.
3. Educate their children well.
4. Study well themselves.
5. Encourage husbands & children to work & study well.
And kindness & cleanliness are taught.

These 5 things are put forward as being important work which women can do for their country & they accept this. 9189 women in Shanghai have succeeded in them all & they are called *activists*. There are 4 in the group I visited.

Study groups for women
Newspaper reading.
Literary classes.
Meetings & lectures.
Cinemas.
Organization of a small library.

Birth Control
Discussed in the reading groups & at lectures given by doctors. And the women go to doctors.

Religion
Most still attend Buddhist temples, Christian churches & Muslim mosques. They are much less superstitious now. They do not publicise birth control among Catholics & Muslims. Respect their beliefs.

APPENDIX VII
Shanghai

Seven years before, Shanghai was a semi-feudal, semi colonial city with a population of 6 million of which 2% were criminals. In addition, there were loafers or professional beggars, pickpockets, gangsters, swindlers, blackmailers, brothel keepers, opium den keepers, gamblers, homosexuals & prostitutes. And the Department of Social Transformation was set up immediately.

The Kuo-Min-Tang worked with the gangster organizations which had spheres of influence with a leader at the top of each group to whom all loot or profit was handed. Some KMT officials were actual leaders themselves.

The corruption of the government & the social system were the cause of all this vice & crime: insecurity of jobs & poverty drew people into criminal activities & to eradicate it, a policy of re-education was decided upon.

In the first period, the leaders who had committed crimes were sentenced according to law while the general run when caught in a crime were sent to the Security Bureau where they were offered re-education & if they refused, had it forced upon them. KMT officials & employees who had not committed crimes were left in their jobs where they helped to reveal information. Beggars did not like & understand the policy at first & had to be forced.

In the 2nd period after 1951, those who undertook to reform themselves were allowed to do so & those who refused to be re-educated were allowed to go but if caught committing the same crime again, were taken by force.

Prostitutes. In 1950 all brothel keepers were warned to close down & made responsible for the health of prostitutes. Before that it was common for them to murder diseased girls. In 1951 all the remaining brothels were banned & the prostitutes persuaded that re-education was good. No force was used. The majority agreed when told that it would lead to jobs & security.

At the same time the rest of the population was educated to live less corrupt lives & the demand for prostitutes dropped. Also the new marriage laws changed things for concubines had sometimes been obtained from brothels.

Re-education. 2-3 year courses linking productive labour with ideological education. It was explained to them why they were as they were — the social system — & the evil of being parasites.

But the remoulding of character is very difficult. Some were recalcitrant & some suspicious. Many escaped or ran away. Some agreed to enter a reformatory then changed their minds when they got there. Many prostitutes, characteristically, wanted a comfortable life & did not want to use their brains & when they came up against real work, did not like it & made a fuss & ran away. Also, they were not accustomed to a collective, organized, disciplined life. And they cannot earn so much so easily.

Those who had served their term were sent to their homes in the country or into jobs in industry or state farms. 60,000 prostitutes & criminals have been reformed in 6 years & the prostitute problem has been practically eliminated. The rest reformed themselves. Just over 1000 left. There are, of course, still a few private ones.

Reasons for success 1. The closing of the brothels. 2. The banning of the selling of girls. 3. Education of the whole population. 4. Large scale economic construction.

I met Mr Chin, a re-educated capitalist, and on the 16th March, recorded what he told me.

APPENDIX VIII

Shanghai — Mr Chin

Before the revolution he had 250,000 yuan (dollars) invested in a dispensary business employing 10 workers. He was a middle capitalist. He spent half his life in giving parties, gambling, racing & Mah jong etc., which were all necessary to do business. Except for the 4 great families who were closely connected to the government & held monopolies in all the main things, the capitalists were weak in China (unlike Russia) & business was precarious & difficult with prices up one day & down the next & there was cut-throat competition.

They were patriotic nationalists on the one hand & profit makers on the other. They would think nothing of selling stale ort harmful goods. When the revolution came the 4 families fled to Taiwan & the majority of the remaining capitalists went to the schools (3 months) & co-operated with the new government.

They continue to draw dividends on their capital & they receive a salary. Salaries in Mr Chin's family range from 260-750 yuans. He draw the first as an assistant director of his own business which has now been enlarged & employs 600 workers.

60% of Shanghai's 100,000 capitalists are re-educated & organized & 5% of these are leaders of groups who go on trying to help the remaining 40% who have not yet seen the light. The schools are still open for those who voluntarily choose to go to them.

The organized capitalists work a joint state/private system but eventually the state will take over altogether. There is nothing against owning & inheriting property. You can be rich — as long as you do not have power over others & exploit others.

In Russia, the capitalists were very strong & powerful & refused to co-operate. In one town only 6 out of the total number came over to the govt. As a body they resisted the revolution & so had to be exprotriated by force. Lenin wanted to do it by persuasion but couldn't. In China, too much force was used at first. Then, they learnt from their own mistakes & Russia's & changed their policy to one of persuasion & re-education. And it is working well.

In Russia, during the first years of agrarian reform output fell. In China it rose. He did not know why.

APPENDIX IX

Boat People of Canton

There are 60,000 boat people in Canton. Seamen on junks, ferrymen, fishermen & boat dwellers.

Before Liberation in 1949, they were not allowed to go ashore unless they paid tribute to the Kuo-Min-Tang police & other rascals. They were not even allowed to moor near the bank & paid highly for the right to moor far out in the river. They bought their necessities from boat shops only.

They drank the river water & buried their dead in the river. They had no doctors, no help in childbirth & there was heavy infant mortality. Boat thieves robbed them, There were no schools. They suffered great poverty, hunger & cold & were stoned by the people on the shore. All the river people in China were looked down upon & treated in this way.

Now. Divided into 8 areas. There are 8 primary schools (650 children in the school I saw) 5000 attending altogether, the majority going on to middle school ashore. There are early morning & evening literacy schools for adults (300 in the one I saw). And handicraft classes for women. In 2 years time there will be no boat people left. Villages are being built for them & large numbers are already being absorbed into the community.

I also noted down some odd pieces of information:

1. Two years ago all cats & dogs were killed to eradicate fleas & lice — the causes of typhus. The use of human excrement as manure also causes typhus — in the plants & in the dust which blows everywhere. This accounts for their horror of dust & their masks.

2. In the Gobi desert where geological surveys are going on, the foreign scientists have to be guarded. The local Muhammedans would shoot at them.

3. The forests in northern China were all cut down to eradicate robbers. Result — soil erosion & a change in the climate. No rain & new trees are difficult to grow.

4. Meat is not inspected & tapeworm is prevalent. It can develop 5 years after eating infected food.

5. There is a section of the China coast where the sea is full of bacteria which gets into the pores of the skin, into cuts etc. & causes tumours.

APPENDIX X

Speakers at the Congress on Meditation

Swami Bhavayananda of the
Ramakrishna Vedanta Centre

"...What are we supposed to look forward to in the depths of our meditation? That is an experience which cannot be put into words... As Sri Ramakrishna puts it, "If someone has not tasted melted butter can you tell him what it tastes like? He can only know by tasting it himself"... When we go down into our deeper Self it is 'the flight of the alone to the Alone' as Plotinus puts it. But it is not an escape from the world, not a state of trance but a state of enhanced consciousness in which the Self is revealed in all its glory and in that stage of illumination no doubts remain: it is its own proof. We discover it is the light of Self or Reality, that lights everything... We live in constant awareness of Truth and this frees us from all craving and want. To experience this Truth while still living in this life is the purpose of meditation... But I must warn you that it is not easy. The Upanishads describe it as "walking on the edge of a razor"

Dr Edith Schnapper, Newnham College, Cambridge.

"... Any true spiritual search is concerned with transcending the dualities in their many shapes and guises. We must allow what C. G. Jung has called the transcendent function to operate in us. This involves facing and enduring the tension resulting from the clash of the opposites and doing so again and again. What must not be done is to evade the problem by opting for one side to the exclusion of the other. ..."

Applied to meditation this means that we have to go through the experience of the dichotomy of the two worlds ... and not side-step the issue by affirming the reality of one and denying it to the other ... and the temptation is great. To have discovered the existence and intense reality of the inner life is a revolutionary experience which can and often does attract us to such a degree that we seek to explore it more and more and enter even deeper into the new reaches of reality opening out before us. In comparison the material life appears illusory and unreal. If we follow this trend it will lead us to a life of partial or even total withdrawal, the monastic life in some form.

Most of us here, I think, have chosen a middle course. . . However, if we are completely honest with ourselves we have to admit that this is not enough to bring about a spiritualization of life itself. In fact, the major trends in the world today appear to be moving in the opposite direction, in the almost total neglect of the life of the Spirit. We all know that meditation holds the key for the reversal of this development; but what is the method that will meet the challenge?

In our endeavour to draw nearer to our goal of union with God or the Ultimate, we aspire upwards; out meditations are based on an ascending motion; our gaze is fixed on the heights. . . The question is whether such an upward directed aspiration is in itself sufficient to bring about the desired radical change in our lives and the world we live in. The answer appears to be that it is not. . . It is still only a partial solution . . . leaving the rest of our nature basically unchanged. Moreover, it does not even help us to transcend the dichotomy of the two worlds, in fact it can aggravate it by producing a split between our inner and outer life.

Years of yogic experiences drove Sri Aurobindo to the conclusion that the time had come for a new spiritual venture. He saw that the only way to break the impasse lay in an attempt to compliment our upward directed search by bringing down into ordinary life the higher spheres of awareness. . . What, in this context is meant by a bringing down? The one major difference between Sri Aurobindo's Integral Yoga and other systems is the decisive emphasis on a downward motion. . . The ascent is the first step, he says, but it is a means for the descent. The descent of the new consciousness attained by the ascent. . . A force or energy is felt to descend into us. . . It acts as an agent for change . . . and, according to the need of the seeker is experienced initially as a descent of peace or silence, a gentle flow of a vibrant force, an inrush of energy, or a downpour of knowledge, light or love.

. . . It will in time open our inner centres of consciousness one by one down to the vital and physical levels, and it will do so from above and not, as in other yogas, in the reverse direction . . . at every step it will implant the higher into the lower, thus there is here no sudden uprush of a vital power from below but a gradual infiltration of a purifying and transmuting energy from above. . . .

303

... In the Integral Yoga there is a total identification of Yoga and Life — all Life is Yoga. . . "It is there above you", Sri Aurobindo wrote to a disciple, "and if you can once become conscious of it, you have then to call it down into you ". . . .

... The hidden source of this inner opening is discovered to lie behind the physical heart; we experience an awakening or a call going out from it to which we respond by concentrating our attention on it, by trying to draw it out from its veiled recess. As it emerges slowly and usually intermittently, we recognise it as our true self and give ourselves to its promptings and guidance. And this, traditionally, is seen as an inner birth, the coming forward of the Psychic Being or Soul . . . the major link with the indwelling Divine Presence, the Guide and Master of our Works.

... It seeks Divine Union and abhors all separation. In its light, divisions are seen as a play of the ignorance and in this realisation, the opposition of Matter and Spirit as well as Yoga and Life, are the first to fall victims. . . .

What the Psychic Being asks of us and what the Force working in us presses us to do is to allow the Divine to take possession of our entire life. For most of us this means a struggle. . . What lies ahead, Sri Aurobindo describes as the ascent of the Sacrifice. It is the Baghavad Gita way of turning every action godwards, of claiming nothing our own, neither the result of our actions, nor the act itself, nor the idea of being the doer of action. All we do and all we are is thus sacrificed . . . it is made holy . . . a full identification of the outer and inner worlds becomes a possibility and we are enabled to stand back from the turbulence of life in the midst of life and to remain yet deeply concerned, held in the knowledge of the essential oneness of all that is. It will also gradually bestow upon us that peace and luminous silence which we sought at the beginning of our quest and which we now realise is the one thing needful for the higher ranges of consciousness that lie beyond the mental spheres, called by Sri Aurobindo the Supramental or Truth Consciousness, to descend and take root in mankind, in the World and ultimately in the earth nature.

Is this to envisage the impossible? Not more so than to speak of the Kingdom of Heaven. If this means anything it means exactly this, the divinisation of earthly existence. . . .

Looking at the world as it is today, perhaps we feel that we are speaking of some paradaisal state after death. The fact is that we are speaking of the goal of a vast transformatory process whose first manifestations are working in and around us now and whose full realization we can hasten or hinder; it is up to us."

The Rev Brother Simon Tugwell. Society of Jesus.

"This life is a life in the spirit, a life whose subject is Christ 'I live now not I but Christ lives in me', my spirit, as the Greek Fathers say, being 'mixed' with the Holy Spirit. And the faculty by which this takes place, is faith: by faith Christ lives in our hearts. I would like to draw your attention to various words which are correlated in the scriptures and in the Tradition round this idea of meditation and faith.

. . . One of the distinctive contributions, I am told, of Israel to world religion is the Holy War, and it is here that faith gets its origin. In going to a Holy War, the chosen people are to rely solely on the strength of God for the defeating of their — and His — enemies. Quite how literally this was ever put into practice we shall never know but it comes out very markedly in one of the stories of the crossing of the Red Sea when the rabble of people who had been slaves for generations, led out into the desert by Moses, with the sea in front of them and the Egyptians behind, begin to complain, "It would have been better for us to stay with the Egyptians than to die in the wilderness". But Moses said to them, "fear not, stand firm, and see the salvation of the Lord, which he will work for you today. The Lord will fight for you, you have only to be silent. ". . In Hebrew the word faith is connected with the root which means 'stand firm, which is in fact the root 'Amen' 'Truth'. . . . When the mountains are toppling into the sea — a pretty catastrophic situation — what the Hebrew actually says is: "Relax, and know that *I* am God. *I* will be lifted up, or as the New English Bible says, 'Let be, and learn that *I* am God. . . . The Hebrew says, 'Relax, let be', the Greek says, 'Be quiet, be at leisure', the latin says, 'be empty: and the English, 'be still'. And there, more or less, is the doctrine of meditation. . .

. . . We have not created the world, we do not structure reality, reality is not on our terms. . . We must accept it on its own terms, and this reality in the last analysis is the glory of God — this is what Christians believe. Let be and know that *I* am God, *I* will be lifted up. And for this to happen, we must accept the total 'naughting' as the Medieval English mystics said, of our souls: we must put off absolutely everything and stand naked before God, with no attempt, no ambition to re-structure the world in our own image, for our own satisfaction.

. . . There is a very remarkable sermon by Eckhart on Detachment and there he is asking the question: which is the chief virtue? And he says, people say love is, people say humility is: I say that

305

detachment is, because the main point about love is that it makes me love God, but the point about detachment is that it makes God love me, because if I clear myself totally out of the way, if I make myself a totally empty vessel, then God cannot help but pour Himself in. . . ."

The Rev K. G. Cuming, an Anglican clergyman, qualified doctor and spiritual healer

"It is my purpose in this talk to endeavour to show how the practice of meditation can be, if used with mental and spiritual understanding, of great value in promoting healing both of the body and of the mind, besides leading to those states of spiritual health and wholeness towards which the whole of humanity is sincerely striving. . . .

I would like to begin by reminding you of the Rev, Dr Leslie Weatherhead's definition of a miracle: "A miracle is a law-abiding event by which God accomplishes his redemptive purposes through the release of energies which belong to a plane of being higher than any with which we are normally familiar."

After a long disquisition on meditation, he goes on:

"So far we have dealt with the physical, mental and emotional. Now we come to the state of healing itself and we will assume that by whatever meditative method you have used . . . your conscious mind is now open to the super-conscious mind. With mind and body duly prepared, as the raised consciousness opens like a flower to the rays of the sun, so the mind opens to the rays of divine love and the whole being is flooded with spiritual light. The Master Jesus said, "If thine eyes are single then shall thy body be filled with light". Now this surely is a supreme state of meditation, an esctasy of communion with the divine. Whether this mysterious statement about thine eye being single be taken as meaning that the whole heart and mind and will is one-pointed and bent upon achieving mystical communion with the divine, or whether you take it as an esoteric injunction to open the third eye — either way you should by this time have reached the state of bliss and at-onement. Maybe this is one sense in which Jesus said, "I and the Father are one."

Here if you wish is the affirmation, the Christian revelation, I am poised and centred in the Christ mind and nothing can disturb the calm and peace of my soul. In this state of spiritual communion the Christian may find new and important meaning in the words of

306

the service of Holy Communion. . . "the body and blood of our Lord Jesus Christ to preserve thy body and soul unto everlasting life". It may well be that these words may be changed before many years have passed to a concept more suited to our spiritual needs and perhaps we will think of the bread of life and the wine of the spirit.

You will remember that in the definition of a miracle these energies were said to belong to a plane of being higher than any with which we are normally familiar. If we have meditated properly, successfully, we shall have reached that state of being, if our eye is single and our whole being is filled with light, then we are indeed absorbing and radiating these healing energies. Our next task is to achieve the gradual descent of the spiritual mountain, bringing down with us those energies into every part of the body, and so using our will consciously mentally focussing it on the problem areas. These problem areas may be mental or emotional in nature, our own problems or those of others.

Archbishop Anthony Bloom. Metropolitan of Sourozh.

"The subject which was suggested for my talk was Meditation and Prayer, and my intention is to speak on three points which relate to the subject but which obviously do not cover it. The first point is named after a book, "The Journey Inwards", so the title is stolen. The second point is something about Prayer and the third something about meditation — and when I say something, I mean it."

After saying 'something', a great deal in fact, about the terrors of the journey and about freeing ourselves from the tentacles of greed and possessiveness, he goes on:

"There are several types of prayer. There is in the Christian experience the kind of prayer which is centred round an event which we do not manufacture, the sacramental event, the real overpowering presence of God to which we respond. There are those prayers which wind their way discursively speaking to God, and holding our thoughts, our minds, our whole being, our whole life before God, trying to see all its meanderings in the light of God. Then there is the prayer on which I would like to say a few words which is the prayer for stability par excellence in the Orthodox Church, the Jesus Prayer. This is a prayer for stability because there is nothing in it but standing before God with one's mind rooted in one's heart. Mind and heart silent, immobile,

307

gazing Godward. The words are just 'Lord Jesus Christ, Son of God, have mercy on me'."

After talking at great length about Mercy and about the differences between prayer and meditation, he ends:

"We complain very often that our meditation, our prayer, does not lead us straight on to God, straight into the tiger's cage, straight into the fire of God. We can enter into the power of God if we are capable of being in the burning bush, not if we are straw or wood. We must learn to be grateful to God that he allows us to struggle on year after year putting barriers between Him and us so that we can gradually become capable of coming one step nearer, and one step nearer again, until we are purified and free of our selfishness, of our greed, of our desire, of our false imagination, until we are able to meet God and stand naked before Him and say, Have Mercy. It is death in Life. You are the goal to me. Let it be Life and only Life."

U Maung Maung Ji. Founder President,
London Buddhi: *London Buddhist Vihara Society*

"We are very fortunate indeed to have inherited an ancient teaching of eternal wisdom, the Doctrine of the mind with its spiritual message and power of healing. . .

Self-observation is a pathway to comprehend the mind and to awaken in us an awareness of the arousing of consciousness from its unconscious subsoil. This arising is not sudden but a gradual shifting of the centre of gravitation, a change of emphasis in our lives enabling us to sense the occult forces and to turn them from the unity of the Universe to the harmony within ourselves. . .

This awareness can help us evolve towards the knowledge of the higher worlds. We have the power to perfect and transform ourselves step by step. We can rise only with the help of thoughts that evoke in us respect and veneration for human beings, animals and things around us. Our spiritual eyes are opened and we begin to see the wider range of the world. . .

Silent and unnoticed we are truly treading the Path of Mindfulness and yet still doing our duties as before and attending to our business without those around us noticing an occult change in our lives. The transformat ɔn goes on only in the life within, hidden from the outward gaɀe."

Sir George Trevelyan

". . .It is quite clear that in all the movements represented here, meditation is sensed as being of paramount importance at the present stage of our thinking. We represent a great many different lines and we learn in each conference of this sort how to meet each other. . . In the climbing of this mountain we have obviously each to choose our own route, and not every route is suitable to everybody. It must not discourage us that others of greater wisdom and skill are taking some other path. Our path may be a very simple one but it is our path, "a poor thing, an ill-favoured thing, but our own" and we must realise that we are all concerned with one great quest, which is the climbing of this mountain towards expanded consciousness, and a deeper understanding of the human and spiritual crisis which faces mankind today.

Our society really needs missionaries to propagate the very idea of God once more. So many have lost God and have above all lost the sense of the super-sensible world, the reality of higher worlds. The world is divided into those who take the agnostic, atheist or materialistic view and those who realise that there exists a higher world . . . and that the core of man belongs to this higher world. Many talk about the spirit and spiritual values, implying . . . art, music, altruism and the churches as opposed to politics, economics and money making. But these values are not what we understand by the living spirit, the dawning in our consciousness of the truth that we are in fact in touch with higher beings, that higher planes of consciousness exist and that we are destined to move on to these planes because that kernel in every human being is eternal and part of the whole consciousness of the living God. The implications of this emerging view are obviously enormous. It is terrific news, if one might put it that way.

After talking about the limitations and shut-inness of the body and our release from it when its usefulness is over, and about our loneliness and separation from the great living one-ness of things, he goes on:

"Now the great step in our thinking is to grasp that there are planes of consciousness, and by planes we mean different frequencies, different vibratory rates. A higher frequency can simply pass through lower rates unimpeded. These walls and our bodies are being passed through continuously by television and wireless and there is no difficulty in grasping that. It is possible for a place on a higher plane to be co-existent on this spot, or fields, or a river with higher beings walking beside it. Space is an illusion. These wonderful realms are not far away. They are very close.

309

The sense of distance is due simply to our lack of vision and the decaying of those organs of perception which exist in us all.

"This is a completely different idea from the more orthodox concept that human consciousness starts at conception, the soul evolving through a life and then passing on perhaps to eternal life. The concept of the levels of consciousness means obviously that *we were there before we were born*. Once we grasp the concept of pre-existence it ceases to be necessary to discuss whether there is survival after death. This becomes axiomatic. We are eternal, therefore we didn't start at conception. We were there before birth. What started was only the beginning of this housing for the soul. . . .

"Birth into the body is indeed a form of death, and release from the body at what we call death is the great rebirth. That is the turn round in our thinking which our age has got to achieve. It is of vital importance because the world is teetering upon the edge of disaster. Even the great scientists are saying that there is grave danger of our so polluting the world that life on this planet is threatened. We may even blow it up in our vast, wise ignorance. Like children we are playing with wonderful toys. This is not to belittle the fantastic achievement of mankind in making a moon rocket or an atom bomb. It is an amazing example of creative group activity and it opens vistas of immense hope if man can only use his sense and see that the universe is spiritual in essence. . . ."

APPENDIX XI

Additional lines in Anna Morduch's talk –
'The Golden Thread of Gnosis'

...The actual process of the initiation into the temple mysteries in Egypt and Greece has never been fully revealed. But we do know that there were stringent tests for the candidate to pass and probably certain draughts containing stimulants such as LSD which brought about a loosening of the physical body followed by visions and experiences which changed the candidate's life. After initia-tion the veil was removed and he became an epopte: one who knew that man was indeed the image of God, that the whole cosmos was reflected in man according to the formula ' as above so below '... and he would have lost the fear of death and would have turned from the things which men covet and seek. It is this sense of whole-ness which our time is desperately trying to recover but however hard we try and whatever slogans we use the third dimensional world of unenlightened man is neither one nor a world of brothers. We try to live in a house without a roof and when torrents sweep our bits and pieces away, we blame God. Unless we can find the 'Father' — we are not brothers.

And she ended:

...the toe of Brahman, described in the Upanishads, where the spirit dwells in man's body. There is a little lotus flower and it is in a little space wherein are lodged both heaven and earth, sun and moon, lightning and stars. It is the Self free from evil, ageless, deathless, hungerless, thirstless, real of desire, real of purpose. Who can tell what memories half remembered may stir among the children who call themselves hippies or love children. We have called this golden thread, the threat of Ariadne, which links us with the king's daughter who helped Theseus to find his way out of the labyrinth at Knosses... This is the point at which we find ourselves historically and personally. If we want to find our way out of the labyrinth we must be guided by the thread of love and wisdom. The symbol for this reversal is the Shepherd's Crook.

APPENDIX XII

Anna Morduch's letter

". . . Like Gandhi I should like to go into a long fast because of the things I have heard and had to believe about a friend I loved and trusted and for all that — *still* love. I do not wish to discuss it — it is all too painful and ugly and I do not want to hear any explanations . . . It is not for me to deal with all this but for *you* my dear and I beg you to do so squarely and fairly. I shall try to put it out of my mind and think of it as a fever which will pass and leave you sane and sober again when my friendship will be open to you. Baraka must work and it does with John. If he were a red devil or an evil magician you would experience things you can hardly credit. . . . However he commanded me severely to give you the following message 'You are not to play with fire any more'. This is a serious warning. If you write any more libellous letters he will take you to court and see you punished for it. I pleaded for his compassion and he said there was no need for me to remind him of that. He had deep compassion for anyone who could do such things. Much prayer will go up for you because I can only think that you had done too much, tried to cope with far too many heady things and the result is akin to some fever of the brain. . . I hold you in the Light where Love can reach you. . .

As for my own affairs . . . order has now been restored and Pir Vilayat has made his wishes clear. I can continue the work in the way it has been given to me and naturally I feel thankful and happy . . . the two completely separate parts of the work can continue and there need be no animosity, no shadow between us . . . although I could not compromise about the basic principles, we can begin a new phase.

Do not answer now my dear and let this ugly thing die down. Just concentrate on your work . . . just give yourself peace and quiet and as much sunshine and normal living as possible. I shall be connected with you and try to help you but I think it wise to wait a while before we meet again. Blessings to you."

She had always known that I believed Ross had an evil side. There was nothing new in my letter to Elizabeth — only its racy descriptions and style. As to meeting again and the restoration of our friendship, she knew that I had stopped coming to her meetings and was avoiding her at every turn, but she was too conceited in her spirituality to admit this to herself.

Note: Using her pendulum, after her estrangement from Pir Vilayat and demotion, on account of her attachment to John Ross, she telephoned me early one morning to tell me that Pir was dead. The pendulum had told her during the night. She was, in effect, practising black magic herself. She wanted him dead.

Not long after this Pir supplanted her as Head of the Order in Britain with someone else — although she would not acknowledge this. Continuing her activities, there were two Heads confusing the Path of the devotees.

APPENDIX XIII

Frances Bank's monologue

"I am finding peace. I am at peace. I am absorbed into the peace that is here. I no longer need to strive and struggle as I did on earth. Always there I worked too hard. I battled forward. I followed every path. I obeyed the precepts, followed the doctrines, studied and examined all the theories of the spirit; drove myself with the whip of an iron will, read, marked, digested the sciences of the human mind, the human psyche and of the occult. All for the bliss and glory of a break-through to spirit. And now as I look back I realise that so much was illusion. I sought the Spirit and the Spirit was there all the time. 'He came unto His own and his Own received Him not'.

As I rest now in this Reality I see, with sadness, the truth of those words, 'I knew Him not'. I struggled, fasted, sought for what was already present, perfect and everlasting within me. I looked for the Spirit to reveal itself when all that was necessary was the letting go of Self — relaxation unto God. I, who longed so much for the touch of the divine, who dedicated my life to religious work, read the lives of the saints for their examples, denied myself all sensual pleasures and fulfilments — tried truly to obey the Master; I, who had done all this had not accepted the simple Reality of those words, 'Behold, I am with you even unto the end'. I had not been able to let go and let the Spirit absorb me, the very tenseness of my striving was my undoing. The more I battered at the Veil which hid the Face of Divinity, trying to tear it away, the more did I create illusion. For the Veil was, as I now realise, the Veil of my own setting.

Light, Divinity, Reality — all-pervading consciousness were there for my *acceptance*. Relax and allow the Spirit to stream through you. Swim with the tide of the Spirit. That is the great lesson I am learning as I review my mistakes. There was no 'break-through' of which I once so glibly talked. There is only a gradual absorption of that amount, or degree of Spirit which the open soul can accept.

I am aware too that I repeated old struggles, that none of it was new. No adventure into matter is ever entirely fresh or untried. It has been worked to its end perhaps hundreds of times before, though under different circumstances, perhaps in different worlds. I can not be sure of that yet; and it will be worked again and again until we learn that the purpose of life in matter is to illumine it with Spirit.

Even here, in my new life, I have been rushing hither and thither in search of adventure, experience, progress. But now I let go. I seek for nothing. I absorb and am absorbed by the Spirit of Light, Love, Beauty. . . ."

INDEX TO "THE GOLDEN THREAD"

India 226; 228; 262; 274; 316; 320; 323-4; 351; 374

Ione 111; 180 the laughing clown; 195

Irwin, Lady 247; 249 Delhi Hunt

Irwin, Lord — the Viceroy 227; 231-2; 233 invited to lunch; 234 commissions a portrait; 235-7; 237-8 visit to Viceregal Lodge — the banquet; 239 assassination attempt; 243; 249 Delhi Hunt; 251; 316

Irish peer 220; 222-3

Jack 36-8

Jaipur, HH the Maharajah 322-4 in London; 328-21 arrive in Jaipur — the lover; 332; 336

Jaipur State 328-9 palaces & treasure

Jane 257

Jammu 315; 318

Jean (in Los Angeles) 70; 75; 78; 83

Jerusalem 92

Jesus Christ 143

Jessie 183

John, the widower 148; 154; 164-5; 166 the wedding; 167; 173-5; 176 the drunken quarrel; 177 he leaves; 178-9

Just, Mrs 152-4; 173

Jungle, east & west, a 342L

Kalka 240; 280; 285

Karl (Los Angeles) 72

Karl Marx 224; 259

Kasauli 266-8; 314

Kashmir, HH the Maharajah & Maharani 293; 298-9; 309; 316; 318

Kelly, Miss (Los Angeles) 45

Kensington 14; 16; 321

Kensington Gardens 25

Kentish Town 196

Kiddle, Miss 87; 92-4; 99-100; 111 'dear old thing'; 114 so cruel; 119; 134; 179; 184 taken ill & dies

Kinko, Colonel (see Waterhouse)

King Edward 22

King & Country 34 recruiting

King George III 71

Kindrochit House 209

Kutab Minar 256

Lancers, 15th/19th (see Gage)

Lantz, Charles 61; 62 the dying man & a smart thing; 66 reward

Laurier, Sir Wilfrid 26

Lennox, Mrs 46-7; 101

Leach, Dame Florence 106-9 a holiday together; 148 the poor widower; 178 will not be a witness

Lewellyn-Davies, Mrs 23 Peter Pan

Lewisham 165

Lethe 303

London, Bishop of (see Winnington-Ingram)

Los Angeles 42; 55-6; 57-8 hot months; 59 'city of the quick or the dead'; 70; 73 a warm-hearted place; 75 burglaries; 78 the clairvoyant; 83; 96 news of Yen; 98

Lucknow Week 342

Luker, Ada 11; 13-16; 20; 24; 89

Luker, Amy 20; 87-9; 105-6; 111; 118; 120-1 selling old clothes; 134; 166 at the wedding; 172-3 the death of Mars; 177; 263 the wedding present

Luker, Frank 219; 221; 243

Luker, Louie (see Burrell)

Luker, Noel 16; 18; 24

Luker, William 13-15; 23

Luker, William junior 15; 19 a pampered monster; 23 torments; 89; 178; 199; 227

Lummis, Charles 59 desert dwelling; 60 the portrait; 140

Lutyens, Sir Edwin 338

Mad maid (see Batten)

Mad mountain dream 312; 315 ends

Madeleine 305; 307; 308-9; 311; 315; 319

Maggie 19

Maidens Hotel 242; 304; 311; 312 lunch with John; 338-9; 341-2 fudge hostess; 343 Ali; 344 fudge factory; 348

Marie Louise, HH Princess (see Schleswig-Holstein)

Mackenzie-King, Mr 26

Mara, Sir John & Miss 29-30

Mars 162; 165; 166-7; 172 his death

Martha 219-21 great & grim; 243

Mary, HRH Princess 131-2 Prize-giving Day

Maud 27; 29 nurse in Ottawa

INDEX TO "THE HORSES AND THE CHARIOTEER"

L, Ls — letter, letters N — notes P — Philippa G — Gordon M — Mother

328

331

INDEX TO "THE DANCE OF THE OPPOSITES"

L = letter   N = notebook